STUDIES IN MORAL, POLITICAL,
AND LEGAL PHILOSOPHY

General Editor: Marshall Cohen

A list of titles in the series
appears at the back of the book

SPEAKING OF EQUALITY

An Analysis of the Rhetorical Force
of 'Equality' in Moral and
Legal Discourse

Peter Westen

PRINCETON UNIVERSITY PRESS
PRINCETON, NEW JERSEY

Library of Congress Cataloging-in-Publication Data

Westen, Peter, 1943–
Speaking of equality : an analysis of the rhetorical force of
equality in moral and legal discourse / Peter Westen.
p. cm. — (Studies in moral, political, and legal philosophy)
Includes bibliographical references.
ISBN 0-691-07858-0 (alk. paper)
1. Equality. I. Title. II. Series.
JC575.W49   1990
320'.01'1—dc20   90-8159

This book has been composed in Linotron Palatino

Princeton University Press books are printed on acid-free paper,
and meet the quidelines for permanence and durability of the
Committee on Production Guidelines for Book Longevity of the
Council on Library Resources

Printed in the United States of America
by Princeton University Press,
Princeton, New Jersey
10 9 8 7 6 5 4 3 2 1

To

Marianne

Remembering the way to Keshwa Chaca,

and other journeys

Philosophy is a battle against the bewitchment of our intelligence by means of language.

—Wittgenstein

It is characteristic not only of the use of legal concepts, but also of many concepts in other disciplines and in ordinary life, that we may have adequate mastery of them for the purpose of their day-to-day use; and yet they may still require elucidation; for we are puzzled when we try to understand our own conceptual apparatus. We may know how to use these concepts, but we cannot say how or describe how we do this in ways which are intelligible to others and indeed to ourselves. We know, and yet do not fully understand . . . much in the way perhaps that a man may know his way about a familiar town by rote without being able to draw a map of it or explain to others how he finds his way about the town.

—H.L.A. Hart

It is precisely because everyone thinks he knows what equality is, that it appears to be difficult to explain exactly what it is.

—Albert Menne

CONTENTS

CONTENTS

PREFACE

The proposed Equal Rights Amendment to the U.S. Constitution testifies to the rhetorical power of 'equality'. The text of the ERA begins with the word 'equality':

Equality of rights under the law shall not be denied or abridged by the national government or by the states on account of sex.

Yet as a legal matter, the word 'equality' is superfluous: the ERA would retain the same meaning in law if, like the Nineteenth Amendment guaranteeing the right to vote without regard to sex, it omitted 'equality' altogether. The Nineteenth Amendment does not state that "*Equality* in the right to vote shall not be abridged or denied." It simply states:

The right to vote shall not be abridged or denied by the national government or by the states on account of sex.

The authors of the ERA, too, could have saved themselves unnecessary language by succinctly stating:

Rights under the law shall not be denied or abridged by the national government or by the states on account of sex.

The congressional reports of the ERA do not reveal why its authors inserted a word that added nothing in law to what they were seeking to accomplish.[1] What lawyers may not understand, however, statesmen surely do: by formulating their demands in the language of equality, the framers of the ERA associated their cause

[1] The original version of the ERA, the so-called Lucretia Mott Amendment introduced in the House of Representatives in 1923, was worded somewhat differently. Rather than speaking of "[e]quality of rights," it provided: "Men and women shall have equal rights throughout the United States and every place subject to its jurisdiction." The current version of the ERA, which Congress adopted and sent to the states for ratification in 1972, derives its wording from amendments introduced by the Senate Judiciary Committee in May of 1943. See Sealander, "Feminist against Feminist," p. 150. The reports of the Senate Judiciary Committee do not make any reference to the committee's reasons for the change in wording. See S. Report No. 267, 78th Cong., 1st Sess., to accompany S.J. Res. 25, 28 May 1943. For histories of the ERA, see Berry, *Why ERA Failed*; Mansbridge, *Why We Lost the ERA*.

with an ancient and powerful rhetorical tradition, a tradition that reaches back at least as far as Plato and Aristotle's definition of social justice—and Jesus of Nazareth's statement of the brother-hood of mankind—in terms of 'equality'.[2]

The rhetoric of equality is persuasive for many reasons. One reason, surely, is that some of the most significant and acclaimed moral crusades in history have been fought and won under the banner of 'equality', including the abolition of chattel slavery, the elimination of feudal privilege, the outlawing of caste, the disestablishment of religion, the spread of universal suffrage, the opening of careers to talent, the outlawing of racial discrimination, and the emancipation of women. By making claims in the name of equality, an advocate today reaps the vicarious benefit of earlier triumphs won in its name.

Yet these previous successes cannot fully account for the rhetorical appeal of 'equality' because, as Plato and Aristotle implicitly

---

[2] We have shown that both the unjust man and the unjust act are unfair or unequal; now it is clear that there is also an intermediate between the two unequals involved in either case. And this is the equal; for in any kind of action in which there is a more and a less there is also what is equal. If, then, the unjust is unequal, the just is equal, as all men suppose it to be, even apart from argument.

Aristotle, *Nicomachean Ethics* V.3.1131a (trans. Ross). See also Aristotle, *Eudemian Ethics* VIII.9.1241b ("both justice seems to be a sort of equality and friendship also involves equality, if the saying is not wrong that 'love is equality' "; trans. Solomon); Aristotle, *Politics* III.5.1280a, III.6.1282b, V.1.1301.

[T]he true and best equality is hardly so patent to every vision. 'Tis the very award of Zeus. Limited as is its scope in human life, wherever it has scope, in public affairs or private, it works nothing but blessings. For it assigns more to the greater and less to the lesser, adapting its gifts to the real character of either. . . . It is this, Clinias, at which we must aim, this equality on which we must fix our gaze, in the establishment of our nascent city. And if others would found other such societies, they should shape their legislation with a view to the same end—not to the interest of a handful of dictators or a single dictator, or the predominance of a populace, but always to justice, the justice we so explained to be a true and real equality, meted out to various unequals. ·

Plato, *Laws* VI.757 (trans. Taylor). For the Christian view of the brotherhood of man, see Matthew 5:43–45, 7:11–12, 23:8–9; Acts 17:26, 29; 1 Corinthians 12:14–26; Colossians 3:11, 4:1 ("Masters, give unto your servants that which is just and equal; knowing that ye also have a Master in heaven"); Galatians 3:21–29; Romans 2:6–12, 10:12–13, 14:8–11; James 2:8–9 ("If ye fulfil the royal law according to the scripture, Thou shalt love thy neighbour as thyself, ye do well: But if ye have respect to persons, ye commit sin"); 1 John 4:19–21. See Lakoff, "Christianity and Equality," p. 119 (describing Galatians 3:28 as expressing "the Pauline Christian conception . . . that all human beings are equal in the eyes of God").

For an anthology of writings on equality from the Bible and Herodotus to *Brown v. Board of Education*, see Abernethy, *The Idea of Equality: An Anthology*.

attest, 'equality' has possessed rhetorical force since the dawn of recorded political discourse. Nor does 'simple justice' account for its appeal, because 'equality' can also be invoked to assert highly controverted claims, such as the expropriation and redistribution of private property, the opening of national borders to unimpeded immigration, the emancipation of children from the supervision of their parents, and the adoption of and resistance to racial quotas.[3] Rather, I believe that the source of much of equality's rhetorical appeal is *conceptual* in nature—that is, 'equality' derives its persuasiveness not only from the things to which it refers, but from the kind of *word* it is. In particular, I shall argue that 'equality' possesses two paradoxical features that combine to lend it singular rhetorical force.

The first of equality's paradoxical features is that it appears to have at the same time both a single meaning and a variety of divergent meanings.[4] Thus, on the one hand, 'equality' seems to refer to a definite state of affairs, in a way that a word like 'beauty', for example, does not. We learn from an early age that beauty is largely subjective. To say something is beautiful means that it is attractive to a particular beholder. Equality, however, is not a relationship defined by reference to an ever-changing observer. It is a certain kind of relationship among persons or things or numbers. Particular persons or things or numbers are either equal or they are not. $2 + 2$ *is* equal to 4; it is *not* equal to 5. Blacks and whites are not juridically equal in South Africa; they are juridically equal in Zimbabwe. Equality is "one idea"[5] with a "definite,"[6] "objectiv[e],"[7] and "universal"[8] meaning.

On the other hand, while people seem to share the concept of equality, they have very different conceptions of equality. Consider the difference of opinion that exists about what "equality"

[3] For competing views regarding the justice of various kinds of economic equality, see Flew, *The Politics of Procrustes*, and Green, *The Pursuit of Inequality*.

[4] See Rae, *Equalities*, p. 5 (referring to equality as "a single abstract conception"); Tawney, *Equality*, p. 92 (characterizing equality as having "a variety of divergent meanings").

[5] Lakoff, *Equality in Political Philosophy*, p. 6 ("Formally there is one idea of equality").

[6] Stone, "Equal Protection and the Search for Justice," p. 2 ("Partially because of its kinship to mathematics, equality seems to have a definite meaning in a sense in which notions of 'justice' or even 'fairness' do not").

[7] Stone, "Justice Not Equality," p. 98 ("The notion of equality [carries] a certain *soupçon* of logically or mathematically demonstrable certainty and objectivity").

[8] Rae, *Equalities*, p. 3 (referring to "the universal use of equality as a category of thought").

on grounds of "sex" means under the Equal Rights Amendment. Everyone agrees that the ERA would render men and women equal under the law, but people have different conceptions of what such sexual equality means. Some people contend, and some deny, that it will require men and women to be treated interchangeably for purposes of military combat duty. Others contend, and others deny, that it mandates subsidized abortions for indigent women, legitimates homosexual marriage, or outlaws separate athletic teams and events for men and women.[9] Indeed, the seventeen states that have adopted ERAs of their own differ considerably in their interpretations of what such equality means.[10]

To be sure, some of these competing conceptions of equality may depart from what the authors of the ERA specifically intended, and from what a majority of Americans consider fair and just. Yet they all constitute bona fide conceptions of equality. Consider the question of maternity leaves for women. There is much disagreement about whether employers ought to be required by law to offer nonmandatory maternity leaves to pregnant employees. Some people favor such maternity leaves; others do not. Significantly, however, the two groups cannot easily resolve their dispute in terms of equality, because both groups plausibly claim to be treating men and women equally. Advocates of maternity leave argue that maternity leaves treat men and women equally by giving working women the same opportunity as working men to engage in "reproductive activity" without jeopardizing their work.[11] Opponents of maternity leave argue that the only policy which treats men and women equally is one which either grants both men and women parental leaves or denies them both parental leaves.[12] Both groups wish to treat men and women equally, but

[9] Compare Lee, *A Lawyer Looks at the Equal Rights Amendment*, pp. 43, 55, 64–66, 78–79, with Emerson and Lifton, "Should E.R.A. Be Ratified?" pp. 233–34. See also Steiner, *Constitutional Inequality*.

[10] See Driscoll and Rouse, "Through a Glass Darkly," p. 1282; Williams, "Equality Guarantees in State Constitutional Law," p. 1195. Cf. Karasik, "Equal Protection of the Law under the Federal and Illinois Constitutions," p. 263.

[11] Herma Hill Kay makes a pointed case for the "equality" of maternity leaves. See Kay, "Equality and Difference," p. 27:

> In order to maintain a woman's equality of opportunity during her pregnancy, we should modify as far as reasonably possible those aspects of her work where her job performance is adversely affected by the pregnancy. Unless we do so, she will experience employment disadvantages arising from her reproductive activity that are not encountered by her male co-worker.

[12] See Williams, "The Equality Crisis," pp. 196–98. See also Williams, "Equality's Riddle," p. 331.

they have contrary and inconsistent conceptions of equality. The first paradox, then, is that equality appears to be one thing to all people and yet different things to different people.

The second paradox is that 'equality' has favorable connotations, and yet is not itself an evaluative term. Thus, like 'justice', 'equality' is a word with favorable associations. It is a "virtue word,"[13] a word which tends to refer to relationships which are desirable. That is why advocates find it easier to argue in favor of equality than against it. Arguments in the name of equality put opponents "on the defensive." Equality is a "loaded word." We "feel constrained by the very word ['equality']—to deny equality is almost to blaspheme."[14]

Yet unlike 'justice', 'equality' is not an evaluative term. An evaluative term is a word which denotes value. 'Justice' is an evaluative term, because to say something is "just" *means* that it is right and good. Not so with equality. To say something is "equal" is not to say that it is right and good. Hence the irony in Anatole France's description of French law: "The law in its majestic equality, forbids the rich as well as the poor to sleep under bridges, to beg in the streets, and to steal bread."[15] Anatole France recognized that laws against theft and vagrancy create a kind of equality, but in calling it such, he scarcely meant to commend it. Equality has laudatory connotations, but a person can condemn particular equalities without in any way contradicting himself. Some equalities are desirable, while others, like the equality in Hitler's concentration camps and the equality of cruel Procrustes, are notoriously unjust.

Now it may be suggested that there is an easy solution to this second paradox of equality. The reason 'equality' has laudatory connotations, it may be argued, is that 'equality' for adults is something like 'sweets' for children. The word 'sweets' has laudatory connotations for children, because it refers to something which most of them happen to relish most of the time. Unfortunately, this solution to the second paradox is inconsistent with the import of the first paradox. 'Equality' does not refer to a single thing which people can either like or dislike; rather, as the debate

[13] Pennock, Introduction to *Equality*, p. ix ("Equality . . . is a 'virtue word' ").

[14] Kristol, "Equality as an Ideal," p. 110 ("Every inequality is on the defensive"); de Cervera, "The Paradoxes of Equality," p. 238 (equality is a "loaded word"); Ryan, *Equality*, p. 3 ("We feel constrained by the very word—to deny equality is almost to blaspheme").

[15] Anatole France, *Le Lys Rouge* (1894), quoted in John Bartlett, *Familiar Quotations*, 14th rev. ed. (Boston: Little, Brown, 1968), p. 802a.

over the ERA demonstrates, it encompasses a range of "mutually exclusive" "antagonistic," and "incompatible" conceptions about which people inevitably disagree.[16]

These paradoxical features (i.e., that it has both one meaning and many meanings, and that it is a virtue word which does not always refer to virtuous things) combine to give 'equality' great rhetorical force. Together they mean that

—Because 'equality' lends itself to so many diverse conceptions, an advocate who wishes to state his claim in the language of equality can often find a way of doing so.

—Because 'equality' also expresses a single concept, an advocate who makes his claim in the language of equality appears to be seeking the same things as sought in previous crusades for equality.

—Because 'equality' is a virtue word, an advocate who wears the mantle of equality puts his adversaries on the defensive.

—Because 'equality' does not *by definition* signify as something right and good, advocates who argue that equality is right and good cannot be accused of begging the normative question in dispute.

This essay is a study of the foregoing paradoxes and their role in the rhetorical force of 'equality'. It investigates some of the reasons why expressing claims in the language of equality tends to invest them with greater weight than stating them in alternative modes. Studies of equality come in different forms. Some, like John Rawls's seminal *Theory of Justice*, are essentially apologetic, consisting of arguments in favor of, or against, the justness of particular conceptions of equality. Others are essentially historical, tracing the rise and fall of diverse conceptions of equality over time. Still others are economic, analyzing the feasibility of certain equalities, or sociological, studying popular attitudes toward equality. This study is none of these. It is an exercise in "analysis."[17] It is an attempt to understand the persuasiveness of equality claims by examining the language of equality.

[16] Rae, *Equalities*, pp. 2, 4, 132, 138–40 (emphasis omitted).

[17] For a discussion of the distinction between "analysis" and "evaluation," see White, *Grounds of Liability*, pp. 2–6. See especially pp. 5–6:

Evaluative judgments can be argued for, supported, and justified; they can be accepted or rejected for good or bad reasons. One can be brainwashed, converted, or persuaded into them. But they are not taught and learned like scientific or analytic truths. Teaching someone how highly the freedom of the

This is an analysis of how the words 'equality' and 'equal' work in ordinary discourse. What is it to be equal? What is it that people or things are when they are equal? What does it mean to state that people are "equal" in law and morals? The questions are essentially conceptual. The advantage of conceptual analysis is that, being grounded in ordinary language, it rests on matters on which each of us is already an authority. As such, it is both modest and immodest in its aspirations: immodest, because it purports to reveal significant features of language of which we have hitherto been unaware; modest, because, even when successful, it creates the impression of belaboring the obvious—of reminding us of things that, in some sense, we realize we have always known.

The disadvantage of conceptual analysis is that I shall have nothing to say about what many people above all wish to know—nothing about what equalities actually exist or ought to exist. In return, however, I hope to cast light on some central paradoxes of equality, including the fact that equality can be both one thing to all people and different things to different people; that equality tends to be laudatory without being defined as laudatory; that things which are equal in one respect are necessarily unequal in others; that all rules, however much they may discriminate among people, nevertheless treat people equally; that complying with a rule treats people equally, while violating a rule does not always treat them unequally; that treating people equally does not always mean treating them as equals; that "equals should be treated equally" also means that "unequals should be treated unequally"; that normative disputes are never about "Whether equality?" but always about "Which equality?"; and that, just as *all* normative disputes are about equality, *none* is really about equality.

This essay is an outgrowth of a conceptual thesis that I advanced in a series of articles published in the early 1980s. I first advanced the thesis in an article entitled, perhaps unhappily, "The Empty Idea of Equality"—unhappily because the title caused some people to assume that I considered statements of normative equality to be

---

innocent is rated by Roman law, by the Church, by his neighbours, or by God, or showing him the correct analysis of the notion of freedom is not teaching him to rate this freedom highly. Knowing how highly to rate it is no more like knowing how highly it is rated than knowing what to call your dog is like knowing what your neighbour's dog is called. For scientific or analytic answers one turns to a clever or learned man, for evaluative answers to a wise man. Skill and knowledge are the qualities of the former; judgment of the latter.

meaningless, whereas I meant that they are *derivative*. As a consequence of response to the article, and further reflection on my part, I have modified my original views in several respects. While I continue to believe that much of the thesis has validity, I now believe that equality in mathematics may differ fundamentally from equality elsewhere; that a certain class of rights may indeed be usefully viewed as "equality rights"; that the so-called presumption of equality has plausible force; and that the inherent ambiguities of equality, which I once considered solely a vice, may be a virtue in some contexts.

I am deeply grateful to friends and colleagues for intellectual exchange that has brought me to my present understanding of equality. Terrance Sandalow, in a faculty-student seminar on "The Idea of Equality," first introduced me to the philosophical literature on equality. My colleague Don Regan, with his customary generosity and acuity, engaged in a long and critical correspondence with me in the early years when I was still groping my way. Gerald MacCallum, Chaim Perelman, Felix Oppenheim, Jeremy Waldron, Carl Wellman, and Alan White, in their studies of freedom, justice, rules, property, and rights, provided models of the kind of conceptual analysis I chose to pursue. Steven Burton, Edwin Chemerinsky, Anthony D'Amato, William Cohen, Kent Greenawalt, Kenneth Karst, Michel Rosenfeld, and Kenneth Simons all wrote original and thoughtful essays in response to my initial essay. Ken Simons, after five years of trying, finally persuaded me that there is a place for "rights" of equality in normative discourse. Tom Green and James Boyd White helped me think through my motivations in undertaking this investigation. Several of my friends and colleagues were kind enough to read and comment on the manuscript. Tom Green, Leo Katz, Jim Krier, Terrance Sandalow, Fred Schauer, and Brian Simpson generously set aside time to read and annotate it from beginning to end. Bruce Frier, James Boyd White, and Nicolas White all read portions of it. Jan Opdyke, my gifted freelance copyeditor, helped me express myself the way I wished.

I am also profoundly indebted to others for support. The John Simon Guggenheim Memorial Foundation supported the leave of absence during which I wrote "The Empty Idea of Equality." The William W. Cook Fund of the University of Michigan Law School supported my research during the summers of 1987 and 1988. Barbara Vaccaro of the reference department of the University of Michigan Law Library responded to my every plea for help. Barbara Brown, my secretary, with her usual calm and efficiency, helped me prepare the manuscript for copyediting. Penguin Books Ltd. granted me permission to reproduce portions of Hugh Tredennick's translation of the *Phaedo* in *The Last Days of Socrates* (Penguin Classics, revised edition, 1969), copyright Hugh Tredennick, 1954, 1959, 1969. Russell Hardin and the editors of *Ethics* were kind enough to publish an earlier version of Chapter 8. Bobbie and David Krueger opened their house to me in Antigua, Guatemala, in the winter of 1988 as a quiet retreat in which to complete the manuscript, and my friends there, including Pamela Hirst-Prins, Michael Hopkins, Howard and Nancy Jewell, Xenii Nielsen, and Dennis and Louisa Wheeler, have made me long to return.

I owe much to many people, some of whom I have failed to mention. What I have received from my wife, Marianne, and my children, Jonathan, Carla, and Anna, in happiness of family, is beyond measure.

SPEAKING OF EQUALITY

INTRODUCTION

One day, while on vacation in Guatemala, I go to a *campesino* market to buy food for dinner. I ask a vendor for one pound of black beans. He puts a brass weight marked "one pound" in one pan of a hand-held balance and pours beans into the other pan until the two come into balance. "Bueno," he says, "ya son iquales" ("Good, now they're equal").

What does the vendor mean when he says that the two pans of the scale are "equal"? Does he mean that they are absolutely identical in weight? Does he mean that they are highly similar in weight? Or does 'equal' mean something different from—something in between—'identical', on the one hand, and 'similar', on the other?

I try to buy a newspaper, but the vendor cannot make change for a $10 bill. I ask the pharmacist for change. She takes the $10 bill and gives me two $5 bills, while counting aloud, "5 + 5 = 10."

What does the pharmacist mean by saying "5 + 5 = 10"? Does 'equal' have the same meaning in arithmetic as it does for the *campesino*? If the pharmacist means something different, where does the difference lie—in the meaning of the word 'equal' or in something to which the 'equal' refers? Is there any core meaning of 'equality' that remains constant in both usages?

After buying snacks for my three children, I sit in a cafe and read the newspaper. I read that the people of Guatemala have recently adopted a new constitution, which states that "in Guatemala, all people are free and equal." What does it mean to say in law that all people are equal? Does the legal equality of one Guatemalan to another differ from the mathematical equality of "5 + 5 = 10" and the descriptive equality of the two pans of the balance scale? Is there any sense in which the meaning of equality remains the same in all three instances? Why does the concept of equality in the Guatemalan constitution seem more elusive, more complex, and more controversial than the equality of "5 + 5 = 10"? And if the former equality is more enigmatic than the latter, where does

3

the enigma lie—in the concept of equality itself, or somewhere else?

I return home with the snacks for the children—chocolate for my son, gum for my daughters. "Because I want to treat you all equally," I say, "I have brought each of you your favorite treat." My son likes the chocolate but not my explanation. "I agree that you're treating us fairly," he says, "but you're not treating us equally because you're bringing us different things." Who is right? Am I right that I treated my children equally, or is my son right that I did not? Or is it possible that both of us are right?

My older daughter has a different problem with the gum. Like her younger sister she would rather have gum than chocolate, but unlike her sister, she does not care much for any kind of sweet. She would rather have the money than the gum. "I know you're trying to be fair," she says, "but it's not really equal to give the same thing to both of us if it's something she likes more than I do."

Am I right in thinking that I am treating my daughters equally by giving the same quantity of gum to each without further distinguishing between them? Or is the older child right when she says that no distribution is really equal which has a disparate impact on them by giving one more pleasure than the other? Are we both right? Or does the answer lie in the distinction some commentators draw between treating people "equally," on the one hand, and treating them "as equals," on the other? Have I succeeded in treating the girls equally and yet failed to treat them as equals? Or is it sophistic to distinguish between equal treatment and treatment as equals?

The older daughter's complaint also raises a question about the relationship between fair treatment and equal treatment. What is the connection between treating a person fairly and treating her equally? Why does she regard it as a form of moral criticism to call the treatment "unequal"? Is unequal treatment a moral concept, or is it a purely descriptive concept? Is it both?

I am still thinking about the relationship between equal treatment and fair treatment when my wife calls us to dinner. My wife serves the meal to the children by giving the largest portion to our son, who is a teenager and has the largest appetite, the next largest portion to the older daughter, who is going through a growth spurt, and the smallest portion to the youngest, who never eats much at dinner. She also gives everyone a glass of water. Everything goes smoothly until I suggest that we have treated the children equally by treating them in accordance with their needs. My son does not like my use of 'equal'.

"I don't get it," he says. "The more you talk about equality, the less I understand it. 'Equal' means giving us each the same amount: It means taking food and dividing it by the number of people at the table. What Mom did with the glasses of water was equal. What she did with the meal was proportional—dividing the meal in proportion to our needs. 'Equal' is equal; it's not proportional."

I resist the temptation to say that while some commentators agree with him, others (including Aristotle) disagree. Some agree that per-capita distributions are the only truly equal distributions. Others believe that, while per-capita distributions differ in substance from distributions in accord with needs (or in accord with merit, or effort, or wants), per capita distributions are no more inherently equal than other principled distributions.

Nor do I tell my son that some commentators would question the proposition he regards as self-evident, namely, that his mother treated him and his sisters equally by giving them each a glass of water. Whether it is truly equal, they would say, depends upon her *reason* for giving him a glass of water. If she gave him the glass of water because (and *only* because) she had already given water to his sisters, then she treated him equally. If, however, she gave him the glass of water because she believes every child is entitled to at least one glass of water per meal (and not because she had already given glasses of water to his sisters), then she did not treat him equally with his sisters. This is so, they say, because treatment is equal if and only if it is treatment to which a person is entitled only by virtue of its having already been given to others.

After dinner several children from the neighborhood come to the door soliciting contributions for their parish church's Lenten celebration. Each holds out a tin can asking that we favor him with our donation. Our girls both want to give a portion of their allowance, but they don't know how they should distribute it. My wife, not seeing any basis for distinguishing among the children, feels we should divide the donation among them equally. "Unless someone gives me a good reason for preferring one child over the others," she says, "I really think we have to treat them the same."

My son, who is embarrassed by the throng of children, doesn't feel presumptively obliged to treat them equally. "I don't see why it's up to us to find reasons for treating them differently; it's up to them to show us reasons for treating them the same. Why do we have to resolve doubts in their favor?"

The difference of opinion between my wife and son is the difference between competing normative propositions—competing maxims—regarding equality. My wife is proceeding in accord with what some call "the presumption of equality," that is, the normative proposition that "people ought to be treated equally unless there are good reasons for treating them differently." My son, feeling no presumption one way or the other, may be unconsciously proceeding in accord with what is sometimes called the "principle of equality," namely, the principle that "equals should be treated equally, and unequals should be treated unequally."

Which of the two propositions of equality is the more persuasive? Are they consistent with one another? What do they both mean in the context at hand? Who are the "people" who are to be treated equally within the meaning of the "presumption of equality"—only those children who are soliciting contributions at our door, or all the door-to-door solicitors in town? What would constitute a "good reason" for treating the children unequally within the meaning of the presumption? Is a personal preference for redheads a good reason? Who are the "equals" who are to be treated equally within the meaning of the "principle of equality"—the first child to approach us, or the one we wish most to please? And what is the meaning of "equal treatment" within both propositions of equality—to donate to the most courteous child, or to all the children per capita?

I turn on the evening news to hear about a controversial campaign by Guatemalan women in favor of affirmative action. Advocates on both sides of the controversy adopt the language of equality. I am reminded of other controversies in which both sides invoke 'equality' in support of their contrary positions—controversies over the use of sex tables in computing life insurance, the use of height and strength requirements for fire departments, and the maintenance of separate athletic events for men and women. How does the concept of equality accommodate such mutually exclusive positions, and what is the source of its compelling rhetorical force? Why is it easier to argue in favor of equality than against it? Why is inequality always on the defensive? Is it because equality is inherently desirable, or presumptively desirable? If either, how can equality also lend itself to the most controverted of social causes? How can equality be simultaneously both desirable and controversial?

In one sense, these questions regarding equality differ significantly. Some involve descriptive statements of equality; others involve prescriptive statements of equality. Some look to whether rules are equal on their face, others to whether rules are equal as applied. Some concern the meaning of 'equals', others the meaning of 'equal treatment'. Some probe the relationship between equality and per-capita distribution, others the relationship between equality and rights of nondiscrimination. Some involve propositions of equality ("equals should be treated equally"), others the rhetorical force of equality. Yet in another sense the questions are also the same. They all call for an analysis of language—an inquiry into ordinary usages of the word 'equality'. Their answers turn not on contested moral propositions but on linguistic analysis of the concept of equality in moral and legal discourse.

It is fitting that these questions of equality should differ from one another and yet be the same, for equality is itself a relationship that uniquely straddles the gap between "different" and "same": things that are equal, being distinct things, are necessarily different; and yet, being equal, they are also the same. Moreover, the general concept of equality that underlies particular relationships of equality has both a fixed element, which remains the same in all its usages (at least regarding persons and things we perceive through the senses), and a variable term, which can differ greatly from one statement of equality to another. The key to understanding the meaning and rhetorical force of 'equality' in law and morals, I believe, lies in identifying the kinds of variable terms that enter into moral and legal statements of equality.

PART ONE

THE ORDINARY MEANING OF 'EQUALITY'

The words 'equality', 'equal', and 'equally' have meanings which range over various settings. Sometimes they signify descriptive relationships, e.g., "Carla and Amy are equal to one another in height." Sometimes they signify prescriptive relationships, e.g., "All human beings are equal in the sight of God." Sometimes they straddle descriptive and prescriptive relationships, as in complaints by children that their parents have not "treated" them "equally."

What happens to 'equality' and its cognates as they range from one setting to another? Is 'equality' a word like 'square', which has many different meanings depending upon whether one is talking about a Euclidean "square," a "square meal," "St. Mark's Square," "Melvin, the square," "the square of the number 25," to "square" accounts, or a draftsman's compass and square? Is 'equal' a word like 'rectangle', which has the same meaning in every setting? Or is it, perhaps, a word like 'game', which (as Ludwig Wittgenstein has shown) has usages that at most share certain "family resemblances"?[1]

Interestingly, 'equality' seems to differ from all of the foregoing words. It differs from 'rectangle' because it appears to have more than one meaning. It differs from 'square' because its various meanings seem to have something in common. Yet it also differs from 'game' because the different meanings of 'equality' have more in common than mere family resemblances. Thus, 'equality' seems to *combine* the features of words (like 'rectangle') that retain their meaning in every setting and words (like 'square') that change their meaning from one setting to another: 'equality' appears to have both a single and constant meaning in all its usages

---

[1] For a discussion of Wittgenstein's views regarding "universals," including his discussion of "games," see Chapter 2, pp. 47–51.

and a wide range of variable meanings. In that sense 'equal' works like the word 'sequence'. A sequence is typically defined as "the following of one thing after another in a continuous, logical or recurring order of a certain kind."[2] Every sequence is in some sense the same, because every sequence is a continuous, logical, or recurring order of a certain kind; yet sequences come in an infinite variety, because there are infinite ways in which things can be ordered to follow one after the other. 'Sequence' has the capacity to retain its meaning while constantly changing its meaning because it expresses a concept that consists of both a fixed term, which remains constant in all settings, and a variable term, which changes from one setting to another.

'Equality', I believe, has the same semantic structure as 'sequence', at least with respect to persons and tangible things; for equality, too, is a concept that consists of a fixed term which remains constant in all its usages and a "variable"[3] term that can take a nearly infinite variety of forms. To understand the relationship between these fixed and variable terms in the language of equality, we shall start by analyzing simple and uncontroverted statements of descriptive equality and mathematical equality. Then, having formulated a tentative definition of 'equality' in those settings, we shall apply it to more elusive and problematic statements of prescriptive equality.

[2] *Webster's New World Dictionary*, p. 1299.

[3] Let us, then, . . . take up our problem again from the very beginning. The question is to find a formula of justice which is common to the different conceptions we have analyzed. This formula must contain an indeterminate element—what in mathematics is called a variable—the determination of which will give now one, now another, conception of justice. The common idea will constitute a definition of formal or abstract justice. Each particular or concrete formula of justice will constitute one of the innumerable values of formal justice.

Perelman, *The Idea of Justice and the Problem of Argument*, p. 15. See also Feinberg, *Social Justice*, p. 100 (quoting from a doctoral dissertation by Louis Katzner in which Katzner refers to the principle of equality as containing "a completely unspecified variable").

O N E

DESCRIPTIVE EQUALITY

Statements of equality seem simple, even self-evident, in the area of weights and measures. Perhaps by analyzing how 'equality' works in such seemingly self-evident statements, we will learn something about how it functions in the more perplexing and elusive language of law and morals. Thus imagine the following:

Making a Pound Cake

I decide to make a pound cake. The recipe calls for a pound each of flour, butter, and sugar. I take a spring-mounted digital scale from the cupboard. The scale measures weight in increments of ounces by displaying the number of ounces that an object weighs, to the nearest full ounce. The scale is accurate to within .01 ounces, meaning that, if the scale indicates that an object is closer to 16 ounces than to any other weight in full ounces, it *is* that, plus or minus .01 ounces.

I pour cake flour into the pan of the scale until the flashing numbers stop at "16." I empty the measured flour into a bowl and repeat the process with the sugar and butter until I have 16 ounces of each. I now have "equal" amounts of flour, sugar, and butter.

Notice that I use a digital scale (which measures weight in whole numbers) rather than an analog scale (which measures weight continuously), and that it is a spring scale (which weighs individual objects) rather than a balance scale (which weighs one object against another). I shall postpone for now discussing the implications for equality of shifting from a digital scale to an analog scale and from a spring scale to a balance scale. I will also delay examining the implications of the fact that the digital scale is accurate only to within .01 ounces. It suffices in the meantime that we can meaningfully say, and ordinarily do say, that the flour, sugar, and butter are all "equal" in weight.

The foregoing equalities—like equalities of speed and size—are

11

simple and evident. We use them every day without the slightest difficulty. They are among the first things we teach our children. We shall begin our inquiry, therefore, by identifying precisely what we mean by 'equality' in these simple settings that we seem implicitly to understand. What precisely do we mean when we say that the pans of flour and sugar are "equal"? What do we mean when we say the same about two lengths of rope, or two volumes of water? What essential elements, if any, do such statements have in common? What, if anything, is the distinctive "generic"[1] concept of equality that underlies them?

The Constitutive Elements of Descriptive Equality

Plurality

Simple descriptive equalities have three features in common. First, they all involve "plurality," that is, they all involve a relationship between two or more things. Thus we say "The pan of flour is equal to the pan of sugar." We do not say "The pan of flour is equal"—not without simultaneously making reference, either explicitly or implicitly, to the thing or things the flour is equal *to*. This suggests that 'equality' is a term we use to refer to a relationship obtaining between at least two things.[2] The same is true of the term 'inequality'. We may sensibly say "The pan of sugar and bowl of butter-and-flour are unequal in weight." But we do not say "The pan of sugar is unequal"—not, at least, without referring, explicitly or implicitly, to the thing or things to which the pan of sugar is unequal.

Difference

Second, the simple equalities under discussion here all involve a relationship between things that are distinguishable in one or more respects. Thus, while we say "The pan of flour and the pan of sugar are equal," we also distinguish between the items being described. "The pan of flour" and "the pan of sugar" are not different descriptions of the same thing; they are contrasting descriptions of two different things.

---

[1] Adler and Hutchins, "The Idea of Equality," p. 304 (discussing "the generic notion of equality"). See also p. 319 (discussing "the root meaning running throughout the use of 'equality' ").

[2] See Menne, "Identity, Equality, Similarity," pp. 50, 51 (statements of equality and inequality "presuppos[e] two objects").

Indeed, if we were using two different descriptions to refer to the same underlying thing, we would never assert them to be "equal." To illustrate, assume that having measured out a pound of flour for the pound cake, I place it in a blue bowl. I could plausibly say "The flour in the blue bowl *is* the flour I measured for the cake," or "The flour in the blue bowl is *the same* as, or *identical to,* the flour I measured for the cake." But I would not say that the flour in the blue bowl "equals" the flour I measured for the cake. As Hugo Bedau puts it, "Equality . . . not only does not imply identity, it implies non-identity."[3]

Comparison

The third feature the equalities we are discussing have in common is that they all involve a *comparative* relationship. When we say "The flour and sugar are equal in weight," we are not merely describing each of them by reference to weight; we are comparing them by reference to weight. We do the same when we say that one thing is longer than another—or larger, or faster, or more expensive, or more beautiful. We are describing the flour and the sugar not in isolation, but in reference to one another.

To illustrate the significance of comparative statements, consider the sentence "The flour and sugar are both white." This statement tells us something about both the flour and the sugar: it describes them by reference to color. But it tells us nothing more than the two sentences "The flour is white" and "The sugar is white." It tells us nothing about the flour and sugar that we would not know by inspecting them in isolation from one another. In contrast, the statements "The flour and sugar are equal in weight" and "The flour is more finely ground than the sugar" tell us something about the flour and sugar that we cannot learn about either the flour or the sugar by examining them in isolation from one another. What they tell us about the flour is dependent upon what they simultaneously tell us about the sugar, and vice versa.

This comparative element of equality is itself complex, however, and warrants fuller investigation. How, analytically, does one go

[3] Bedau, "Egalitarianism and the Idea of Equality," pp. 3, 12. See also Menne, "Identity, Equality, Similarity," p. 57 ("[In the case of both 'identity' and 'equality'] we are confronted with two names, but in the case of identity there is only one object corresponding to the name whereas in the case of equality we are dealing with two objects").

about making a comparison? What are the essential presuppositions of comparisons? There are several.

Common Standard of Measurement. Comparisons of two or more things presuppose a common standard of measurement. We cannot say that one thing is longer, or hotter, or more beautiful than another without first having a common standard of length or heat or beauty by which to measure them. Nor can we say that the pan of flour and the pan of sugar are equal in weight, or unequal in weight, without first having a common standard of weight by which to measure them. "You wouldn't be understood," Elizabeth Wolgast observes, "if you said that a rose and a hyacinth were unequal, not unless it was understood what standard of comparison you had in mind. There might be such a measure—depth of color, for instance, or size, or even fragrance. But the judgment of inequality and a measure go together, the former requires the latter."[4]

To demonstrate, imagine the task of comparing two things without a common standard of measure. Imagine, for example, that a shopkeeper places a hefty sack of flour in a room equipped with a scale calibrated in grams, and another hefty sack of flour in an adjoining room equipped with a scale calibrated in ounces. The shopkeeper orders his assistant, who does not know the formula for converting grams to ounces, to determine whether the two sacks are equal or unequal in weight. What will the assistant do? Presumably he will conclude that he cannot determine whether the sacks are equal or unequal in weight because he cannot compare them in weight, and that he cannot compare them in weight because he has no common standard by which to measure them.

Furthermore, comparisons not only presuppose the *existence* of a common standard of measurement, they also presuppose that the subjects of comparison are themselves *measurable* by the common standard.[5] Imagine trying to compare things that are not amenable to a common standard. Imagine that a professor of Aesthetics directs a student to determine whether a certain rosebush and a certain poem are equal or unequal in fragrance. How will the student respond? He might respond by offering to determine

[4] Wolgast, *Equality and the Rights of Women*, p. 38.

[5] Aristotle may have been the first to make this observation—see *Physics* VII.4.248b6–10—but it has also been well made by others. See, for example, Adler and Hutchins, "The Idea of Equality," p. 318 ("[E]quality supposes some element of sameness. There must be some basis of comparability. . . . Between things such as Aristotle, a hard surface, a loud noise, a red flag, there is mere diversity; hence no question of equality or inequality").

whether the rosebush and poem are equal in some *other* respect—say, in respect of their ages. Or he might offer to determine whether the rosebush and the book in which the poem appears are equal in weight, or in cost. But he cannot even try to determine whether the rosebush and poem are equal or unequal in fragrance because he cannot compare them for fragrance; and he cannot compare them for fragrance because poems are not measurable for fragrance.

Finally, all comparisons of two or more things presuppose not only that the things have been jointly measured by a common standard, but also that their respective measures have been juxtaposed to determine the extent to which they differ. Imagine, for example, a shopkeeper with a poor memory who sets about to determine whether two sacks of flour are equal or unequal in weight. He takes the first sack, weighs it on a scale calibrated in grams, notes the weight on a slip of paper, and places the piece of paper in his pocket. He then takes the second sack of flour, weighs it, too, on the scale, notes its weight on a second slip of paper, and puts that slip in his pocket as well. Remembering the two slips of paper in his pocket but forgetting what they say, he asks himself, "Are the two sacks of flour equal or unequal in weight?" How will he answer his question? Presumably he will realize that, although he has taken the step of subjecting both sacks to a common standard of measure, he cannot know whether the sacks are equal or unequal in weight without taking the additional step of juxtaposing their respective measures by that standard to determine whether they differ.

Measurement of "More or Less": Aristotle. Some commentators, including Aristotle, have argued that when one compares two or more things to determine whether they are equal, one necessarily uses a standard of comparison that is designed to determine whether one thing is "more" or "less" than another. Determining equality, they argue, means determining that the things being compared are neither more nor less than one another as measured by a standard for determining more or less.[6]

Aristotle's generalization holds true for many determinations of equality, particularly the most common descriptive equalities of weight, length, volume, speed, temperature, cost, and number. Consider, for example, our earlier conclusion that the pan of flour

---

[6] See Aristotle, *Metaphysics* I.4.1055b10–1056a23; Aristotle, *Nicomachean Ethics* V.3.1131a10–20. See also Plato, *Parmenides* 169d; Russell, *The Principles of Mathematics*, pp. 159, 167–68, 218–19.

and the pan of sugar were equal in weight. To make the determination, we first measured each pan by a standard designed to determine whether things are more or less heavy, on a scale of one-ounce increments. Then, having measured each pan and determined that each weighed 16 ounces, we juxtaposed their respective weights to determine whether one was more or less than the other. We concluded that the two pans were equal when we determined that their respective measures were neither more nor less than one another.

Nevertheless, Aristotle's generalization fails to account for all uses of 'equality'. While it does account for equalities based on standards that measure for increments of "more" or "less," it fails to account for equalities based on binary standards that measure in terms of "either/or."[7] Binary standards of equality measure what Mortimer Adler and Robert Maynard Hutchins call "differences of type" as opposed to "differences of degree."[8] Such standards can be used not only to measure entities that differ in type *rather than* degree, but also to measure entities that differ in type *and* degree, by determining whether they fall within what John Rawls calls a certain "range" of degree.[9] Binary standards of mea-

---

[7] This is not to say that Aristotle ignored cases of identity by reference to standards of "either/or." He recognized their existence but took the position that we refer to them not in the language of "equality," but in the language of "likeness." See Aristotle, *Physics* VII.4.249b1–3. Like Aristotle, I think that we use the language of likeness to refer to such identities, but I believe that the language of likeness is not exclusive, and that we *also* sometimes use the language of equality for such identities.

[8] Some [equalities], however, are of such a sort as to admit of degrees, whereas others do not. All citizens, for example, are equal as citizens and have equal political rights (*isopoliteia*). But not all citizens have equal political power (*isokratia*). The President is no more a citizen than an ordinary voter is, yet he obviously possesses much greater power.
   This example reveals still another distinction among equalities. It is the distinction between what we will call a *difference of degree* and a *difference of type*. In the one case, men are equal or unequal with respect to a trait, such as political power, that may be possessed in varying degrees. In the other case, there is no question of degree but merely of the presence or absence of a trait, such as citizenship.

Adler and Hutchins, "The Idea of Equality," p. 306. See also Benn, "Egalitarianism and the Equal Consideration of Interests," pp. 63–64.

[9] See Rawls, *A Theory of Justice*, p. 508 (discussing the measurement of "range properties"):

   Moreover, it is not the case that founding equality on [people's] natural capacities is incompatible with an egalitarian view. All we have to do is to select a range property (as I shall say) and to give equal justice to those meeting its conditions. For example, the property of being in the interior of the unit circle

16

surement are particularly important in moral and legal discourse because, as we shall see in Chapter 3, prescriptive equalities are frequently based on binary standards of comparison. However, they can also form the basis for descriptive equalities.[10] For example:

Ping-Pong Balls

My neighbor is a serious ping-pong player. He insists on using new ping-pong balls when he plays, but he lets the neighborhood children use the old balls to play among themselves. To distinguish among the balls, he marks them according to their condition, as follows:

—he leaves new balls unmarked;

—he marks used balls that possess surface defects with a "D," regardless of how major or how minor the surface defects happen to be;

—he marks all other used balls with an "O," regardless of how much or how little they have been used.

To maintain order, he posts a sign for the neighborhood children which reads, "Please keep balls of equal rank together!"

What does my neighbor mean when he refers to ping-pong balls of "equal" rank? What standard of comparison is he implicitly applying to the balls? Obviously, he is not measuring the balls by whether they are "more" or "less" used or more or less defective, because he regards all used balls as equally used and all balls with surface defects as equally defective. Rather, he is using binary standards to determine *whether they are new or used* (regardless of how more or less used they may be) and *whether they possess or do not possess surface defects* (regardless of how more or less defective

---

is a range property of points in the plane. All points inside this circle have this property although their coordinates vary within a certain range. And they equally have this property, since no point interior to a circle is more or less interior to it than any other interior point.

[10] But see Wolgast, *Equality and the Rights of Women,* p. 45 (arguing that relationships of equality are confined to comparisons based on standards of "more or less" and that it is a misnomer to speak of the "equality" of persons who are identical by binary standards of "either/or"):

There is no measure according to which one human qua human can be said to be greater or less than another. . . . But if that is what is meant by men being equal, the idea is most unfortunately expressed. It is one thing to say that all men are equal, which implies that there is a measure applicable [by which they can be graded], and quite another to say that men are equal *because no [such] measure of them exists.* For the latter claim to be plausible, it should say that neither equality nor inequality apply to human beings.

they may be). By balls of "equal rank," he means balls that have been measured by binary standards; that have been compared to one another, as measured by those binary standards; and that have been found to be indistinguishable as measured by those standards.

Comparative and Noncomparative Standards of Measurement. We have seen that statements of equality are invariably *comparative*, meaning that in order to say two things are "equal," one must first subject them to a common standard of measurement and then juxtapose their resulting measures to see whether they differ. The underlying standards of measurement themselves, however, may be either noncomparative or comparative. The difference is that noncomparative standards of measurement are capable of performing only a single function—the function of measuring each discrete object by itself—thereafter leaving it to the person doing the measuring to perform the additional step of juxtaposing the resulting measures to determine whether they differ. Comparative standards, in contrast, are both more limited and more flexible—more limited because they are incapable of measuring individual objects by themselves, more flexible because they consolidate into a single process the otherwise separate steps of measuring two objects and juxtaposing their respective measures for purposes of comparison.

Recall the spring scale used in "Making a Pound Cake." A spring scale employs a noncomparative standard for measuring weight because it measures *individual* objects with respect to how much they weigh, in this case in whole ounces. The most the scale can do is weigh objects separately; it cannot also *juxtapose* the resulting weights to see how they compare. Thus, in determining that the pan of flour and the pan of sugar were equal in weight, we first used the scale to ascertain the weight of each pan by itself. Then, having weighed each item separately, we put the scale aside and ourselves performed the next step of juxtaposing the two weights to see whether they differed from one another in whole ounces.

In contrast, balance scales employ comparative standards of measurement. Balance scales (the kind held in the medieval representation of blind Justice) are still commonly used by merchants in developing countries.

A Moroccan Market

Jim, on a trip to Morocco, goes to the market in Marrakesh to purchase 200 grams of myrrh. The vendor uses a hand-held balance scale consisting of two empty pans, accurate to within 3 grams. He places a 200-gram brass cylinder in one pan, causing that pan to sink and the other to rise. He then pours myrrh into the second pan until the two pans are even, or balanced, to the naked eye. He removes the 200-gram brass cylinder and gives Jim what he has just determined to be an "equal" amount of myrrh.

A balance scale lacks the capacity to weigh individual objects by themselves because, being predicated on a comparative standard of measurement, it can measure objects only in relation to one another, by disclosing whether one object weighs *more* than another, weighs *less* than another, or weighs *neither more nor less*. As it happened, of course, Jim already knew the weight of the brass cylinder—200 grams. But, if Jim had not known, the balance scale alone could not have told him. Nor could it have told him how much the myrrh alone weighed. But, while it cannot measure objects individually, a balance scale possesses a capacity that spring scales lack: it can weigh two objects and simultaneously juxtapose their respective weights. Indeed, a balance scale not only can perform the two operations simultaneously, but *must* perform them simultaneously, because, being predicated on a comparative standard of measurement, it can measure an object only by reference to another object. Thus, the Moroccan balance scale measured the myrrh for its weight—and measured the brass cylinder for its weight—by disclosing that neither object was lighter and neither was heavier than the other.

These distinctions between spring scales and balance scales, and between noncomparative and comparative standards of measurement, are matters of curiosity at this stage of the inquiry. But it is important to understand the difference between noncomparative and comparative standards of measurement in simple statements of descriptive equality, because the difference becomes significant in the area of prescriptive equalities. We shall see in Chapter 6 that prescriptive equalities not only can but (according to some commentators) *must* be predicated on comparative standards of measurement.

The Distinctive Comparative Relationship of "Equality"

We have identified three features that simple descriptive equalities share. We have seen that in order to make statements of descriptive equality, (i) we must start with two or more things, (ii) these things must differ from one another in some respect, and (iii) we must compare them—by subjecting them to a common standard of measurement and then juxtaposing the resulting measures to determine whether they differ.

What distinguishes descriptive "equality" from other comparative relationships, however, is the *precise kind* of descriptive comparison it signifies. To identify the nature of that relationship, we shall proceed by contrasting equality with several related comparative relationships: the comparative relationship that obtains among things that are identical in a given *dimension*; the relationship that obtains among things that are identical in *all respects*; and the comparative relationship that obtains among two or more distinct things that are *similar*. One can find examples of the first two relationships in Plato's discussion of equality.

Plato's Phaedo

Plato discusses the concepts of equality and inequality in several contexts, some of which anticipate Aristotle's more systematic analysis. Plato's best-known reference to equality occurs not in the later dialogues as a conceptual analysis of equality, but in the *Phaedo* as part of an extended proof of the preexistence of the human soul.[11] Unfortunately, in the course of his discussion, Plato makes untested assumptions about the meaning of equality—or what he calls "absolute equality"—that depart from the way 'equality' is ordinarily used, and by doing so he undermines both his discussion of equality and his proof for the preexistence of the soul.

Plato, speaking through Socrates and Simmias of Thebes, uses equality as an example of something of which human beings have knowledge that they cannot have acquired through experience in the world. We have all had the experience of seeing, touching, and hearing things that are equal, says Socrates, like two sticks that are equal or two stones that are equal. Yet these things which we per-

---

[11] The *Phaedo* as a whole is an inquiry into the immortality of the soul. The argument regarding equality is one that Socrates eventually abandons, not because it fails to demonstrate the preexistence of the soul, but because proof of the *pre*existence of the soul does not also satisfy his goal of demonstrating the *post*existence, or immortality, of the soul. Plato returns to the concept of equality, to discuss it in more abstract terms, in the later dialogue *Parmenides*.

ceive through the senses, though equal in one sense, invariably fall short of being what we would all regard as "absolutely equal":[12]

> [SOCRATES:] We admit, I suppose, that there is such a thing as equality—not the equality of stick to stick and stone to stone, and so on, but something beyond all that and distinct from it—absolute equality. Are we to admit this or not?
> [SIMMIAS:] Yes indeed, said Simmias, most emphatically.
> [SOCRATES:] And do we know what it is?
> [SIMMIAS:] Certainly.
>
> . . . .
>
> [SOCRATES:] Well, now, what do we find in the case of the equal sticks and other things of which we were speaking just now? Do they seem to us to be equal in the sense of absolute equality, or do they fall short of it in so far as they only approximate to equality? Or don't they fall short at all?
> [SIMMIAS:] They do, said Simmias, a long way.[13]

The task for Socrates is to reconcile our universal knowledge of "absolute equality" with our lack of experience of it. We certainly have knowledge of absolute equality, he says, because without it we would not realize that things we perceive through the senses fall short of attaining it. Yet we cannot have acquired the notion of absolute equality through seeing or hearing or touching things in the world, because no two tangible things are ever absolutely equal. The solution, he suggests, is that our souls come into the world already possessing a knowledge of absolute equality which they acquired elsewhere. The dialogue resumes:

> [SOCRATES:] Then we must have had some previous knowledge of equality before the time we first saw equal things and realized that they were striving after equality but fell short of it.

---

[12] Plato's reference to what Tredennick translates as "absolute equality," as well as the entire discussion in *Phaedo* 74b–c, has been the subject of vigorous and extended debate among classical scholars. David Gallop argues that what Tredennick translates as "absolute equality" should instead be translated as "the equal itself." Gallop, *Plato: Phaedo*, p. 121. My colleague James Boyd White has suggested in personal conversation that it should be translated as "equality itself." For an analysis of *Phaedo* 74b–c and a review of the exegetical debate, see Gallop, *Plato: Phaedo*, pp. 119–26. For present purposes, I do not believe it matters which of these proposed translations one accepts.

[13] Plato, *Phaedo* 74a–c (trans. Tredennick).

[SIMMIAS:] That is so.

. . . .

[SOCRATES:] So before we began to see and hear and use our other senses we must somewhere have acquired the knowledge that there is such a thing as absolute equality. Otherwise we could never have realized, by using it as a standard for comparison, that all equal objects of sense are desirous of being like it, but are only imperfect copies.

[SIMMIAS:] That is the logical conclusion, Socrates.

[SOCRATES:] Did we not begin to see and hear and possess our other senses from the moment of birth?

[SIMMIAS:] Certainly.

[SOCRATES:] But we certainly admitted that we must have obtained our knowledge of equality before we obtained them.

[SIMMIAS:] Yes.

[SOCRATES:] So we must have obtained it before birth.

[SIMMIAS:] So it seems.

. . . .

[SOCRATES:] When do our souls acquire this knowledge? It cannot be after the beginning of our mortal life.

[SIMMIAS:] No, of course not.

[SOCRATES:] Then it must be before.

[SIMMIAS:] Yes.

[SOCRATES:] Then our souls had a previous existence, Simmias, before they took on this human shape they were independent of our bodies, and they were possessed of intelligence.[14]

Plato's argument for the preexistence of the soul thus rests on an assumption—the assumption that we humans have a notion of absolute equality which the comparison of tangible things can never approach. Unfortunately, Plato does not explain what he means by absolute equality. The failure is serious, because neither of the two things he may plausibly mean coheres with ordinary notions of equality. These two possible meanings are "identical in a given dimension" and "identical in all respects."

Identical in a Given Dimension

One possibility is that by "absolute equality" Plato means the relationship that obtains between two or more things that have been

[14] Plato, *Phaedo* 74b–76c (trans. Tredennick).

jointly measured and found to be indistinguishable in at least one dimension—such as weight, height, speed, volume, or temperature.

"Things we perceive through the senses can never be absolutely indistinguishable in a given dimension," he would presumably say, "because the more minutely we examine them in a given dimension the more we inevitably perceive differences of degree between them. Look at the things we ordinarily take to be equal— sticks that we take to be equal in length or stones that we take to be equal in weight. If the sticks appear to be equal in length, it is only because we are using a standard of measurement—in inches, centimeters, or something even finer—that is too crude to identify the more minute differences that inevitably obtain between them. If we were continually to refine the standard for measuring length, we would inevitably discover that the two sticks, though indistinguishable by some measures, are not indistinguishable by the finest measure of length." Or so the argument goes.

Plato, in denying that tangible things can ever be absolutely equal, may have had the foregoing argument in mind. Yet one must doubt it, because the argument is flawed. For one thing, there is no logical or empirical reason why things we perceive through the senses cannot be indistinguishable in length or weight or some other dimension by even the finest standards of measure. The finer or more precise the standard of measure, the less likely that any two objects will be indistinguishable by that standard; but the improbability that any two objects will be indistinguishable by a given standard does not negate the possibility that they might be. All material objects consist of atoms and subatomic particles. There is no reason to believe that two objects cannot consist of the same number of atomic or subatomic particles—and thus be indistinguishable from one another by even the finest measures.

Furthermore, even if there were no other respect in which tangible things are indistinguishable by the finest standards of measure, there is at least one respect in which many things are—that is, in respect of their number. Regardless of how finely one counts them, one pile of ten stones is always indistinguishable in number from every other pile of ten stones.

Finally, in denying the possibility of absolute equality, Plato does not appear to be denying that tangible things may be indistinguishable in a given dimension by the most minute measures of that dimension. For if he were, he would have to concede that some tangible things at least *appear* to be absolutely equal. He would have to concede, for example, that sticks of wood which are indistinguishable in length to the naked eye also appear to be absolutely equal. Yet he clearly means to reject that possibility. Speaking through Socrates, he persuades Simmias that sticks of wood will not only always fall short of being absolutely equal, but always fall short by "a long way." It follows that in arguing that no two tangible things are ever absolutely equal, Plato cannot sensibly mean that there is no single dimension in which such things are truly indistinguishable.

Now it might be suggested that, while the foregoing is not what Plato meant when he denied the possibility of absolute equality, it is nevertheless what we today mean when we refer to equality. The trouble is that this would preclude us from using the language of equality in the areas in which we are accustomed to using it most. We are accustomed to invoking equality to describe things that are neither more nor less than one another as measured by what Aristotle called standards of "more" or "less." Yet things that are neither more nor less than one another by one such standard can nearly always be shown to be more or less by some still finer standard for measuring the same dimension. If we were indeed precluded from using the language of equality to compare things measured by standards of more or less, we would have to confine ourselves to using it solely to describe things by *number* or by the binary standard of *either/or*. We would be precluded from referring to things as being "equal" in height, weight, length, or speed, because we ordinarily lack the most precise standards for measuring those dimensions. Needless to say, we do refer to such "equalities," and we do so without any apparent failure of communication.

Identical in All Respects

It is more likely—given Plato's apparent acceptance as paradigmatic of what we shall discover in Chapter 2 to be the kind of equality that obtains in mathematics[15]—that by "absolute equality" Plato meant the relationship that obtains among things that are indistinguishable in *all respects*. If so, Plato is certainly right to conclude that the kinds of distinct things we perceive through the senses necessarily fall short—indeed, fall a "long way" short—of attaining that relationship. For it is axiomatic that things that are

[15] See Chapter 2, especially the Conclusion.

truly indistinguishable in *all* respects are not distinct things, but one and the same thing.[16] As Craig Dilworth writes, following Leibniz:

> [I]f an entity A is the same as an entity B, then, and only then, is it identical with B. Thus when A is said to be identical with itself, or with B, what is being said is that A does not differ from itself, or does not differ from B. And when A and B are identical . . . we are not dealing with two things, but with one thing under different labels or characterizations.[17]

If by "absolute equality" Plato means "identical in all respects," however, he makes a linguistic mistake—the mistake of defining 'equality' in terms of 'identity'. It is a linguistic mistake not because we lack the experience of complete identity, and not because we lack the experience of perfect descriptive equality, but because our concepts of complete identity and descriptive equality are mutually exclusive. Equality, as we conceive and employ it descriptively, is a relationship that presupposes the existence of two or more distinct things; and thus presupposing them, it excludes the possibility of complete identity. Complete identity, on the other hand, is a relationship we conceive and employ with respect to things that are one and the same; thus conceived, it excludes relationships of descriptive equality.

To illustrate the mutually exclusive relationship between complete identity and descriptive equality, and the confusion that results from conflating them, consider an example:

Identical Twins

Mary and Agnes are identical twins. They were born on the same day and at the same hour; they both weighed 6 pounds, 3 ounces, at birth; they have always been the same height in inches. Nevertheless, like all material objects, Mary and Agnes occupy different time and space and consist of different molecules. In addition, they also have very different personalities and life stories:

---

[16] The axiom that things which are the same in every respect are the same thing is commonly known as Leibniz's "principle of the identity of indiscernibles." See Rabinowicz, *Universalizability*, pp. 24–25, 113–14; Perelman, *Justice, Law, and Argument*, p. 35; Cartwright, "Identity and Substitutivity," p. 121 (describing as "Leibnitz's Law," or the "Principle of Identity," the proposition that X is identical to Y if every property of X is a property of Y).

[17] Dilworth, "Identity, Equality, and Equivalence," p. 89.

—Mary is sociable and gregarious. She married her high-school sweetheart, John, and has a baby boy, Joey.

—Agnes, in contrast, is retiring, overweight, childless, and single.

We can imagine twins like Mary and Agnes, and we know how we would talk about the relationships which obtain between them. We would say that the two sisters are "equal" in age (in years, days, and hours), "equal" in height (in feet and inches), and "equal" in birth weight (in pounds and ounces). And we could also say that Mary and the sister of Agnes and the wife of John and the mother of Joey—being one and the same person—are "identical" in all respects. But we would not say that these Mary-persons are "equal" to one another. Why not? Not because they are *not* identical in all respects, but precisely because they *are* identical in all respects and hence lack the feature of being distinguishable that the concept of descriptive equality presupposes.

By the same token, we would not say that the two sisters, Mary and Agnes, are "identical" in all respects, because Agnes and Mary are not the same person and hence do not possess the feature that complete identity presupposes. If Agnes could somehow momentarily become identical in every respect to Mary (in the way that Mary and the wife of John are identical)—that is, if they could both occupy the same time and space and consist of the same molecules and possess the same life histories—Agnes would not suddenly *attain* absolute equality with Mary; rather, she would instantly *lose* her relationships of equality with Mary. Our "ordinary concept of equality," according to Hugo Bedau, "does not admit of our saying that Tully is equal to Cicero, or that water is equal to H_2O, or that any two things are equal to each other unless we are ready to deny the possibility of their identity. . . . Equality thus does not imply identity, it implies nonidentity."[18]

Now it might be argued that the very nature of the relationship of equality between Agnes and Mary (that is, the relationship of being less than identical in all respects) illustrates the precise point Plato was making. The argument would go as follows:

Major Premise: As human beings, we can imagine two or more distinct persons or things (such as Agnes and Mary) as being identical in all respects, a concept we can call "absolute equality."

[18] Bedau, "Egalitarianism and the Idea of Equality," p. 8.

26

Minor Premise: None of the distinct persons or things we perceive through the senses (such as Agnes and Mary) are ever identical in all respects.

Conclusion: As human beings, we have a concept that we can call "absolute equality" that transcends any relationship between persons or things that we perceive through the senses.

The fallacy in the foregoing argument is the major premise. It is a mistake to believe that we can imagine persons or tangible things that are, at the same time, both distinct and indistinguishable. We can imagine one person or tangible thing with multiple descriptions, like "Mary" and "John's wife," whose referents are indistinguishable in all respects; and we can conceive of distinct persons or things, like Agnes and Mary, which are equal in some respects and distinguishable in others. But we cannot imagine persons or tangible things that are, at the same time, both distinct and indistinguishable, because to say two or more persons or things are distinct *means* that they are distinguishable in one or more respects.[19]

Similarity: The Meaning of 'Relevance'

Plato's argument for the preexistence of the soul rests on a misconception regarding the meaning of equality. To say two or more persons or tangible things are equal does not mean that they are the same thing, or that they are identical, or that they are indistinguishable in all respects. 'Equality', though sometimes interchangeable with 'sameness', is not always a synonym for 'sameness'.[20]

---

[19] "[If] two individuals x and y have the identical property F but are themselves not identical, then they must differ at least in a property G." Menne, "Identity, Equality, Similarity," pp. 53–54.

[20] The terms 'equal' and 'same' are sometimes interchangeable, as in the sentences "I gave Mark and Paul equal amounts of cake" and "I gave Mark and Paul the same amounts of cake." But, as Hugo Bedau so acutely demonstrates, the two terms are not *always* interchangeable:

[The] requisite condition of substitutivity for synonym-pairs fails for this pair. If I gave Mark and Paul *equal* servings, I did not give them the *same* serving; what I did was to serve them the same amount, servings of the same size. If I gave you the same answer I gave him, I didn't give you an answer equal to the one I gave him: I gave you the very answer I gave him. To say a man is equal to the task is not to say the man is the same as the task, but that he is up to performing the task.

Bedau, "Egalitarianism and the Idea of Equality," p. 7.

Alternatively, however, it might be argued that 'equality' is a synonym for 'similarity'. Indeed, similarity and equality have much in common. They both presuppose the existence of at least two distinct things. One would not say of people or things that are identical in all respects that they are "similar" (one would not say of John's wife and Joey's mother that they are "similar" to one another). Also, equality and similarity are both comparative relationships. One cannot declare two persons or things to be "similar" without positing a common standard by which to measure their similarity (one cannot say that Mary and Agnes are "similar" in appearance without making reference to common standards for assessing appearance).[21] What precisely do we mean, then, when we measure two or more distinct persons or things by a common standard and declare them similar? What does the meaning of 'similar' reveal about the meaning of 'equal'?

We appear to use the word 'similar' in two different ways. Sometimes by declaring two or more things to be similar, we mean that (1) we have jointly measured them by a certain standard of measure, (2) we have juxtaposed their respective measures by that standard to determine whether they differ, and (3) we have ascertained that although some of their respective measures differ, either *most* of their respective measures or the *most important* of their respective measures are indistinguishable. Consider, for example, the relationship in appearance of the Polish and the Indonesian national flags, as shown in Figure 1. Most of us would say, I expect, that as national symbols the Indonesian and Polish flags are similar. But what do we mean by that? Obviously we do not mean that as national symbols the two flags are indistinguishable in all respects, because if they were, they would symbolize the same nation or nations. We mean, rather, that as measured by the standard we deem appropriate for assessing such symbols, the two flags, though distinguishable in some respects, are indistinguishable in most—or in the most significant—respects.[22] The standard we deem appropriate here is a standard of appearance. We implicitly measure the appearance of flags by a complex standard that distinguishes them according to (i) the colors they employ, (ii) their patterns, and (iii) their words and icons, if any. Measured by

[21] See Brennan, *The Open-Texture of Moral Concepts*, pp. 52–53 ("The question, as I mentioned, turns on the notion of 'similarity'. . . . Similarity is a triadic relation of the form: A is similar to B in respect of C").

[22] See Goodman, "Seven Strictures on Similarity," p. 443 (to say things are "similar" means they are identical in most important respects).

INDONESIAN FLAG

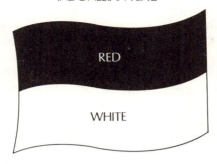

POLISH FLAG

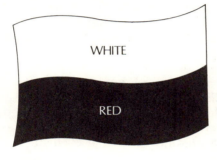

FIGURE 1. An illustration of 'similarity': the Indonesian and Polish national flags.

the foregoing three-part standard, the Polish and Indonesian national flags are indistinguishable in all but their patterns. The two flags are "similar" because, although they are precisely the converse of each other in one relevant respect, they are indistinguishable in most—and in the most important—relevant respects.[23]

To be sure, in order to declare two things to be identical or nonidentical in "relevant" respects, one must be able to identify the respects in which the things are relevant. The word 'relevance' comes from the Latin *relevare*, meaning to relieve, aid, or assist. To say something, X, is relevant means that it assists, advances, con-

---

[23] Interestingly, the word 'similar' appears to have this meaning in geometry, too; for in geometry, polygons are said to be "similar" (for which the symbol is ≈) if they are identical in most of the ways in which polygons are measured—meaning that they have the same number of sides, they have corresponding angles, their corresponding angles are congruent, and their sides are in proportion, even though they are of different sizes.

duces toward, connects up with, or serves the purpose of some other thing, Y, which one wishes to accomplish.[24] To say that two things are identical (or nonidentical) in relevant respects means that they have been measured and ascertained to be identical (or nonidentical) by a standard of comparison that itself is a suitable measure of what conduces toward Y. To declare things to be identical in relevant respects, therefore, one must first possess a *suitable* standard of comparison—or what J. Lucas calls a "criterion of relevance."[25] Things are identical in relevant respects to the extent that they possess the same features in common as measured by a standard of comparison that is deemed suitable to the task at hand.

To illustrate, assume that the National Basketball Association finds it useful to assess potential players by measuring them by what it calls a "composite scale"—a composite standard for measuring players in a number of different respects, including their height (in inches), weight (in pounds), and speed (in tenths of a second). Two players, A and B, are measured and found to be identical in height (in inches), weight (in pounds), and speed (in tenths of a second). Player B now wishes to demonstrate that he is actually 5 millimeters taller than player A, and 10 grams heavier, and 2 hundredths of a second faster. The NBA dismisses B's efforts, telling him that those differences are "irrelevant." By "irrelevant" the NBA does not mean that B's features are of no importance to anyone. It means, rather, that those features and the respective standards by which they are measured (millimeters, grams, hundredths of a second) do not serve the NBA's purposes at hand.

In contrast to the usage of 'similar' described above, we also use

[24] "To say 'x is relevant' . . . means 'x is actually or potentially related in an instrumentally helpful or harmful way to the attainment of a given end. . . .' " Blackstone, "On the Meaning and Justification of the Equality Principle," p. 241.

Anyone who calls for the use of an *irrelevant* characteristic within any competition, therefore, is asking most certainly for some new or expanded purpose to be recognized and for a change in the winning rule. Just as there was a purpose or policy goal served by excluding blacks from law school, so there can be a purpose or policy goal served by introducing "because he's black" as an active consideration to include a man in a law school class. Just as exclusion served racial segregation, so inclusion will serve racial integration. Someone who urges admission of a candidate because he is black has spoken relevantly or irrelevantly, it would appear, depending on the purpose of policy served by the contest in question.

Bronough, Introduction to *Philosophical Law*, p. 47.
[25] Lucas, *The Principles of Politics*, p. 245.

the word 'similar' to signify the relationship that obtains between distinct things that, although not entirely indistinguishable in most (or most important) respects, are *nearly* indistinguishable in all or most important respects. Consider

Peaches and Nectarines

Peaches and nectarines are both fruits of the *prunus persica* tree. Both are pit-type fruits with hard, furrowed stones containing a single seed. The differences are that peaches have a downy skin and slightly muted coloration, while nectarines, being mutations, have a smooth skin, unmuted coloration, fruit with a somewhat waxy texture, and a distinctive flavor.

Although most people would describe nectarines and peaches as "similar" fruits, this does not mean that they are indistinguishable by the standards we ordinarily use to identify fruit—standards of size, shape, external color, texture, thickness of skin, internal color, and taste. Rather, it means that, as measured by the foregoing standards on scales of more or less, and compared with other fruits, nectarines and peaches are relatively close to one another. Thus, although nectarines differ from peaches by the standards of appearance, texture, and taste that we ordinarily apply in distinguishing fruit, nectarines are closer in those respects to peaches than to any other fruit, and closer than most fruits are to one another. Nectarines and peaches are similar because in most relevant respects they are relatively close to being indistinguishable.[26]

Needless to say, although the concept of similarity presupposes a standard of comparison, it does not itself prescribe particular standards. It operates by reference to whatever standard is appropriate, or itself "relevant," to the purpose at hand. A relevant standard for one purpose may be irrelevant for another. A student of language, for example, might wish to compare the names of fruits on the basis of their phonetics or their orthography. For that purpose, the relevant standard of comparison is not the size or shape of fruits but the sound and spelling of their names. By the latter standards, 'nectarine' is similar to 'mandarin', but not at all similar to 'peach'.

In sum, we use 'similarity' in two distinct ways: sometimes we use it to describe a relationship between two or more distinct

---

[26] In mathematics, the term 'approximately equal' (for which the symbol is $\cong$) is used in place of 'similar' for quantities that are nearly identical.

things that, measured by a relevant standard of comparison, are indistinguishable in most but not all respects; at other times, we use it to describe a relationship of two or more distinct things that, measured by a relevant standard of comparison, are relatively close to one another in most if not all relevant respects. Both meanings of 'similarity' are themselves similar to the concept of equality, because equality, too, is a comparative relationship that obtains among two or more distinct things that have been jointly measured by a common standard. But, despite their similarity (indeed, *because* of their mere similarity), the concepts of similarity and equality are not indistinguishable in all respects. They are not one and the same concept, the measure of their difference being that, while we sometimes use them interchangeably, we often carefully distinguish between them. Thus, we describe the Polish and Indonesian flags as similar but not equal in appearance, and nectarines and peaches as similar, not equal, fruits. By the same token, we would say that the two bands of color on the Polish flag are equal, not similar, in width—just as we say that the sum 2 + 2 is equal, not similar, to 4.

Identical in Relevant Respects

We have contrasted equality with three comparative relationships. Each differs significantly from equality, yet each also possesses distinctive features in common with equality. By identifying those distinctive features, we can construct the unique comparative relationship we mean to express when we speak of equality.

Equality possesses one important feature in common with *identity*: to say that two things are equal does not mean they are nearly identical or mostly identical in relevant respects; it means that they are entirely identical in those respects.[27] Thus, when we say that the 16-ounce pans of flour and sugar are equal in ounces, we mean that they are entirely indistinguishable from one another in that

[27] It is true that we can say that two men have equal yet different abilities—e.g., that one has a creative mind, the other a keen, critical intellect, or that two women are equally beautiful although having different styles of beauty, the one a cold, remote beauty, the other a warm, vibrant, vital beauty. But in each case we should, if pressed, seek to justify our claim about the equality of ability, or of beauty, in terms of some ultimate identity of some sort. Otherwise if we could not point to some such identity, we should withdraw the word 'equally' and say that both are very able or very beautiful but in different ways.

McCloskey, "Egalitarianism, Equality, and Justice," pp. 54–55.

respect. Equality also possesses something in common with relationships of *identity in a given dimension,* for to say that two things
are equal does not mean that they are one and the same thing; it
means that, although they are identical in a certain respect, they
differ in other respects. Finally, equality possesses something in
common with *similarity:* to say two things are equal does not mean
that they are identical in a certain dimension as measured by the
finest conceivable measures of that dimension; it means that they
are identical in *relevant* respects, whose relevance is measured by
whatever standard of comparison is deemed suitable to the task at
hand. Thus, when we say that Agnes and Mary were equal in
birth weight, we do not mean that they were identical as measured
by the finest conceivable standards of weight; we mean that they
were identical as measured in pounds and whole ounces, because
the latter was the particular standard deemed suitable at the time
for measuring babies.

Descriptive equality, then, is the *identity* (as opposed to similarity) that obtains among things that are indistinguishable in *relevant*
respects (as opposed to all respects), as measured by relevant *standards of measurement* (as opposed to relevant dimensions). It is the
relationship that obtains among two or more distinct things that
have been jointly measured by a common standard of comparison
and found to be indistinguishable by reference to that standard.[28]
Inequality, in contrast, is the relationship that obtains among two
or more distinct things that have been jointly measured by a common standard of comparison and found to differ from one another
by reference to that standard.

To illustrate, let us return to the discussion we postponed:

The Nature of Digital and Analog Scales

A digital scale measures weight—and other continuous quantities—in numbers: when an object is placed on the scale, the
weight as displayed on the scale "jumps" from one number

---

[28] Equality is a name of a relation. We speak of two things as being equal, or
as being made equal. When we speak in this way we can be called upon to
explain in what respects they are equal—e.g., in weight, size, length, worth,
ability. To treat them as being equal is to treat them as being identical in some
important respect relevant to our purposes.

McCloskey, "Egalitarianism, Equality, and Justice," p. 54. See also Bedau, "Egalitarianism and the Idea of Equality," p. 7 ("Things that are equal in a certain respect
will normally be quite dissimilar to each other in other respects; whereas in the
respect in which they are equal they are not merely similar but *the same*") (emphasis
added).

to the next number until it reaches the number representing the weight of the object. Thus, in weighing ingredients for our pound cake, we used a digital scale calibrated in ounces, which weighs objects by displaying the number of ounces that an object weighs, to the nearest full ounce.

An analog scale works by measuring weight—and other continuous quantities—continuously, rather than by "jumping" in unit amounts. Thus, a scale consisting of a needle set against a dial marked in ounces is an analog scale. When an object is placed on the scale, the needle comes to rest at the portion of the dial that most closely represents the object's weight. One "reads" the face of the scale by reference to the proximity of the needle to the surrounding marks.

We decide to reweigh the pans of flour and sugar. We place each pan separately on the digital scale, which comes to rest each time on the number 16. We then place each pan on the dial scale. With respect to the flour, the needle comes to rest slightly below the 16-ounce mark; with the sugar, the needle comes to rest well beyond the 16-ounce mark, though below the 16½-ounce mark.

What can we say now about the pans of flour and sugar—are they equal or unequal? The answer should be evident by now: their equality depends upon what is deemed to be the relevant standard of comparison. The digital scale measures objects in whole ounces, to the closest full ounce that an object weighs. Taking this as the relevant standard, the two pans are equal, because *they are identical in weight, each weighing closer to 16 ounces than to either 15 or 17 ounces.* The dial scale provides more information. Like the digital scale, it shows that the two pans weigh closer to 16 than to any other full number of ounces; and, if that remains the relevant standard, then the dial scale, too, reveals the two pans to be equal. But unlike the digital scale, the dial scale also shows that the weight of the flour is slightly less than 16 ounces, while the sugar is considerably more than 16 ounces. If the relevant standard of comparison is weight to the nearest one-half ounce, the dial scale reveals the two pans to be *unequal* because they are *nonidentical* as measured by that standard (see Figure 2).

To be sure, it is always potentially ambiguous to say that two objects are "equal in weight," because "equal" is a function of a particular *measure* of weight, while "weight" is a dimension to be measured. To say objects are equal in weight without specifying

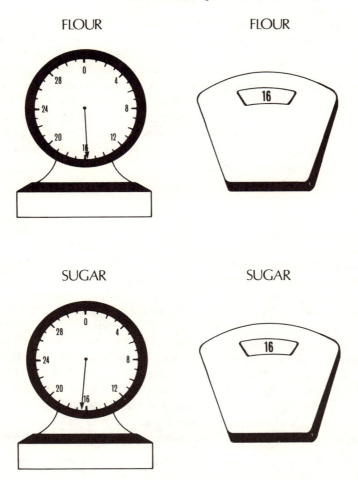

FIGURE 2. An illustration of the varying measures of weight revealed by weighing determinate quantities of flour and sugar first on an analog dial scale, and then on a digital scale calibrated in whole ounces.

the standard by which they have been measured, therefore, can be misleading. The ambiguity is relatively innocuous when the controlling standard is understood; thus, when the two objects are weighed on the digital scale and found to be identical, it is relatively harmless to say "They are equal in weight" because it is understood that one means they are equal in weight *as measured by the digital scale*. The ambiguity is more serious when two objects are weighed on different scales and found to be identical by one standard but nonidentical by the other. Then to say that the objects are equal in weight is misleading because the objects are known to be unequal by at least one standard for measuring weight. This does not, however, mean that the objects are unequal in weight—for they *are* equal as measured by the standard of one scale.[29] It means, rather, that instead of saying ambiguously "They are equal in weight," one could more perspicuously say "They are equal *in pounds*" (or *ounces*, or *grams*, or whatever one deems to be a controlling measure of weight).

Margins of Error

Few scales are completely accurate; most are accurate only to a certain degree. By way of example, let us assume that the digital scale and dial scale are both accurate to within a hundredth of an ounce, that is, each displays an accurate measure of the object it is weighing plus or minus .01 ounces. Let us further assume that both scales adhere to the convention of "weighing upward," that is, the convention of treating objects that weigh exactly midway between two full-ounce measures as corresponding to the higher of the two measures. The margin of error in this case will have no effect on the way we read the dial scale because .01 ounces is too slight a difference to be detected visually on the dial. But it may have an effect on the digital scale because that scale may indicate that two objects weigh closer to 16 ounces than to any other full ounce where, as measured by a finer instrument, they might be revealed

---

[29] Kenneth Simons has noted that it is "odd" to say that objects found to be identical by one measure of volume, and nonidentical by another measure of volume, are nonetheless equal. He argues:

> If, according to precise calibration, one bottle is 1.0001 liters in volume and the other is 0.9998 liters, then the first in fact has slightly more volume than the second. . . . Once the precise measurement is made, one can no longer truly say that the two bottles are equal in volume, but only that they are very close to equal [even though] they are 'equal' as measured imprecisely by integral liters.

Simons, "Equality as a Comparative Right," p. 404 n. 28. Simons is right if by "odd" he means "ambiguous," because it is indeed ambiguous to say that the two bottles are equal in volume when it is known that they are unequal by at least one measure of volume. However, it is not odd to say that the bottles "are equal in volume *in liters to the closest whole liter*." Nor, indeed, is it ambiguous to say "They are equal in volume," if everyone understands liters-to-the-closest-whole-liter to be the relevant measure.

to weigh 15.49 and 16.50 ounces, respectively, and, hence, to be closer to 15 and 17 ounces, respectively.

What can we say, then, about the equality of two objects, which, for all we know, *may* weigh closer to 15 and 17 ounces, respectively? We might be tempted to say that, although the two objects appear equal, they may not "really" be equal because a more accurate scale might reveal differences in weight. If we said this, however, we would be guilty of misusing language, because we would be conflating "equality" with a standard of comparison which we have not yet determined to be relevant. The equality of the two objects—like the descriptive equality of any two persons or things—is a feature of the standard of comparison that is relevant to the purpose at hand.[30] If we take as relevant "the number of ounces an object weighs, to the nearest full ounce to within .000001 ounces," we cannot know whether the two objects are equal or not, because the digital scale cannot measure to that degree of accuracy. If, however, we take as relevant "the number of full ounces displayed by the digital scale" (or "the number of full ounces an object weighs, to within *.01* ounces"), the two objects are not just approximately equal, they are *completely* equal, because they are completely indistinguishable by those standards.

Now it has been suggested that we can say still more about things that are descriptively equal besides that they are "identical by relevant standards of comparison." Thus, Elizabeth Wolgast argues that to say two things are equal means that they are interchangeable, or what she calls *"substitutable."* She asks us to imagine that a lumberyard stores planks of wood in such a way that only the ends are showing. A purchaser who is looking for planks of a certain length is told by the lumberyard that the planks stored together are all "equal." By learning that the planks are equal, she says, the purchaser knows more than that they are identical by a given standard of measure; he also knows that they are interchangeable. In her words:

Suppose you went to the lumberyard looking for a plank to use for a job of repairing. As you look at a stack of planks seeing only the ends, you would be interested to hear that they are all equal, that they measure the same. What is im-

[30] Evans, "Equality, Ambiguity, and Public Choice," p. 1393 ("Whether or not persons or things are equal depends on the scales used to compare them. Two distances may be the same when measured in miles, but different when measured with a micrometer").

portant about knowing this? What difference does it make? This: from the remark that they are equal, it follows that one plank is substitutable for any other. You can choose one randomly and without regard to individual differences, without discrimination; you can do this *because* they equal.

Planks may be unequal in color or clarity even while they are equal in length, so it is sometimes necessary to specify that respect in which they are being compared. But to say things are *simply equal* will normally imply that for ordinary and understood purposes one can be freely substituted for another.[31]

Wolgast is correct that descriptively equal things are sometimes interchangeable. But she is wrong to argue that they are *always* interchangeable and wrong to suggest that saying they are equal *means* that they are interchangeable for a given purpose. To say things are descriptively equal means that they have been measured and found to be indistinguishable by a standard of comparison that is deemed suitable to the task at hand. The standard may be suitable as the sole standard bearing upon a task at hand or as one of a set of combined standards bearing on a task at hand. Things that are descriptively identical by standards of the first kind are, indeed, interchangeable; things that are descriptively identical by standards of the second kind, however, are *not* interchangeable. To illustrate, consider Wolgast's hypothetical stack of lumber planks. The lumberyard wishes to store and display its inventory of oak planks by their lengths (say, in inches) for purposes of maximizing its available space; the customer wishes to purchase oak planks by the combined criteria of their lengths (in inches) and color (as judged by the customer's discriminating eye) for the purpose of laying a parquet floor. For the lumberyard, length is the sole criterion that bears upon the task of storing and displaying oak planks, and, hence, planks that are equal in length are also interchangeable for that task. For the customer, however, length is only one of several criteria that bear upon the task of selecting oak planks for a parquet floor, and, hence, planks that are equal in length are not interchangeable for that purpose.

Conclusion

We have undertaken in this chapter to analyze the meaning of the word 'equality' as we ordinarily use it to describe people and tan-

[31] Wolgast, *Equality and the Rights of Women*, pp. 39–40.

gible things as we believe they actually *are* (in contrast to the way we think they ought to be). We concluded our analysis by formulating a working definition of 'equality' (as we ordinarily use the word to describe people and things perceived through the senses). 'Equality', as we have defined it, signifies the comparative relationship that obtains between two or more distinct persons or things by virtue of their having been jointly measured by a relevant standard of comparison and found to be indistinguishable by reference to that standard. Thus, our previous statement that the twin sisters Agnes and Mary were "equal" in weight at birth means that they were both weighed by an appropriate standard and found to be indistinguishable by that standard—in their case, a standard for weighing newborns, in pounds and ounces, to the nearest ounce.

This definition of 'equality', if sound, serves several purposes. It identifies the general meaning of 'equality'—the basic semantic formula which underlies particularized statements of descriptive equality. It also demonstrates the validity and invalidity, respectively, of two common assertions about equality: (i) "Things that are equal in one respect are unequal in others"; and (ii) "Things that are equal to the same thing are equal to each other." Let us examine these statements in more detail.

"Things That Are Equal in One Respect Are Unequal in Others"

The truth of this statement, which appears as early as the writings of Plato,[32] is analytic; that is to say, the truth of the statement lies in the meaning of its constituent terms—in this case, the terms 'things', 'equal', and 'unequal'. 'Equal things' refers to the descriptive relationship that obtains among two or more distinct things that have been measured, compared, and found to be indistinguishable by reference to a relevant standard of comparison. 'Unequal things' refers to the descriptive relationship that obtains among two or more distinct things that have been measured, compared, and found to differ from one another by reference to such a standard. It follows that things that are descriptively equal in one respect not only *may* be descriptively unequal in other respects but *must* be descriptively unequal in other respects, because, as we

---

[32] See Plato, *Parmenides* 129. For an argument that Plato meant to be making the same statement in *Phaedo* 74b, see Haynes, "The Form Equality, as a Set of Equals," pp. 20–21.

have seen, things that are indistinguishable in every respect (that is, indistinguishable by every standard of comparison) are not distinct at all but are one and the same thing, and thus cannot be the subject of meaningful statements of descriptive equality.

"Things That Are Equal to the Same Thing Are Equal to Each Other"

This axiom, which is as old as Euclid,[33] depends for its truth on the standards by which such "equality" is measured; for the axiom is true with regard to some standards but untrue with regard to others. The axiom is true of equalities based on noncomparative standards used to determine whether objects either possess a feature or do not, such as the binary standards used in the "Ping-Pong Balls" example in separating new ping-pong balls from used balls. If we determine that ball 1 equals ball 2 in being used, and that ball 2 equals ball 3 in being used, then we can confidently conclude that ball 1 also equals ball 3, because to say that the latter balls are "equal" means that they both possess the binary feature of being used as opposed to new.

The maxim also holds true for equalities based on noncomparative standards used to determine whether things possess "more" or "less" of a certain quality, such as the noncomparative standard we used to weigh the ingredients in "Making a Pound Cake." Once we determined, by using a spring scale, that the flour equaled the sugar (each weighing 16 ounces, to the nearest ounce to within .01 ounces), and once we determined that the sugar equaled the butter (each weighing 16 ounces, to the nearest ounce to within .01 ounces), then we knew that the flour also equaled the butter.

Nonetheless, the maxim "Things that are equal to the same thing are equal to each other" is not valid with respect to *comparative* standards used to measure things for "more" or "less." Things that are equal to the same thing by such comparative standards are not necessarily equal to each other. They do not possess the property mathematicians call "transitiveness."[34] Consider, for

---

[33] See Euclid, *Elements*, Bk. I, axiom I, in *The Thirteen Books of Euclid's Elements*, vol. I, p. 222. The axiom is true in mathematics because the relevant measures in mathematics are noncomparative (e.g., numerical), rather than comparative.

[34] To say that terms possess the property of "transitiveness" means that if A has a relation to B, and B has it to C, then A has it to C. See Russell, *The Principles of Mathematics*, p. 159. Russell, regarding equalities in mathematics as paradigmatic, believed "transitiveness" to be present in all equalities.

example, the hand-held balance scale used in "A Moroccan Market" to weigh myrrh. A balance scale cannot make a noncomparative determination of how much an object alone weighs without reference to other objects; it can make only the comparative determination of whether an object weighs more, or less, or neither more nor less, than another object. In this case, the vendor used a hand-held balance scale that was accurate to within 3 grams—that is, a scale that, when in balance, reveals objects to be equal in weight, plus or minus 3 grams. Using the scale, the vendor determined that a certain quantity of myrrh was equal in weight to a 200-gram brass cylinder, meaning that each weighed to within 3 grams of the other. Imagine now that we remove the 200-gram brass weight from the balance scale and replace it with enough frankincense to bring the scale back into balance with the myrrh. Do we now know that the latter quantity of frankincense also equals the 200-gram brass weight to within 3 grams? Not necessarily, because the brass weight could equal the myrrh on the balance scale even if the myrrh weighed only 197 grams, and the myrrh could equal the frankincense even if the frankincense weighed only 194 grams. In that event, the 200-gram brass weight and the frankincense would both equal the myrrh on the balance scale, and yet, being separated by a full 6 grams of weight, would not equal each other on the balance scale. Thus, when measured by comparative standards, "things that are equal to the same thing" are not always "equal to each other."

The principal lesson to be learned from analyzing these two maxims is that the crucial step in determinations of descriptive equality is the specification of standards of measurement. Descriptive equality is the relationship that obtains among two or more distinct things that have been jointly measured by a common standard and found to be indistinguishable, or identical, as measured by that standard. Things that are equal by one standard of comparison are inevitably unequal by other standards, and vice versa. It therefore follows that the things of this world that we are capable of measuring are not *either* equal *or* unequal. They are *both* equal *and* unequal.

MATHEMATICAL EQUALITY

Equality is "an easily understood concept in mathematics," Thomas Sowell has observed, and yet "a bottomless pit of complexities anywhere else."[1]

Sowell is surely correct about the simplicity of equality in mathematics. Although we may occasionally despair of understanding particular equations in mathematics, we have no trouble understanding the *concept* of equality that underlies them. This concept of equality is so obvious, so pellucid, that it is taken for granted in the most elementary books of arithmetic.[2] Sowell is right, too, when he goes on to say that 'equality' is a word that causes both "confus[ion]" and "controversy" outside mathematics, particularly in the realms of law, morals, and politics. The clarity that the concept of equality possesses in mathematics seems to disappear in normative discourse.

Sowell also advances an explanation as to why equality seems simple in mathematics but so complex everywhere else. The reason, he suggests, is that the "concept" of equality changes from one context to another: the definition itself is more complex in normative discourse than elsewhere, and its complexity will persist, he says, until we "defin[e]" what equality means in the realms of moral and legal discourse.

The suggestion that 'equality' has a different, simpler meaning in mathematics than it has elsewhere is not unique to Sowell. It is as old as Plato and as recent as Wittgenstein.[3] Mortimer Adler and Robert Maynard Hutchins have observed that "[t]here has always been a suspicion, and it is a suspicion that still exists, that equality

---

[1] Sowell, "We're Not Really Equal," p. 13.

[2] For discussions of the concept of equality in mathematics, see Russell, *The Principles of Mathematics*, pp. 21, 24, 159, 167–68, 218–19, 339; Waismann, *Introduction to Mathematical Thinking*, pp. 29ff., 55–56.

[3] Wittgenstein suggested that the measure of dimensions (e.g., time and distance) is never as exact as, say, equations in mathematics. Wittgenstein, *Philosophical Investigations*, § 88.

as applied to things human is at best a derivative idea and that its primary place lies in the mathematical order; and hence, too, that carrying it over into social and political discussion may be to some extent illicit, confusing, and metaphorical in no helpful way."[4] Jacques Maritain expressed the same thought when he said, "When applied to man, this idea [of equality], from the very outset, puts the philosopher to the test" because "it is surrounded by geometrical imagery" as to which he must "work constantly against the grain."[5]

Maritain and others may ultimately be right that 'equality' has a categorically different meaning in mathematics than it has elsewhere. Nevertheless, as I believe we shall see in this and subsequent chapters, theirs is not the only plausible position. One can also argue that although "conceptions" of equality differ from one realm to another, they are all based on a single "concept" of equality, that the concept itself is as clear and simple in normative discourse as in mathematics, and that the challenge of equality is not to search for distinctions among equalities but to identify what they have in common.

We concluded the preceding chapter by defining the meaning of 'equality' in descriptive statements. We shall now inquire whether it means the same thing in mathematical statements. We shall see, I believe, that the tentative definition of 'equality' formulated in the previous chapter fits some ordinary statements of mathematical equality, but it hardly fits them all. Indeed, it fails to fit what many people would regard as the purest and most commonplace instances of mathematical equality. By analyzing its fit, and lack of fit, and the reasons for them, we shall try to reformulate the definition in such a way as to accommodate statements of both descriptive and mathematical equality.

Numbers as Description

Crazy Eights

Two sisters are playing the card game Crazy Eights. The rules of the game are simple. Each player is dealt an equal number cards, anywhere from eight to ten. The remaining cards are left in a pile between them with the top card turned face up. The first player attempts to "match" the exposed card by lay-

---

[4] Adler and Hutchins, "The Idea of Equality," p. 303.
[5] Maritain, "Human Equality," p. 1.

ing down a card from her hand that is either of the same suit or equal in number. If she can make the match, she does, thus completing her turn. If she cannot, she must draw one or more new cards from the pile until she can make the match. Thus, if the exposed card is a five of clubs, the first player must match it by laying down the five of diamonds, five of spades, or five of hearts, or laying down some other card in the suit of clubs, or she must draw cards from the pile until she can match it. The first person who succeeds in laying down all her cards wins the game.

The game of Crazy Eights involves numerical equalities: each player receives an equal number of cards, say ten; the players are able to discard cards by laying down those that are equal in number or suit to the card on the table. The total cards each player initially receives, and the particular matching-number cards she lays down, also display numbers that are equal. Yet these numerical equalities are no different, conceptually, from the descriptive equalities we have previously discussed. They all involve the relationship that obtains among distinct things that have been measured, compared, and found to be identical in their respective properties by a relevant standard of measurement—in this case, the standard of number.

Consider the statement "Each player, having been dealt ten cards, possesses an equal number of cards." To say the two sets of cards are "equal" does not mean that they are identical in every respect, for if they were identical in every respect, they would not be two distinguishable sets of cards. Nor does it mean that they are identical in *most* respects, or *nearly* identical in relevant respects, in the way things are that we describe as being "similar." Rather, it means that they are descriptively equal: while distinguishable by many standards for measuring tangible objects, they are indistinguishable by the one standard that the rules of Crazy Eights render relevant to the initial distribution of cards to players—the standard of *number*.

The same descriptive relationship of equality may exist even where numbers are detached from tangible objects. Consider the following episode:

The Benefits of Arabic Numerals

A schoolteacher is instructing her students on the benefits of systems of arithmetic notation based on the concept of zero.

She does so by juxtaposing two systems on the blackboard—the arabic and the Roman systems of numerical notation:

I	=	1
II	=	2
III	=	3
IV	=	4
V	=	5
VI	=	6
VII	=	7
VIII	=	8
IX	=	9
X	=	10
XX	=	20
XXX	=	30
XL	=	40
L	=	50
C	=	100
M	=	1000

"Notice," she says, "that both systems have a way of noting the number 'one hundred', and that the respective notational forms of 'one hundred' equal one another in number:

$$C \quad = \quad 100$$

Yet the arabic system utilizes a zero and thus possesses the notational advantage of being able to express 'one hundred'—and all other numbers—by combinations of no more than ten separate symbols: 1, 2, 3, 4, 5, 6, 7, 8, 9, and 0."

The equations the teacher has written on the blackboard consist solely of numerals. Yet the relationship of equality that obtains between the numerals is still descriptive because the teacher is talking about numbers qua notations. She is stating the equations not solely to express the abstract integers they represent, but also to indicate various notational forms for expressing those integers. She thus means to say that the respective numerals are identical in one relevant respect, but nonidentical in others: identical with respect to the abstract integers—the *numbers*—they represent, yet nonidentical with respect to their notational form.[6]

[6] See Frege, "Function and Concept," p. 22 (distinguishing between "numerals" as "characters," on the one hand, and the "numbers" [or "arithmetical objects"] for which they stand, on the other).

Numbers as Abstractions

More often we use mathematical equations rather differently. We use them not to express descriptive relationships among tangible things (e.g., 3 apples + 3 apples = 6 apples), and not to describe relationships among different forms of symbolic notation (e.g., 3 + III = VIII − 2), but to represent the complete identity that obtains between the abstractions to which symbolic notations on each side of an equal sign refer.

Solitary Confinement

A political prisoner in a repressive society is subjected to solitary confinement for many months at a time. Because he is something of a "numbers cruncher," he sets out to maintain his sanity by doing complicated mathematical computations in his head. He starts with two-digit numbers:

$$13 \cdot 18 = 234$$
$$36 \cdot 52 = 1872$$
$$87 \cdot 91 = 7917$$

and so forth. During the initial weeks, he does the calculations by visualizing the numerical symbols in his mind. But after a time he discovers that he has so internalized the calculations that he can do them without visualizing the symbols, by merely thinking about the *idea* of the numbers themselves, and that he can do them not only with two-digit numbers but with three- and sometimes four-digit numbers. As he does so, he comes to realize that the respective equivalents in mathematical equations do not in any sense constitute different things, but rather are different manifestations of the very same thing—that, as *integers*, as *numbers*, the concepts of "3 + 3" and "6" are so completely identical in the only dimension they occupy that each could be sensibly defined in terms of the other.

The prisoner's insight into the nature of mathematical equalities appears to contradict what we have thus far supposed regarding descriptive equalities. Equality in mathematics appears to be a relationship among abstractions that are inherently identical in the only dimension they possess—that is, the dimension of number.[7]

[7] See Frege, *Grundgesetze der Arithmetik*, quoted in Dilworth, "Identity, Equality, and Equivalence," p. 87 ("I use the expression 'equal' to mean the same as 'coincid-

Although the arithmetic operation of adding "3 + 3" differs from the operation of subtracting "9 − 3," the arithmetic products of the two operations are one and the same number; and, of course, the consummate equation of "6 = 6" consists of the same number on each side of the equal sign.[8] That is what students of mathematics mean when they say that equalities in mathematics possess the property of being "reflexive" (i.e., for a term like the number '3' to be equal to anything it must also be equal to itself).[9] Yet, according to what we have thus far determined, descriptive equality is a relationship among things that not only *may* be distinguishable, but *must* be distinguishable in some respects. How, then, can we reconcile these two different usages of 'equality'?

One possibility is what might be called "anticonceptualist." A "conceptualist" believes that the various usages of significant words often reflect underlying "core" meanings; hence, he endeavors to unpack such meanings by analyzing the way words are used in ordinary language.[10] In contrast, anticonceptualists be-

---

ing or identical with', and this is just how the sign of equality is actually used in arithmetic"). See also Frege, "Function and Concept," p. 22:

> I must here combat the view that, e.g., 2 + 5 and 3 + 4 are equal but not the same. This view is grounded in the same confusion of form and content, sign and thing signified. It is as though one wanted to regard the sweet-smelling violet as differing from the *Viola odorata* because the names sound different.

For commentary on Frege's view of identity and equality in mathematics, see Caton, "The Idea of Sameness Challenges Reflection," p. 177; Bernhardt, "Frege on Identity."

[8] See Frege, "Function and Concept," p. 23:

> [W]e shall have to recognize that the expressions '2,' '1 + 1,' '3 − 1,' '6:3' stand for the same thing, for it is quite inconceivable where the difference between them could lie. Perhaps you say: 1 + 1 is a sum, but 6:3 is a quotient. But what is 6:3? The number that when multiplied by 3 gives the result 6. We say '*the* number,' not 'a number'; by using the definite article, we indicate that there is only a single number. . . . The different expressions correspond to different conceptions and aspects, but nevertheless always to the same thing. . . . By recognizing only two real roots, we are rejecting the view that the sign of equality does not stand for complete coincidence but only for partial agreement.

Craig Dilworth argues that "3 + 3" is *not* identical in all respects to "9 − 3" because the former represents a different mathematical operation than the latter. Yet he concedes that the result of performing those operations is one and the same number, and he appears further to concede that the equation "6 = 6" is a limiting case in which the same concept is expressed twice. Dilworth, "Identity, Equality, and Equivalence," pp. 87–88.

[9] Russell, *The Principles of Mathematics*, pp. 159, 219.

[10] For a description of conceptualism, see White, *Grounds of Liability*, chap. 2. For an account of various kinds of efforts to find the "common core" meanings of words, see Swanton, "On the 'Essential Contestedness' of Political Concepts," pp. 812–13. For exemplary illustrations of the effort to define concepts, see MacCallum,

lieve, with Wittgenstein, that the meanings of words consist solely in their usage, not in the entities (or "universals") to which they refer, and that the proper posture for students of language is not to assume or seek the existence of unifying definitions but to suspect definition.[11] Although Wittgenstein's has been the more fashionable view in recent years,[12] conceptualism is presently experiencing something of a revival, perhaps in part because of John

"Negative and Positive Freedom," p. 312 (an analysis of the concept of freedom); Hohfeld, *Fundamental Legal Conceptions* (an analysis of the concept of rights); Lukes, *Power*, pp. 9–27 (an analysis of the concept of power); Oppenheim, *Political Concepts* (an analysis of the concepts of power, freedom, and egalitarianism); Waldron, "What Is Private Property?" p. 313 (an analysis of the concept of private property).

[11] Wittgenstein's classic example is his analysis of the meaning of the word 'game', in which he demonstrates that, rather than having a single core meaning, 'game' refers to a variety of things that have at most only a certain "family resemblance." Wittgenstein's references to "games" and "family resemblances" are scattered throughout his writing. Exemplary statements, however, can be found both in *The Blue Book* and in *Philosophical Investigations*. "This craving for [conceptual] generality," he writes,

> is the resultant of a number of tendencies connected with particular philosophical confusions. There is . . . the tendency to look for something in common to all the entities which we commonly subsume under a general term. We are inclined to think that there must be something in common to all games, say, and that this common property is the justification for applying the general term 'game' to the various games; whereas games form a *family* the members of which have family likenesses. Some of them have the same nose, others the same eyebrows and others again the same way of walking; and these likenesses overlap.

Wittgenstein, *The Blue Book*, p. 17.

> Consider for example the proceedings that we call "games". I mean board-games, card-games, ball-games, Olympic games, and so on. What is common to them all?—Don't say: "There *must* be something common, or they would not be called 'games' "—but *look and see* whether there is anything common to all.—For if you look at them you will not see something that is common to *all*, but similarities, relationships, and a whole series of them at that. . . .
>
> And the result of this examination is: we see a complicated network of similarities overlapping and criss-crossing: sometimes overall similarities, sometimes similarities of detail. . . .
>
> I can think of no better expression to characterize these similarities than "family resemblances".

Wittgenstein, *Philosophical Investigations*, §§ 66–67.

[12] See Waldron, "What Is Private Property?" p. 317, where he states:

> Conceptual definition is a complicated business and the idea that it always involves the precise specification of necessary and sufficient conditions [for the correct use of a term] must be regarded as naive and outdated in the light of recent philosophical developments.

Interestingly, however, Waldron goes on to say that Rawls's distinction between "concepts" and "conceptions" has rightfully revived interest—including his own—in the enterprise of defining concepts.

Rawls's influential distinction between "concepts" and "conceptions."[13]

An anticonceptualist would find nothing disturbing in the apparent dissonance between descriptive equality and mathematical equality. "It shows," he would say, "that the usage of 'equality' depends on context. We use the word descriptively to express a relationship between things that are inherently distinct, yet we also use it in mathematics in precisely the opposite way—to express a relationship between abstractions that are inherently *indistinguishable*. Searching for a single, common definition of 'equality' in both contexts is futile: either the search will yield nothing or it will produce a definition of 'equality' that is too general or too indistinguishable from that of other relational terms to be of any utility."[14]

[13] Rawls distinguishes between "the concept of justice" and "the various conceptions of justice." He defines the difference in several ways. The concept of justice, he says, is a "set of principles for assigning basic rights and duties [to members of society] and for determining . . . [a] proper distribution of the benefits and burdens of social cooperation." In contrast, a conception of justice is a particular set of such principles, based on particular views of what rights and duties are basic and what distributions are proper. People do not disagree about the concept of justice, but they do disagree over conceptions of justice. By the same token, Rawls says, we all have a concept of "just" institutions, because we all believe that just institutions are ones that make "no arbitrary distinctions . . . between persons in the assigning of basic rights and duties [and that] determine a proper balance between competing claims to the advantages of social life." But we have different conceptions of just institutions, because we have different "notions" of what constitute "arbitrary distinction[s]." See Rawls, *A Theory of Justice*, pp. 4–5. See also p. 10 ("The concept of justice I take to be defined, then, by the role of its principles in assigning rights and duties and in defining the appropriate division of social advantages. A conception of justice is an interpretation of this role").

Ronald Dworkin, relying on Rawls, also gives prominence to the distinction between "concepts" and "conceptions" in his philosophy of law, including his discussions of equality. See Dworkin, *Law's Empire*, pp. 70–72, 90–101; Dworkin, *Taking Rights Seriously*, pp. 103, 134–36 (contrasting the "concepts" of fairness and cruelty with competing "conceptions" of fairness and cruelty).

For criticism of the attempt to control the direction of political debate by artfully defining political concepts, see Stevenson, "Persuasive Definitions." For provocative reflections on "conceptual" approaches to intellectual and cultural life, and a plea, instead, for a "linguistic-literary" view of life, see White, "Thinking about Language."

[14] For a view much like the one in the text, see Ilham Dilman's discussion of his and Wittgenstein's views. Dilman sees a genuine difference

in the way equality is established in physics and in mathematics. The crucial difference is that in mathematics there are no degrees of accuracy: two sums are either equal or not, and if they are equal they are so absolutely. Whereas the equality between two logs, established by measurement, admits of degrees of accuracy. One could say that there is no such thing as an absolutely accurate measurement; meaning that to speak of absolute accuracy, to speak of equality in absolute terms, here is a misunderstanding (see [*Philosophical Investigations*]

The anticonceptualist may be right in believing that our usage of 'equality' varies from one context to another, but this does not mean that 'equality' has no useful meanings. Rather, based on the analysis thus far, it would seem that 'equality' has at least two useful meanings: one for the description of things that are distinct, and one for mathematical relationships. Each is discrete, and each is useful, provided that it is confined to its respective sphere. Accordingly, to that extent it would seem that the proper aim of analysis would be not to lament the lack of a single meaning of 'equality', but simply to avoid conflating its usage in one sphere with a contrary usage in another.

Nevertheless, there remains another possibility, one that is consistent with Wittgenstein's recognition[15] of the possibility of nec-

---

§ 88). Yet this grammatical feature of physical equality may be construed as some sort of defect: The equality we find between two logs can never be perfectly neat, the logs can only be more or less equal—as if they had been cut by a lumberjack with defective eye-sight.

What is exercising one is that the employment of the term 'equals' is not governed here by strict criteria, as it is in pure mathematics. It seems that where there are no criteria, where a word cannot be defined in terms of the necessary and sufficient conditions of its employment, its meaning has been only imperfectly determined or not determined at all.

Dilman, "Universals," pp. 40–41.

[15] [Wittgenstein] does not deny that in some cases, it is possible to delimit the use of a concept in terms of necessary and sufficient conditions that govern it. For instance the concept of mass. This is also true of geometrical concepts.

Dilman, "Universals," p. 41. See also Bambrough, "Universals and Family Resemblances," pp. 211–12.

To be sure, to be able to define a concept (that is, to be able to specify the necessary and sufficient elements for all its known usages) is not necessarily to be able to deduce its correct use solely from its definition. Wittgenstein himself is said to have believed that, even where we are able to specify the necessary and sufficient conditions for the proper use of a word, we can never know through deduction alone whether those conditions are present, and, hence, can never deduce from definitions alone how to use the word accurately in future cases. See Bambrough, "Universals and Family Resemblances," p. 214; Dilman, "Universals," pp. 43–44:

That is, even if all the cases in which it is correct to apply a particular word shared a common essence, this would still not do for us what we hope from it. This hope cannot be fulfilled in the case of *any* word.

We [justify] the application of [a] term deductively [from the definition of the necessary and sufficient conditions of its proper use] and this pleases us. We then notice that this justification presupposes that the conditions from which it follows deductively that [the usage is correct] are satisfied in the particular case. But the claim that [the conditions] are satisfied cannot itself be supported deductively.

If the foregoing view is correct, no definition of 'equality' can ever suffice by itself to tell us everything we need to know in order to use 'equality' correctly in future

essary and sufficient definitions. Despite its apparently different usages in description and mathematics, 'equality' may nonetheless possess a single, common meaning. If so, the key to its common meaning lies in the differences between the subjects of descriptive equality and the subject of mathematical equality. The subject matter of descriptive equality is tangible things that *possess* dimension, and can be measured for their dimension, without also *consisting* of measures of dimension. Thus, a piece of cloth possesses length, and can be measured for its length, without in any sense being defined in terms of length. In contrast, the subjects of mathematical equality not only possess dimension but are defined in terms of dimension. Numbers not only possess ordinal magnitude; they also consist of ordinal magnitude, in the sense that they can be defined as ordinal magnitudes. The same is true of angles, lines, circles, polygons, and solids: they not only possess shape and dimension; they are also defined in terms of shape and dimension.

This difference in the subject matter of descriptive and mathematical equalities may explain how 'equality' can possess a single meaning and yet produce such different prototypes. When one describes two tangible things as "equal," one says something *about* them—something about their identity in a certain dimension, something that cannot possibly exhaust everything that distinguishes one from the other because they do not consist solely of dimensions. In contrast, when one states that two mathematical entities are "equal," one also *completely defines* them. One asserts their identity in a certain dimension and, thus, necessarily exhausts everything that can be said about their identity, because they consist solely of dimension. As Adler and Hutchins put it, "There is no need to specify the respect in which lines or numerical results are to be judged equal or unequal, since lines are only lengths and numbers are, as it were, pure multitudes."[16] This suggests that the difference between descriptive equality and mathematical equality is not that the former means partial identity and the latter means complete identity, for 'equality' in both cases means "identity by the relevant standard of measure." The difference is that the subjects of descriptive equality *possess* dimension,

---

cases. Nonetheless, although a definition of the necessary and sufficient conditions for the proper use of 'equality' may not itself tell us *everything* we wish to know about how to use it, it does tell us *something* about how to use it: it tells us that, where the conditions for its use are present, it is correct to use it, and that, where the conditions for its use are not present, it is not correct to use it. See Dilman, "Universals," p. 44.

[16] Adler and Hutchins, "The Idea of Equality," p. 322.

rather than merely *consisting* of dimension; hence, the subjects of descriptive equality, though equal, also necessarily differ from one another. In contrast, the subjects of mathematical equality consist of dimension, as well as possess it; being equal, they are necessarily identical. Accordingly, we can no longer say, as we did in Chapter 1, that equality is a relationship between things that are definitely *distinct*, because the sets of terms in a mathematical equation are essentially indistinguishable from one another. Rather, we may say that equality in descriptions and mathematics is

(1) the relationship that obtains among two or more entities, whether tangible or intangible,

(2) that have been jointly measured and compared by reference to a common standard of measurement,

(3) and that, though not identical by all measures of their dimensions to the extent that they consist of more than dimension,

(4) are nevertheless indistinguishable by reference to the relevant standard of measurement.

Proportional Equality

The relationship between distributive justice and equality can be traced back to Plato.[17] Plato believed, with Aristotle, that to distribute goods "justly," a society should distribute them "equally."[18] Plato emphasized, however, that the equality that corresponds to distributive justice is of a particular kind. There are "two kinds" of equality, he said,[19] numerical and proportional. A distribution

[17] "To everyone the idea of justice inevitably suggests the notion of a certain equality. From Plato to Aristotle, through St. Thomas Aquinas, down to the jurists, moralists and philosophers of our own day runs a threat of universal agreement on this score." Perelman, *The Idea of Justice and the Problem of Argument*, p. 12.

[18] See the Preface, note 2.

[19] It is an old saying, and as true as old, that equality gives birth to friendship; that maxim is most sound and admirable. But 'tis none too clear what sort of equality it is that has these effects, and the ambiguity makes havoc with us. There are, in fact, two equalities under one name, but, for the most part, with contrary results. The one equality, that of number, weight, and measure, any society and any legislator can readily secure in the award of distinctions, by simply regulating their distribution by the lot, but the true and best equality is hardly so patent to every vision. 'Tis the very award of Zeus. Limited as is its scope in human life, wherever it has scope, in public affairs or private, it works

is "numerically equal" to the extent that it treats all persons as indistinguishable (e.g., distributions of goods to persons based either on lot or on per-capita shares). A distribution is "proportionately equal" to the extent that it treats all persons in proportion to what they deserve (e.g., distributions of honors to people in proportion to their demonstrated merit). The distinction was normatively significant for Plato because, in his view, proportional equality is always normatively just, while numerical equality is only contingently just.[20]

There has always been a suspicion (to which we shall return in Chapter 7) that Plato's notion of "proportionate" equality is "geometric" sleight-of-hand, that it is a derivative metaphor with questionable application to human affairs,[21] and that the only genuine equality regarding distributions is what Plato dismisses as equality of "number."[22] Although Plato's substantive views on distributive

---

nothing but blessings. For it assigns more to the greater and less to the lesser, adapting its gifts to the real character of either. In this matter of honors, in particular, it deals proportionately with either party, ever awarding a greater share to those of greater worth, and to their opposites in trained goodness such share as is fit. For we shall in truth find that this sheer justice is always also the statesmanlike policy. It is this, Clinias, at which we must aim, this equality on which we must fix our gaze, in the establishment of our nascent city. And if others would found other such societies, they should shape their legislation with a view to the same end . . . always to justice, the justice we explained to be a true and real equality, meted out to various unequals.

Plato, *Laws* VI.757 (trans. Taylor).
For the comparable views of Isocrates and Aristotle regarding the difference between numerical and proportional equality, see notes 23 and 26 below, and Chapter 7, note 12.
[20] Plato concedes that in order to "avoid disaffection among the masses," it will sometimes be necessary to "introduce some use of equality of the lot"; but he urges men, when they do so, to "breathe a prayer to God and good luck to direct even the fall of the lot to the justest issue." Plato, *Laws* VI.757 (trans. Taylor). See the quotation in note 19 above ("There are, in fact, two equalities under one name, but, for *the most* part, with contrary results").
[21] Plato uses the terms 'proportionate equality' and 'geometric equality' interchangeably. Compare Plato, *Laws* VI.757, with Plato, *Gorgias* 507e–508a ("But it seems to me that you pay no attention to these things in spite of your wisdom, but you are unaware that geometric equality is of great importance among gods and men alike, and you think we should practice overreaching others, for you neglect geometry"; trans. Woodhead).
For the argument that Plato and Aristotle exploited proportional and geometric equality as mathematical metaphors in political discussion in order to subvert the Greek ideal of "equality pure and simple," i.e., democratic equality, see Harvey, "Two Kinds of Equality," pp. 126–29. Cf. del Vecchio, *Justice* (referring to Aristotle's use of "geometric proportion" as a model of equality as an "artifice").
[22] See Frankena, "Some Beliefs about Justice," p. 96, describing Aristotle's formula of proportional equality as "inequalitarian"; Lakoff, *Equality in Political Philosophy*, p. 18, describing Aristotle's scheme of proportional equality as an attempt to

justice fall outside the scope of this study, it is appropriate to observe that "proportional" equality is as genuine an "equality" as any other. Indeed, it should have been evident since the time of Aristotle's lectures on ethics that, far from being derivative, proportional equality is a truly generic notion of equality with respect to distributions, and that proportional equality necessarily includes all arguably just "numerical" distributions.

Aristotle agreed with Plato that a just distribution is always a proportionately equal distribution, and vice versa.[23] But he also demonstrated that proportional equality is a mathematical notion that leaves room for considerable disagreement about substantive matters of right and wrong and good and bad, including whether a proportionately equal (and, therefore, just) distribution will eventually correspond with the results of a numerically equal distribution.[24] Aristotle's analysis of the relationship between justice and proportional equality consists of six steps:

"combine elements of hierarchy and social aristocracy with elements of *equality*," thereby implying that hierarchy is inconsistent with real equality; Popper, *The Open Society and Its Enemies*, pp. 95–96, referring to Plato's and Aristotle's notion of proportional equality as "anti-equalitarian"; and Rae, *Equalities*, p. 60 ("Proportionate equality . . . is not ordinarily conceived of as egalitarian. . . . [For] its effect is to legitimate most or many inequalities endemic to market systems").

[23] Aristotle, *Politics* V.1.1301a; Aristotle, *Nicomachean Ethics* V.3.1131b. It should be noted that Aristotle's equation of proportional equality with justice is confined to *distributive* justice, as opposed to rectificatory justice. Aristotle distinguishes between "absolute" justice and "particular" justice, and, within "particular justice," between "distributive justice" and "rectificatory justice." Distributive justice concerns the proper distribution of offices, honors, and goods; rectificatory justice concerns justice between individuals based on voluntary (contractual) and involuntary (tortious or criminal) transactions. Aristotle asserts that, while distributive justice is based on proportional equality, rectificatory justice is based on numerical equality. Aristotle, *Nicomachean Ethics* V.3.1131a25–35. For a discussion of Aristotle's views of equality in general, and of his distinction between distributive and rectificatory justice in particular, see von Leyden, *Aristotle on Equality and Justice*, pp. 13ff.

Given Aristotle's conception of proportional equality as a relationship between two persons and two things, however, it is not clear why the same conception does not also apply to rectificatory justice, which also involves two persons and one misappropriated thing, which stands in relation to each person as a geometric mean. For an argument that Aristotle's formula of proportional equality is broad enough to subsume both distributive and rectificatory justice, see Marc-Wogau, "Aristotle's Theory of Corrective Justice and Reciprocity." Cf. Isocrates, *Areopagiticus* 20–23 (describing the "kin[d] of equality" that "gives to each man his due" as one which "rewards *and punishes* every man according to his deserts"; trans. Norlin) (emphasis added).

[24] Aristotle, *Nicomachean Ethics* V.3; Aristotle, *Politics* III.9 and V.1.1301b26–1302a15. For Aristotle's distinction between proportional and numerical equality, and for the extent to which the former subsumes the latter, see note 23 above and note 26 below.

(1) Equality in the distribution of goods to persons entails at least four terms: two or more persons (P_1, P_2); and two or more respective distributions to such persons (D_1, D_2).

(2) The distributions of D_1 to P_1, and D_2 to P_2, can be stated in the form of ratios—the ratios $D_1:P_1$ and $D_2:P_2$.

(3) By definition, ratios are "equal" when the proportions underlying them are the same; for example, the ratio 4:2 "equals" the ratio 8:4 (that is, 4:2 = 8:4), because the same proportion, 2:1, underlies each set.

(4) The ratio $D_1:P_1$ "equals" the ratio $D_2:P_2$ when $D_1:D_2$ equals $P_1:P_2$; and the latter two ratios are equal when the same proportion underlies each of them.

(5) To determine the proportion of one person to another for moral purposes—that is, the moral proportion $P_1:P_2$—one must possess a moral standard for measuring and comparing persons.

(6) There is one, and only one, universally accepted moral standard for measuring persons with respect to distributions—namely, measuring them on the basis of "merit."[25]

THEREFORE: When the proportion of one distribution to another ($D_1:D_2$) is the same as the proportion of one person's merits to another's ($P_1:P_2$), then, and only then, are the distributions of D_1 to P_1 and D_2 to P_2 morally proportionate—morally equal and just—because then, and only then, is each distribution proportionately equal to each recipient's merits.

Aristotle's argument is compelling. It demonstrates that all distributions of goods to persons which are "just" are also morally "proportionate" and "equal" distributions (and vice versa), the proportions all being based on the ratio between what each person

[25] Aristotle, *Nicomachean Ethics* V.3.1131a22–b14 (trans. Thomson) (referring to "merit").

I understand Aristotle to be using the term 'merit' broadly to refer to all cases in which it is deemed that a person, A, ought to receive some social good, X, by virtue of traits he possesses—whether because of backward-looking considerations of "desert" or forward-looking considerations of the "good" that will thereby come about. Cf. Wilson, *Equality*, p. 67 (defining 'merit' broadly). For other definitions of what Thomson translates as 'merit', see Aristotle, *Nicomachean Ethics* V.3.1131a25 (trans. Ross) ("merit"); Aristotle, *Politics* V.1.1301b35–40 (trans. Rackham) ("worth"); Aristotle, *Politics* V.1.1301b35–40 (trans. Sinclair) ("value"); Aristotle, *Politics* V.1.1301b35–40 (trans. Barker) ("desert").

receives and what he deserves. Therefore, the argument also demonstrates that per-capita distributions, where just, are also proportionately equal, because they are all based on the proportion 1:1.[26] Unfortunately, as Aristotle further demonstrates, the foregoing argument is normatively incomplete because it does not contain an accepted standard for measuring "merit." Different people have different views regarding the appropriate standard. "Democrats," Aristotle said, believe that a person's merit should be measured by whether he possesses the status of a free man; thus they believe that goods should be distributed on a per-capita basis to all free men. "Oligarchs" believe that a person's merit should be measured by the extent of his wealth or social position; thus they be-

---

[26] As explained in the text, Aristotle demonstrates that all distributions involving two or more people (including per-capita distributions) necessarily take the form of ratios of people to things and, hence, necessarily involve "proportional" equality whenever the same proportion underlies each ratio. This suggests that proportional equality subsumes numerical equality whenever the same proportion of 1:1 underlies all ratios of people to things. Indeed, Aristotle implicitly says as much, because he maintains that all "just" distributions are proportionately equal (see Aristotle, *Politics* V.1.1301a; Aristotle, *Nicomachean Ethics* V.3.1131b), and that some per-capita distributions are just (see Aristotle, *Politics* V.2.1302a2–15; Aristotle, *Eudemian Ethics* VII.9.1241b33–40).

On the other hand, Aristotle also appears to agree with Plato's distinction between proportional equality and numerical equality with respect to distributions:

> But equality is of two sorts. One sort is numerical equality: the other sort is equality proportionate to desert. 'Numerical equality' means being treated equally, or identically, in the number and volume of things which you get; 'equality proportionate to desert' means being treated on the basis of equality of ratios.

Aristotle, *Politics* V.1.1301b (trans. Barker). See also Aristotle, *Eudemian Ethics* VII.9.1241b33–40. This suggests that proportional equality may not subsume numerical equality.

Thus the paradox: either proportional equality subsumes numerical equality, in which case Aristotle should not have distinguished between them, or proportional equality and numerical equality are mutually exclusive, in which case numerical equality can never be proportional, and, hence, never just.

Despite these apparent inconsistencies, there is at least one reading that reconciles the texts. It appears that by "proportional" distributions Aristotle means *normatively* proportional distributions, that is, those and only those distributions which reflect *normatively just* proportions between people (including per-capita distributions when they are just), and that by "numerical equality" he means all distributions per capita and by lot, regardless of whether or not they are just. This reading explains how Aristotle can simultaneously maintain that justice is proportional equality and vice versa (see *Nicomachean Ethics* V.3.1131b10–15) *and* that proportional equality includes and does not include numerical equality. Proportional equality is always just because it is defined as consisting of proportions that are just, including per-capita distributions wherever the latter are just. Numerical equality is not always proportional—and hence must be distinguished from proportional equality—because it is not always just.

lieve that goods should be distributed in accordance with a person's wealth or social status. "Aristocrats" believe that a person's merit should be measured by the extent of his noble birth; thus they believe that goods should be distributed in accordance with a person's ancestry.[27] Each proposed distribution is asserted to be just; each, if truly just, is proportionately equal to what each person deserves. Yet the three distributions differ because they rest on different standards for measuring merit.

It follows, therefore, that the normatively significant question is not whether just distributions are proportionately equal (because they obviously are) but how one measures merit with respect to distributions, and that the latter is a normative question about which the mathematical notion of proportional equality has nothing to say. To be sure, it is possible that in speaking of "proportional equality" Plato was referring, not to the formal principle that goods should be distributed equally "to each according to merit," but to the particular contested view, which Aristotle happened to share, that a person's merit should be measured by his moral excellence.[28] In that event, Plato's argument for proportional equality is indeed normatively significant (and controversial). Yet, in that event, it is also an argument that must be validated in moral and political theory, rather than in mathematics, because it is an argument, not for proportional equality as opposed to numerical equality, but for one particular measure of proportional equality ("to each according to his moral excellence") as opposed to others ("to each according to his wealth," "to each according to his number," and so on).[29]

---

[27] Aristotle, *Nicomachean Ethics* V.3.1131a20–30; Aristotle, *Politics* V.1.1301a27–b5. See also Aristotle, *Politics* III.3.1280a. It should be noted that Aristotle uses 'aristocracy' in different ways—sometimes referring to a regime in which privilege is based on birth (see Aristotle, *Politics* III.7.1281b14–1283b45), and sometimes referring to a regime in which privilege is based on civic excellence (see *Nicomachean Ethics* V.3.1131a29).

[28] Those who contribute most to an association of this character [i.e., those who contribute most to good action] have a greater share in the polis [and should therefore, in justice, receive more recognition from it] than those who are equal to them (or even greater) in free birth and descent, but unequal in civic excellence, or than those who surpass them in wealth but are surpassed by them in excellence.

Aristotle, *Politics* III.9.1281a1–10 (trans. Barker).

[29] See *The Politics of Aristotle*, trans. Barker, p. 205 n. 2, in which Barker, relying on Newman, notes that in normative contexts, proportional equality does not itself supply a standard of desert but rather is a formula for incorporating standards of desert by reference.

Conclusion

'Equality' may or may not have a fundamentally distinct meaning in mathematics, depending on whether the complete identity which obtains among mathematically equal entities forms part of a unique concept of equality in mathematics, or whether it is simply a necessary consequence of applying a unitary concept of equality to the unique subject matter of mathematics. In either event, it is important to recognize that mathematically equal entities are completely identical, whereas descriptively equal entities are not—important because it means that equalities in the one area cannot be coherently adjudged by equalities in the other.

To illustrate the danger of conflating the use of 'equality' in mathematics with its usage in descriptions, consider again Plato's statement that no two things in the world are ever "absolutely equal." We have seen above that this statement is true only if one attributes to 'equality' a meaning it does not possess in relation to tangible things, namely, "identical in every respect." One therefore wonders: How could Plato, whose understanding of words was both great and subtle, attribute to 'equality' a meaning it does not possess? How could he be so mistaken? The answer, perhaps, is that he was not mistaken about what 'equality' means. He may have known perfectly well what 'equality' means in mathematics. He may, instead, have made the mistake of judging the equality of tangible things by the equality of mathematics.[30] He may, in other words, have made what Gilbert Ryle calls a "category mistake," the mistake of applying to the description of tangible things a feature of equality that is categorically confined to the realm of mathematics.[31]

[30] Dilman, for example, assumes that when Plato speaks of "absolute equality" in *Phaedo* 74b, he has mathematical equality in mind. See Dilman, "Universals," p. 40.

[31] See Ryle, *The Concept of Mind*, pp. 16–18.

THREE

PRESCRIPTIVE EQUALITY

Distributing the Pound Cake

The pound cake is out of the oven and is ready to be eaten. I am uncertain, however, as to how I should distribute it among my three children.

—One of the children has refused to do his chores for a week and has admitted to pilfering his sister's allowance money, knowing that denial of dessert has sometimes been a penalty in our family for misbehavior.

—Another child is overweight. But I promised all the children that whoever brought home a perfect report card would get a special treat, and he is the only one who has done so.

—The third child did her best to help me make the cake without asking for anything in return, while the others refused to lend a hand.

I seek guidance in Scripture, remembering St. Paul's message to the Galatians, "All of God's children are equal in his eyes."[1]

I feel I, in turn, should proceed from the proposition that "all my children are equal in my eyes," but I wonder what that signifies in the matter at hand.

Equality is more than a descriptive and mathematical concept. It is also a subject of moral and political contention. "Few issues," it has been said, "have sparked more controversy or held more sway over the course of history than has equality. Ships have been launched, lives given, governments toppled—all in the name of this one ideal."[2]

These controversies, as Aristotle observed,[3] involve a different

---

[1] See Lakoff, "Christianity and Equality," p. 119 (describing Galatians 3:28 as expressing "the Pauline Christian conception . . . that all human beings are equal in the eyes of God").

[2] Verba and Orren, *Equality in America*, p. 1.

[3] Aristotle, *Politics* III.5.1280a15–25 (everyone "agree[s] as to what constitutes

59

kind of equality than that which we have studied thus far; for people do not generally disagree about whether X and Y are equal in weight, or whether $3 + 3 = 6$. People disagree about propositions of a different sort—propositions such as "all men are created equal," "all human beings are equal in God's eyes," "all persons are equal before the law," and "all men and women"—or all blacks and whites, old and young, rich and poor, married and unmarried, able and disabled, Christians and non-Christians, heterosexuals and homosexuals, legitimate and illegitimate—are "equal to one another in their rights."

The propositions of equality examined in Chapters 1 and 2 have one thing in common: they are statements of "is," not statements of "ought"; they depict things as they are, not as they ought to be. To say, as we did in "Making a Pound Cake," that the pan of flour and the pan of sugar are "equal" in weight states a fact, not a right or a duty. To be sure, when we selected the digital spring scale as the relevant standard of comparison, we did so because we believed it would serve the purposes we already had in mind. And when we measured out equal amounts of flour, sugar, and butter, we did so because we believed these equalities were essential to something we wished to do—perhaps even something we believed we ought to do. In that sense, all the equalities we take the trouble to ascertain are linked in some way to things we wish to do or believe we ought to do. But there is a significant difference between determinations of equality that are linked to a duty or necessary to a duty, on the one hand, and determinations that are the *source* of a duty, on the other. The equalities that obtained among the flour, sugar, and butter may have been necessary for the making of a pound cake, and they may even have been necessary for the fulfillment of a duty to make a pound cake, but they were not the source of a duty to make a pound cake. When we measure out equal amounts of flour, sugar, and butter pursuant to a duty to make a pound cake, we do so because we possess the duty before we establish the equalities; and, once we measure out equal amounts of ingredients, the amounts remain equal, without regard to any duty involved in the use of them.

In contrast, the equality invoked as a starting point in "Distributing the Pound Cake" ("all my children are equal in my eyes") is not descriptive; it is prescriptive. It represents a relationship, not

equality in the thing, but dispute as to what constitutes equality in the person"; trans. Rackham).

of "is" (or not solely of "is"), but of "ought." It represents things, not as they are (or not solely as they are), but as they ought to be. To say that my three children are "equal" in my eyes (or equally deserving of love, equally worthy of respect, or equally entitled to concern) is not to state a verifiable fact about the world that is either true or false. Rather, it is to state a normative principle of conduct that is right or wrong. These equalities are not merely linked to rights and duties; they are *statements* of rights and duties. The acknowledgment that children are equal members of a family implies something about the treatment to which they are entitled.

As one might expect, prescriptive equalities are controversial in ways that descriptive equalities are not. Descriptive equalities are rarely the subject of serious dispute. People may occasionally disagree about whether a particular standard of measure is appropriate for a particular comparison; and, having selected a standard, they may disagree about whether the subjects measured are indeed indistinguishable by reference to that measure. (Thus, people might disagree as to whether a digital spring scale accurate to within .01 ounces is the appropriate measure for making a pound cake; and having decided to use the digital spring scale, they might disagree as to how to read the scale). But such disagreements tend to lend themselves to objective resolution because we assume they rest on verifiable assertions of fact. Prescriptive equalities are controversial in an entirely different way. When people disagree on such issues as whether all human beings are equal in worth, or whether human fetuses are equal to full-term babies in their right to life, or whether all people are equal in their claim to the world's resources, they are not disagreeing about verifiable questions of fact. They are disagreeing about inherently contestable questions of value.

Interestingly, prescriptive equality appears to be more than merely controversial in the way that all normative relationships are. It is also singularly and profoundly enigmatic. Thus, prescriptive equality has been variously described as "strange and difficult," "complex," "intricate," "ambigu[ous]," "elusive," "slippery," and "mysterious."[4] It is ironic that prescriptive equality

[4] Adler and Hutchins, "The Idea of Equality," p. 303 (equality is a "strange and difficult" idea); Blackstone, Introduction to *The Concept of Equality*, p. v ("complex"); Dallmayr, "Functionalism, Justice and Equality," p. 10 ("intricate"); Verba and Orren, *Equality in America*, p. 1 ("ambigu[ous]"); Evans, "Equality, Ambiguity, and Public Choice," p. 1385 ("elusive"); Cauthen, *The Passion for Equality*, p. 2 ("slippery"); Dworkin, "What Is Equality? Part 1, Equality of Welfare," p. 185

should seem so complex and enigmatic, because it is identical to descriptive equality in all but one respect. Prescriptive equality and descriptive equality are both "equalities"—they are both relationships of identity that obtain among two or more distinct things that have been jointly measured and compared by a common standard of measurement and found to be indistinguishable by reference to that standard. The sole difference, as we shall see below, is in the nature of the standard of measurement.

Elements of Prescriptive Equality

Prescriptive equality has several elements in common with descriptive and mathematical equality. The latter, as we have previously defined it, is

(1) the relationship that obtains among two or more entities, whether tangible or intangible,

(2) that have been jointly measured and compared by reference to a common standard of measurement,

(3) and that, though not identical by all measures of their dimensions to the extent that they consist of more than dimension,

(4) are nevertheless indistinguishable by reference to the relevant standard of measurement.

Prescriptive equalities certainly share elements (1), (2), and (3): one cannot declare people to be morally or legally "equal" without having compared them, and one cannot compare people without having jointly measured them by one or more common standards of measurement. And, as with descriptive equalities, in declaring different people to be "equal," we do not mean that they are identical by all possible measures; for if they were, they would not be "equal" persons but, rather, one and the same person.

The interesting question is whether prescriptive equality also shares element (4)—in other words, is prescriptive equality (like descriptive and mathematical equality) also a relationship of *complete* identity by reference to a *relevant* standard of measurement? There are several possibilities:

("mysterious"). See also Laski, "Liberty and Equality," p. 26 ("No idea in the whole realm of political science is more difficult than the concept of equality").

(A) Prescriptive equality may be the comparative relationship that obtains among persons who are identical in *all* prescriptive respects.

(B) Prescriptive equality may be the relationship that obtains among persons who are identical in *some* prescriptive respects.

(C) Prescriptive equality may be the comparative relationship that obtains among persons who are similar—that is, the relationship that obtains among persons who are either *nearly* identical in relevant respects or completely identical in *most* relevant respects.

(D) Prescriptive equality may be the comparative relationship that obtains among persons who are completely identical in relevant prescriptive respects.

Neither A nor B can be the pertinent relationship, though for reasons that are the converse of one another. Relationship A cannot be the one which underlies prescriptive equality because, as we shall see, no two people in mature societies are ever identical in *all* prescriptive respects.[5] Relationship B does not work because all people in mature societies are prescriptively identical in at least *one* respect—all persons in a mature society are, for example, legally entitled to the benefits and burdens which the law prescribes for them.[6]

Relationship C appears to have more validity because, just as we commonly say that "people who are equal should be treated equally," we also say that "people who are similarly situated should be treated similarly," thus suggesting that in realms of prescriptive equality, 'equal' and 'similar' may be synonymous. Yet that cannot be so, because if 'equal' and 'similar' were synonymous, it would follow that "people who are merely similar should be treated equally" and "people who are equal should be treated merely similarly," neither of which is true. To illustrate, consider

Voting in Surlandia

The nation of Surlandia enacts a constitution declaring that "all adult, competent, and law-abiding citizens are equal in their right to vote for the office of president."

[5] See the discussion of "Two Surlandian Brothers" below in this chapter.
[6] See the discussion of "equal before the law," pp. 74–79 below.

—An "adult" is any person who is twenty-one years of age or older.

—A "competent" person is anyone who understands the nature of casting a vote and holding elective office.

—A "law-abiding" person is anyone who has not been convicted of a felony for which he has not been pardoned.

—A "citizen" of Surlandia, in turn, is any person who has been either born or naturalized in Surlandia.

John of Surlandia is the youngest of three brothers. He would like to vote, as his brothers do, in national elections. Like them, he was born in Surlandia, graduated from college with honors, and has never been convicted of a crime. The only relevant difference between John and his brothers is that they were all twenty-one years old when they registered to vote, while John is twenty years, eleven months, and twenty-seven days old.

With regard to the qualifications for voting, John is "similar" to his brothers in two senses. He is similar in that he is identical to them in *most*, that is, three out of four, relevant respects (citizenship, competency, and law-abidance). He is also similar in the sense of being *nearly* identical in all relevant respects (identical in three respects and nearly identical in the fourth, age). Yet, obviously, he is not prescriptively "equal" to them, for he cannot vote. So, being prescriptively equal must mean more than being mostly identical or nearly identical in relevant prescriptive respects. Prescriptive equality is the relationship which remains under alternative D—the relationship which obtains among persons who are *completely* identical in relevant respects.

Now it might be said that, while prescriptive equality and descriptive equality both share elements (1) through (4), they differ with respect to the *multiplicity of the standards of comparison* that they may incorporate by reference. We have seen that the concept of descriptive equality can incorporate a nearly infinite number of standards for measuring things in their various dimensions. In contrast, some commentators have suggested that while there are many standards of descriptive equality (and, hence, many descriptive equalities), there is only one genuine standard of prescriptive equality (and hence, only one genuine prescriptive equality). Thus, it has been said that, while there are many components to prescriptive equality (equality in economics, equality in politics, and so on), the components are "interconnected" by virtue of an "indivisib[le]" and single "value" or "ideal" of prescriptive equality.[7]

It may be true that there is a single, generic standard of prescriptive equality from which all other standards can be derived. Thus, it may be true, as Kant and others suggest, that subsidiary moral norms can be derived from the basic norm "treat every person as an end and not solely as a means"—a basic standard by which all persons are "equals" in that respect.[8] But, even if such a norm can be established, it must also coexist with innumerable subsidiary rules, which classify people identically for some purposes and differently for others, because all just societies, including Kantian societies, must classify people differently for some purposes than for others.[9]

The Nature of Prescriptive Standards

The significant difference between prescriptive equality and descriptive equality lies in the nature of their underlying standards of comparison. In the case of descriptive equalities, the standards of comparison are themselves descriptive. That is to say, the standards of comparison that underlie descriptive equalities are stan-

[7] Verba and Orren, *Equality in America*, p. 25 ("interconnected"; "indivisib[le]" [quoting Pole, *The Pursuit of Equality in American History*]); Dworkin, "What Is Equality? Part 1, Equality of Welfare," p. 185 (prescriptive equality is an "ideal"); Bork, "The Impossibility of Finding Welfare Rights in the Constitution," p. 701 (a "value").

[8] See Williams, "The Idea of Equality," pp. 115–18 (describing Kant's categorical imperative as a norm of "equality" from which other norms can be derived); Gutmann, *Liberal Equality*, pp. 27–41 (same); Charvet, *A Critique of Freedom and Equality*, pp. 69–81 (an analysis of Kant's moral imperatives). See also del Vecchio, *Justice*, p. 150 (arguing that "rights" can be derived from the "supreme postulate of justice," namely, that all persons are entitled to equal respect); Dworkin, *A Matter of Principle*, pp. 181–204, and *Taking Rights Seriously*, pp. 180–83, 272–78 (suggesting that liberties can be derived from the norms "Treat everyone as an equal" and "Treat everyone with equal respect and concern"). On the question of whether Dworkin's norm is comparative or noncomparative in nature, see notes 21–22 below, and Chapter 4, note 10.

[9] [Virtually] all government action involves the making of choices and the drawing of lines in ways that entail favoring some over others. Every political decision makes distinctions among persons, groups, and interests and decides who should win and who should lose in the competition for attention, concern, favor, and resources.

Bator, "Equality as a Constitutional Value," p. 21. See also *Toll v. Moreno*, 458 U.S. 1, 39 (1982) (Rehnquist, J., dissenting) ("All laws classify"); *Clements v. Fashing*, 457 U.S. 957, 967 (1982) (opinion of Rehnquist, J.) ("classification is the essence of all legislation").

dards for comparing people and things solely with respect to what they actually are, as opposed to how they ought to be treated. Thus, in "Making a Pound Cake" we measured and compared the flour, sugar, and butter for their weight in full ounces as displayed by a digital scale that measures weight to within .01 of the nearest full ounce. We determined the ingredients to be equal because by that standard they were indistinguishable, each weighing 16 ounces on the digital scale, each sharing the same description.

The standards of comparison which underlie prescriptive equality do share something significant with the standards underlying descriptive equality, for, just as the latter *are* descriptive standards, the former necessarily *contain* descriptive standards. We can see why this is so by isolating the steps involved in concluding that particular persons are prescriptively equal with regard to the treatments they deserve. First, one cannot say that a particular group of persons deserve identical treatment unless one is able to distinguish those who are members of the group from those who are not. And, second, one cannot identify particular persons as members of a group without possessing a descriptive standard which specifies the features that together characterize them as members.[10]

To illustrate the descriptive component that underlies all prescriptive equalities, consider the equality involved in "Voting in Surlandia." To say that certain people in Surlandia are prescriptively "equal" with respect to voting means that they have been measured by a common standard regarding voting and found to be identical in possessing the right to vote. Yet, in order to identify and distinguish that group of people from others, the standard of comparison must contain descriptive criteria by which such persons can be known—in the case of Surlandia, the descriptive cri-

[10] See Adler and Hutchins, "The Idea of Equality," pp. 303, 328 (arguing that every prescriptive equality is premised on a relevant description); Coons, "Consistency," p. 73 ("Rules, then, consist at least of description and judgment"); Hart, "Definition and Theory in Jurisprudence," p. 34 (referring to Bentham's injunction to reduce prescriptive terms to descriptive ones); Rees, *Equality*, p. 104 ("To justify equality of treatment there must be equality of the attributes of the persons concerned, otherwise the move from factual premises to moral principle is unwarranted"). But see Evans, "Thinking Clearly about Equality," p. 102 ("A statement that people *are* equal in fact is logically unrelated to a statement that people *should* be treated equally"); Frankena, "Some Beliefs about Justice," p. 97 (referring to commentators who believe that prescriptive equalities are not always based on descriptive ones); McCloskey, "Egalitarianism, Equality, and Justice," p. 50 ("The evaluative claims are usually linked with these factual claims, but they need not be so linked and they are not always so linked").

teria require that a person be (i) twenty-one years of age or older, (ii) born or naturalized in Surlandia, (iii) capable of understanding the nature of voting, and (iv) untouched by felony conviction. People who satisfy all four criteria are descriptively equal because, measured by the relevant descriptive component, they are identical in their descriptions.

To be sure, while some descriptive criteria are nonnormative (e.g., "twenty-one years of age or older"), others incorporate external prescriptions by reference (e.g., the description "naturalized," which incorporates by reference rules regarding "naturalization"). Yet, even though a specified group of people may be described initially by reference to external prescriptions, the group can always be redescribed in nonnormative terms, because the external prescriptions themselves, to be known and applied, must contain or refer to nonnormative criteria for identifying the people to whom they apply. Thus, people who are initially described as having been "naturalized" can be redescribed in nonnormative terms, because the prescriptions governing "naturalization," to be known and applied, must contain or refer to nonnormative criteria for identifying the people to whom they apply.

The standards of measurement that underlie descriptive equalities, it will be recalled, come in two distinct forms: continuous standards for measuring things in terms of "more or less"; and binary standards for measuring things in terms of "either/or."[11] A scale calibrated in ounces measures things as being "more or less" because it measures how much more or less one thing weighs than another. Litmus paper measures things as being "either/or" because it determines whether some substance is base (blue) or acid (red). Interestingly (and, perhaps, not surprisingly), the same two kinds of standards may also underlie descriptive components of prescriptive equalities. Thus, taxpayers who are prescriptively equal with respect to the amount they owe in income tax are people who, when measured by how much *more or less* they have earned in taxable income, are descriptively identical in the amounts they have earned. On the other hand, citizens of Surlandia who are prescriptively equal in possessing the right to vote are people who, when measured by the *binary* standard of being *either* twenty-one years of age or older *or* less than twenty-one years old, are descriptively identical in being twenty-one years of age or older.

[11] See the "Ping-Pong Balls" example above in Chapter 1.

It follows, therefore, that the standards of comparison that underlie prescriptive equalities must contain at least two components. They must contain a descriptive component, because they incorporate descriptive criteria for identifying the persons to whom they apply. They must also contain something *more* than a descriptive component—something normative in nature—because, as a consequence of measuring and comparing people by the standards underlying prescriptive equalities, we not only identify a class of people who are identical with respect to what they *are*, but also know something about how they *ought to be treated*. Hence the query: what is the nature of such standards? What kind of thing contains both descriptive criteria for identifying a class of persons and normative specification of the treatment such persons either owe or deserve?

The answer should be clear by now: a specification that persons of a certain description owe or deserve certain treatment is what we ordinarily call a moral or legal "rule." As W. Twining and D. Miers explain, a rule is a compound of description and prescription:

> Any rule, however expressed, or even if it has not been expressed, can be analyzed and restated as a compound conditional statement of the form "If X, then Y." The first part, "if X," which is known as the *protasis*, is *descriptive*—it indicates the scope of a rule by designating the conditions in which the rule applies. The second part, "then Y," known as the *apodosis*, is *prescriptive*—it states whether the type of behavior governed by the rule is prohibited ("may not," "ought not"), required ("ought" or "must"), permitted ("may") and so on.[12]

A rule may take the form of a "right," that is, a justified claim on the part of a described group of persons, A, to do or receive something with respect to a specified group of persons, B. Or it may take the form of a correlative "duty," a justified obligation on the part of a described group of persons, B, to do or refrain from doing something with respect to a specified group of persons, A.[13] A rule

---

[12] Gottlieb, *The Logic of Choice*, p. 40; Twining and Miers, *How to Do Things with Rules*, pp. 137–38. See also Friedman, "Legal Rules and the Process of Legal Change," pp. 786–87; Schlag, "Rules and Standards," p. 381, esp. n. 11.

[13] For a generic definition of 'rights', see Finnis, *Natural Law and Natural Rights*, p. 205:

> [We] may safely speak of rights whenever a basic principle or requirement of practical reasonableness, or a rule derived therefrom, gives to A, and to each

may be justified in law, or in morals, or in both law and morals. A rule may be conditional or unconditional, defeasible or indefeasible. In any event, a rule is a "prescription"—a prescription specifying that persons of a certain description deserve or owe something with respect to other persons of a certain description.

In short, the standards of comparison that underlie prescriptive equalities are themselves prescriptions. Just as descriptive equality is the relationship that obtains among persons or things that have been jointly measured, compared, and found to be indistinguishable in fact by reference to specified standards of description, so prescriptive equality is the relationship that obtains among persons who have been jointly measured, compared, and found to be indistinguishable in their rights or duties by reference to specified prescriptions. And just as descriptive "equals" are persons or things that are identical in their descriptions as measured by relevant standards of description, prescriptive equals are persons who are identical in what they owe or deserve as measured by relevant prescriptions. In short, prescriptive equals are persons who fall within the same descriptive class—who possess the same description—for the purpose of a given rule of conduct.

Conversely, prescriptive "inequality" is the relationship which obtains among persons who, having been measured and compared by reference to a specified prescription, are *distinguishable* in their respective rights or duties—people who are *not* identical in what they owe or deserve as measured by relevant rules of conduct and do *not* fall within a descriptive class of persons for whom common treatment is prescribed.

The Relation between Descriptive and Prescriptive Equality: The Link between "Is" and "Ought"

Aristotle complained that every political faction tends to argue that because it is equal in some particular respect, it ought to be treated equally in all respects. Thus, he said, aristocrats argue that be-

---

and every other member of a class to which A belongs, the benefit of (i) a positive or negative requirement (obligation) imposed upon B (including *inter alia*, any requirement not to interfere with A's activity or with A's enjoyment of some other form of good) or of (ii) the ability to bring it about that B is subject to such a requirement, or of (iii) the immunity from being himself subjected by B to any such requirement.

For an illuminating account of Hohfeldian analysis of rights and duties, see Wellman, *A Theory of Rights.*

cause they are all equal in the nobility of their birth they ought to be politically equal in every respect, while democrats argue that because they are all equal in being freeborn, they ought to be politically equal in every respect. Each faction, he concludes, selects one descriptive criterion in terms of which its members "are" equal, and on that basis argues that they are entitled to equal treatment in all respects.[14]

Given our analysis of prescriptive equalities, we can appreciate Aristotle's complaint. Equality is not an alchemy for transmuting an "is" into an "ought." One cannot infer from the fact that people *are* equal in height, or beauty, or wealth, or flute-playing, that therefore they *ought to be treated* in a certain way.[15] Rather, when we reason that prescriptive equals, being descriptively identical, ought to be treated identically, we are not inferring an "ought" from an "is," but are applying an existing statement of "ought" to the persons to whom it applies. We are giving effect to a rule that itself links an "is" to an "ought"—a rule that prescribes certain treatment for persons of a certain description. Having identified persons who are identical (viz., "equal") in sharing the description contained in the rule, we give them the treatment prescribed for them by the rule. We give them that treatment not because *we* are inferring an "ought" from an "is" but because the *rule* containing the description by which they are equal states that everyone who is identical in sharing that description ought to receive that treatment.

As an illustration of the relationship between descriptive and prescriptive equality, consider the prescriptive equality set forth in the Surlandian constitution:

> All adult, competent, and law-abiding citizens are equal in their right to vote for the office of president.

To have declared such persons equal is to have measured them, compared them, and found them to be indistinguishable by a common standard of measurement. The standard cannot be solely descriptive, because people who are identical solely by descriptive

---

[14] Aristotle, *Politics* III.7.1281b14–1283b45. See also III.5.1280a7–35; V.1.1301a27–b5.

[15] See Hawkins, *The Science and Ethics of Equality*, pp. 11–12; Lloyd, *Introduction to Jurisprudence*, p. 87 ("The idea of equality or nondiscrimination is essentially a value-judgment which cannot be derived from any assertions or speculations regarding the nature of man"); Oppenheim, "The Concept of Equality," p. 107 ("[n]ormative principles cannot be derived from factual generalizations; neither equality nor inequality of characteristics entails the desirability of either egalitarian or inegalitarian treatment"). See also Aristotle, *Politics* III.12.1282b23–1283.

standards are at most descriptively equal. To be prescriptively equal (that is, equal with respect to the treatment they owe or deserve), people must also be measured and compared by a standard that prescribes the way people ought to be treated. At least two implicit prescriptions may underlie the Surlandian declaration of equality:

P_1: Every adult, competent, and law-abiding citizen is eligible to cast one and only one vote for the office of president.

P_2: If *any* adult, competent, and law-abiding citizen is allowed to cast a vote for the office of president, every *other* adult, competent, and law-abiding citizen shall be allowed to cast a vote for such office.[16]

These prescriptions obviously differ in their content. As we shall see, P_1 is a "noncomparative" right, while P_2 is a "comparative" right. Yet both prescriptions describe an identical group of persons, who possess a common right to vote, by specifying the descriptive features that such persons must have in common. Measured by such descriptive standards, certain persons—namely, any and all "adult, competent, and law-abiding citizens"—are descriptively indistinguishable, and being descriptively indistinguishable, they are entitled to common treatment with respect to voting. They are prescriptive equals because, under both rules, they all fall within the descriptive class of persons for whom a common treatment is prescribed. They are prescriptive equals, not because we infer the "ought" of common treatment from the "is" of descriptive identity, but because we start with implicit standards of comparison that themselves prescribe common treatment for persons who are identical in possessing certain descriptive features.

Ambiguity Regarding the Substance of the Underlying Prescription

Prescriptive equality is a relationship that obtains among persons by reference to moral or legal rules, that is, it is the identity that obtains among persons who have the same rights or duties under controlling rules of conduct. To say that people are prescriptively equal is to make implicit reference to the substance of a given rule

[16] I do not mean to suggest that there are only two possible implicit prescriptions that may inform the Surlandian constitution. There may be as many different prescriptions as are entailed by the many different meanings of "equality in voting." For an analysis of the plethora of electoral systems masked by the term 'equality', see Still, "Political Equality and Election Systems."

of conduct by referring to the identity the rule creates among them. Prescriptive equality, then, is an oblique way of talking about rules by reference to the common classifications they create among people.

This does not mean that rules are in any way temporally *anterior* to prescriptive equalities. Some commentators (including myself) have said that prescriptive equalities stand in a "consequential" relationship to rules, thereby implying that rules stand in a sequential relation to prescriptive equalities such that rules come first and prescriptive equalities thereafter.[17] That is not so. Rules and prescriptive equalities are coeval, not sequential. Prescriptive equalities presuppose rules, just as rules presuppose prescriptive equalities. The two arise simultaneously, because they are alternative ways of expressing the same normative judgment.[18]

To say that prescriptive equality is a way of talking about rules, however, is not to say that prescriptive equality is a *perspicuous* way of talking about rules. On the contrary, being an oblique and ambiguous way of talking about rules, the language of prescriptive equality tends to obscure the content of the rules it reflects.[19] The ambiguity has several sources, two of which are discussed below: the ambiguity of prescriptive equalities as to whether they are based on comparative or noncomparative rules of conduct; and the tendency to express prescriptive equalities elliptically, thereby failing to make explicit the precise terms of the underlying rules one has in mind.

Comparative and Noncomparative Rules

Just as comparative and noncomparative standards of measurement may inform descriptive equalities, so, too, they may both inform prescriptive equalities. A noncomparative standard of measurement, it will be recalled, is a standard by which one can measure a thing, A, without reference to any other thing, B. Thus, an

[17] Browne, "Nonegalitarian Justice," p. 52; Westen, "The Meaning of 'Equality' in Law, Science, Math and Morals," p. 653 (quoting Browne favorably).

[18] See Chapter 9, notes 39 and 41, and the accompanying text.

[19] Browne, "Nonegalitarian Justice," p. 53 (referring to the tendency of 'equality' to "distort and obscure" the content of underlying principles of justice). See also Carr, "The Concept of Formal Justice," p. 223 (equality "serves only to blind us to the actual workings and character of the practice of doing justice"). Cf. Raz, *The Morality of Freedom*, p. 228 (the practice of expressing noncomparative principles in the language of 'equality' is "less perspicuous, *i.e.*, less revealing of their true grounds, than some non-egalitarian formulations of the same principles"). For the extent to which Raz's point about noncomparative principles also holds for comparative principles, see Chapter 6, pp. 144–45.

ordinary spring-mounted bathroom scale is based on a noncomparative standard because it can ascertain how much a particular person weighs without reference to the weight of anyone else. A comparative standard of measurement, in contrast, is a standard for measuring one thing, A, by reference to some other thing, B. Thus, the balance scale held in the medieval representation of blind Justice incorporates a comparative standard because it measures only whether an item in one pan of the scale weighs "more," "less," or "neither more nor less" than items in the other pan.

By the same token, a noncomparative rule is a rule by which the rights or duties of one particular person, A, can be determined without reference to his relations to other persons, and a comparative rule is a rule by which the rights or duties of A are determined by reference to his relations to another person or persons, B.[20] Rules formulated in the language of equality can be ambiguous as to whether the underlying principle is comparative or noncomparative. An example is what Ronald Dworkin refers to as the "right to equal concern and respect."[21] To speak of every person's right to "equal concern and respect" is ambiguous (and, indeed, Dworkin's statements themselves are ambiguous)[22] as to whether one means:

[20] The distinction between comparative and noncomparative justice was introduced by Joel Feinberg in "Noncomparative Justice," p. 298:

> A way of achieving still more unity [in one's understanding of justice] is to separate the data of justice as neatly as possible into two categories. Perhaps this can be done in a variety of ways, but the one in which I am interested here sorts the various contexts, criteria, and principles of justice into those which essentially involve comparison between various persons and those which do not. In all cases, of course, justice consists in giving a person his due, but in some cases one's due is determined independently of that of other people, while in other cases, a person's due is determinable *only* by reference to his relations to other persons. I shall refer to contexts, criteria, and principles of the former kind as *noncomparative*, and those of the latter sort as *comparative*.

For further discussion of Feinberg's views, see Chapter 6, pp. 134–37. Joseph Raz discusses noncomparative rules in *The Morality of Freedom*, p. 225:

> Under [noncomparative] principles each person's right is independent of that of other people. He has it because the reason for the right applies to him. Other people may or may not have the same right. If they do that is because there is in their case too a reason (the same one) to give them a right to G.

[21] The "right to equal concern and respect" has come to be associated with Ronald Dworkin, who has made it the normative foundation of his philosophy of law. See Dworkin, "Liberalism," p. 125. Dworkin appears to take the notion of equal "respect and concern" from John Rawls. See Dworkin, *Taking Rights Seriously*, pp. 180–83; Rawls, *A Theory of Justice*, pp. 504–12; Rawls, "A Kantian Conception of Equality," p. 94 (referring to "equal respect and consideration").

[22] In his earlier writing, Dworkin appears to view the "right to equal concern and

R_1: *Every* person is entitled to be treated with a certain concern and respect.

or

R_2: If *any* person is treated with a certain concern and respect, every *other* person shall be entitled to the same concern and respect.

R_1 is a noncomparative rule because the concern and respect that it accords an individual person, say "Jack," are independent of—and can be ascertained without reference to—the way other persons happen to be treated. R_2, in contrast, is a comparative rule because the concern and respect it accords to Jack are entirely a function of the concern and respect that happens to be accorded to others, say "Jill." R_2 is the less beneficent of the two rules because it is indifferent as to whether all persons are treated *with* a certain concern and respect or *without* any concern and respect.

R_1 and R_2 differ, then, in their normative content, and yet they have one thing in common. Both are prescriptions by which Jack and Jill are "equal" regarding their right to concern and respect. As a result, they illustrate an ambiguity that inheres in the language of prescriptive equality: to say that two persons are prescriptively "equal" regarding X is inherently ambiguous—ambiguous as to whether (by virtue of a noncomparative rule) each possesses an independent right or duty regarding X, or whether (by virtue of a comparative rule) one person possesses a right or duty to X only insofar as others are accorded X. To that extent, statements of prescriptive equality are less perspicuous than an explicit statement of the rules to which they implicitly refer.[23]

Elliptical Formulations of Prescriptive Equalities: The Example of "Equality before the Law"

Statements of prescriptive equality also tend to be elliptical. They tend to refer to rules obliquely, thus omitting constituent elements in rules that full statement would make explicit. The omissions are

---

respect" as a comparative right, that is, a right to "concern and respect" *if and only if* such concern and respect is granted to others. See Dworkin, *Taking Rights Seriously*, pp. 356–57. More recently, however, he speaks of the right to "equal concern and respect" as a noncomparative right of each person to be treated in "the way the good or truly wise person would wish to be treated." Dworkin, "Liberalism," p. 127. Most commentators assume that Dworkin means to be expounding a noncomparative rule of treatment. See Chapter 4, note 10.

[23] See Raz, *The Morality of Freedom*, p. 233.

of two kinds: sometimes statements of prescriptive equality fail to specify the *persons* to whom rights and duties apply, and sometimes they fail to specify the *rights and duties* such persons possess.

The failure to describe persons fully may be illustrated by considering again the voting provisions ("V") of the Surlandian constitution:

V: All adult, competent, and law-abiding citizens are equal in their right to vote for the office of president.

The foregoing statement of equality is explicit about the class of persons to whom it applies: it specifies all the features they must possess in order to have the right to vote. Yet the norm which this statement expresses can be stated in terms that are less explicit, and hence, less clear. Thus, in lieu of V, one could just as well say:

V_1: *All persons who are* adult, competent, and law-abiding citizens are equal in their right to vote for the office of president.

And just as one can express V by referring to the equality of "all persons" in V_1, one can, if one so intends, express the latter elliptically by stating:

V_2: All persons are equal in their right to vote for the office of president.

—*meaning*, but *not stating*, that "all persons *who are adult, competent, and law-abiding citizens* are equal in their right to vote for the office of president." Statement V_2 is true because all persons *are* equal under the Surlandian constitution with respect to the right to vote—equal in that every person has a right to vote *if* he or she is an adult, competent, and law-abiding citizen.[24] Yet the statement of equality in V_2 is less specific—and hence less perspicuous—than an explicit statement of the rule (P_1 or P_2) to which it implicitly refers.

Some statements of prescriptive equality also fail to specify the rights and duties to which they refer. An example may be found

[24] [We] may be all equal before the law, in the sense that the law applies to everybody, but in this sense our being equal before the law is compatible with the law's assigning to different people very different rights and duties. In this sense, a law which hangs coloured men for raping white women, but does not hang white men for raping coloured women applies equally to all men; that they are *all* hanged *if* they are coloured, treats all men alike in just the same way as does a rule that they are hanged *if* they are murderers.

Harrison, *Hume's Theory of Justice*, pp. 193–94.

in the axiom "All persons are equal before the law."[25] To ascertain whether the axiom is true, and what it means, one must first identify the specific relationship to "the law" with respect to which all people are asserted to be equal. Yet the axiom, by referring to this relationship elliptically, fails to specify the terms of the underlying prescription. There are at least seven noncomparative prescriptions to which the axiom may refer (to which one could add an equivalent set of seven comparative prescriptions):

P_a: *Consistency.* The law shall not distinguish among persons except in accord with the traits and activities by which they are legally classified.[26]

P_b: *Immunity.* The law shall not classify any person in such a way as to render him or her wholly unanswerable to, or wholly unprotected from, other persons.[27]

P_c: *Due Process.* The justiciable disputes of all persons shall be resolved by impartial tribunals after hearing from all sides.[28]

P_d: *Prospectivity.* The law shall always be promulgated in advance of the conduct to which it applies.[29]

P_e: *Indigence.* Courts of law shall be open to all persons without regard to their financial ability to pay.[30]

[25] Canada has recently codified the axiom as part of its fundamental law:

> Every individual is equal before and under the law and has the right to the equal protection and equal benefit of the law without discrimination and, in particular, without discrimination based on race, national or ethnic origin, colour, religion, sex, age or mental or physical disability.

Canadian Charter of Rights and Freedoms § 15(1).

[26] This is the principle that some commentators believe the framers of the Fourteenth Amendment had in mind when they prohibited the states from denying "any person" the "equal protection of the laws." See Berger, *Government by Judiciary*, pp. 18–19 (arguing that the framers intended the equal protection clause as a requirement that the executive branch of government give blacks the protection to which they are entitled under the "privileges or immunities" clause of the Fourteenth Amendment).

[27] J. R. Lucas has identified a number of principles, including the present principle, that are commonly subsumed under the phrase "equality before the law." See Lucas, *The Principles of Politics*, p. 253 ("nobody is so lowly as not to have recourse to the courts, nobody is so mighty as not to have to answer to the courts: anybody can invoke the courts' aid, everybody must render them obedience").

[28] See Lucas, *The Principles of Politics*, pp. 246–56 (the courts shall decide all disputes "fairly and impartially, without fear or favor," after "hearing argument on both sides").

[29] See Lucas, *The Principles of Politics*, pp. 246–56 (the law shall regulate all people in accordance with "antecedently promulgated" rules).

[30] Cf. Lucas, *The Principles of Politics*, pp. 246–56 (the courts shall ensure that both sides to disputes are "evenly matched" in their access to counsel).

P_f: *Rationality*. The law shall not distinguish among people on the basis of arbitrary classifications.[31]

P_g: *Procrustes*. The law shall not distinguish among people on any basis whatsoever.

These prescriptions all have one thing in common: each is a rule by which "all persons" are rendered prescriptively indistinguishable (hence, "equal") before "the law." Yet they differ dramatically in their normative content:

—P_a ("Consistency") merely makes explicit what is necessarily implicit in every mature legal system, namely, that the state shall give to every person the treatment to which he is legally entitled. The principle is formal in nature because it adds nothing of substance to what the law already provides: it requires that a person receive the treatment to which he has a right, but it does not itself specify such rights. It merely incorporates by reference whatever rights and duties the law otherwise prescribes. It is consistent with the specifics of all legal systems, including systems based on slavery, peonage, and racial apartheid.[32]

—P_b ("Immunity) is a substantive norm but one that is no longer controversial. It prohibits the state from treating any person as either wholly above the obligations of law (in the way, perhaps, that the king of England was once above the law) or wholly outside the protection of the law (as "outlaws" once were).[33]

---

[31] This is the principle that Justice John Paul Stevens believes informs the equal protection clause of the Fourteenth Amendment. See *City of Cleburne v. Cleburne Living Center*, 105 S. Ct. 3249, 3261 (1985) (Stevens, J., concurring). See Note, "Justice Stevens' Equal Protection Jurisprudence."

[32] Consider the legal status of persons of color in America before the Civil War. In most antebellum states free persons "of color" were by law treated like whites for some purposes, and like slaves for other purposes: like whites, they were generally entitled to marry, contract, own personal property, and sue and be sued; like slaves, they were generally prohibited from voting, from serving as jurors, from testifying against whites, and from holding public office. See Berlin, *Slaves without Masters*, pp. 3–132; Litwak, *North of Slavery*, pp. 3–112. The law thus purported to draw no distinctions among whites, free persons of color, and slaves, except in accord with the various traits and activities by which they were legally classified. In that respect, all antebellum persons were "equal before the law."

This is not to say that the principle in question is meaningless. On the contrary, it is a prescription that governments should obey the law—that governments should give people the treatment to which they are entitled. The principle is one that every government accepts in theory, and that different governments implement with differing degrees of success, but that no government ever fully succeeds in putting into practice.

[33] See *Chisholm v. Georgia*, 2 U.S. (2 Dall.) 419, 458 (1793) ("But in the case of the

77

—P_c ("Due Process") is a rule of judicial procedure that has been controversial in recent years. Criminal defendants through much of the nineteenth century were not allowed to testify in their own defense. Today prisoners in many jurisdictions are still barred from filing civil suits.

—P_d ("Prospectivity") is a rule of notice. It requires that the state give its subjects notice in advance of the coercive norms by which they will be governed. In American constitutional law, P_d applies to the formulation of criminal norms, but it is still largely inapplicable to civil norms.[34]

—P_e ("Indigence") is a rule of judicial procedure that also remains controversial. In American constitutional law, criminal defendants today are entitled to the assistance of counsel without regard to whether they have the means to hire an attorney, but civil litigants are not.[35]

—P_f ("Rationality") is potentially the most contestable of these rules. It prohibits the state from distinguishing among people on certain grounds, i.e., on "arbitrary grounds," in spite of the state's wish to do so. To be sure, "arbitrary" is a protean word which may refer to discrimination based on race, discrimination based on race or sex, discrimination based on race

King, the sovereignty . . . [while] it vested him with jurisdiction over others, it excluded all others from jurisdiction over him. With regard to him, there was no superior power; and consequently, on feudal principles, no right of jurisdiction"); *United States v. Burr*, 25 F. Cas. 30, 34 (C.C.D. Va. 1807) (No. 14,692d) ("It is a principle of the English constitution that the King can do no wrong, that no blame can be imputed to him, that he cannot be named in debate. . . . By the constitution of Great Britain, the crown is hereditary, and the monarch can never be a subject"); Gray, *The Nature and Sources of the Law*, p. 27 (the king of England is "commonly" said to be a person "who has rights though no duties").

Regarding "outlawry," see Blackstone, *Commentaries*, pp. *319–20 ("anciently, an outlawed felon was said to have *caput lupinum*, and might be knocked on the head like a wolf, by anyone that should meet him, because, having renounced all law, he was to be dealt with as in a state of nature, when everybody that should find him might slay him"); *Drew v. Drew*, 37 Me. 389, 391 (1854) ("The word *outlaw* has a distinct technical signification, and when used in that sense refers to persons, and not to things. Thus, an outlaw is one who is put out of the law; that is, deprived of its benefits and protection. In earlier times he was called a *friendlesman*; one who could not, by law, have a friend. An outlaw was said *caput genere lupinum*, by which it was meant, that anyone might knock him on the head as a wolf, in case he would not surrender himself peaceably when taken"). Interestingly, Thomas Jefferson tried unsuccessfully in 1779 to revive the obsolete institution of "outlawry" by urging the Virginia legislature to adopt legislation that would have declared any "white woman" who failed to leave the state within one year of having a child "by a negro or mulatto" to be "out of the protection of the laws." *Papers of Thomas Jefferson*, p. 471.

[34] See Munzer, "A Theory of Retroactive Legislation," p. 425.
[35] See *Lassiter v. Department of Social Services*, 452 U.S. 18 (1981).

or sex in the absence of "rational" (or perhaps "compelling") reasons to the contrary, or discrimination of other sorts. Regardless of what "arbitrary" is determined to mean, however, P_f clearly limits what the state may lawfully do.

—P_g ("Procrustes"), as we shall shortly see, is the converse of P_a. Just as every mature society subscribes to P_a, no mature society can take P_g seriously, for every mature society must draw legal distinctions among people based on their respective circumstances.[36]

Societies differ in their perceptions of the justness of these rules. Although every mature society accepts P_a, and none embraces P_g, they have widely differing views about the remaining rules. The axiom "All persons are equal before the law," however, is linguistically capable of referring to each of the rules because each provides for "equality before the law" in one form or another. As a consequence, "equality" possesses the character of a mask—a mask which conceals a range of widely different prescriptions.

Prescriptions by Which People Are Simultaneously both Equal and Unequal

Statements of prescriptive "equality" are ambiguous for an additional reason. They are less explicit than direct statements of the respective rules to which they implicitly refer because, with respect to some rules, the same people may be both prescriptively equal and prescriptively unequal regarding the very same treatment, depending upon how one characterizes the rule. Hence, to say that people are equal or unequal regarding treatment prescribed by such rules is inherently unilluminating.

Rules can be divided into two sets. One set classifies people by reference to a single trait and prescribes joint treatment for all persons possessing that trait. The other set either classifies people by reference to multiple traits or, having classified them by reference to a single trait, prescribes individualized treatment for persons possessing the relevant trait. The distinction between the two sets is significant, because rules in the first set classify people as pre-

[36] See "Two Surlandian Brothers" below. See also Rees, *Equality*, p. 98 ("the attempt to conceive [of] . . . a society [in which all persons are treated equally in every respect] faces [the same] number of formidable obstacles, so much so that it must lead one to wonder if it really is a coherent notion"); Berlin, "Equality as an Ideal," p. 137 (describing a world of "absolute" prescriptive equality as a "perhaps absurd ideal").

scriptive equals without also classifying them as unequals, while rules in the second set classify people as both equals *and* unequals.

Single-Trait Rules versus Multiple-Trait Rules

Rules that classify people solely by reference to single traits create classes of persons who are prescriptively identical with respect to their rights and duties. Rules that classify people by reference to multiple traits create two classes of persons: a general class of persons who are identical in that they all possess *one* of the relevant traits; and a subclass of persons who are identical in that they all possess *all* the relevant traits. People who fall within the subclass (like people who are classified by reference to a single trait) are prescriptively equal without being prescriptively unequal, because they are treated identically without any further distinction being drawn among them. People who fall within the general class, however, are prescriptively equal in one relevant respect and prescriptively unequal in others. They are prescriptively equal in that, *if* they possess certain *additional* traits, they will all be treated the same. They are prescriptively unequal in that those who possess the additional traits will be treated differently than those who do not.

To illustrate the difference between single-trait and multiple-trait classifications, consider the difference between two provisions of the Surlandian constitution: P_1, regarding the right of citizens to vote, and P_3, regarding their right to petition the government for redress of grievances:

P_1: Every adult, competent, and law-abiding citizen is eligible to cast one and only one vote for the office of president.

P_3: Every citizen is entitled to petition the government for redress of grievances.

P_3 classifies people solely by reference to their possessing the single trait of being a "citizen," and grants a privilege to all citizens without drawing distinctions among them. It thus creates a single class of persons, citizens, who are prescriptively equal and in no way unequal to one another.

P_1 is more complex, for it classifies people by reference to a set of traits. It prescribes common voting rights for every citizen who possesses the additional traits of being "adult," "competent," and "law-abiding." It thus creates at least two classes of persons: (1) a class of persons who possess the trait of being citizens; and (2) a subclass of persons who also possess the traits of being adults, competent, and law-abiding. People who fall within the subclass are equal in the same way as persons who are classified in reference to a single trait, for P_1 prescribes identical treatment for all of them without in any way distinguishing among them. People who fall within the larger class of "citizens," however, are both relevantly identical and relevantly nonidentical in the treatment they deserve—hence, they are both prescriptively equal and prescriptively unequal. They are prescriptively equal because they all possess a prescriptive opportunity that other persons do not have: they all have a right to vote for president *if* they can show that they are competent and law-abiding adults. Yet they are also prescriptively unequal because P_1 treats those who are competent, law-abiding adults differently from those who are not. P_1 both classifies them as a unit and subclassifies them into separate units. It treats them as identical and distinguishes among them. It defines them as equals and treats them as unequals.

The distinction between single-trait and multiple-trait classifications depends very much on how the underlying rule is formulated. Consider P_3 again. This rule can be formulated as either a single-trait rule or a multiple-trait rule without incurring a change in meaning. It can be formulated (as above) as

P_3: Every *citizen* is entitled to petition the government for redress of grievances.

or, alternatively, as

P_3': *Every person who is a* citizen is entitled to petition the government for redress of grievances.

Substantively, P_3 and P_3' are identical, producing the same normative results in every case. Formally, however, they differ significantly. P_3 creates a single, general class of "citizens" whose members are prescriptively equal without in any way being prescriptively unequal. P_3', in contrast, creates a general class of "persons" and a subclass of "citizens." Now the members of the general class are at the same time prescriptively equal and prescriptively unequal—equal because they all possess the privilege of petitioning the government for redress of grievances *if* they can show that they are citizens, unequal because only citizens possess that privilege.

81

The relationship between P_3 and P_3' is significant because it happens that every rule taking the form of P_3 can be reformulated as P_3'. In other words, every rule that creates rights or duties in persons who possess a single trait, X, can be reformulated as creating rights or duties within an initial class of "persons" who also possess the additional prescribed trait X. In that sense, *all* people are equal under *all* moral and legal rules, because as "persons" they all have prescribed rights and duties *if* they can show that they possess whatever additional traits the rules may require. Yet people are also unequal under most moral and legal rules because most rules also distinguish among persons by treating those who possess particular traits differently from those who do not.

The distinction between single-trait and multiple-trait classifications also bears upon whether people who are prescriptively equal are also interchangeable. We have previously seen that to say things are descriptively equal does not mean that they are fully interchangeable.[37] Interchangeability (or what Elizabeth Wolgast calls "substitutability")[38] is a contingent rather than a necessary property of things that are descriptively equal; whether such things are interchangeable depends upon whether the underlying standard of comparison is the sole measure which bears upon the task at hand. The same analysis applies to whether prescriptively equal persons are interchangeable: people who are prescriptively equal are interchangeable if, and only if, the prescription by which they are identical is the sole standard of comparison that bears upon the propriety of the conduct at hand. Consider the four-part standard that governs who is eligible to vote for president in Surlandia (i.e., the requirement that voters be "adult, competent, law-abiding citizens"). Two people who are identical in all respects by that four-part standard are also interchangeable for eligibility purposes because the four-part standard is the sole prescription that bears upon eligibility to vote. In contrast, two people may be identical in only one of the four respects made relevant by the standard (say, in being "citizens" of Surlandia). Such persons are identical in the sense that, *if* both were also adult, competent, and law-abiding, both would have a right to vote. Moreover, in that limited sense they are also interchangeable—interchangeable in both being persons who, if they are also adult, competent, and law-abiding, have a right to vote. But they are not interchangeable in hav-

[37] See Chapter 1, pp. 37–38.
[38] Wolgast, *Equality and the Rights of Women*, p. 40.

ing or not having the right to vote, because they are *nonidentical* by reference to the three remaining criteria governing the right to vote.

Joint Treatment versus Individualized Treatment

Just as multiple-trait rules render people both equal and unequal, so, too, do rules prescribing "individualized" treatment for members of a prescriptive class. The distinction between "joint" treatment, on the one hand, and "individualized" treatment, on the other, is the distinction between an undivided share in the whole of something (e.g., a pay-television viewer's undivided viewing share in the whole of a broadcast) and a divided share of something (e.g., a corporate shareholder's proportionate share of the profits). Joint treatment is treatment extended on a "non-competitive"[39] and nonexclusive basis to all members of a prescriptive class; individualized treatment is treatment divided, allocated, and parceled out among members of the class for their exclusive possession.

To illustrate the difference between individualized and joint treatment, compare

P_a: The law shall accord all persons the treatments prescribed for them by law.

and

P_4: Every citizen is entitled to the possession and privileges of a national passport.

P_a and P_4 both prescribe common treatment for their respective beneficiaries, but the treatments differ. The treatment that P_a prescribes, that the state adhere to the rule of law, is a nonexclusive and nondepleting public good. The treatment is joint because, rather than being divided and parceled out severally in such a way that each recipient receives an exclusive share, it is fully extended to every recipient for his nonexclusive enjoyment every time it is invoked. In contrast, the treatment P_4 prescribes is individualized. Although passports are a nondepleting good, and they may be distributed to every citizen, they are an exclusive good in the sense that each citizen receives his own distinct passport.

---

[39] Zaitchik, "On Deserving to Deserve," p. 379 ("A noncompetitive case is one in which the amount received by one person will not adversely affect the amount that others can receive").

This distinction between joint and individualized treatment is significant because under rules of joint treatment people are prescriptively equal without being unequal, while under rules of individualized treatment people are both prescriptively equal and prescriptively unequal. Thus, P_a treats people equally without treating them unequally, by giving all persons the undivided benefit of living under a rule of law. P_4 treats citizens both equally and unequally—equally by giving all of them passports, unequally by giving each a different and exclusive passport.

Single Rules versus Multiple Rules

That a particular class of persons should, simultaneously, be both prescriptively equal and prescriptively unequal is hardly unusual. Nor is the phenomenon confined to individual rules that classify people by reference to multiple traits or that prescribe individualized treatment. The same thing occurs under multiple rules that classify people by one trait (or set of traits) for one purpose and by another trait (or set of traits) for another purpose. People who possess only one of the traits (or sets of traits) in common will be equal in one prescriptive respect and unequal in another.

Now it might be thought possible to formulate moral and legal rules in such a way that most (or, at least, many) people will in fact possess the relevant traits in common, thereby creating situations in which most (or many) people will be prescriptively equal without also being unequal. But that is nearly inconceivable. Indeed, in any mature moral or legal system, it is practically impossible that *any* two people will possess in common all the traits that the system's rules deem relevant. Consider, for example,

Two Surlandian Brothers

Alfonse and Gaston are identical twins. From their earliest infancy their lives were rendered as identical as possible. They enrolled in the same schools, took the same classes, spent the same amount of time studying, participated in the same extracurricular activities, shared the same interests. As adults, they continued to meld their lives as much as possible. They applied for driving licenses together, opened joint bank accounts, rented and purchased property jointly, and worked for the same company at the same job. They married twin sisters in a double-marriage ceremony, and each of their wives became pregnant at the same time, giving birth to girls within

minutes of one another. Their lives appeared to mirror one another until one day when
—Alfonse's wife contracted appendicitis.
—His daughter collided with another car while driving her mother to the hospital.
—Alfonse left work for the afternoon to attend to his wife.
—He signed his wife into the hospital.
—He ordered himself lunch in the hospital cafeteria.

Alfonse and Gaston have organized their lives in such a way as to have precisely the same rights and duties at all the same times. Yet even they will have failed under the rules of any plausible mature legal system because, by virtue of his wife's becoming ill, Alfonse now has rights and duties that Gaston lacks. Under the rules governing medical insurance, leave from work, tax deductions for medical expenses, medical care of one's relatives, contractual liability for one's purchases, and vicarious liability for the torts of one's children—indeed, under any plausible system of norms—Alfonse now has traits that relevantly distinguish him from his brother, and in distinguishing one from the other, render them prescriptively unequal.[40]

"Two Surlandian Brothers" demonstrates, in a microcosm, the way every mature normative system inevitably treats people prescriptively as both equals and unequals. Every such system treats people as "equal before the law" by regarding them as identical in deserving such rights and duties as the system prescribes for persons with their respective traits. Yet every system also treats people as prescriptive unequals by regarding them as nonidentical in accord with the relevantly nonidentical traits they inevitably possess.

It follows, therefore, that people stand in the same relationship to prescriptive equality and inequality as they stand to descriptive equality and inequality. We discovered in Chapter 1 that people and things that are equal by one descriptive standard of comparison are necessarily unequal by other descriptive standards of comparison, and vice versa. We see now, too, that people who are

---

[40] To be sure, Alfonse and Gaston remain prescriptively identical in many respects. For example, they are both people who, *if* their daughters negligently collide with other drivers, will be liable for their daughters' torts. At the same time, however, they are prescriptively unequal under the same rule because they possess relevantly different traits with respect to the rule: Alfonse's daughter *has* collided with another driver, and Gaston's has *not*.

equal by one prescriptive standard are invariably unequal by other prescriptive standards, and vice versa.

The Combination of Description and Prescription:
Descriptive Standards of Comparison Predicated
on Prescriptive Baselines

We have assumed thus far that, when prescriptions enter into the determination of equalities, they enter as standards of comparison—that is, as standards for measuring and comparing people with respect to how they ought to be treated. In fact, prescriptions can also be used as baselines within descriptive standards of comparison for measuring and comparing people with respect to how much, if at all, any actual or hypothetical treatment departs from their prescribed treatment. The difference between using a prescription as a standard of comparison, on the one hand, and using it as a baseline within a descriptive standard of comparison, on the other, is highly significant. For when prescriptive standards are used to compare people with respect to how they ought to be treated, they yield "prescriptive" equalities, that is, equalities that represent things as they ought to be. In contrast, when prescriptive standards are used as baselines to compare people with respect to how much certain actual or hypothetical treatment departs from prescribed treatment, they yield "descriptive" equalities that may or may not be desirable.

Prescriptions as Standards of Comparison

Rules of conduct are statements about how people ought to be treated. As such, they can be used (as we have used them thus far) to measure and compare particular persons with respect to how they ought to be treated. To do so, one must:

(1) Identify an initial group of persons whom one wishes to measure and compare.

(2) Consult the relevant rule for the descriptive traits that persons must possess in order to receive the treatment the rule prescribes.

(3) Identify within the initial group of persons the subset of particular persons who actually possess—and the subset of those who do not possess—the relevant descriptive traits.

(4) Draw the obvious conclusion that all those who actually possess—and all those among themselves who do *not* possess[41]—the relevant descriptive traits are prescriptively "equal" to one another, because they are identical with respect to the treatments which the rule states they ought to receive.

The conclusion that two persons or groups of persons are equal thus means that they both fall within—or both fall without—the class of persons for whom the relevant rule prescribes common treatment. Their equality is the identity that obtains among them by reference to how they ought to be treated.

To illustrate, consider how one would measure and compare people by reference to P_1.

P_1: Every adult, competent, and law-abiding citizen is eligible to cast one and only one vote for the office of president.

One proceeds (1) by identifying an initial class of persons whom one wishes to measure and compare by P_1, say, the class of all persons living in Surlandia; (2) by consulting P_1 for the descriptive criteria that a person must possess as a condition of being entitled to vote; and (3) by identifying within that class the subclass of persons who satisfy those criteria in being adult, competent, law-abiding citizens. To say that these persons are "equal" is a way of talking about the terms of P_1—talking about P_1 by reference to the identity in treatment that P_1 would create among people if it were faithfully applied.

Prescriptions as Baselines within Descriptive Standards of Comparison

Rules may also be used as a measure of something quite different. They may be used as baselines within descriptive standards for measuring how much, if at all, certain treatments depart from prescribed treatments.

As everyone knows, rules of conduct are enforced with differing

---

[41] We have demonstrated thus far that people who fall *within* the terms of a rule are prescriptively equal, because they all ought to *receive* the treatment prescribed by the rule. For completeness of statement, we have also asserted—but *not yet* demonstrated—that people who fall *outside* the terms of a given rule are also prescriptively equal, because they ought all to be *denied* the treatment prescribed by the rule. For the validity of the latter assertion, see the discussion of the truth of the maxim "Unequals should be treated unequally" in Chapter 9.

degrees of fidelity. A given rule on a given occasion may be fully followed, or fully violated, or partially followed and partially violated. Accordingly, given individuals may all be accorded, or all be denied, or some be accorded and some denied, the treatment that a given rule prescribes for them. Moreover, individuals can be measured and compared with respect to whether they differ in actually receiving the treatments that they ought to receive. To compare individuals in this respect, however, one cannot use prescriptive or descriptive standards alone. One must use a combination of the two—a descriptive standard that incorporates a prescriptive standard as a baseline—thus *describing* people by reference to whether or not they are identical in the extent to which they actually receive the treatment they ought to receive. To apply the combined standard, one must first perform the prescriptive step of identifying the group of persons who are identical with respect to the treatment they *ought* to receive (steps [1] through [3]). Then, one must take the additional descriptive step of measuring and comparing the persons in this group by reference to how fully their prescribed treatment corresponds to an actual course of treatment. Altogether one must:

(1) Identify an initial group of persons whom one wishes to measure and compare.

(2) Consult the relevant rule for the descriptive traits that persons must possess in order to receive the treatment the rule prescribes.

(3) Identify within the initial group of persons the subset of particular persons who actually possess—and the subset of those who do not possess—the relevant descriptive traits.

. . . .

(5) Focusing on the subset of persons identified in step (3), consult the relevant rule for a description of the treatment prescribed for them.

(6) Using the prescribed treatment determined in step (5) as a standard, measure the extent to which an actual course of treatment departs from that prescribed treatment.

(7) Compare the results of such measurements for every person identified in step (3) to determine which persons are identical—and which are not—regarding the extent, if any, to which an actual course of treatment departs from the treatment they ought to receive.

(8) Draw the obvious conclusion that those who are identical in the extent, if any, to which actual treatment departs from their prescribed treatment are "equal," and that those who are not identical are "unequal."

To illustrate, consider again the class of persons who were previously determined in steps (1) through (3) to be prescriptively equal, namely, all citizens of Surlandia who are competent, law-abiding adults. Now assume that the government of Surlandia, being corrupt, permits 60 percent of these persons to vote and prohibits the remaining 40 percent from voting. What can we say about the groups as a whole? Are they equal or unequal? The answer depends upon the standard by which we measure them. If we measure them by reference to the treatment they ought to receive, we will invoke the prescriptive standards of P_1 and conclude that they are equal—indeed, *prescriptively* equal. But, if we measure them for the difference, if any, between that prescribed course of treatment and an actual course of treatment, we will invoke a descriptive standard that uses P_1 solely as a baseline, and we will conclude that 60 percent are *descriptively unequal* to the remaining 40 percent because the former have received the treatment which P_1 prescribes for them while the latter have been denied it.

Notice what this means. It means that rules of conduct can yield two distinct kinds of equality, depending upon whether they are used as prescriptive standards of comparison or as baselines within descriptive standards of comparison. The former equalities deal with what "ought to be"; the latter equalities deal with what "is." To be sure, in some cases the two equalities will correspond with one another, namely, when actual courses of treatment correspond with prescribed courses of treatment. But the two equalities cannot correspond when people are denied the treatment to which they are entitled. In those cases the language of equality is ambiguous. So, to say people are "equal" may mean that a rule has been faithfully enforced. Or it may mean that a rule has been violated. Or it may have to do not with the enforcement of a rule at all but with how the rule states people ought to be treated.

Conclusion

Philosophers today are puzzled that Plato and Aristotle could have said things about equality that seem so patently false. Like Plato,

Aristotle believed that justice is equality, and equality is justice. In Aristotle's words:

> We have shown that both the unjust man and the unjust act are unfair and unequal; now it is clear that there is also an intermediate between the two unequals involved in either case. And this is the equal; for in any kind of action in which there is a more and a less there is also what is equal. If, then, the unjust is unequal, the just is equal, as all men suppose it to be, even apart from argument.[42]

Philosophers today consider it "obvious"[43] that equality can sometimes be unjust. Equality can be unjust, they say, because equality itself looks only to the sameness of treatment, not to its justice. "Equality itself," in Douglas Rae's graphic words, "is as well pleased by graveyards as by vineyards."[44] William Frankena makes the same point by way of example. "If a ruler were to boil his subjects in oil, jumping in afterwards himself," he says, "it would be an injustice, but it would be no inequality in treatment."[45] G. Del Vecchio concludes that Plato and Aristotle are simply wrong to have maintained that justice and equality are one and the same:

> It cannot, however, be maintained (as many [ancient] authors have thought) that the idea of justice resolves itself simply into that of equality, and can be sufficiently defined thereby. Even for the conscience of the ordinary man (always a useful guide in this matter) an injustice repeated with perfect equality in every possible case does not on that account become justice.[46]

[42] Aristotle, *Nicomachean Ethics* V.3.1131a10–15 (trans. Ross). See the Preface, note 2, and Chapter 9, note 1.

[43] Lucas, *On Justice*, p. 171.

[44] Rae, *Equalities*, p. 129.

[45] Frankena, "The Concept of Social Justice," p. 17. Vlastos makes the same point: "Would any of us feel that no injustice was suffered by Soviet citizens by the suppression of *Doctor Zhivago* if we were reliably informed that no one, not even Khrushchev, was exempted, and that the censors themselves had been foreign mercenaries?" Vlastos, "Justice and Social Equality," p. 62. See also Feinberg, "Noncomparative Justice," p. 312 (suggesting that one form of equal treatment would be to take people who are all entitled to be free and enslave them). My colleague Brian Simpson has acutely pointed out that Frankena's example is *not* the example of equal treatment Frankena thinks it is, because while the ruler *kills* all his subjects, he merely *commits suicide* himself.

[46] Del Vecchio, *Justice*, p. 86 n. 3. See also del Vecchio, "Equality and Inequality in Relation to Justice," p. 46.

We can now understand the real nature of the dispute between these ancient and modern philosophers. Their dispute is not about the meaning of 'equality'. They would all agree, I believe, that equality regarding people is the relationship that obtains among persons who are identical as measured by a relevant standard of comparison. Nor do they disagree about the nature of the standards of comparison by which the equality of persons ought to be determined, for both the ancients and, I believe, the moderns would agree that for purposes of equality, people should be measured and compared by their "relevant" traits, relevance being measured by considerations of justice. Their real dispute is the product of one of the many ambiguities that the language of equality tends to create—in this case an ambiguity in the standards by which people are compared.

Plato and Aristotle, in concluding that equality is always just, are speaking of *prescriptive* equality, the relationship which obtains among people who, when measured by their relevant traits, are identical *with respect to how they ought to be treated*. Such equalities, if given effect, will always be just because by definition they are relationships that ought to be given effect. That is what it means to say that prescriptive equality is the relationship which obtains among people with respect to how they ought to be treated.

The moderns, in contrast, are not speaking of prescriptive equality, although they are using prescriptive standards as baselines. Rather, they are speaking of the identity which obtains among people who, when measured by the extent, if any, to which an actual or hypothetical course of treatment departs from prescribed treatment, are identical *with respect to whether they receive the treatment to which they are entitled*. Such equalities are not always just, because people are sometimes identical in being denied the treatment to which they are entitled.

The difference between the ancients and the moderns appears to be philosophical, a normative dispute about right and wrong, but it is not. It is a dispute which has its source not in conflicting moral standards but in an ambiguity of the language of 'equality'. To say that two individuals are equal with respect to a certain prescribed treatment may mean

—that they all *ought to receive* identical treatment, regardless of whether they have in fact received such treatment;
—or that they all ought to receive identical treatment and, in fact, *have all received* such treatment;

91

—or that they all ought to receive identical treatment but, in fact, *have all been denied* such treatment.

The ancients have the first meaning in mind, their modern counterparts the third. They appear to have a philosophically significant difference of opinion, but in fact they are talking past one another.

F O U R

EQUAL TREATMENT

A younger child refuses to go to bed while the older child is
allowed to stay up.

"It's not fair!" she says. "How come he gets to stay up and
I don't?"

"Because," the brother responds, "when I was your age, I
had to go to bed early, too."

"I know," she says, "but that was different. When you were
my age, you didn't have an older brother who was allowed to
stay up."

Parents know from personal experience what Piaget would teach
them, that young children are quick to develop a moral sense of
equality.[1] Given our conclusions thus far, analyzing what it means
to treat children equally should be relatively straightforward.
'Equal treatment', after all, consists of only two terms—'equal' and
'treatment'. We have already analyzed 'equality' and its cognates
in the three basic contexts in which they occur: descriptions, mathematical relationships, and prescriptions. It would seem that our
only remaining task is to analyze the meaning of 'treatment' in
light of our previous understanding of 'equal'.

Unfortunately, the persistent ambiguities of 'equality' combine
with 'treatment' to create difficulties that deserve further attention. In addition to those difficulties, courts and commentators
have raised two special questions of equality in the area of equal
treatment, namely, whether there is a difference between treating
people "equally" and treating them "as equals"; and whether
rules that do not explicitly discriminate among particular persons,
but that inevitably have a "disparate impact" on them because of
the differential traits they possess, are indeed rules of equal treatment.

[1] See Piaget, *The Moral Judgment of the Child*, pp. 276–95.

The Elements of Equal Treatment

In the context of equal treatment, the term 'equal' can be used both descriptively and prescriptively: it can be used to refer to actual courses of treatment and to courses of treatment people ought to receive. Yet its capacity to straddle both descriptive and prescriptive meanings can also be a source of confusion. To clarify such ambiguities, we shall first examine the meanings of 'treat' and 'treatment'. Then, we will attempt to identify what 'equally' and 'equal' add to these meanings.

The Meaning of 'Treatment'

'Treatment' signifies behavior that a person manifests toward himself or toward another person or thing. To "treat" is to manifest such behavior. The behavior may be conscious or unconscious; active or passive; benevolent, neutral, or malicious; good, bad, or neither good nor bad. A person treats wood by rubbing it with furniture polish. He treats himself well by attending to his health. He treats his spouse badly by forgetting her birthday. Moreover, just as a person can act singly in treating himself or others, he can join with others in rendering collective treatment. A fraternal association can treat itself to an annual banquet. A government can treat its people fairly or unfairly.

Treatments can be singular or plural—singular when they consist of a single behavior toward a single person, plural when they consist of multiple behavior toward a single person or single behavior toward more than one person. Singular treatments can be measured by reference to their constituent elements, that is, by reference to *who* is manifesting *what* behavior toward *whom*. By the same token, one can compare plural treatments by first measuring two or more of them by a common standard of measure and then juxtaposing their respective measures to determine the extent, if any, of their differences.

The Meaning of 'Equal'

Generally speaking, 'equal' means the same thing in 'equal treatment' and 'treating equally' as elsewhere: to speak of "equal treatment" or "treating equally" is to refer to treatments that have been measured, compared, and determined to be identical by a relevant standard for comparing treatments. Like the standards for comparing people studied thus far, standards for comparing treatments may be descriptive or prescriptive: descriptive insofar as they measure treatments for what they *are* (regardless of what they ought to be); prescriptive insofar as they measure treatments by what they *ought to be* (regardless of what they are). Moreover (and, again, like prescriptive standards used to compare people), prescriptive standards may be used prescriptively to compare the treatments which people ought to receive, or they may serve as baselines within what are otherwise purely descriptive standards and be used to compare actual or hypothetical treatments by reference to how much, if at all, they depart from the treatments which people ought to receive.

To illustrate the foregoing differences, imagine

A School Orchestra

A local elementary school has a program for introducing its students to instrumental music. The school requires that each fifth-grade student elect a musical instrument to study for the year. Students may elect instruments that they are studying already, or they may use instruments they already possess. However, no student is expected to buy an instrument, because the school promises to lend an instrument of choice to each fifth-grade student who does not possess an instrument of the kind he or she wishes to study.

Anna, Karin, Linda, and Peter are fifth-grade students. Anna, who possesses a cello, tries to persuade the others to choose the cello, too. All agree—except Peter, who thinks that cellos are for girls. He chooses the trumpet. The school promises to supply cellos to Karin and Linda and a trumpet to Peter.

The Difference between Descriptive and Prescriptive Standards for Comparing Treatments

"A School Orchestra" illustrates the differences between descriptive and prescriptive standards for comparing treatments. Let us begin with descriptive comparisons. Is the school's proposed treatment of the four children descriptively equal or unequal? The answer depends upon the standard of measure one regards as relevant. Assume the following descriptive standards (DS) for comparing the school's proposed treatments of the children:

DS_1: whether the school lends trumpets to fifth graders.

DS_2: whether the school lends musical instruments of their choice to fifth graders.

DS_3: whether the school lends musical instruments of choice to fifth graders who do not possess instruments of their choice.

To determine whether the school's proposed treatment is equal, one must select one of the foregoing descriptive standards and, using it, measure and compare the treatment of the four children. The results depend upon which standard one selects.

—Measured by DS_1, *none* of the children will be treated equally, because no two children will be treated identically in being given a trumpet (though three of them will be treated identically, and hence equally, in *not* being given trumpets).

—Measured by DS_2, three of the children will be treated equally, because three will be treated identically in being given a musical instrument of their choice, though Anna will not.

—Measured by DS_3, *all* of the children will be treated equally, because all will be treated identically in being given musical instruments of their choice if they do not already possess one.

The same analysis applies to determining whether the school's proposed treatments are prescriptively equal. To determine whether the school proposes to treat the children equally from a normative standpoint, one must identify a relevant norm, or "prescription," to govern the distribution of musical instruments. In this case, we can take prescription P as the relevant prescription because this is the rule by which the school system believes it ought to be bound:

P: The school should lend a musical instrument of choice to each fifth-grade student who does not already possess one.

Measured by P, the school's proposal treats all the children equally because it treats them identically by reference to itself. Indeed, in that respect, *to adhere to a rule is necessarily to treat people equally by reference to the rule* because every rule prescribes treatments for people that are necessarily identical as measured by the scheme of treatment the rule prescribes. That is what Chaim Perelman means in saying, "Equality of treatment is merely the logical consequence of the fact of keeping to [a] rule."[2]

By the same token, when measured by P, the school also proposes to treat some students *unequally* because it proposes to give nonidentical treatments to students who are prescriptively unequal by reference to the school's rule. Thus, the school proposes to treat Peter and Karin differently, by giving a trumpet to Peter and a cello to Karin, by virtue of their having chosen those different instruments in accord with the school's rule. In that sense, *to adhere to a rule that classifies people is also necessarily to treat them unequally by reference to the rule* because every rule that classifies people as nonidentical with respect to what they deserve also prescribes treatments for them that are nonidentical in that respect.

It follows, then, that every rule, as adhered to, that classifies people treats them both *equally and unequally* by reference to its own terms: equally, by giving them all the very treatments prescribed for them by the rule; unequally, by giving nonidentical treatments to people whom the rule classifies as prescriptively nonidentical. Thus, the school's proposed rule treats fifth graders both equally and unequally: equally, because it promises students that *if* they do not already possess a musical instrument of their choice the school will provide one; unequally, because the rule

---

[2] Perelman, *The Idea of Justice and the Problem of Argument*, p. 38 (referring by "equality of treatment" to *prescriptive* equality of treatment). A. M. Honoré makes the same point:

> The notion of conformity to a rule can be made to yield the notion that like cases should be treated alike. If we think of those species of rule that prescribe that certain people be treated in a certain way when certain conditions are fulfilled, the demand that such rules should be observed entails the demand that the cases falling within the conditions mentioned should be treated in the way prescribed in the rule, that is that people who are alike in the relevant respect should be treated alike.

Honoré, "Social Justice," p. 82. See also Gewirth, "Political Justice," p. 124 ("equality is involved in the very idea of rules"); Ross, *On Law and Justice*, p. 273 ("equality . . . simply means the correct application of a general rule"); Flathman, "Equality and Generalization," p. 38 ("To treat people equally is to treat them in the same way. To treat people in the same way is to treat them according to a rule"); Raz, *The Morality of Freedom*, p. 220 ("All principles are statements of general reasons. As such they apply equally to all those who meet their conditions of application. Generality implies equality of application to a class").

carefully distinguishes between students who already possess an instrument of choice (such as Anna) and those who do not (such as Karin, Linda, and Peter)—denying the former something that it gives to the latter.[3]

The Difference between Prescriptions as Standards of Comparison and Prescriptions as Baselines

"A School Orchestra" illustrates the difference between descriptive and prescriptive standards for comparing treatments. In some cases, however, descriptive standards of comparison may themselves contain prescriptive elements, namely, when they incorporate prescriptions as baselines by which to compare actual or hypothetical treatments by reference to how much, if at all, they depart from the treatments people ought to receive. This difference between prescriptive standards of comparison and descriptive standards that incorporate prescriptions as baselines is significant because, when prescriptions are used as standards of comparison (as in "A School Orchestra"), the resulting equalities and inequalities are ones that *ought* to exist. When, on the other hand, prescriptions are used as baselines within descriptive standards of measure, the resulting descriptive equalities and inequalities may be ones that ought *not* to exist. To illustrate, let us take the orchestra example one step further.

The Day of Reckoning

The day arrives for the distribution of instruments. As expected, the music teacher gives a trumpet to Peter and a cello to Karin. The teacher does not have a cello for Anna because Anna possesses a cello of her own. Unfortunately, because of an unanticipated demand for cellos, the teacher also has no cello for Linda. The teacher explains to Linda that he tried

---

[3] Felix Oppenheim puts this point particularly well:

It is logically impossible for any rule of distribution to treat either equals unequally or unequals equally, in the sense of allotting the same benefit or burden (in the same amount) to persons who differ [with respect to] the characteristics singled out by the rule, or different shares to persons whom the rule places in the same category.

Oppenheim, *Political Concepts*, pp. 119–20. See also Oppenheim, "The Concept of Equality," p. 103 ("Every conceivable rule treats equals [in some specified respect] equally and unequals unequally").

very hard to find a cello for her, but none was available. He apologizes to Linda and urges her to choose another instrument.

Linda complains to the school board. "It's not fair," she says, "to single me out for different treatment. You're treating me unequally!"

How is Linda using the word 'unequal'? Needless to say, she is not using it purely descriptively, because she intends "unequally!" to be a normative criticism. Nor is she using it prescriptively—that is, she is not using it to refer to unequal treatments that *comply* with the school's rule. Rather, she is using it to refer to unequal treatments that *violate* the school's rule, treatments that are descriptively unequal by reference to whether they are what they ought to be—descriptively unequal in that the treatments differ in the extent to which they comply with what the rule *prescribes*. In other words, using P as a baseline for describing its actual treatment of the children, the school has treated Anna, Karin, and Peter equally and Linda unequally because the school has given Anna, Karin, and Peter—and denied Linda—the treatment that the relevant rule of conduct prescribes.

The Ambiguities of Equal Treatment

The terms 'equal treatment' and 'treating equally' contain the same ambiguities as statements that people are "equal"—not surprisingly, since the ambiguity inheres in the term 'equal'. Thus, 'equal treatment' and 'treating equally' are ambiguous regarding (1) whether they express a descriptive or prescriptive standard for comparing treatments; (2) whether such standards are comparative or noncomparative; (3) if prescriptive, what the precise terms of the prescriptions are; and (4) if descriptive, whether they are purely descriptive or whether they incorporate prescriptions as baselines for measuring departures from prescribed treatment.

In addition, 'equal treatment' and 'treating equally' reflect further ambiguities—ambiguities that tend to predominate in statements of "treatment," although they are present in statements that people are "equal" as well. These ambiguities arise when rules of conduct are used as baselines within descriptive standards for comparing treatments with respect to how much, if at all, they depart from what they ought to be, that is, for determining whether treatments differ in departing from what the baseline of the rule prescribes. Ambiguities arise from the differing normative implications of the resulting equalities and inequalities, depending upon whether the baseline rules are comparative or noncomparative. The difference may be formally stated as follows: (1) courses of treatment that comply with a relevant rule, whether comparative or noncomparative, are always descriptively equal as measured by that rule; and (2) courses of treatment that violate certain kinds of *comparative* rules are always descriptively unequal as measured by the baseline rule, although those that violate *other* kinds of comparative rules and those that violate *noncomparative* rules are not always descriptively unequal.

We have previously seen that treatments can be compared by reference to whether they differ, descriptively, by reference to the baseline rule determining what they ought to be. Treatments that comply with a moral or legal rule are always descriptively equal in that respect. They are always descriptively equal because they do not differ with regard to what they ought to be—that is, they are identical in being the treatments which they ought to be.

It is tempting to assume that, just as treatments that comply with a rule are always descriptively *equal* as measured by the baseline rule, treatments that violate a rule are always descriptively *unequal* in that respect. Indeed, it is true that the violation of certain comparative rules is always descriptively unequal as measured by the extent to which the recipients are receiving the treatments they ought to receive. This is true of what Kenneth Simons calls "universal" comparative rules, that is, comparative rules of the form "If any person in the protected class X receives benefit B, all persons in the protected class X shall receive benefit B."[4] A comparative rule of that kind can be violated only by denying some *but not all* protected members of class X the treatments to which they are entitled. In violating a comparative rule of that kind one necessarily treats protected members of class X unequally as measured by the extent to which one is giving them the treatments the rule prescribes for them.

However, the violation of other kinds of comparative rules and of noncomparative rules is not necessarily unequal, descriptively, by reference to what such rules prescribe. Consider, for example,

[4] See Simons, "Equality as a Comparative Right," pp. 452–56, esp. n. 155. See Chapter 6, note 28.

a comparative rule of the form "If persons in class X receive benefit B, persons in the protected class Y shall receive benefit B, too." A comparative rule of that kind can be violated without treating protected persons unequally vis-à-vis one another if *all* members of the protected class Y are denied the treatment to which they are entitled—for, measured by the extent to which they receive the treatments they ought to receive, they are treated equally if they are all denied such treatment. The same is true of noncomparative rules. Thus, given the baseline of the school's noncomparative rule in "The Day of Reckoning," the school is treating fifth graders unequally when it gives musical instruments of choice to Karin and Peter but not to Linda. The school is not treating Karin, Peter, and Linda unequally, however, if it denies instruments of choice to all of them.

These truths about the equality of treatments also apply to the equality of persons. Compliance with a rule always renders people descriptively equal, as measured by the baseline of the rule, because it always yields people whose treatments are descriptively identical as measured by what the rule prescribes. Noncompliance with certain comparative rules always renders people descriptively unequal as measured by what the rules prescribe. Yet, as in the case of unequal treatments, noncompliance with other comparative rules, and with noncomparative rules, does not always render persons descriptively unequal, as measured by the baseline of the rule, because noncompliance may deny *all* the subjects of a rule *all* of the treatment the rule prescribes for them.

It follows, then, that the terms 'equal treatment' and 'unequal treatment' are normatively ambiguous. One can use them purely prescriptively, to refer to treatments that are identical or nonidentical in precisely the ways treatments ought to be identical or nonidentical; in that event, the terms 'equal treatment' and 'unequal treatment' are always laudatory. One can also use them descriptively by reference to a prescriptive baseline, to refer to treatments that are identical or nonidentical in the extent, if any, to which they *depart* from what they ought to be. In that event, even though 'equal treatment' is always laudatory with respect to certain comparative rights, it is sometimes condemnatory with respect to noncomparative rights, depending upon whether all persons are granted the treatments they ought to receive or all are denied them. As a result, the words 'equal' and 'unequal' are both capable of referring to just treatments *and* unjust treatments, depending upon the nature of the standard of comparison and the subject matter being compared.

Treating People "Equally" versus Treating Them as "Equals"

Some commentators, of whom Ronald Dworkin is the most prominent, distinguish between 'equal treatment', on the one hand, and 'treatment as an equal', on the other.[5] They argue that 'equal treatment' not only means something different from 'treatment as an equal', but is also normatively less fundamental. Dworkin argues that treating people "equally" means giving them "an equal distribution of some opportunity or resource or burden," while treating a person "as an equal" means giving him "the same respect and concern as anyone else."[6] And because Dworkin believes that a person's right to be treated with the same respect and concern as others is more fundamental than the right to an equal distribution, he also believes that the "right to treatment as an equal" is more fundamental than the "right to equal treatment." "If I have two children," he says, "and one is dying from a disease that is making the other uncomfortable, I do not show equal concern [though I do provide equal treatment] if I flip a coin to decide which should have the remaining dose of a drug. This example shows that the right to treatment as an equal is fundamental, and the right to equal treatment derivative."[7]

Dworkin's distinction between 'treatment as equals' and 'equal treatment' is essentially the same as Plato's and Aristotle's distinction between proportional and numerical equality.[8] Like Plato and Aristotle, Dworkin may be right in believing that treating people with "respect and concern" is normatively more fundamental than giving them per-capita shares. The correctness of his views, however, is ultimately a normative, not an analytical, issue (although it may be an analytical task to determine precisely what is meant by the words 'respect' and 'concern'[9] and whether 'equal' adds anything to their meaning).[10] Dworkin is also free to stipulate that,

---

[5] Dworkin, *Taking Rights Seriously*, pp. 226–29.

[6] Dworkin, *Taking Rights Seriously*, p. 227. For more on Dworkin's right of equal respect and concern, see Chapter 3, notes 21–22, and note 10 below.

[7] Dworkin, *Taking Rights Seriously*, p. 227.

[8] See Chapter 2, pp. 52–57.

[9] For inquiries into what Rawls and Dworkin mean by "respect" and "concern," see Hart, "Between Utility and Rights," p. 844 n. 42; Smith, *Liberalism and American Constitutional Law*, pp. 186–97.

[10] For the argument that the word 'equal' does not add anything to what Dwor-

in his terminology, 'treatment as an equal' refers to distributive justice of the former kind and 'equal treatment' to distributions of the latter kind. Without such a stipulation, however, it is misleading to attribute a normative significance to the distinction between 'treatment as an equal' and 'equal treatment' because conceptually the two terms are largely interchangeable: to treat people as equals *means* to give them the equal treatment to which they are entitled under prevailing rules of conduct; and to give people prescriptively equal treatment *means* to treat them as the prescriptive equals they are.

As we saw in Chapter 3, to say that people are prescriptively "equal" means that they have been measured, compared, and determined to be identical by reference to a relevant rule of conduct. To "treat" such people "as equals" is to give them the equal treatments that a rule prescribes for them. It follows, therefore, that prescriptively one cannot treat persons as equals without also giving them the equal treatment to which they are entitled, nor can one give them prescriptively equal treatment without also treating them as equals.

To illustrate the correlation between equal treatment and treatment as equals, consider Dworkin's hypothetical case: the case of distributing a life-saving drug between two children, one dying and the other merely uncomfortable for lack of the drug. We cannot treat the children either "equally" or "as equals" in any

kin means by "concern and respect," see Hart, "Between Utility and Rights," p. 845:

> When it is argued that the denial to some of a certain freedom, say to some form of religious worship or to some form of sexual relations, is essentially a denial of equal concern and respect, the word 'equal' is playing an empty but misleading role. The vice of the denial of such freedom is not its inequality or unequal impact: if that *were* the vice the prohibition by a tyrant of all forms of religious worship or sexual activity would not increase the scale of the evil as in fact it surely would, and the evil would vanish if all were converted to the banned faith or to the prohibited form of sexual relationship. The evil is the denial of liberty or respect; not *equal* liberty or *equal* respect: and what is deplorable is the ill-treatment of the victims and not the relational matter of the unfairness of their treatment compared with others.

See also Postema, "Liberty in Equality's Empire," pp. 68–69; Raz, "Professor Dworkin's Theory of Rights," p. 130:

> When Dworkin talks of a right to equal concern and respect, he really has in mind a right to concern and respect. He adds 'equal' to indicate that none has a greater right than another; but this again follows not from any conception of equality but from the fact that he is here referring to a group with equal claim to have the right.

prescriptive sense without possessing a "prescription," or rule of treatment, by which to determine the equalities. Yet, once we have identified a relevant rule of treatment, we invariably treat the children both as equals and equally merely by virtue of complying with the rule. Assume, for example, that we take the proper rule of treatment to be P_A:

P_A: All marketable goods, including life-saving drugs, shall be distributed among people by lot, leaving it to them to redistribute such goods among themselves through voluntary market transactions, as they may wish.

Proceeding on that basis, we treat the children both "as equals" and "equally," prescriptively, by distributing the drug upon the flip of a coin: as equals by considering them identical in their right to obtain the drug by the laws of chance; equally by giving the drug to whichever of them wins the flip of the coin. If, on the other hand, we take the proper rule of treatment to be P_B, our treatment of the children will be different:

P_B: All life-saving drugs shall be distributed among children wholly on the basis of their vital needs.

Under this rule we treat the children both as equals and equally by giving the life-saving drug to the dying child: as equals by considering them identical in their right to life; equally by distributing the drug between them wholly on the basis of their vital needs. In neither case do we treat the children as equals without also treating them equally, or equally without also treating them as equals. Notice, however, that by virtue of being rules that distribute goods among persons on an individualized basis, P_A and P_B also treat the children both "as unequals" and "unequally." P_A, like all rules of distribution based on lot, treats the children both as unequals and unequally by distinguishing between them in accord with the results of the lottery. P_B also treats the children as unequals and unequally by explicitly distinguishing between them on the basis of their needs. Each rule treats the children both as equals and as unequals, equally and unequally. Yet, just as neither rule treats the children equally without also treating them as equals, neither treats them unequally without also treating them as unequals.

Why, then, if "equal treatment" always correlates with "treatment as equals" (and if "unequal treatment" always correlates with "treatment as unequals"), do commentators try to differentiate between them? Why is it assumed that people can be treated as equals without being treated equally, or be treated as unequals without being treated unequally? To answer these questions we shall proceed in three steps: first, we shall try to determine just what these commentators are doing, *conceptually*, when they distinguish between treatment 'as an equal' and 'equal treatment'; second, we shall try to identify their *normative purpose* in drawing the distinction; and, third, we shall attempt to understand how the *language of equality* happens to serve their normative purposes.

The Conceptual Step

Commentators who distinguish between 'treatment as an equal' and 'equal treatment' are not distinguishing between different concepts of equality. They have a single concept of equality in mind. Rather, they are distinguishing between different conceptions of equality based on competing prescriptive standards of comparison. They use 'equal treatment' to refer to the consequences of measuring treatments by what Plato and Aristotle called a "numerical" standard of comparison, that is, a prescriptive standard that treats people as interchangeable. They use 'treatment as an equal' to refer to the consequences of measuring treatments by what Plato and Aristotle called a "proportional" standard of comparison, that is, a prescriptive standard that treats people on the basis of what is "due" them.[11] To be sure, people sometimes ought to be treated interchangeably, and in those cases "treatment as equals" and "equal treatment" will come to the same thing. Where the two standards prescribe different courses of conduct, however, treating people on the basis of their "due" (hence, as equals) will not produce "equal treatment"; and treating people as interchangeable (thus extending them equal treatment) will not be treating them "as equals."

Consider, for example, Dworkin's hypothetical distribution of life-saving drugs on the basis of the flip of a coin. What does he mean in saying that the distribution affords the children "equal treatment" while failing to treat the children "as equals"? By what standard or standards does he measure the treatments in deter-

---

[11] 'Due' for Aristotle has both a broad and a narrow meaning. The broad meaning refers to that to which a person is entitled by virtue of his possessing a trait which a speaker regards as a proper measure of desert. The narrow meaning refers to that to which a person is entitled by virtue of his possessing the particular traits which *Aristotle* regarded as the proper measure of a person's desert. I am using 'due' here in the broader of the two senses. See Chapter 2, note 25.

mining them to be, simultaneously, both equal and not equal? The answer, it seems, is that he is invoking the specified treatments of both P_A and P_B. He uses P_A's specification of treatment (that children be treated interchangeably) as a measure of whether they are receiving equal treatment, and P_B's specification of treatment (that children be treated on the basis of what is due them in accord with their needs) as a measure of whether the children are being treated as equals. Accordingly, when he says that distributing life-saving drugs by lot succeeds in giving the children equal treatment but fails to treat them as equals, he means that such a distribution

—does, indeed, give them equal treatments as measured by the specifications of P_A,
—but does *not* give them equal treatments as measured by the specifications of P_B.

Conversely, if distributing life-saving drugs on the basis of vital needs does not give the children equal treatment but does treat them as equals, it is because the distribution

—does not give the children equal treatments as measured by P_A,
—but does give them equal treatments as measured by P_B, by treating them both on the basis of their vital needs.

The Normative Step

Dworkin does more, however, than simply distinguish between two competing standards of distribution—more, that is, than distinguish one competing conception of equality from another. Like Plato and Aristotle, he also expresses a distinct preference for one conception over the other, believing that the obligation to treat children on the basis of their vital needs predominates over any obligation to treat them interchangeably. To be sure, these two distributive formulas do not always conflict, for there are cases in which one can simultaneously treat people interchangeably and on the basis of their medical needs, and in that event one is free to invoke whichever conception one prefers. Thus, Dworkin recognizes that there are cases in which it is just to treat people interchangeably.[12] In the event of conflict between the two rules, how-

[12] The first is the right to *equal treatment*, which is the right to an equal distribution of some opportunity or resource or burden. Every citizen, for example, has a right to an equal vote in a democracy; that is the nerve of the Supreme

ever, he believes that the treatment specified in P_B is the appropriate measure of the justice of treatments, because he believes that P_B is the normatively relevant rule of conduct.

The Linguistic Step

Having distinguished between two conceptions of equality, and asserted one to be always just and the other not, Dworkin employs specific terminology to distinguish the former equality from the latter—using 'treatment as equals' for the equality he regards as always just and 'equal treatment' for the equality he does not regard as always just. His choice of terms is no coincidence; it reflects what appear to be their different connotations in common usage. The term 'equal treatment' is ambiguous as to whether it is based on descriptive or prescriptive standards of comparison. In contrast, the term 'treatment as equals' appears to be commonly used to refer solely to treatments based on prescriptive standards of comparison, treatments that are identical as measured by the relevant rule of conduct. Thus, people are not ordinarily said to be treated "as equals" if they are denied the treatment to which they are entitled, or if they are treated equally in accord with descriptive standards of comparison that are unjust. Rather, people are said to be treated "as equals" only when they are given the equal treatment to which they are entitled. To treat people "as equals" is *to treat them as the prescriptive equals they are.*[13]

In that respect, Dworkin is right to use 'treatment as equals' to refer to treatment he regards as just, and 'equal treatment' to refer to treatment he does not always regard as just, because the former term always refers to the equalities that result from rules of conduct by which it is assumed people ought to be measured, while the latter term can also refer to equalities that result from descriptive standards of comparison that are unjust. By the same token, it is also misleading to base a normative distinction upon the two terms because, while 'equal treatment' sometimes refers to de-

---

Court's decision that one person must have one vote even if a different and more complex arrangement would better secure the collective welfare.
Dworkin, *Taking Rights Seriously*, p. 227.

[13] Cf. Raz, "Professor Dworkin's Theory of Rights," p. 130 ("The truth is that Dworkin's invocation of the right to be treated as an equal is no more than a rhetorical device to enlist the sympathies of those who are moved by appeals to equality. For Dworkin has nothing more to say about it other than to identify it with the right to equal concern and respect").

scriptive equalities, it can also refer to prescriptive equalities, and thus can refer to the same rules of conduct that define 'treatment as equals'.

"Disparate Adverse Impact" as Unequal Treatment

We have concluded thus far that treatments are equal when they are identical by reference to relevant standards of measure. Also, treatments are equal by prescriptive standards when they are identical by reference to relevant "prescriptions." It would seem to follow, therefore, that rules that do not explicitly distinguish among particular classes of persons—that is, rules that are facially *neutral* regarding particular classes of persons—must, if faithfully applied, treat such persons equally.

Some American courts and commentators appear to assert the opposite. They argue that rules that are facially neutral regarding particular classes of persons do not treat such persons equally if, by virtue of factual differences among the classes, the rules in fact *affect* the classes differently.[14] The issue most often arises in litigation under Title VII of the Civil Rights Act of 1964. Section 703(a)(2) of the act makes it unlawful for an employer

> [1] to . . . classify his employees or applicants for employment [2] in any way which would deprive or tend to deprive any individual of employment opportunities . . . [3] because of such individual's race, color, religion, sex, or national origin.[15]

The question raised under section 703(a)(2) is: To what extent does an employer unlawfully "classify" his employees and applicants

---

[14] In law, the "disparate adverse impact" argument tends to be confined to adverse impact on disparate *groups* as opposed to *individuals* because laws tend to define their subjects not by name, but by reference to general traits. In principle, however, the argument applies to any facially neutral treatment of two or more persons who are so factually situated that facially neutral treatment will have a disparate adverse impact on one as opposed to the other. See Greenawalt, "How Empty Is the Idea of Equality?" p. 1171.

"Disparate adverse impact" arguments can be raised by any group that feels itself disadvantaged by rules that are neutral on their face, but they are most frequently asserted by women who argue that rules that do not distinguish on their face between men and women nonetheless treat them "unequally." Perhaps the most powerful and potentially the most global of such assertions is Catharine MacKinnon's argument that, regardless of their intent and facial neutrality, laws treat women unequally to the extent that they effectively reinforce male domination. See MacKinnon, "Difference and Dominance."

[15] Civil Rights Act of 1964. For an illuminating study of these issues, see Rutherglen, "Disparate Impact under Title VII," p. 1297.

for employment by applying employment practices that, though neutral on their face regarding "race, color, religion, sex, [and] national origin," have an adverse impact on persons of a particular race, color, religion, sex, or national origin? The question in *Griggs v. Duke Power Company*,[16] for example, was whether an employer classified applicants on the basis of race, in violation of section 703(a)(2), by using intelligence tests as a condition for employment and promotion where evidence showed that 58 percent of all whites, but only 6 percent of all blacks, passed such tests. The U.S. Supreme Court held that even though the employer's use of intelligence tests was facially neutral regarding race, the practice had a "discriminatory" effect on blacks, and therefore, absent a justification, was invalid. The Court stated:

> The [Civil Rights] Act proscribes not only overt discrimination but also practices that are fair in form, but discriminatory in operation. The touchstone is business necessity. If an employment practice which operates to exclude Negroes cannot be shown to be related to job performance, the practice is prohibited.[17]

Commentators disagree about *Griggs* and its successor cases. Some commentators argue that treating protected groups "equally" under Title VII means applying facially neutral rules that are not intended to disadvantage protected groups, despite the adverse impact the rules may have on such groups.[18] Some assert the opposite—that treating protected groups equally under Title VII may also require treating them in accordance with rules that have a neutral impact on them.[19] Others suggest that the controversy over "disparate impact" is a dispute between differing notions of equality.[20] In the opinion of Martha Chamallas, the dispute over

---

[16] 401 U.S. 424 (1971). For more recent Supreme Court adjudication regarding section 703(a)(2), see *Connecticut v. Teal*, 457 U.S. 440 (1982); *New York City Transit Authority v. Beazer*, 440 U.S. 568 (1979); *Nashville Gas Company v. Satty*, 434 U.S. 136 (1977); *Dothard v. Rawlinson*, 433 U.S. 321 (1977); *Washington v. Davis*, 426 U.S. 229 (1976).

[17] 401 U.S. at 431.

[18] George Rutherglen takes essentially this position, arguing that Title VII prohibits employment practices that are either overtly adopted to disadvantage, or pretexts for disadvantaging, members of protected groups. See Rutherglen, "Disparate Impact under Title VII," p. 1311. See also Gold, "*Griggs*' Folly," p. 429.

[19] See Friedman, "Redefining Equality, Discrimination, and Affirmative Action under Title VII," pp. 60–61; Jacobs, "A Constitutional Route to Discriminatory Impact Statutory Liability for State and Local Government Employers," pp. 316–17.

[20] See Belton, "Discrimination and Affirmative Action," pp. 539–41 (referring to "two basic concepts of equality"—an "equal treatment [conception]" and an "equal

disparate-impact analysis under Title VII is a dispute between "two distinct conceptions of equality": the proponents of disparate-impact analysis advocate an "equal opportunity or equal achievement conception of equality," while its opponents advocate an "equal treatment conception of equality."[21]

The controversy over disparate impact is not about the meaning of equal treatment. Rather, it is about the rules by which equal treatment should be measured. If a facially neutral rule is a legally relevant standard for assessing the treatment of all the people to whom it applies (that is, if the rule is a legally appropriate measure of how all such people ought to be treated), applying the rule necessarily treats them equally as measured by the baseline of the rule. Conversely, if a facially neutral rule is a legally inappropriate measure of the way some of the people to whom it applies ought to be treated, then applying the rule treats them unequally by reference to the baseline of how they ought to be treated, by giving some and denying others the treatments to which they are legally entitled. It follows, therefore, that to complain of disparate impact is simply to assert that a given rule is an inappropriate—an unjust—measure of the way some of the people to whom it applies ought to be treated.

To illustrate, consider

The Case of the Disadvantaged Firewomen

A municipal fire department requires that all applicants seeking to become firefighters pass a physical fitness test. The test consists of a number of obstacles, including the requirement that candidates be able to lift a hundred-pound weight and carry it for a distance of fifty yards within twenty seconds or less. The test allegedly duplicates the tasks which firefighters might face under actual firefighting conditions. Unfortunately, test scores show that, although women do as well as men on other parts of the test, women are ten times as likely

---

opportunity [conception]"); Fiss, "A Theory of Fair Employment Law," pp. 237–49 (referring to "two senses of equality"—an "equal treatment [sense]" and an "equal opportunity" or "equal achievement [sense]").

[21] Each of the theories of liability corresponds to a recognized conception of equality. The disparate treatment theory [i.e., the theory that an employer discriminates only if he either classifies employees on the basis of a prohibited trait or intends to disadvantage members of a protected class] reflects the equal treatment conception of equality. The disparate impact theory fits well with what is known as the equal opportunity or equal achievement conception of equality.

Chamallas, "Evolving Conceptions of Equality under Title VII," p. 316.

as men to fail the weight test. As a consequence, because of the weight test and the lower rate at which women seek fire-fighting jobs, only 2 percent of all firefighters are women.

A feminist organization challenges the weight test on the ground that it limits the opportunities of women to become firefighters in the same proportion as men. It sues the fire department under a municipal ordinance that requires municipal agencies to "treat men and women equally," arguing that, because the weight test has an adverse impact on women, it does not "treat" men and women "equally."

The fire department, in its defense, argues that it is necessarily treating men and women equally, because it is applying the same weight test to all applicants without regard to sex.

This dispute, which is stated in the language of equal treatment, concerns the standard by which equality of treatment ought to be determined. The fire department, in defending as equal its treatments of men and women applicants, is implicitly asserting that their treatments ought to be measured by prescriptive standard P:

P: No person ought to be certified as a firefighter unless he or she is able to carry a hundred pounds for a distance of fifty yards within twenty seconds or less.

Measured by the baseline of P, the fire department is treating men and women applicants equally because it is giving them treatments that are identical to what P prescribes.

The feminist plaintiffs, in complaining that the weight test treats women unequally, in violation of the law, are necessarily arguing that P cannot lawfully be applied to women. (Note that *Griggs* confines the plaintiffs to challenging the weight test for its impact on women, rather than for its impact on both men and women, because *Griggs* is a comparative rule for the protection of adversely impacted minorities, not a noncomparative rule for invalidating unwise employment practices.)[22] The feminists are thus implicitly arguing that the legally appropriate standard for measuring the fire department's treatments of applicants is not P, but P as modified by P':

P': . . . , provided that women are not required, as a condition for becoming firefighters, to carry a hundred pounds for a distance of fifty yards within twenty seconds.

[22] See Rutherglen, "Disparate Impact under Title VII," p. 1339 and n. 175.

111

If the feminists are right that the fire department's employment practices ought to be assessed by the baseline of P as modified by P', then they are also right that the fire department is treating men and women unequally because, by failing to comply with P', the fire department is according men, but denying women, treatments to which they are entitled.

To be sure, in order to show that P is invalid as a measure of the way women ought to be treated, the feminist plaintiffs must first prove that P violates Title VII. Commentators differ in their interpretations of what Title VII requires in the way of proof. Some argue that evidence of disparate impact suffices to invalidate an employment practice unless the employer can show that the practice is a valid business necessity. Others claim that such evidence suffices to invalidate an employment practice unless the employer can show that the practice is not a pretext for intentional discrimination. The two interpretations differ in theory, proof, and remedy,[23] and litigants who prevail under one interpretation may fail under the other. Under both, however, disparate impact is merely evidence of unlawful inequality, not coextensive with unlawful inequality. To show that a facially neutral rule subjects applicants to unequal treatment in violation of the law, plaintiffs must do more than present evidence of disparate impact. They must show that the employment practice to which they have been subjected is *invalid*, because to say that a facially neutral rule treats people unequally in violation of the law is to say that the rule is being applied to a subset of persons to whom it cannot lawfully be applied.

True, the disparate impact of facially neutral rules is always *descriptively* unequal because it always reflects a descriptive difference in the way the rules affect people who possess different traits. Indeed, descriptively, every rule has a disparate impact on people who possess different traits. That is why it can be truthfully said that "to treat two people equally in one respect will always be to treat them unequally in others."[24] Descriptive inequalities, however, are relationships of "is," not relationships of "ought." In order to complain legitimately about descriptive inequality, one must also show that the disparate impact involved is unequal by prescriptive standards—in other words, one must show that the facially neutral rule treats some people differently than they ought

---

[23] For an evaluation of these two interpretations of section 703(a)(2), see Rutherglen, "Disparate Impact under Title VII," pp. 312–16.

[24] Note, "Developments in the Law—Equal Protection," p. 1164.

to be treated and, hence, is invalid with respect to some of the people to whom it applies.

Conclusion

The parable "Laborers in the Vineyard," from the Book of Matthew, is about many things, including what it means to treat people "equally." Jesus tells of a householder who

> went out early in the morning to hire laborers into his vineyard. And when he had agreed with the laborers for a penny a day, he sent them into his vineyard. And he went out about the third hour, and saw others standing idle in the marketplace, and said unto them: "Go ye also into the vineyard, and whatsoever is right I will give you." And they went their way. Again he went out about the sixth and ninth hour, and did likewise. And about the eleventh hour he went out, and found others standing idle, and saith unto them, "Why stand ye here all the day idle?" They say unto him, "Because no man hath hired us." He saith unto them, "Go ye also into the vineyard; and whatsoever is right, *that* shall ye receive."[25]

When evening came, the owner of the vineyard told his steward to pay the laborers their "hire," starting with those hired last.

> And when they came that were hired about the eleventh hour, they received every man a penny. But when the first came, they supposed that they should have received more; and they likewise received every man a penny. And when they had received it, they murmured against the goodman of the house, saying, *"These last have wrought but one hour, and thou has made them equal unto us, which have borne the burden and heat of the day."* But he answered one of them, and said, "Friend, I do thee no wrong: didst not thou agree with me for a penny? Take what thine is, and go thy way: I will give unto this last, even as unto thee. Is it not lawful for me to do what I will with mine own? Is thine eye evil, because I am good?"

Those who had labored the whole day believed, perhaps rightly, that the owner of the vineyard had treated them unjustly. From a rhetorical standpoint, they also appear to have believed that they could best express their grievance by reproaching the owner for

[25] Matthew 20:1–16.

treating them "equally" with laborers who had worked fewer hours. If so, they may have been mistaken. For, as we shall later see, the semantics of 'equality' tend to favor those who advocate equality over those who oppose it. 'Equality' has favorable, even "sacred,"[26] connotations, which place those who oppose it on the defensive.[27] By arguing against "equal" treatment, the disgruntled laborers put themselves at a rhetorical disadvantage vis-à-vis the vineyard owner. Moreover, instead of allowing the rhetoric of 'equality' to work against them, they could have used it to their advantage: instead of complaining that the vineyard owner treated them "equally" when he ought to have treated them unequally, they could legitimately have reproached him for treating them "*unequally*."

To understand the reproach of "unequal" treatment, it is important to identify the kind of standard of comparison that underlies pejorative references to unequal treatments. Criticism of treatments for being unequal are not predicated on purely descriptive standards of comparison (for, if the standards were purely descriptive, 'unequal' would not have pejorative connotations). Nor are such criticisms based on purely prescriptive standards (for, if the standards were purely prescriptive, 'unequal' would have laudatory connotations). Rather, pejorative references to "unequal" treatments are predicated on a combination of description and prescription: they reflect descriptive standards for measuring whether treatments are identical or nonidentical in the extent, if any, to which they depart from what they ought to be. To criticize treatments for being "unequal" is to state that some people are being treated less favorably than others with respect to the baseline of how they all ought to be treated.

The disgruntled laborers, believing that they should be paid in accord with their labor, felt that the owner of the vineyard had treated them unfairly. Their grievance may have been based on the fact that the owner told those hired later in the day that he would pay them "whatsoever is right." If one penny was regarded at the time as a "right" wage for one hour of work,[28] then it was a

---

[26] Robert Nisbet, quoted in Flew, *The Politics of Procrustes*, p. 20 ("There are certainly signs that equality is taking on a sacred aspect among many minds today").

[27] See the Preface, note 14. For a fuller discussion of the "emotive" meaning of 'equality', see Chapter 11.

[28] Commentators differ as to whether "one penny"—or literally one "denarius"—was an adequate day's wage. Compare Brown, *The Jerome Biblical Commentary*, p. 97 ("*denarius*: A coin representing subsistence wages at the lowest level for a day"), Argyle, *The Gospel according to Matthew*, p. 150 (a "usual day's wage"), and

grossly inadequate wage for twelve hours of work. Moreover, if employers are morally obliged to pay their laborers a right wage in accord with the following rule:

A Right Wage: An employer should pay his employees a right wage based on their labor.

then the owner not only treated the twelve-hour laborers unfairly but also treated them *unequally*, because, measured by the baseline of "A Right Wage," the owner granted the one-hour laborers and denied the twelve-hour laborers the respective treatments they deserved.

The owner of the vineyard might deny that he had treated his laborers unequally by reference to the relevant baseline rule. He might deny, for example, that "A Right Wage" is the appropriate standard of comparison in cases in which laborers *contract* to work for a specific wage. He did, in fact, make a point of reminding the disgruntled laborers that they expressly agreed to work the whole day for one penny ("Friend, I do thee no wrong: didst not thou agree with me for a penny?"). Thus, the owner of the vineyard might contend that the appropriate rule under the circumstances is not "A Right Wage" but "Free Contract":

Free Contract: An employer should pay his employees a fair wage unless, because of necessity, they expressly agree to work for less than a fair wage.

If "Free Contract" is taken to be an acceptable rule of conduct, the owner could legitimately contend that he treated his laborers "equally" by paying them all in accord with their contracts. The problem with "Free Contract" is that it legitimates any bargain to which desperate laborers agree, however unconscionable its terms.

Alternatively, instead of challenging the baseline rule, the owner of the vineyard might dispute the facts. He might maintain that one penny *was* a fair wage for a twelve-hour day and that he paid the one-hour laborers at a higher rate, not because they earned it, but as a form of charity. Indeed, perhaps that is what he meant in saying: "Is it not lawful for me to do what I will with mine own? Is thine eye evil, because I am good?" He may have been acting in accord with an implicit rule of charity:

Laymon, *The Interpreter's One-Volume Commentary on the Bible*, p. 634 ("*a denarius* . . . considered generous for a full day's work").

Charity: A person who makes gifts to people beyond what he owes them may rightfully distribute gifts in any way he chooses.

The vineyard owner may be right in claiming that charity is something supererogatory—something beyond duty—to which recipients have no right and, hence, to which donors have no obligations.[29] If so, by giving extra money to some laborers and not to others, the vineyard owner treated them all equally, by reference to the relevant baselines, because he treated them in accord with the combination of what "A Right Wage" prescribed and "Charity" allowed.

Yet there remains something troubling about the owner's explanation and about his principle "Charity." He speaks as if, having paid everyone what he owed them, he then gave the one-hour laborers additional gifts of charity. But that is not what he *said* he was doing when he paid the laborers, for, in giving each of them one penny, he said he was paying them *wages for their work* (or what he called their "hire"). By distributing charity under the pretense of compensation, he wrongly disparaged the work of the twelve-hour laborers by implying that their full day of work was worth no more than one hour of work by others.[30] If such disparagement is unacceptable, it must be because "Charity" itself is unacceptable and, hence, must be modified, perhaps along the following lines:

Honest Charity: A person who makes gifts to people beyond what he owes them may distribute gifts in any way he chooses—provided, however, that he does not wrongly disparage the work of some of his employees, vis-à-vis others, by distributing his gifts under the pretense of paying wages.

Measured by the baseline of "Honest Charity," the owner of the vineyard treated his employees, not equally, but *unequally*—unequally because he discriminated against the twelve-hour laborers in violation of the rule by disparaging their work vis-à-vis the work of the one-hour laborers.

"Laborers in the Vineyard," then, is paradoxical in several respects. Morally, it is a paradox because it tells of an employer who appears to have behaved arbitrarily, yet it presents the story as a

[29] See, generally, Heyd, *Supererogation*.
[30] I am indebted to H. J. McCloskey for this observation. See McCloskey, "Utilitarian and Retributive Punishment," p. 106.

metaphor of divine justice. Rhetorically, it is a paradox because it tells of laborers who appear to have suffered "unequal" treatment, yet it presents them as complaining of "equal" treatment. Why did the author of the parable cause the laborers to complain of "equal" treatment when they might more effectively have complained of "unequal" treatment? And what is the connection between the first paradox and the second?

The answers, I think, lie in the normative ambiguity of the term 'equal treatment'. 'Equal treatment' has two connotations, depending upon whether it is used prescriptively or descriptively. When it is used prescriptively, it has laudatory connotations: to say that treatments are prescriptively equal means that they have been measured by the relevant rule of conduct and found to be identical in the way they ought to be. But when 'equal treatment' is used descriptively, it is normatively neutral: to say that treatments are descriptively equal means that they have been measured and found to be identical by a descriptive standard that may or may not be normatively appropriate.

The author of the parable had a choice of two ways to express the disgruntled laborers' grievance, both based on descriptive standards of comparison. As we have seen, the vineyard owner's behavior could have been measured by a

descriptive standard based on a normative baseline—namely, the extent, if any, to which the treatments departed from what the laborers believed they ought to have been.

Measured by that standard, the vineyard owner treated the disgruntled laborers, not equally, but "unequally," by treating them worse than the others by reference to how they believed they all ought to have been treated. Alternatively, the vineyard owner's conduct could have been measured by a

purely descriptive standard—namely, the extent, if any, to which the treatments represented per-capita distributions.

Measured by this standard, the vineyard owner treated the disgruntled laborers "equally," by distributing all wages on a per-capita basis. Rhetorically, the disgruntled laborers' grievance could have been conveyed more effectively by the former standard than by the latter because 'unequal' by the former standard is a pejorative term, while 'equal' by the latter standard is normatively neutral.

This brings us to the author's possible reasons for causing the disgruntled laborers to complain of "equal" rather than "unequal" treatment. He may have done so because the ambiguity of 'equal treatment' reinforces the ambiguity of the parable itself. A principal theme of the parable is that worldly justice sometimes differs from divine justice—that a certain kind of per-capita treatment, which mankind may regard as wrong, God in His mercy regards as right. The normative ambiguity of per-capita treatment is reinforced by the semantic ambiguity of 'equal treatment', for the term is ambiguous as between description and prescription. When used descriptively, it is normatively neutral; when used prescriptively, it is laudatory. The author of the parable exploits the ambiguity by using the single word 'equal' to tell the story simultaneously from both mundane and divine points of view. From the disgruntled laborers' point of view, the vineyard owner treated his employees "equally" because, descriptively, the wages he paid were identical by a per-capita standard of comparison. From God's point of view, the vineyard owner also treated his employees equally because, prescriptively, the wages he paid were identical as measured by what they ought to have been. The disgruntled laborers use 'equal' as part of a grievance; the author of the parable uses 'equal' as a term of praise. Thus, in response to the disgruntled laborers' complaint that the owner of the vineyard treated them "equally," the author of the parable implicitly declares, "Indeed he did!"

F I V E

SUMMARY

We began this portion of our inquiry by posing two questions: (1) What, if anything, is the generic meaning of 'equality' that underlies the many and varied usages of 'equality'? (2) Why is equality so much more elusive, and controverted, in moral discourse than in physical science? If our analysis has been sound, we should now be in a position to propose answers.

The Generic Meaning of 'Equality'

Some observers react to the apparent multifariousness of 'equality' by concluding that it has no generic meaning. In his analysis in *Equalities*, Douglas Rae argues that, rather than having a "single" and "universal" meaning, "the notion of equality . . . splits itself into many distinct notions"—at least as many as 108, and perhaps as many as 720, "structurally distinct interpretations of equality."[1] Philip Kurland goes even further, arguing that "the concept of equality . . . [has] no more definition than the shape of an amoeba":

> Equality is the subject of many learned works—ancient and modern—no two of which are in complete accord as to its meaning or form. The concept of equality, except in mathematics, would appear to have no more definition than the shape of an amoeba. And that definition must differ depending upon the time at which it is viewed, the perspective from which it is viewed, the purpose for which it is viewed, and—perhaps most importantly—the idiosyncracies of the viewer. For after all, equality is a concept that appeals to instinct, rather than intellect.[2]

[1] Rae, *Equalities*, pp. 127, 128, 132–33 and n. 3.
[2] Kurland, "Ruminations on the Quality of Equality," p. 1.

Rae is surely right that there are a great many conceptions of equality—indeed, probably more than his hypothesized total number consisting of "four or perhaps five digits."[3] It does not follow, however, that no single concept of equality underlies them all. If our analysis thus far is sound, equality appears to be a single concept—at least with respect to persons and tangible things—which lends itself to multifarious and contradictory conceptions. Equality regarding persons and tangible things is:

(1) the relationship that obtains among two or more persons or things which,

(2) although distinguishable in one or more respects,

(3) have nevertheless been jointly measured,

(4) compared, and

(5) ascertained to be indistinguishable

(6) by reference to a relevant standard of comparison,

(7) a standard which, until specified, can be represented as "X."

Thus, equality is a concept that possesses both fixed terms and a variable term. The fixed terms, which remain constant throughout all statements of equality, are (1) through (6). The variable term, which changes from one conception of equality to another (and from one relationship of equality to another), is the "relevant standard of comparison," X. Therefore, equality is both a single concept and a multitude of conceptions—both "one idea" and "many" ideas[4] —depending upon whether the variable standard of comparison remains unspecified.

Of course, all persons and tangible things are identical in some respects because they are identical in possessing mass and occupying space. By the same token, all persons and tangible things are nonidentical in some respects because they are nonidentical in the particular mass they consist of and the particular spaces they occupy. The significant question for purposes of equality, therefore, is whether persons and tangible things are identical in *relevant* respects. Something is "relevant" to the extent that it is conducive to or useful or instrumental in furthering some state of

[3] Rae, *Equalities*, pp. 133–34.

[4] Lakoff, *Equality in Political Philosophy*, p. 6 ("Formally there is one idea of equality; substantively there are many") (emphasis omitted).

affairs one wishes to bring about. Commentators differ as to whether relevance is a matter of "fact" or a matter of "value."[5] In reality it is both: whether a particular consideration furthers a given goal is a factual question; whether a particular goal is one which one wishes to bring about is an evaluative question.[6] The further question whether something *ought* to be a goal, and whether considerations *ought to be allowed* in furtherance of it, are normative questions.

In order to declare people identical in "relevant" respects, therefore, one must possess a standard of comparison that is an appropriate measure of the state of affairs one wishes to bring about. To declare people identical in *normatively* relevant respects, one must possess a standard of comparison that is a *normatively* appropriate measure of the state of affairs one wishes to bring about. Persons or tangible things are identical in (normatively) relevant respects to the extent that they are identical as measured by standards of comparison that are (normatively) appropriate to states of affairs one wishes to bring about. The concept of equality does not itself contain criteria for judging standards of comparison; it presupposes them. Equality is a relationship that obtains among persons or things by reference to *such standards of comparison as have been independently established as appropriate to the states of affairs one wishes to bring about*.

The difference between descriptive equalities (e.g., "Jack and Jill are equal in height") and prescriptive equalities (e.g., "Jack and Jill are equal before the law") is not a difference in terms (1) through (6) of equality. Descriptive and prescriptive equalities both consist of terms (1) through (6), for they are both relationships of identity among two or more distinct persons or things by reference to "such standards of comparison as have been independently established as appropriate." The difference is in the nature of the variable standard of comparison. Descriptive equalities are based on descriptive standards, that is, standards for comparing persons or things with respect to how they *are*. Prescriptive equalities are themselves based on prescriptions—standards that specify the particular treatments that persons with particular traits *ought to receive*. Just as descriptive equals are persons or things that are identical in the descriptions they possess as measured by relevant descriptive standards, prescriptive equals are identical in

[5] See Williams, "The Idea of Equality," pp. 112–14.
[6] I have been persuaded of this by Oppenheim, "Egalitarianism as a Descriptive Concept," pp. 147–48.

what they owe or deserve as measured by relevant prescriptions. Prescriptive equals are persons who fall within the same descriptive class—persons who possess the same description—for purposes of relevant rules of conduct.

The Elusiveness of Prescriptive Equality

There are several reasons why prescriptive equalities are more elusive than descriptive equalities. A principal reason is the mistaken assumption that controlling standards of comparison are descriptive when they are really prescriptive, which leads to a futile search for factual answers to inherently normative questions. Consider D. A. Lloyd Thomas's argument in his essay "Equality within the Limits of Reason Alone."[7] Thomas argues that there are five presuppositions to the conclusion that all humans are prescriptively equal:

(1) that, empirically, there is some quality that all humans possess;

(2) that humans possess the quality uniquely;

(3) that the quality is "relevant" to the normative conclusion that follows from it;

(4) that the quality is possessed in equal amounts by all persons;

(5) that elements (1), (2), and (4) are open to empirical confirmation.

Thomas is right to conclude that descriptive equality is a necessary prerequisite of prescriptive equality: one cannot conclude that persons as a group ought to be treated equally unless one possesses a descriptive standard for identifying "persons." For centuries, moral philosophers, arguing that all human beings are prescriptively equal, have searched for a descriptive standard by which humans are in fact equal. For the Stoics, the descriptive standard was the possession of reason; for the Epicureans, it was the capacity to experience happiness; for Christians, it was knowledge of good and evil; for Hobbes, it was the capacity to kill and be killed; for Kant, it was rationality; for John Rawls, it is "moral personality," a capacity to make plans and give justice; and for others, it is

---

[7] Thomas, "Equality within the Limits of Reason Alone," p. 538.

the state of being "conscious beings who necessarily have intentions and purposes and see what they are doing in a certain light."[8]

It is a mistake to assume, however, as some commentators do,[9] that because descriptive equality is necessary, it is also *sufficient*. Descriptive equality is an "is," not an "ought." One cannot infer that, because people *are* equal, they *ought to be treated* equally. To make the move from descriptive to prescriptive equality, one must do what is always necessary in moving from an "is" to an "ought": one must engage in moral or legal reasoning toward the formulation of a norm, a proposition that persons of a certain description deserve treatment of a certain kind. Without such norms, prescriptive equality is impossible because there is no standard by which people can be compared with respect to what they owe or deserve. With such norms, prescriptive equality is as obvious as any descriptive equality because it is simply the identity which obtains among people who fall within a descriptive class of persons for whom certain treatment is prescribed by rule.

This is not to say that Thomas commits the fallacy of inferring an "ought" from an "is." Despite his emphasis on the controlling nature of factual identity, he invokes a word that avoids the naturalistic fallacy—the word 'relevant'. He recognizes that, before descriptive equality can render people prescriptively equal, it must be shown to be *relevant* to the normative conclusion that follows from it. What he fails to make explicit, however, is that normative relevance is a function of the normative appropriateness of an implicit norm, or rule, specifying that people of a certain description ought to be treated in certain ways. It is the rule that determines which of people's various descriptive qualities are prescriptively relevant.[10]

[8] See Sigmund, "Hierarchy, Equality, and Consent in Medieval Christian Thought," p. 138 (on Stoic conceptions of equality); Pole, *The Pursuit of Equality in American History*, pp. 6, 7 (on Epicurean conceptions of equality); Lakoff, "Christianity and Equality," p. 115 (on Christian conceptions of equality); Hobbes, *Leviathan*, Pt. I, chap. 13, p. 94; Kant, *The Fundamental Principles of the Metaphysics of Morals*, excerpted in Abernethy, *The Idea of Equality*, pp. 153–55; Rawls, *A Theory of Justice*, pp. 505–12; Williams, "The Idea of Equality," p. 117. With respect to Kant, it should be noted that he argued that rational moral agency itself is a transcendental characteristic rather than an empirical capacity, though one must wonder: if rational moral agency is not an empirical characteristic, how can one distinguish creatures who are rational moral agents from those that are not?

[9] See, e.g., Weale, *Equality and Social Policy*, pp. 20, 22; Williams, "The Idea of Equality," pp. 112–14.

[10] See Wilson, *Equality*, p. 121 ("[In] framing a rule, we have ipso facto accepted certain characteristics as relevant and others as irrelevant").

The Contestedness of Prescriptive Equality

In his essay "Essentially Contested Concepts," W. B. Gallie argues that there are some concepts whose use is controversial not because some people use them incorrectly, but because their "proper use . . . inevitably involves endless disputes about their proper uses on the part of their users."[11] The examples Gallie gives are the concepts of art, democracy, and "the American way of life." His followers have added justice, freedom, power, rights, and private property, among others.[12] These concepts are controversial, Gallie maintains, because it is in their *essence* to be contested. In effect they are "essentially contested concepts."

Gallie's thesis, which is itself controversial,[13] may not apply to all the concepts for which it has been claimed. Nevertheless, because of the relationship which obtains between prescriptive equality and its underlying norms, Gallie's thesis appears to hold true for prescriptive equality. As noted above, prescriptive equality is the relationship of identity in rights or duties which obtains among two or more persons by reference to a relevant norm, or rule, of conduct. As such, it consists of two elements:

(i) a rule of conduct, which has been independently established as the appropriate standard for measuring how people ought to behave, describing the treatments that people of various descriptions owe or deserve;

(ii) the application of the rule, which is accomplished by identifying persons who do and do not possess the descriptive features required for the respective treatments.

Step (ii) is uncontroversial, because application of a rule involves the same empirical procedure as is used to determine descriptive equalities—a matter of measuring and comparing people for their identity and nonidentity by reference to given descriptive standards. The controversial element is (i), i.e., the establishment of a

---

[11] Gallie, "Essentially Contested Concepts," p. 169.

[12] See Lukes, "Relativism," p. 184 (justice); Gray, "On Liberty, Liberalism, and Essential Contestability," p. 385 (liberty); Lukes, *Power* (power); Waldron, "What Is Private Property?" p. 313 (private property); Connolly, *The Terms of Political Discourse*, pp. 140–73 (freedom).

[13] For criticism of Gallie's thesis, see Connolly, *The Terms of Political Discourse*, chap. 6; Clarke, "Eccentrically Contested Concepts," p. 122; MacDonald, "Is 'Power' Essentially Contested?" p. 380; Lukes, "Reply to MacDonald," p. 418; Swanton, "On the 'Essential Contestedness' of Political Concepts," p. 811.

certain rule as the relevant standard by which to measure behavior. It is something about which people endlessly disagree because it is ultimately a matter of defining just behavior.

The same point about the inherent contestedness of prescriptive equality can be made in terms of "relevance." Every proposed rule is a standard for identifying people who are prescriptively "equal" because every rule creates one or more classes of persons whose prescribed treatment is identical. Furthermore, every rule is a standard for identifying prescriptively "equal treatment" because every rule creates one or more classes of treatment for the persons to whom it applies. Finally, as commentators often observe, every rule treats "equals" "equally" because every rule necessarily prescribes identical treatment for the persons it defines as identical.[14] It follows that the controlling question will always be "Which rule, of the many available rules, is the one by which people *ought* to be measured and compared?" That, however, is a question for which answers must be sought not in conceptions of equality (which coincide with, rather than precede, the formulation of rules), but in external theories of justice and justification.

To illustrate, consider the example introduced at the beginning of Chapter 3:

Distributing the Pound Cake

The pound cake is out of the oven and is ready to be eaten. I am uncertain, however, as to how I should distribute it among my three children.

—One of the children has refused to do his chores for a week and has admitted to pilfering his sister's allowance money, knowing that denial of dessert has sometimes been a penalty in our family for misbehavior.

—Another child is overweight. But I promised all the children that whoever brought home a perfect report card would get a special treat, and he is the only one who has done so.

—The third child did her best to help me make the cake without asking for anything in return, while the others refused to lend a hand.

Not surprisingly, the children, who disagree about how the cake ought to be distributed, see the issue as a matter of equality.

Child 1: "Mom and Dad are always saying 'All-our-children-are-equal-in-our-eyes.' That means that we should be treated

[14] See Chapter 4, pp. 96–97.

equally. Treating us equally means giving us equal amounts of cake."

Child 2: "You're right about what Mom and Dad say. We *are* all equal in their eyes, and they *should* treat us equally. But treating us equally doesn't mean giving us equal amounts of cake. It means giving all of us an equal right to earn extra pieces of cake by bringing home perfect report cards. They made the same promise to all of us. It's not my fault that I am the only one who took them up on it."

Child 3: "Sorry, you are both wrong. You don't understand what Mom and Dad mean by 'equal in our eyes.' They mean the same thing God means. It's what we learned in Sunday School: when God says 'All my children are equal in my eyes,' he means 'I regard all my children in the same way until they do things that cause me to regard them differently.' That's how he distinguishes between saints and sinners. It's the same with Mom and Dad. They regard us equally until we do things to make them regard us differently. You both have done things to make them regard you differently—stealing my allowance, gaining too much weight, and refusing to help with the cake—so we are not equal anymore, no more equal than sinners are to saints after they offend God."

The children appear to be disagreeing about equality, and in a sense they are. They agree that their parents should treat them equally but disagree about *how* they ought to do it. That is no accident. Analytically, in fact, such is always the case, for every proposed rule treats people equally by giving all people the treatments prescribed for persons possessing their traits. Every normative dispute can be framed as a contest between one proposed rule and another—hence, between one proposed equality and another. That may be what Douglas Rae means when he states that, in normative disputes, "the question is not 'Whether equality?' but 'Which equality?' "[15]

[15] Rae, *Equalities*, p. 19. See also Benn, "Equality, Moral and Social," p. 41 (Equality . . . usually . . . means getting rid of one system of distinctions and replacing it with another"); Cooper, *The Illusions of Equality*, p. 14 ("The point being made is neither trivial nor merely 'slick' for at least two reasons. First, many of the interesting debates are not about the bare question, 'Should we have equality?', but about which of various competing equalities we should have. Indeed, all debates must, au fond, be of this sort, given that each equality demanded carries an inequality with it, and vice versa"); Karst, "Equality and Community," p. 191 ("The achievement of one form of equality necessarily implies the imposition of corresponding

By the same token, however, insofar as all normative disputes are about equality, none of them is about equality. They are about the prescriptive standards of comparison—the rules—by which equalities are measured. Thus, although the three children speak the language of equality, their dispute is about which of three implicit rules is the relevant standard for measuring the conduct of their parents:

P_1: Dessert shall be distributed among the children of the family on a per-capita basis.

P_2: Dessert shall be distributed among the children in accord with what has been promised them.

P_3: Dessert shall be distributed among the children on a per-capita basis, except that children who have disqualified themselves by their misconduct or by overeating shall receive none.

The children have different conceptions of equality because they have different rules in mind. They have different rules in mind because they have different conceptions of justice.

---

inequalities"); Lucas, "Against Equality Again," p. 261 ("If we set out to establish equality in one respect, we shall thereby establish some other inequality in another respect"); Mortimore, "An Ideal of Equality," p. 222 ("In practice, egalitarians have been concerned merely to replace one type of discrimination with another").

PART TWO

SOME MORE EQUAL THAN OTHERS

George Orwell's *Animal Farm* is a fable of farm animals who begin by creating a democracy in which "[a]ll animals are equal" and end by submitting to a dictatorship of pigs in which "all animals are equal, but some animals are more equal than others."[1]

The irony of *Animal Farm* works on several levels. Part of it is that, as heirs of the French and American Revolutions, we regard "equality" and political oligarchy as mutually inconsistent. Yet that is not its essential irony, nor one which would have impressed Aristotle and his contemporaries, who considered it plausible to discuss "aristocracy" and "oligarchy" in terms of "equality."[2] What even Aristotle would have found ironic, however, is that the pigs' rhetoric of equality betrays their hypocrisy. A person can truly be said to be "first among equals" (*primus inter pares*), for this means merely that he and other members of a group are identical in the respect in which they are "equal" and nonidentical in the respect in which he is "first."[3] Not even a pig, however, can truly say that, among equals, some are "more equal" than others,[4] for relationships of equality are not relationships of degree. People who are capable of being compared are either equal or unequal, not "more" or "less" equal. To say "Some are more equal than others" is more than a semantic mistake: it reveals a public wish to honor equality, animated by a private intention to subvert it.

[1] Orwell, *Animal Farm*, p. 112.

[2] Aristotle, *Politics* III.9–12.1280a7–1283a23.

[3] For example, it is often said without irony that, as one of nine members of the Supreme Court of the United States, the chief justice is "first among equals." That means that the chief justice and other members of the Supreme Court are equal in some relevant respects (e.g., in their authority to vote on cases before the Court) and unequal in others (e.g., in their authority to preside over deliberations of the Court).

[4] We sometimes say X is "more equal than Y" when we mean that neither X nor Y is equal to something else, Z, but X is more nearly equal to Z than Y is. That cannot be what the pigs of *Animal Farm* have in mind, because they claim to believe that "[a]ll animals are equal."

129

Nevertheless, although one cannot straightforwardly say that some people are "more equal than others," one can plausibly argue that certain *conceptions* of equality are more egalitarian—more closely linked to the logic of equality—than others. Among the many rival conceptions of equality, three conceptions (or sets of conceptions) are commonly assumed to have such a special pedigree. One set, which we shall discuss in Chapter 6, comprises the equality produced by a certain class of comparative rights—"anti-discrimination rights" of the form *Whatever benefits are extended to X shall be extended to Y, too*. Another set of conceptions, the subject of Chapter 7, comprises what Plato and Aristotle referred to disparagingly as "numerical equality." The third, the subject of Chapter 8, is the set comprising "equal opportunity."

S I X

ANTIDISCRIMINATION RIGHTS

[N]or shall any State deprive any person of life, liberty, or property without due process of law, nor deny to any person within its jurisdiction the equal protection of the laws. —Fourteenth Amendment

The Fourteenth Amendment to the U.S. Constitution is the source of most of the personal rights that people of the United States possess vis-à-vis state governments. Fourteenth Amendment rights can be classified in various ways, including by reference to whether they are noncomparative or comparative in nature. To say that A has a "noncomparative right" means (as we have seen)[1] that his entitlements can be determined without reference to the relative status of others. To say that A has a "comparative right" means that his entitlements are a function of his relations to other persons. For example, the right of a person to the privacy of his home is a noncomparative right because it can be ascertained with-

[1] See Chapter 3, pp. 72–74. We previously distinguished between comparative and noncomparative rules. We are now distinguishing between comparative and noncomparative "rights," in part because our reference is the U.S. Constitution, which employs the language of rights. By 'rights', however, I am not referring solely to American constitutional rights, nor to what Ronald Dworkin calls trumping "principles" as opposed to nontrumping "policies." See Dworkin, *Taking Rights Seriously*, pp. 22–31, 84–86, 180–82, 191, 227, 273; Dworkin, *A Matter of Principle*, pp. 359–60, 370–72. I am using the word 'rights' broadly, in what Wesley Hohfeld called its "generic" sense, to include all entitlements, privileges, liberties, powers, and immunities created in persons by rules. Hohfeld, *Fundamental Legal Conceptions*, pp. 42, 71. For an illuminating definition of rights, see Finnis, *Natural Law and Natural Rights*, p. 205, quoted above in Chapter 3, note 13.

For other, inclusive definitions of 'rights', see Feinberg, "The Nature and Value of Rights," pp. 143, 155 ("To have a right is to have a claim against someone whose recognition as valid is called for by some set of governing rules or moral principles"); Gewirth, "The Basis and Context of Human Rights," pp. 119, 120 ("A person's rights are what belong to him as his due, what he is entitled to, hence what he can rightly demand of others"); Ginsberg, On *Justice in Society*, p. 74 (rights are all claims that can justly be made by or on behalf of an individual or group of individuals to some condition or power); McCloskey, "Rights—Some Conceptual Issues," p. 99 (rights are "entitlements to do, have, enjoy, or have done").

out reference to the relative status of other persons. In contrast, the right of black children to attend public schools on the same basis as white children is a comparative right because the rights of black children are determined by reference to the privileges enjoyed by white children.

Comparative rights fall within two subcategories: antidiscrimination rights and remaining comparative rights. An antidiscrimination right is the right of A to such benefits as are extended to B.[2] For example, the statutory right of women under the Equal Pay Act to the same employment compensation as men is an antidiscrimination right because it guarantees women the same compensation as is extended to men. In contrast, the statutory right of military veterans to employment preference over nonveterans is a comparative right that is *not* an antidiscrimination right because, while the rights of veterans are a function of their status relative to other persons, those rights exceed the benefits extended to other persons.

This distinction between antidiscrimination rights and other rights is significant for Fourteenth Amendment purposes because it generally correlates with the division of rights between the amendment's two principal clauses: the equal protection clause, with its guarantee of "equal[ity]"; and the due process clause, with its protections of "life, liberty, [and] property."[3] With some

---

[2] By 'antidiscrimination rights' I mean what Fullinwider, *The Reverse Discrimination Controversy*, p. 223, refers to as "principles of comparative equality"; what Greenawalt, "How Empty Is the Idea of Equality?" pp. 1178–83, calls "substantive principles of equality"; what Raz, "Principles of Equality," pp. 321, 331–34, calls "strictly egalitarian" principles of equality; and what Simons, "Equality as a Comparative Right," p. 416, refers to as "comparative equality rights." Thus, antidiscrimination rights are not confined to the right of a person, X, not to be disadvantaged vis-à-vis Y on the basis of certain *limited* traits, but include X's right not to be disadvantaged vis-à-vis Y on the basis of *any* trait. Specifically, antidiscrimination rights include what Simons calls both "positive" and "negative" nondiscrimination rights. See Simons, "Equality as a Comparative Right," p. 422 n. 74.

The word 'discrimination' has a checkered history. Although it has always referred to the act of distinguishing among persons or things, its connotations have changed over time. In the eighteenth and early nineteenth centuries, it possessed positive connotations, being regarded as synonymous with 'discernment', 'astuteness', 'keenness', and 'tact'. In twentieth-century legal discourse, it has acquired pejorative connotations, being regarded as synonymous with 'bias', 'prejudice', 'favoritism', 'bigotry', and 'intolerance'. Although the change is sometimes assumed to have come about in America as a result of cases in the post–Civil War period dealing with newly emancipated persons of color, 'discrimination' may have first acquired its negative connotations in railroad cases dealing with differential railway rates.

[3] The Fourteenth Amendment also contains a third clause, the so-called privileges and immunities clause, prohibiting the states from abridging the "privileges

exceptions, antidiscrimination rights have been attributed to the equal protection clause, while noncomparative rights and remaining comparative rights have been attributed to the due process clause.[4]

Some commentators have argued that the association of antidiscrimination rights with equality is not only legally correct, but also *conceptually* appropriate—that is, they assert that antidiscrimination rights derive from the Fourteenth Amendment in part *because* it is an "equality" provision.[5] They advance two reasons for believing that antidiscrimination rights stand in a unique and intimate relationship with the concept of equality: first, they assert that,

---

or immunities of citizens of the United States." Although some commentators have argued that the framers of the Fourteenth Amendment intended this clause (rather than the due process clause) to be the repository of noncomparative rights, the Supreme Court very early construed the privileges and immunities clause to be largely a dead letter, thus forcing the Court's subsequent constitutional jurisprudence of noncomparative rights into the due process clause. See Ely, *Democracy and Dissent*, p. 24 (suggesting that the framers of the Fourteenth Amendment intended to assign noncomparative and antidiscrimination rights to the privileges and immunities and the due process clauses, respectively).

[4] For authority that the due process clause is (or ought to be regarded as) a source of noncomparative rights, and the equal protection clause a source of antidiscrimination rights, see Lupu, "Untangling the Strands of the Fourteenth Amendment," p. 981; Perry, "Modern Equal Protection," pp. 1023, 1074–83; Wright, "Judicial Review and the Equal Protection Clause," pp. 1, 17–18. Cf. *Bearden v. Georgia*, 461 U.S. 660, 665 (1983) ("we generally analyze the fairness of relations between the criminal defendant and the State under the due-process clause, while we approach the question of whether the state has invidiously denied one class of defendants a substantial benefit available to another class of defendants under the equal protection clause").

The assignment of antidiscrimination rights and other rights to the equal protection clause and the due process clause, respectively, is not without exception. Some antidiscrimination rights are typically derived from the due process clause; for example, the requirement that the state not discriminate against speech on the basis of its content derives from that clause. See Karst, "Equality as a Central Principle in the First Amendment," p. 20. Conversely, some commentators have argued that the equal protection clause is the source of some noncomparative entitlements. See Karst, "The Supreme Court, 1976 October Term—Foreword," pp. 1, 4 ("The substantive core of the [fourteenth] amendment . . . is a principle . . . which presumptively guarantees to each individual the right to be treated by the organized society as a respected, responsible, and participating member"). For a catalogue of noncomparative and antidiscrimination rights that do not divide neatly between the due process and equal protection clauses, see Simon, "Equality as a Comparative Right," pp. 387, 468–70, 475–78. For a discussion of the difficulty of separating noncomparative from comparative rights under the equal protection clause, see Alexander, "Modern Equal Protection Theories," p. 3.

[5] See Lupu, "Untangling the Strands of the Fourteenth Amendment," p. 1055; Simons, "Equality as a Comparative Right," pp. 389, 405, 408, 415 (arguing that antidiscrimination rights are "the important sense" and "the operative conception" of equality in "constitutional theory," because they are the only rights in law and morals that *"essentially"* rely on demands for equality).

unlike noncomparative rights, antidiscrimination rights and equality are both essentially *comparative* in nature; second, they claim that, in contrast to other rights, the essential *purpose* of antidiscrimination rights is to bring about relations of equality.

This is not the place to debate the history or meaning of the Fourteenth Amendment, or to assess rival theories of constitutional interpretation. Those are substantive, not conceptual, matters. It is appropriate, however, to examine whether antidiscrimination rights are in a sense uniquely "egalitarian in nature."[6] I believe we shall see that, while the first of the aforementioned reasons lacks force, the second has merit in the following sense: although all rights result in equality, and all such equalities possess the same basic features, antidiscrimination rights are "designed to achieve equality"[7] in ways that other rights are not, because unlike other rights, which require single and specified relationships of equality, antidiscrimination rights aim toward, and are satisfied by, *any* relationship of equality between rightsholders and the persons of whose treatment their rights are a function. That is why antidiscrimination rights are commonly, and appropriately, referred to as "equality rights."

Equality, Comparisons, and Comparative Rights

Joel Feinberg, in his influential article "Noncomparative Justice," first introduced the distinction between comparative and noncomparative principles of justice.[8] By 'comparative justice' he appears to mean the general principle underlying all prescriptive equalities, namely, that people who are equal in relevant prescriptive respects ought to be treated equally:

[6] To the extent that you are indeed an authentic egalitarian you are committed to saying that what various persons are to hold is to be determined primarily by reference to what other people have, rather than by reference to what those persons themselves both are or are not, and have or have not done.

Flew, *The Politics of Procrustes*, p. 29. See also Cooper, *The Illusions of Equality* (arguing that it is a necessary condition of egalitarianism that "the ground given for increasing or decreasing some people's amount of X make essential reference to the amounts of X which other people have").

[7] Raz, "Principles of Equality," p. 331. It should be noted that Raz uses his own terminology for what we have called antidiscrimination rights, referring to what in his taxonomy are "(5.2) type principles" and to "strict egalitarian" principles of equality. See Raz, "Principles of Equality," pp. 330–38.

[8] Feinberg, "Noncomparative Justice," p. 297. For a parallel discussion, see Feinberg, *Social Philosophy*, pp. 98ff.

All comparative justice involves, in one way or another, equality in the treatment accorded all members of a class; but whether that equality be absolute or "proportional," whether it be equality of share, equality of opportunity, or equality of consideration, depends on the nature of the goods and evils awarded or distributed, and the nature of the class in which the assignments and allocations take place. Comparative injustice consists in arbitrary and invidious discrimination of one kind or another: a departure from the requisite form of equal treatment without good reason.[9]

Yet, Feinberg's examples of specific "principles" of comparative justice (that is, specific principles resulting in prescriptive equality) are all examples of antidiscrimination or other comparative rights, such as the right of persons not to be discriminated against on the basis of race.[10]

Why is it that Feinberg bases his paradigms of prescriptive equality on examples of antidiscrimination rights as opposed to other rights? Why would one assume that prescriptive equality is a relationship that results solely or especially from antidiscrimination rights as opposed, say, to noncomparative rights? These questions are difficult, perhaps impossible, to answer fairly because Feinberg's terminology is ambiguous[11] and his reasoning more implicit than explicit. Given his emphasis on the *comparative* nature of both prescriptive equality and antidiscrimination rights, however, he may have reasoned as follows:

[9] Feinberg, "Noncomparative Justice," p. 299. See also Feinberg, *Social Philosophy*, p. 99 ("The basic principle of comparative justice is that like cases are to be treated alike").

[10] See Feinberg, *Social Philosophy*, p. 101; Feinberg, "Noncomparative Justice," p. 311.

[11] Feinberg's use of 'comparative' is ambiguous. On the one hand, when he speaks of "comparative justice," he appears to mean the principle "Likes should be treated alike." See Feinberg, *Social Philosophy*, p. 99 ("The basic principle of comparative justice is that like cases are to be treated alike"). Indeed, some commentators understand him to mean precisely that. See, e.g., Montague, "Comparative and Noncomparative Justice," p. 132 (describing Feinberg's "comparative justice" as requiring "the similar treatment of relevantly similar cases and the dissimilar treatment of relevantly dissimilar cases").

On the other hand, Feinberg defines "comparative . . . principles of justice" in the terms that we have adopted here as a definition of "comparative rights," i.e., rights such that "a person's due is determinable only by reference to his relations to other persons." Feinberg, *Social Philosophy*, p. 298. This suggests—and has led other commentators to believe—that by "comparative justice" Feinberg means only such justice as results from comparative rights as opposed to noncomparative rights. See Carr, "The Concept of Formal Justice," pp. 217–22; Simon, "Equality as a Comparative Right," p. 401 n. 25.

Premise (i): Prescriptive equality and antidiscrimination rights are both based on comparative relationships.

Premise (ii): Both comparative relationships mandate equal treatment.

Conclusion: Prescriptive equality and antidiscrimination rights are correlative concepts of equal treatment.

Feinberg may not have intended the foregoing syllogism. Whether he did or not, it is important to understand its fallacy. Premises (i) and (ii) are both true; the fallacy is in the conclusion. Prescriptive equality and antidiscrimination rights are not correlative concepts because the comparisons they presuppose are different: the comparison underlying prescriptive equalities based on noncomparative rights is *prescriptive* in nature and *follows* the formulation of a final rule of conduct, while the application of antidiscrimination rights presupposes an antecedent comparison that is *descriptive* in nature and *precedes* the formulation of a final rule of conduct.

To declare two persons prescriptively equal in their noncomparative rights, one must first identify a relevant noncomparative rule of conduct; having identified the relevant rule, one can then compare the two persons by reference to the rule to see if they are identical in possessing the features specified by the rule. They are prescriptively equal if both possess the traits the rule prescribes as a qualification for common rights or duties. To apply an antidiscrimination right, one must make an additional comparison. One must first compare members of the rightsholding class with the class of persons on whose treatment their rights depend (the "reference class") to see whether the rightsholders are descriptively disadvantaged vis-à-vis the reference class. If the rightsholders are not disadvantaged, the antidiscrimination right has no application. If the rightsholders are disadvantaged, the antidiscrimination right comes into play, requiring the formulation of a new noncomparative rule by which the class of rightsholders and the reference class are identical in the treatments prescribed for them. Thus, both prescriptive equality and antidiscrimination rights involve comparisons, but antidiscrimination rights involve an antecedent comparison of a distinctive kind.

To illustrate, consider the differences between the two kinds of rights—one an antidiscrimination right, the other a noncomparative right—created by the

Twenty-Sixth Amendment

The Twenty-Sixth Amendment to the U.S. Constitution, adopted in 1971, changed the minimum age for voting in federal and state elections in the United States to eighteen years of age: "The right of citizens of the United States who are eighteen years or older to vote shall not be denied or abridged by the United States or by any State on account of age."

In changing the voting age, the amendment created two quite different rights for persons eighteen and older, depending upon whether the elections are federal or state in origin. The difference stems from the mandatory and discretionary nature of federal and state elections, respectively. The Constitution independently requires that certain federal officials (the president, vice-president, U.S. senators, and U.S. representatives) be elected,[12] but it does not require that state offices be filled by election. States are free to decide whether they wish to fill certain offices (judgeships, mayoral positions, executive positions, and perhaps others)[13] by election or by appointment.

[12] Although the Constitution provides for the election of the president, vice-president, senators, and representatives, it also gives the states some authority to define the qualifications of electors. Specifically, it provides that the states shall define the qualifications of presidential and vice-presidential electors, and that a person's qualifications to vote for members of the U.S. Senate and House of Representatives shall be the same as the qualifications the state of his citizenship prescribes as a condition for his voting for members of the state legislature. This might suggest to some that (1) if a state refused to define qualifications for presidential and vice-presidential electors, no one in the state would be qualified to vote for president and vice-president, and (2) if a state abolished its legislature altogether (thereby effectively denying that any of its citizens are qualified to vote for members of the legislature), and if such an abolition were constitutional under the "guaranty clause" (see note 13 below), then citizens of the state would not be eligible to vote for U.S. senators and representatives. However, it should be noted as authority to the contrary that the Supreme Court has construed article I, § 4, clause 1, of the Constitution as empowering Congress to override state voting qualifications with respect to the offices of president and vice-president and members of the U.S. Senate and House of Representatives. See *Oregon v. Mitchell*, 400 U.S. 112, 117–24 (1970)(plurality opinion).

[13] The Constitution does guarantee citizens of states a "republican form of government." However, the federal courts have never been called upon to decide how much of a "republican form of government" must be elected by the people as opposed to appointed—in part because the states tend to use elections even more than the federal government, and in part because the meaning of "republican form of government" has traditionally been thought to be a "political" rather than a justiciable question. Compare *Luther v. Borden*, 49 U.S. (7 How.) 1 (1849), with *Baker v. Carr*, 369 U.S. 186 (1962). Hence, it is possible—though not obvious—that the federal courts would find that a state deprived its citizens of a republican form of government if it chose to fill major legislative and executive positions by appointment.

The Twenty-Sixth Amendment thus created two kinds of rights in citizens of the United States who are eighteen years or older. With respect to federal elections, which are mandatory, it gave them a noncomparative right (NonCR) to vote for the president, vice-president, and members of the U.S. Senate and House of Representatives, essentially as follows:

> NonCR: Every citizen of the United States who is eighteen years or older, and who is otherwise qualified, shall be entitled to vote for president, vice-president, and members of the U.S. Senate and House of Representatives.

With respect to state elections, many of which are discretionary, the amendment gave eighteen-year-olds an antidiscriminatory right (AntiDR) to vote for state offices *if and only if* a state allows persons who are over eighteen to vote for such offices:

> AntiDR: If a state allows persons who are more than eighteen years old to vote in an election, then it shall also allow persons eighteen years old to do so.

The foregoing example illustrates how the comparisons underlying prescriptive equality can differ from the comparisons underlying antidiscrimination rights. Consider the prescriptive equality which obtains among citizens eighteen years and older regarding the right to vote for president. To determine whether eighteen-year-olds and twenty-one-year-olds are equally entitled to vote for president, one first identifies a relevant prescription, or rule of conduct, by which to compare them (NonCR). Having identified NonCR as the relevant rule, one compares them by reference to NonCR, and thereby ascertains that they are identical in possessing the criteria NonCR requires as a qualification for voting for president. In contrast, to determine whether eighteen-year-olds and twenty-one-year-olds are equally entitled to vote in state elections, one *first* compares eighteen-year-olds with twenty-one-year-olds to see whether the former are descriptively disadvantaged vis-à-vis the latter with respect to voting for state officials. If they are not disadvantaged, the antidiscrimination rule (AntiDR) remains inapplicable. If eighteen-year-olds are disadvantaged vis-à-vis twenty-one-year-olds with respect to voting for state officials, AntiDR *then* requires the formulation of a new rule by which the two classes are treated identically in that respect—whether it is a rule by which both classes may vote for such state officials, or neither class may vote for such officials, or both may vote for some such officials and neither may vote for others.

To be sure, once an antidiscrimination right has been applied and a new rule formulated, the class of rightsholders and the reference class become prescriptively equal, and, being equal, they stand in a certain comparative relationship to one another. But the comparative relationship they *then* have is no different from the comparative relationship which exists among eighteen- and twenty-one-year-olds under NonCR and other noncomparative rights—the comparative relationship which obtains among persons who have been compared and found to be identical by reference to a relevant rule of conduct. The distinctive comparative relationship which antidiscrimination rights share with other comparative rights—which justifies calling them "comparative" rights—differs in both nature and timing from the comparison which underlies prescriptive equalities.

Equality Rights, Rights to Equality, Rights to Equal Treatment, and Principles of Equal Rights

Joseph Raz and others have made a further argument for the preferred status of antidiscrimination rights. The reason such rights can uniquely claim to be rights of "equality," they say, is that their "very *purpose*" is to treat people equally.[14] In contrast to other rights, for which equality is "an implication of their form," antidiscrimination rights "have equal treatment as their content."[15] They are "intrinsically egalitarian" because they "take equality as their focal concern or aim."[16] In Kenneth Simons's words, of all rights, antidiscrimination rights alone "*express* . . . a right to equal treatment."[17]

The argument has considerable force. Indeed, as we shall see, there is an important sense in which it is valid. The argument can

---

[14] These [antidiscrimination] principles can be regarded as egalitarian because it is their *purpose* to ensure equality within their sphere of application. It is (part of) the reason for each of their subjects' entitlement to his allotted share that giving him that share will make him equal in his entitlement to the others.

Raz, "Principles of Equality," p. 331 (emphasis added). See also Simons, "Equality as a Comparative Right," p. 397.

[15] Fullinwider, *The Reverse Discrimination Controversy*, p. 223. Cf. Raz, *The Morality of Freedom*, p. 230 (with respect to rights other than antidiscrimination rights, equality is "merely a by-product," rather than "a goal").

[16] Postema, "Liberty in Equality's Empire," pp. 66–67.

[17] Simons, "Equality as a Comparative Right," p. 403.

also be misleading, however, because in a sense *all* rights have the purpose of treating people equally. All rights, after all, are designed to replace former entitlements with new entitlements—and, hence, all rights are designed to replace former equalities with new equalities.[18] Consider the nature of the new right that the Twenty-Sixth Amendment created in persons eighteen years and older with respect to *federal* elections. Before the amendment was ratified, eighteen-year-olds and twenty-one-year-olds were prescriptively unequal because twenty-one-year-olds had a noncomparative right to vote for president and eighteen-year-olds had none. The legal situation then was:

> All citizens who are otherwise eligible shall have a right to vote for president if and only if they are at least twenty-one years old.

or, alternatively:

> All citizens who are otherwise eligible and who are at least twenty-one years old shall be equal in their right to vote for president.

It was decidedly the "purpose" of the Twenty-Sixth Amendment to abolish the foregoing equality and to create a new noncomparative rule by which eighteen- and twenty-one-year-olds would be equal. In that sense, it was the very "content" of the Twenty-Sixth Amendment that eighteen- and twenty-one-year-olds be treated equally, just as it is the content of every rule that certain people be treated equally.

What does it mean, then, to say that the "purpose" of antidiscrimination rights is to treat people equally, when the same can be said of all rights? In other words, in what way is it uniquely the purpose of antidiscrimination rights to treat people equally? There is one such way: while all rights aim toward equality, only antidiscrimination rights aim *solely* toward equality. All rights require, and (if faithfully applied) result in, relationships of equality. But, with respect to most rights, there is one, and only one, relationship of equality which suffices, viz., the relationship in which all rightsholders are allowed to do or receive that to which they are equally entitled. Antidiscrimination rights, in contrast, are satisfied by any relationship in which the rightsholding class and the

---

[18] As Joseph Raz observes, "When several people qualify under a principle, the principle generates equality of rights." Raz, *The Morality of Freedom*, p. 225. For a definition of 'rights', see note 1 above.

reference class are jointly classified—whether it is one in which both classes are jointly allowed something in common or one in which both are jointly denied something in common.[19] In that respect, antidiscrimination rights are indeed "equality rights" because they aim toward equality qua equality. They are "principles of equality," in Raz's words, because "equality is not only their result but is also their purpose. They are designed to achieve equality between their subjects with respect to their subject matter. . . . Equality is part of the ground on which such principles are based."[20]

To illustrate, consider again the difference between the two rights that the Twenty-Sixth Amendment created in persons eighteen years and older:

> NonCR: Every citizen of the United States who is eighteen years or older, and who is otherwise qualified, shall be entitled to vote for president, vice-president, and members of the U.S. Senate and House of Representatives.

> AntiDR: If a state allows persons who are more than eighteen years old to vote in an election, then it shall also allow persons eighteen years old to do so.

With respect to federal elections, NonCR clearly aims to bring about a new relationship of prescriptive equality, one in which eighteen- and twenty-one-year-olds are equal in their right to vote. Yet, it is not *any* equality between eighteen- and twenty-one-year-olds that suffices, but one particular equality, the equality which obtains among persons all of whom are entitled to vote. In contrast, AntiDR is satisfied with any relationship of equality among eighteen- and twenty-one-year-olds (whether it is one in which both groups are allowed to vote, neither is allowed to vote, or both are allowed to vote for some officials and neither is allowed to vote for others) because it has no substantive aims over and above achievement of equality between eighteen- and twenty-one-year-olds. In this sense, antidiscrimination rights have been appropri-

---

[19] [Antidiscrimination rights] reflect the view that it is wrong or unjust for some Fs to have G while others have not. Such inequalities must be remedied. This can be done in one of two ways: either by depriving those Fs who have G of it, or by giving G to all other Fs. So long as some Fs have the benefit while others are denied it the principle applies and the rest of the Fs have the right to G. If their right is satisfied the inequality is eliminated.

Raz, *The Morality of Freedom*, p. 226.
[20] Raz, *The Morality of Freedom*, p. 225.

ately called "equality rights," "rights to equality," "rights to equal treatment," and principles of "equal rights."[21]

Conclusion

Antidiscrimination rights, many people would say,[22] are among the most fundamental and valued principles for which just societies stand (though Raz shows that they do not suffice to constitute just societies).[23] Along with freedom of speech, freedom from torture, and a handful of other noncomparative rights, the principles dearest to many people are rights of nondiscrimination—rights not to be discriminated against on the basis of race, color, sex, religion, country of origin, and a growing list of other protected traits. These are principles of "enormous power," because they express widely shared ideals of common humanity.[24]

Antidiscrimination rights also stand in a special relationship to equality. Like all rights, antidiscrimination rights require and result in equality, in the sense that they prescribe relationships of identity among persons with particular traits. But, unlike other rights, antidiscrimination rights also uniquely aim toward equality because they have no goal beyond bringing about some relationship of identity between rightsholders and the persons on whose treatment their rights depend. Nevertheless, although antidiscrimination rights are uniquely concerned with equality, the converse is not true: equality is not uniquely concerned with antidiscrimination rights because equality is the broader of the two concepts. 'Equality' accurately describes antidiscrimination rights because it exhausts all of what antidiscrimination rights aim toward, which is why they are called *"equality* rights." But the converse is false: 'antidiscrimination rights' does not accurately describe prescriptive equality because, not encompassing

[21] Simons, "Equality as a Comparative Right," p. 389 (referring to antidiscrimination rights as "equality rights" and "rights to equal treatment"); Raz, *The Morality of Freedom*, p. 217 (referring to "principles of equality"); Schneider, "The Dialectic of Rights and Politics," pp. 634–42 (referring to women's antidiscrimination rights as "rights to equality," "equality rights," and "equal rights").

[22] See generally Karst, "Why Equality Matters," pp. 272, 279 (referring to antidiscrimination rights as among the "most deeply held" and "vital substantive values in American life").

[23] Raz, *The Morality of Freedom*, pp. 234–35. Raz goes further and argues that antidiscrimination rights are not only not sufficient, they are not necessary ingredients of a just society. See Raz, *The Morality of Freedom*, pp. 235–44.

[24] Simons, "Equality as a Comparative Right," pp. 481–82 (suggesting a variety of reasons why antidiscrimination rights have such "enormous power").

noncomparative rights, it does not exhaust all of the rights which result in prescriptive equality.

Now, it has been suggested that, just as we commonly use the term 'equality rights' to refer exclusively to antidiscrimination rights, we ought to use 'equality' in law and morals to refer exclusively to the equalities that antidiscrimination rights produce.[25] Yet that would raise several difficulties. For one thing, we are firmly accustomed to using 'equality' to refer to the consequences of noncomparative principles. Thus, we commonly invoke the language of equality to express beliefs in noncomparative principles of justice—such as the right of all persons to live under a rule of law,[26] the right of all persons to a basic standard of living,[27] the right of all persons to be free from torture and inhumane punishments,[28] and the right of all persons to be treated with concern and respect.[29] Furthermore, the subjects of noncomparative rights are "naturally"[30] regarded as being equal for the same reason that antidiscrimination rights are appropriately regarded as equality rights: because the relationship toward which the antidiscrimination rights *aim* is the very relationship that the subjects of noncomparative rights already *possess*—a relationship of identity among

[25] Simons makes this argument, contending that 'prescriptive equality' should be understood as referring only to the operation of antidiscrimination rights. See Simons, "Equality as a Comparative Right," pp. 403–8.

[26] See Chapter 3, pp. 74–79.

[27] See, e.g., Michelman, "The Supreme Court 1968 Term," pp. 12–13, 18; Nagel, "The Meaning of Equality," p. 26 ("equality" can be defined as "the possession of basic rights plus the equal apportionment of certain kinds of benefits that are also regarded as basic").

[28] [Any] just constitution ought to contain an explicit or implicit prohibition against the state's use of torture to obtain criminal confessions. Suppose a state nevertheless tortures an individual. We can say, then, that the right not to be tortured is being violated. But we can also say something else: we can say that the victim is not being treated as an equal in that he is not being treated as immune from torture, as all individuals ought to be treated! Because the human right against being tortured is universal in scope, a constitutional expression of the right must apply equally to each individual within the state's jurisdiction. . . . The violation of equality in the case of the tortured individual lies not in the fact that he is tortured when others are not, but in the fact, simply, that he is tortured. The state does not relieve its violation of equality in this case by proceeding to torture every criminal suspect; it only multiplies the violation.

Fullinwider, *The Reverse Discrimination Controversy*, p. 222. See also Feinberg, *Social Philosophy*, pp. 88–94; Vlastos, "Justice and Equality," pp. 45–53.

[29] For the proposition that the right of "equal respect and concern" should be understood as a noncomparative right rather than an antidiscrimination right, see Chapter 3, note 22, and Chapter 4, notes 6 and 10.

[30] Raz, *The Morality of Freedom*, p. 228.

persons by reference to prevailing rules of conduct. Finally, it would be anomalous to confine 'equality' in law and morals to identities based on antidiscrimination rights alone because 'equality' outside law and morals includes identities based on *all*, not *some*, relevant standards of comparison.

To be sure, if it were useful to do so, one could endeavor to stipulate that 'equality' be used solely in reference to antidiscrimination rights. Raz suggests a reason for doing so. It creates "confusion,"[31] he says, to use the term 'equality' in connection with comparative and noncomparative rights alike because it raises an ambiguity as to which class of rights one has in mind. Moreover, as between the two classes of rights, antidiscrimination rights have a better claim on the language of equality, he says, because other rights can be expressed without any reference to 'equality'—implying that antidiscrimination rights *cannot* be so expressed. To illustrate the superfluousness of 'equality' in connection with noncomparative rights, Raz uses what Ronald Dworkin refers to as "the right to equal concern and respect."[32] Proceeding on the assumption that Dworkin's right to equal concern and respect is a noncomparative right of all persons to be treated as "moral subjects," Raz states that the right "can be expressed with equal ease without invoking equality."[33]

Raz is right that references to "equality" are ambiguous, and he is right that noncomparative rights can be expressed without invoking the language of equality. However, if he meant to suggest that antidiscrimination rights cannot be expressed without invoking 'equality',[34] he is wrong. Antidiscrimination rights can take

---

[31] Raz, *The Morality of Freedom*, p. 228.

[32] For discussion of the right to equal concern and respect, and of whether it is indeed a comparative or noncomparative principle, see Chapter 3, notes 21–22, and Chapter 4, note 10.

[33] It was mentioned above [p. 220] that principles of equal respect and concern . . . often amount to little more than an assertion that all human beings are moral subjects, to an assertion of humanism. Such principles can be expressed with equal ease without invoking equality.

Raz, *The Morality of Freedom*, p. 228. See also p. 221: "many principles commonly thought of as egalitarian (e.g. everyone has a right to free medicine or to education) are normally stated using no such expressions [of 'equality'] at all."

[34] Raz may not, in fact, mean to imply that antidiscrimination rights can only be expressed in the language of equality. Indeed, it is significant that the principles Raz advances as a generic formulation of antidiscrimination rights—i.e., what he calls "(6)-type principles"—make no use of 'equality'. See Raz, *The Morality of Freedom*, p. 225 n. 1 and p. 226. Raz's "(6)-type principles" are what Simons calls "universal comparative rights." See note 35 below.

one of two forms, neither of which makes any reference to 'equality':

F_1: If persons in class X receive benefit B, then persons in class Y shall also receive benefit B.

or

F_2: If any persons in class X receive benefit B, then all persons in class X shall receive benefit B.[35]

Accordingly, we can fully address antidiscrimination rights without mentioning equality, simply by specifying *who* the X's are, *who* the Y's are, and *what* the benefits B are. Thus, to take a paradigmatic example of an antidiscrimination right, the Nineteenth Amendment to the U.S. Constitution states that the right to vote "shall not be denied . . . on account of sex," without further reference to "equality." The same is true of the antidiscrimination principles of the Fourteenth Amendment: whatever one's conception of the Fourteenth Amendment provisions regarding race, one can express them without reference to 'equality'—whether one understands those provisions to mean that no person, or no member of a historically disfavored minority, or no black person, shall be disadvantaged (or disadvantaged in certain respects, or stigmatized) on the basis of race, absent, perhaps, reasons of a certain kind.

Of course, we can also talk about such antidiscrimination rights in the language of equality, by using 'equality' to describe the relationships toward which they aim. Thus, we can talk about the Nineteenth Amendment as an "equality right," or as a right of women to "equality" with men, or as a right of women to be treated "equally" with men. In each case, the language of equality performs the same function as rights in the form of F_1. It does so by referring to the relationships of identity which the Nineteenth Amendment implicitly creates among men and women with respect to voting. Significantly, the language of equality performs this function for antidiscrimination rights, not by *departing* from its general meaning in law and morals, but by affirming it.

[35] Simons calls antidiscrimination rights of this second form "universal" comparative rights. See Simons, "Equality as a Comparative Right," pp. 452–56, esp. n. 155. I am indebted to him for his formulation of the difference between the two.

SEVEN

PER-CAPITA DISTRIBUTIONS

In a well-known passage in *Freedom and Reason*, R. M. Hare asks us to imagine three people who are dividing a bar of chocolate among themselves:

> Suppose that three people are dividing a bar of chocolate between them, and suppose that they all have an equal liking for chocolate. And let us suppose that no other considerations such as age, sex, ownership of the chocolate, etc., are thought to be relevant. It seems to us obvious that the just way to divide the chocolate is equally. And the principle of universalizability gives us the logic of this conclusion. For if it be maintained that one of the three ought to have more than an equal share, there must be something about his case to make this difference—for otherwise we are making different moral judgments about similar cases. But there is *ex hypothesi* no relevant difference, and so the conclusion follows.[1]

Hare's parable contains two suggestions to which we shall return in Chapters 8 and 9, namely, that "similar" cases should be treated similarly and that people presumptively should be treated equally in the absence of reasons for treating them differently. In the meantime, Hare's parable interests us for its unstated assumption about what it means to divide chocolate "equally." Hare means the division of chocolate to be determinate because an inconclusive division would not serve his purpose. Yet, assuming such information to be irrelevant, he does not supply enough information about the ages, needs, entitlements, deserts, labors, etc., of the three people to enable one to divide the chocolate in accord with such considerations. It follows, therefore, that in his use of the word 'equally', Hare does not mean "to each according

[1] Hare, *Freedom and Reason*, p. 118.

to his age" (or "to each according to his needs," etc.), but "to each *per capita*."[2]

Hare is not alone in equating "equal" distributions with per-capita distributions. The same assumption seems to underlie the debate, in which Ronald Dworkin has played a prominent role, as to whether distributive equality means:

Equality of resources: A one-time-only distribution of material resources to people, per capita, leaving it to each person to consume or invest his per-capita share as he wishes in free and informed auctions.

or

Equal outcomes: A continuing process of distribution and redistribution designed to ensure that the per-capita wealth of persons remains as equal as possible throughout their lives, regardless of how much one person's total receipts may differ from another's.

or

Equality of welfare: A distribution of resources designed to ensure that each person ends up with a per-capita share of all available welfare, regardless of how much a needy person's allocation may exceed a nonneedy person's allocation.[3]

These three distributions (and others one could mention) differ dramatically in substance. What they have in common, however, and what seems to underlie the assumption that they are paradigmatic formulas of equality, is that all are based on per-capita standards of measure.

Among recent commentators, none states this assumption more explicitly than Douglas Rae. In the introductory chapter of *Equali-*

---

[2] Since Hare also specifies that the three people all "have an equal liking for chocolate," it is possible that by 'equally' he means "to each according to his liking." However, since in this case "to each according to his liking" coincides with a per-capita distribution, Hare must mean 'equally' in this case to exclude at least any division by which one person receives more chocolate than another.

[3] Although these juxtaposed models are Ronald Dworkin's (see Dworkin, *Law's Empire*, pp. 297–301 [discussing five distinct "conceptions" of equality]), one finds comparable juxtapositions elsewhere. See Nielsen, *Equality and Liberty*, pp. 46–60. For a more complete discussion of Dworkin's two models, "equality of welfare" and "equality of resources," see Dworkin, "What Is Equality?" For a critique of Dworkin's conception of "equality of welfare" and an argument in favor of a revised version of equality of welfare, see Cohen, "On the Currency of Egalitarian Justice."

ties, Rae asks readers to engage in a thought-experiment—to try to identify the features a society must possess if distributive "equality" is to have, not several complex applications, but "one straightforward meaning." For equality to have such a meaning, he says, a society would have to differ greatly from our own: in such a society (1) all members would have to be completely isolated from other societies and atomistic among themselves, having no relations with anyone that they do not also have with everyone; (2) all things of value would have to be distributed once and for all time; (3) all things of value would have to be divided into identical parts, one per member, without diminishing the total value of each thing; (4) all people would have to be alike in their needs and tastes; and (5) all thinking would have to be dichotomous, so that distributions are either equal or unequal but never more equal or less equal.[4] In such a society, equality becomes a "simple and unproblematic notion," one that "can be smoothly translated into policy." It becomes simple because, in such a society, equality "can mean" only one thing: "Given an isolated and indivisible society, once-and-for-all allocation, interchangeable clones, dichotomous thinking, and only finely divisible goods, equality means just one thing: *creating* n *identical lots of each good available to the society and bestowing one lot of each good on each member of society.*"[5]

Rae's thought-experiment is revealing because he eliminates all grounds for distinguishing among the three distributive formulas we considered above. In his admittedly "bizarre"[6] society, the formulas of "equality of resources," "equal outcomes," and "equality of welfare" would all yield the same result—a generic, per-capita distribution possessing the advantages of all three formulas without any of their disadvantages. Yet, more interesting still, by distilling distributions into a single, generic distribution, he makes explicit what he believes to be the essential meaning of distributive equality. He implicitly rejects other equality options that appear to be available in his bizarre society, such as what Ronald Dworkin calls the "libertarian conception of equality,"[7] that of simply leaving all members of society with such property as they already lawfully possess, and what Christine Swanton calls "patterned conceptions,"[8] which distribute social goods equally to all in accord

[4] Rae, *Equalities*, pp. 4–6.
[5] Rae, *Equalities*, p. 7 (original emphasis).
[6] Rae, *Equalities*, p. 12.
[7] Dworkin, *Law's Empire*, p. 297.
[8] Swanton, "On the 'Essential Contestedness' of Political Concepts," p. 817; Swanton, "Is the Difference Principle a Principle of Justice?" p. 419.

with their deserts. Instead, Rae elects as the paradigm of equality a distribution in which all available social goods are divided by the number of persons in society (*n*) and distributed per capita.

It is possible that Rae elects a per-capita distribution not because that is what he thinks 'equality' means, but because in his imaginary society other distributions are *impossible*. Thus, when he defines members of his society as being "interchangeable clones," perhaps he means that they are alike not only in their "needs, tastes, and vulnerabilities" but also in age, size, sex, strength, skill, beauty, labor, effort, accomplishment, and all other possible bases of merit.[9] And, in saying that all things of value in his society are allocated "once and for all time," perhaps he means that, until then, members of society possess nothing of their own. If so, it is true that his society leaves no room for libertarian or patterned conceptions of equality. Yet, notice that this is true only because Rae systematically designs his society so as to exclude such conceptions. He could easily have designed it otherwise—for example, by stipulating that members of the society were alike in all ways *except one*, say, in their "needs." In that event, in lieu of distributing social goods per capita, one could distribute social goods equally to all members of the society in accord with those needs.

Now, it might be argued that in order to delineate a society in which equality has only "one straightforward meaning," Rae was obliged to stipulate that its members possess no distinguishing features because, if the members of a society possess any distinguishing features (say, needs), the society would lend itself to at least two distributive equalities: (1) a per-capita distribution and (2) a distribution based on need. But that argument overlooks the fact that Rae's society also allows for two equalities, namely, a per-capita distribution and a distribution by lot—the two distributions that Plato disparagingly described as "numerical equality."[10] Lotteries treat everyone equally because everyone has an equal chance to win; yet they do not result in per-capita distribution.[11]

---

[9] Compare Rae, *Equalities*, p. 6 (stipulating that all members of the society "are completely alike so far as personal needs, tastes, or vulnerabilities may affect the allocation of values"), with p. 7 (stating that all members of the society are "interchangeable clones") and p. 14 (stating that "there are no relevant differences among persons").

[10] See *Plato*, Laws VI.757.

[11] See Greely, "The Equality of Allocation by Lot," p. 113; Greenawalt, "How Empty Is the Idea of Equality?" pp. 1171–72; Simons, "Equality as a Comparative Right," p. 459 n. 166.

By disregarding the "equality" of distribution by lot, Rae implies that, *conceptually*, the only genuine equality is per-capita equality.

We have dwelt upon Rae's imaginary society as an introduction to the central question of this chapter: What are the grounds for believing that per-capita distributions are paradigmatic equalities? We shall proceed by first reviewing Aristotle's rival conception to the per-capita view, and then discussing two possible arguments in favor of the per-capita view.

Aristotle's Alternative Conception

The ancients were familiar with the idea that the only genuine distributive equality is one in which people are treated as possessing no distinguishing traits (i.e., the equality that results from per-capita distributions or distributions by lot). Plato referred to such equalities as equality "of number," contrasting it unfavorably with what he called "proportionat[e]" and "geometric" equality.[12] As we have seen, it was Aristotle who most thoroughly expounded "proportional equality" as an alternative conception—a conception sufficiently broad to encompass all just distributions, including all arguably just per-capita distributions.[13]

Aristotle's argument can be reduced to three essential steps:

(1) All instances of distributive justice necessarily involve relations between at least two persons (P_1 and P_2) and two respective distributions (D_1 and D_2), including instances in which one person, P_1, gets everything and the other, P_2, receives a distribution, D_2, containing nothing.

[12] See Plato, *Laws* VI.757. For an earlier statement to the same effect, see Isocrates, *Areopagiticus* 20–23 (trans. Norlin):

> But what contributed most to their good government of the state [in the time of Solon] was that of the two recognized kinds of equality—that which makes the same award to all alike and that which gives to each man his due—they did not fail to grasp which was the more serviceable.

Aristotle, as we have seen, also distinguished between "proportional" equality and "numerical" equality. See Aristotle, *Politics* V.1301b26–35. See also Aristotle, *Eudemian Ethics* VII.1241b30–40 (trans. Solomon):

> But since equality is either numerical or proportional, there will be various species of justice, friendship, and partnership; on numerical equality rests the commonwealth, and the friendship of comrades—both being measured by the same standard, on proportional the aristocratic (which is best), and the royal.

[13] For an analysis of Aristotle's conception of proportional equality, see Chapter 2, pp. 52–57, esp. notes 23 and 26.

(2) Distributions of D_1 to P_1, and D_2 to P_2, can be stated in the form of the ratios $D_1{:}P_1$ and $D_2{:}P_2$.

(3) The ratio $D_1{:}P_1$ is equal to the ratio $D_2{:}P_2$ when D_1 stands in the same proportion to D_2 as the "merits" of P_1 stand to the "merits" of P_2.[14]

Aristotle's formula of proportional equality is broad enough to encompass all arguably just distributions, including those based on per-capita shares. It can apply to cases in which goods are distributed to people *proportionately to the degree* to which they possess certain morally relevant traits, and to cases in which goods are distributed to people *proportionately to whether or not* they possess certain morally relevant traits. As Felix Oppenheim observes, "Numerical equality is but a special case of proportional equality."[15]

Consider, for example, the case of

Tornado Fever

A devastating tornado moves quixotically through a town, destroying some homes, partially destroying others, and sparing a lucky few. The path of the tornado also passes through a biological research station, releasing concentrated strains of deadly Venezuelan equine encephalitis, a disease which attacks humans and animals alike.

The town faces two immediate decisions: first, how to distribute its disaster relief funds to victims of the tornado; and, second, how to distribute limited supplies of encephalitis vaccine among the human and animal inhabitants of the town. After a meeting, at which it is decided that every inhabitant older than seventeen years should be allowed to vote, the town resolves as follows:

—Disaster relief funds should be distributed to inhabitants to the extent that their houses have been damaged by the tornado.

—Vaccinations should be reserved for persons, rather than

---

[14] For a discussion of what Aristotle means by 'merit', see Chapter 2, note 25.

[15] Oppenheim, "Egalitarianism as a Descriptive Concept," p. 146. See also Browne, "Nonegalitarian Justice," p. 52 ("It must be insisted that the relational attribute of equality . . . is just one instance of the relational attribute of proportionality"); Miller, *Social Justice*, p. 21 ("The principle of proportion allows us to deal not only with cases in which 'dues' are identical, but with cases in which 'dues' are different, and yet can be expressed as equalities of the same attribute"). But see also Zaitchik, "On Deserving to Deserve," pp. 384–85 (assuming that Aristotle's formula of proportional equality excludes per-capita distributions).

animals, and be made available to all persons in recommended doses of 3 cc. of vaccine per inhabitant.

The town in "Tornado Fever" makes altogether three distributive decisions: (1) to distribute voting power; (2) to distribute disaster relief; and (3) to distribute scarce vaccine. Each decision, if faithfully executed, produces distributions that are proportionate to what their recipients are deemed to "merit," and hence the decisions are normatively equal. Consider the decision to distribute disaster relief. Assume that three adult inhabitants of the town, A, B, and C, have suffered tornado losses of $90,000, $30,000, and $0, respectively, and that the town has sufficient resources to pay for 33 percent of all the damages its inhabitants have suffered. Measured by the degree to which they "merit" relief, inhabitants A, B, and C stand to one another in the normative ratio of 3:1:0, because A has three times as many measurable "units" of merit as B, and C has no units at all. To make normatively equal distributions to A, B, and C, the town must divide the available $40,000 among A, B, and C in sums of $30,000, $10,000, and $0, respectively, because no other sums totaling $40,000 possess the same normative ratio to one another that their recipients, A, B, and C, possess to one another.

The same formula governs the distributions of vaccine and voting power. The difference is that, instead of possessing the normative ratio of 3:1:0, A, B, and C now stand vis-à-vis one another in the normative ratio of 1:1:1 because, regardless of other differences among them, the town has decided that each possesses as much "merit" as the others as regards vaccine and voting power. The town's decision regarding vaccine appears to be the kind of decision Gregory Vlastos discusses in "Justice and Equality."[16] Vlastos argues that "personhood" is a characteristic that cannot be graded because it is not something that comes in quantities of more or less; yet, personhood is a measure of "merit" for the distribution of certain social goods because there are certain goods that all humans—and solely humans—ought to receive solely by virtue of being persons. The town's decision to distribute vaccine to all persons (and only to persons) who inhabit the town appears to be based on the judgment that life-saving medication is something deserved solely by virtue of the recipient's being human.

In contrast, the distribution of voting power, though also per capita, differs from that of vaccine in two respects. First, it is more

[16] Vlastos, "Justice and Equality," pp. 40–53.

"exclusive"[17] than the distribution of vaccine because, instead of extending to all inhabitants of the town, it is confined to inhabitants who are over seventeen years old. Second, rather than being based on an ungradable characteristic that all persons inherently possess, it is based on a gradable characteristic that all people do not possess: the condition of being older than seventeen years. Despite those differences, A, B, and C, being adults, still stand in the normative ratio of 1:1:1 regarding voting power because the town has decided that the *mere existence* of the trait of being older than seventeen years, as opposed to *the degree* to which one is older than seventeen, is the proper measure of merit for allocating votes.[18] It follows that, in order to make normatively equal distributions of vaccine and votes among A, B, and C, the town must divide both the vaccine and votes into shares, which possess the same ratio of 1:1:1, respectively, which A, B, and C possess vis-à-vis one another—that is, the vaccine and votes must be divided into per-capita shares.

Aristotle's formula of proportional equality, then, is a generic conception of distributive equality because it subsumes all distributions that we regard as equal, whether they are based on per-capita shares or not. Yet, despite its conceptual power, Aristotle's formula has not dispelled the presumption that the paradigm of distributive equality is per-capita distribution. We now turn to possible reasons for the persistence of that presumption.

Per-capita Distributions:
Equal without Also Being Unequal?

The presumption that per-capita distributions are paradigmatic may rest on the belief that per-capita distributions are "more" equal than others in that per-capita shares are equal without in any way being unequal by the relevant standard. Consider, for example, the distributions in "Tornado Fever." Prescriptively, the sums of money received by the damage victims A, B, and C are equal because, measured by the relevant prescription, each sum is proportional to the damage suffered by its recipient. Yet, descrip-

---

[17] Douglas Rae uses the term "exclusive" to describe an equality that is confined to a smaller class of beneficiaries than one which is "inclusive." Rae, *Equalities*, pp. 22–27, 43.

[18] See Lukes, *Individualism*, p. 126 (arguing that the mere *existence* of "rationality," rather than the *degree* to which rationality exists, is the relevant ground for distributing certain social goods).

tively, the three sums are also *unequal*, because victim A receives $30,000, while victim B receives only $10,000. In contrast, it might be argued, the distributions of 3 cc. of vaccine each to A, B, and C are both prescriptively equal *and* descriptively equal because they are descriptively identical in amount or number.

This argument is misleading. Per-capita shares are indeed descriptively identical in amount or number because that is how they are defined, but they are not descriptively identical in all respects by per-capita standards, because *no* two distinct shares are descriptively identical in all relevant respects.[19] In the matter of the vaccine, for example, the doses of 3 cc. each for victims A, B, and C are identical in amount or number because, being per-capita shares, they are indistinguishable by reference to the relevant standard for measuring quantity (cubic centimeters).[20] Yet they are not identical in all respects by per-capita standards because, first, A's per-capita dose necessarily differs from B's per-capita dose by reference to the features that render it *A*'s dose as opposed to *B*'s, and, second, A's dose necessarily differs from B's dose by reference to the formula according to which the per-capita doses are distributed, whether the distribution is on a first-come-first-served basis, by place of residence, by lottery, by official discretion, or according to some other formula.

To be sure, there are some goods—those we have referred to as "joint" as opposed to "individualized"[21]—that can be made available to people on an undivided and nonexclusive basis. Examples are the "good" of a clean environment and the "right" of free speech. A town does not distribute a clean environment to its residents (if 'distribute' is even the right word) by dividing the clean environment by the number, n, of its residents and granting each resident an exclusive respective share. It grants the whole of a

---

[19] See Chapter 1, pp. 24–27.

[20] To be sure, the fact that the two doses of vaccine are identical in amount or number by a relevant standard of measurement of volume (e.g., cubic centimeters) does not mean that they are identical in amount or number by all conceivable standards for measuring volume. No two things are likely to be identical by the finest possible standards for measuring objects in any respect, but for purposes of "equality" it is not necessary that they be identical by the finest possible standards of measure. It suffices that they are identical by the *relevant* standard of measure. See Chapter 1, pp.32 –37.

It is true that in actuality some vaccines are administered to people in accord with their body weight, so that children receive smaller doses than adults. In that event, the vaccine cannot be said to be distributed per capita, but rather in accord with need.

[21] See Chapter 3, pp. 83–84.

clean environment to every one of its inhabitants for the nonexclusive enjoyment of each. Accordingly, a joint good can be distributed to citizens A and B without distinction, apart from the inherent distinction between A's relationship to the good and B's relationship to it.

In contrast to goods that are distributed jointly, per-capita shares are equal *and* unequal by the relevant standard—equal as measured by amount or number, unequal as measured by the implicit criteria that necessarily distinguish one distributed per-capita share from another. Per-capita shares are "equal without being unequal" only in the obvious sense that, measured by the relevant standard of quantity, the quantity any one person receives is identical to the quantity every other person receives.

Per-capita Distributions: The Analogy with Mathematics

It might be argued that per-capita distributions are paradigmatically "equal" because they correspond to "equality" in mathematics. As a syllogism, the argument is as follows:

Major premise: Mathematical equality is paradigmatic.

Minor premise: Among distributions, only the equality of per-capita distributions corresponds to equality in mathematics.

Conclusion: Among distributions, only the equality of per-capita distributions is paradigmatic.

Let us begin with the minor premise. On the one hand, there is a sense in which the minor premise is clearly false, for, as Aristotle showed, *all* proportional equalities, including non-per-capita equalities, are equal in the same way that mathematical entities are. All distributions, including non-per-capita distributions, can be expressed as ratios between two or more distributive shares, D_1 and D_2, and two or more persons, P_1 and P_2. By the same token, all distributive equalities, including non-per-capita equalities, can be expressed as mathematical equalities in which the mathematical proportion that underlies the ratio $D_1:D_2$ corresponds to the mathematical proportion underlying the ratio $P_1:P_2$. The difference between the ratios expressing per-capita and non-per-capita equalities is not that the former are mathematically equal and the latter are not but that their underlying proportions are different. Per-capita distributions are mathematically equal in the way that $3:3 =$

1:1, while non-per-capita distributions are mathematically equal in the way that $30{,}000{:}10{,}000 = 90{,}000{:}30{,}000$.

On the other hand, there is a sense in which the minor premise is also true, for per-capita distributions are numerically equal in a way that proportional equalities are not. In per-capita distributions, all recipients are numerically equal to one another and all shares are numerically equal to one another.[22] Consider, again, the numerical relationships involved in the distributions of damage relief and vaccine in "Tornado Fever." Although the town treated inhabitants A, B, and C equally in the sense of giving each of them a sum of money proportionate to his needs, it did not regard their needs as numerically equal, and it did not grant them numerically equal sums of money. Rather, it calculated their needs as being $90,000, $30,000, and $0, respectively, and it granted them sums of money in the respective amounts of $30,000, $10,000, and $0. In contrast, in distributing vaccine the town not only treated A, B, and C proportionately but also treated them as numerical equals— both in counting each of them as "one" in terms of need and in giving them numerically equal doses of vaccine.

To the extent that the minor premise is true, then, the truth of the syllogism depends on the truth of the major premise, "Mathematical equality is paradigmatic." Yet that, in turn, raises a preliminary question: what does it mean to say that mathematical equality is "paradigmatic"? One possibility is that mathematical equalities are regarded as paradigmatic because of the *complete* identity which obtains among entities that are equal in mathematics. For, as we have seen, mathematical entities, when equal, are identical not only by the relevant standard of comparison, but in all measurable respects. However, as we have also seen, being unique to mathematical equalities, the foregoing feature cannot serve as a paradigm for other equalities because other equalities do not possess it: descriptive and prescriptive equalities—including those of per-capita distributions—are relationships among people or things that, though identical by relevant standards of

---

[22] In that respect, per capita distributions are even more numerically equal than Plato's distributions by lot. Distributions by lot treat each person within the lottery as counting for "one," in the sense that each person has an equal chance to win the lottery. Presumably that is why Plato regarded distributions by lot as examples of equality "of number" as opposed to "proportionat[e]" or "geometric" equalities. See Plato, *Laws* VI.757; Plato, *Gorgias* 508. On the other hand, distributions by lot do not divide the distributed bounty into numerically equal shares but operate on a winner-take-all basis.

comparison, inevitably differ by other standards of comparison. Consequently, if mathematical equalities are regarded as paradigmatic for the reason given, then neither per-capita equalities nor any other descriptive or prescriptive equalities among persons could ever be regarded as genuine.

Another possibility is that mathematical equalities are regarded as paradigmatic because the standard of comparison on which they are based—"number"—is considered to be paradigmatic of all equalities. It is true that mathematical equalities are based on number.[23] It may also be true that number is so frequently a part of descriptive and prescriptive standards of measurement that equality comes to be associated with numerical identity.[24] Nevertheless, equalities are not always based on number. For one thing, as we have seen, equalities are often based, not on measures of "more or less," but on binary measures of "either/or."[25] Moreover, some measures of "more or less" are based on measurements other than number. Consider, again, the hand-held balance scale used in "A Moroccan Market" in Chapter 1. A balance scale is a device for determining how much heavier (if at all) one object is than another. A balance scale can be used to determine how much an unknown object weighs in numbers (of ounces, grams, etc.) if known quantities of weight are placed in one pan of the scale and the unknown object in the other. Without known quantities of weight, however, a balance scale cannot determine how much an object weighs in numbers; it can only reveal how much more (if at all) one object weighs than another by how much (if at all) one pan of the scale superficially displaces the other pan. Thus, a balance scale measures whether objects weigh "more or less," yet it is not based on number.

A third possibility is that mathematical equality is regarded as

[23] For the argument that mathematical equalities are identical with respect to "integers," see Russell, *Principles of Mathematics*, p. 158.

[24] Pure numbers, as abstractions, may constitute the relevant standard of comparison only in mathematics. But numbers are often used elsewhere as a metric for other standards of measurement, both descriptive and prescriptive, such as standards for measuring length, speed, weight, time, wealth, etc. Cf. Aristotle, *Nicomachean Ethics* V.3.1131a22–b14 ("So justice is a sort of proportion; for proportion is a property not only of number as composed of abstract units, but of number in general"; trans. Thomson).

Perhaps that is why "equality" is sometimes defined as numerical identity. See *Webster's Third New International Dictionary*, p. 766 ("equal" means, *inter alia*, "identical in mathematical value").

[25] See the "Ping-Pong Balls" example in Chapter 1, and Chapter 3 at note 11.

paradigmatic on *normative* grounds, that is, on the grounds that per-capita distributions are either normatively more important or more common (or both) than other distributions. Per-capita distributions are both common and important. Perhaps the best example is the widely shared belief that all human beings, solely by virtue of possessing features that render them human, are entitled to a certain respect and concern, a belief succinctly expressed in Christian tones by G. K. Chesterton: "All men are equal in the sense that all pennies are equal. Some men are bright or dull, just as some pennies are bright or dull, but all have, in the end, an equal value: for all pennies are stamped with the image of the king, just as all men bear the image of the King of kings."[26]

The real question, however, is not whether per-capita distributions are common or important, normatively, nor even whether they are *more* common or important than other distributions. The question is whether distributions based on *whether* people possess relevant traits are normatively so much more important or more common than distributions based on *the degree to which* they possess relevant traits that only the former can constitute formulas of equal treatment. If circumstances exist under which the Marxist formula "To each according to his needs,"[27] or the more recent "To each according to his efforts,"[28] can properly be regarded as formulas of equality, as many assume they can,[29] the answer must be no.

[26] G. K. Chesterton, quoted in Thomson, *Equality*, pp. 3–4.

[27] The formula "to each according to his needs" comes from Karl Marx's "Critique of the Gotha Programme," pp. 5–7. On the question whether Marx and Engels were egalitarians, see Nielsen, "On Marx Not Being an Egalitarian."

[28] See Milne, "Desert, Effort, and Equality"; Zaitchik, "On Deserving to Deserve." For the argument that justice ought to reward voluntary effort, rather than ability, see Sidgwick, *The Principles of Political Economy*, pp. 505–6, 531.

[29] For the view that the Marxist formula "to each according to his needs" is fundamentally egalitarian, see Rae, *Equalities*, p. 101 ("And to reject need as a basis of person-regarding equality would turn equality into a monstrous parody of itself. It *is* egalitarian to provide medical services to the sick and not to the well"); Spielberg, "A Defense of Human Equality," p. 101; Vlastos, "Justice and Equality," p. 40 (referring to distribution according to need as "the most perfect form of equal distribution"). For another defense of need-based distributions as egalitarian, see Tawney, *Equality*, pp. 49–50:

[E]quality of provision is not identity of provision. It is to be achieved not by treating different needs in the same way, but by devoting equal care to ensuring that they are met in the different ways most appropriate to them, as is done by a doctor who prescribes different regimens for different constitutions, or a teacher who develops different types of intelligence by different curricula. The more anxiously, indeed, a society endeavours to secure equality of consideration for all its members, the greater will be the differentiation of treatment

It is true that per-capita distributions are numerically equal in ways that other distributions are not. In fact, per-capita distributions are the only ones in which all distributive shares are numerically equal and all recipients are numerically equal (though shares and recipients need not be numerically equal to each other). The point is that numerical identity of that kind is the *only* feature that distinguishes per-capita distributions from other formulas of distributive justice. By itself, numerical identity of that kind does not give per-capita distributions either a normative claim or an exclusive analytic claim on the language of equality.

Conclusion

In reviewing Douglas Rae's coauthored book *Equalities*, Brian Barry faults the authors for assuming that all uses of the word 'equality' are "egalitarian," and for failing to realize that some formulas of equality are really formulas for generating "inequality." His comments warrant quotation in full:

> By failing to notice that not all uses of the word "equality" are egalitarian, the authors of *Equalities* manage to produce the illusion that public policies are normally argued about in terms of different conceptions of equality. Thus, . . . the word "equal" occurs in the formula "equal treatment for equals." But if what makes people equal for the purpose of the formula is birth or merit, then this is a formula for generating inequality. The authors admit that this notion of proportional equality "is not normally conceived of as egalitarianism," but fail to follow up this correct observation by asking the obvious question: which, out of all possible uses of the word "equal," are egalitarian?

---

which, when once their common human needs have been met, it accords to the special needs of different groups and individuals among them.

See also Nielsen, *Equality and Liberty*, p. 6:

People must all be treated as moral persons of equal worth; in that way they must be treated as equals. But, anti-egalitarians are quick to remind us, that does not mean that we must or even should treat them equally and this is surely right, *if* it means . . . to treat them identically. A child and a very old and ill person should not be treated the same. But no egalitarian thinks that they should.

For the view that "to each according to his efforts" is egalitarian, see Milne, "Desert, Effort, and Equality." For a discussion of the justice of basing distributions on need or desert, see Miller, *Social Justice*, pp. 209–44.

159

If they had done this, their view of political debate as setting one conception of equality against another would have
disappeared. Instead, they would have seen that the *word*
"equality" crops up in a lot of political contexts, but that only
some of the uses are egalitarian. . . .

Egalitarianism is . . . a rather simple idea. It says that there
is something wrong with a society in which there are systematic differences in the quality of housing, schooling, medical
care, diet, physical security, access to legal protection, and
other almost universally desired things. . . . The point is that
all of these [egalitarians] converge on a call for more equality,
and it is a perfectly comprehensible demand without any further qualification.[30]

Barry's criticism artfully plays on two revealing ambiguities in
the language of equality. First, in the face of a natural assumption
that 'egalitarian' broadly refers to *any* formula of social and political equality, he argues that 'egalitarian' has a narrower meaning
politically and refers only to *some* formulas for social and political
equality. "Equality," he says, "crops up in a lot of political contexts, but . . . only some of the uses are egalitarian." Second, and
even more significantly, he argues that 'equality' itself has two
meanings—a broad one, which extends beyond "egalitarian," and
a narrow one, which coincides with "egalitarian." Thus, he says,
"not all uses of the word 'equality' are egalitarian," but all egalitarians demand "equality"—"a perfectly comprehensible demand
without any further qualification."

Barry has two purposes in distinguishing between the broad
and the narrow meanings of 'equality' with respect to distributive
justice—one analytic, the other rhetorical. Analytically, he wishes
to distinguish between proportional equality, on the one hand,
and egalitarianism, on the other. By proportional equality, he appears to mean the Aristotelian principle of distributing social
goods "to each according to his merits." By egalitarianism, he
means something narrower, describing it as a "simple idea," a distribution by which there are no "systematic differences" in the
quality of goods each person possesses. Although he does not
elaborate, he appears to have in mind a distribution by which people either begin or end with quantitatively equal amounts of social
resources or welfare. In short, he sees egalitarianism as a form of
numerical or *per-capita* distribution.

[30] Barry, "A Grammar of Equality," pp. 38–39.

Barry's rhetorical goal is more interesting still, for he does with respect to 'equality' what Charles Stevenson in his essay "Persuasive Definitions" accuses Plato of doing with respect to 'justice'. Barry takes a familiar word, with favorable "emotive meaning[s]," and redefines it as something contestable, in the conscious or unconscious hope of linking favorable emotive associations with an otherwise controversial political idea (or, perhaps, in the *defensive* desire to prevent Aristotelians from appropriating the favorable connotations of 'equality' on *their* behalf).[31] 'Equality', for reasons we shall explore in Chapter 11, has a strongly favorable emotive meaning, and Barry, consciously or unconsciously, evidently wishes to appropriate its favorable meaning in defense of per-capita distributions, by arguing that nothing else is *really* equal.[32] That seems to be the point in his saying that other formulas of equality are really formulas for "inequality." He wishes to persuade us that the real meaning of equality, its core meaning with respect to distributions, is "per capita."

Barry is not the only person to argue that his is the only "real" conception of equality. Ronald Dworkin and Amartya Sen did so shortly before the appearance of Barry's review in their essays "What Is Equality?" and "Equality of What?" and Kai Nielsen did so later in *Equality and Liberty*.[33] Nevertheless, there is a difference between Barry's claim and theirs. Dworkin, Sen, and Nielsen, in asserting that theirs were the only real equalities, were constrained by the fact that they were making claims of prescriptive equality. As we have seen in our previous discussion of prescriptive equality as an "essentially contested concept," it is part of the meaning of prescriptive equality that it is based on a relevant rule of conduct, because prescriptive equality is defined as an equality that "ought to obtain" among people. A person who advocates a particular formula of distributive justice must take the position that his is the only "real" prescriptive equality because he must believe that his is the only equality that ought to obtain. Barry, on the

[31] Stevenson defines a "persuasive definition" as "one which gives a new conceptual meaning to a familiar word without substantially changing its emotive meaning, and which is used with the conscious or unconscious purpose of changing, by this means, the direction of people's interests." Stevenson, "Persuasive Definitions," p. 331.

[32] See Stevenson, "Persuasive Definitions," p. 334 (a speaker who asserts that his preferred definition of a moral term is what the term "really" means is often advancing a "persuasive definition").

[33] See Dworkin, "What Is Equality?"; Sen, "Equality of What?" pp. 198–220; Nielsen, *Equality and Liberty*.

E I G H T

EQUAL OPPORTUNITY

Along with per-capita distributions and antidiscrimination rights, "equality of opportunity" is commonly said to possess special egalitarian status, particularly within the context of liberal democracies.[1] Yet its claim to being "more equal" than other equalities differs from those discussed in Chapters 6 and 7. Claims made on behalf of antidiscrimination rights and per-capita distributions are essentially *conceptual*, for the relationships of identity that such rights and distributions create are asserted by their proponents to be the only true equalities, the only relationships with legitimate claims to the language of equality. In contrast, the claims asserted on behalf of equal opportunity are *prescriptive*, and its advocates do not lay exclusive claim to the language of equality. Rather, equality of opportunity is said to be "distinctive" because it is the only "normative principle" of equality that "everyone accepts."[2] According to John Schaar, "The one [conception of equality] that today enjoys the most popularity is equality of opportunity. The formula has few enemies—politicians, businessmen, social theorists, and freedom marchers all approve of it."[3]

The very popularity of equal opportunity, however, is something of a paradox. For, if equal opportunity is something that everyone accepts, freedom marchers should have little need to march for it and politicians little need to legislate it. If, on the other hand, equal opportunity is something that must be marched for,

---

[1] See Fishkin, *Justice, Equal Opportunity, and the Family*, p. 1 ("Equal opportunity is the central doctrine in modern liberalism for legitimating the distribution of goods in society").

[2] Rae, *Equalities*, p. 64 ("[Equal opportunity] is the most distinctive and compelling element of our national ideology"); Levin, "Equality of Opportunity," p. 110 ("Equality of opportunity is important because, as noted, everyone accepts it as a normative principle that 'All should have equal opportunity', whether for jobs or for the other good things in life").

[3] Schaar, "Equality of Opportunity, and Beyond," p. 228.

then people must exist who are opposed to it. As Charles Frankel observes, "The universal popularity [of equality of opportunity] should arouse some suspicion. . . . [I]f equality of opportunity is a significant ideal, there ought to be some people who are opposed to it."[4] One possible solution to the paradox, as R. H. Tawney suggests, is that people are simply hypocritical: they pay homage to equal opportunity, yet they "resist most strenuously attempts to apply it."[5] Another possibility, however, the one we shall explore below, is just the opposite—not that people use the language of equal opportunity to mislead others, but that the language of equal opportunity misleads the people who use it by creating the impression of a consensus which does not, in fact, exist.[6]

The task for analysis is to clarify what is meant by 'equal opportunity'. We shall see that both its constituent terms are ambiguous—'equal' because that word can have both descriptive and prescriptive meanings, and 'opportunity' because, like 'equality', it simultaneously represents a single concept and a multiplicity of contradictory conceptions. As a result, 'equal opportunity' signifies different things to different people, enveloping all its uses with favorable connotations.

The Meaning of 'Opportunity'

The first step in analyzing equal opportunity is to clarify "the concept of 'opportunity'."[7] An "opportunity" is a relationship consisting of three distinct elements. Statements of opportunity are ambiguous to the extent that they fail to specify the three elements.

[4] Frankel, "Equality of Opportunity," p. 192.

[5] Tawney, *Equality*, p. 103.

[6] See Goldman, "The Principles of Equal Opportunity," p. 473, suggesting that "radical ambiguity" in the concept of equal opportunity accounts for the fact that political theorists from both the left and the right give it "widespread endorsement." See also Nelson, "Equal Opportunity," p. 157:

> Though equal opportunity is widely regarded as an important social goal, we lack both a clear statement of what it requires and a plausible account of why it is desirable. Even among those who favor equal opportunity, there is disagreement about its meaning. Different people advocate contrary policies in its name, and critics feel free to formulate their own conceptions as objects of attack.

[7] O'Neill, "How Do We Know When Opportunities Are Equal?" p. 177. See also Levin, "Equality of Opportunity," p. 110 ("Before attempting to say what equality of opportunity, or opportunity rights, are, one must say something about what an opportunity is").

Agents

The first element is the agent, or class of agents, to whom the opportunities belong. Opportunities do not float freely about, unattached to persons. Opportunities, by definition, are *of* people—of black people alone, blacks and whites together, women, rich people, poor people, rich and poor together, people from one region alone, older people, children, or whatever.[8] As T. D. Campbell writes, "We may therefore always intelligibly ask about an opportunity—as we may always ask about any liberty or freedom—to whom it belongs."[9]

Goals

The second element in all relationships of opportunity is the goal or set of goals toward which the opportunities are directed. An opportunity is a relationship of an agent to a possible goal. As Alisdair Macleod explains: "Opportunity is always opportunity *to* x—that is, to do, be, become, or receive something or other. Consequently, statements about the existence or nonexistence of equality of opportunity are fully intelligible only if an answer can be supplied to the question, 'opportunity to *what?*' "[10] The goal of an opportunity may be a job, an education, medical care, political office, land to settle, housing, a financial investment, a military promotion, a life of "culture," the development of one's natural abilities, or whatever.[11] The particular goal or set of goals will dif-

---

[8] See, e.g., *Weber v. United States Steel Workers*, 443 U.S. 193 (1979), an affirmative action program for blacks alone; Women's Educational Equity Act of 1978, 20 U.S.C. § 3341(b) (1) (1983 Supp.), providing opportunities for women alone; Naval Petroleum Reserves Production Act of 1976, 10 U.S.C. § 77430(d) (1980), providing an opportunity to major and independent oil producers and refiners to acquire petroleum from naval petroleum reserves; 42 U.S.C. § 5318(b) (1) (1977 Supp.), providing housing and employment opportunities for low- and moderate-income persons; 43 U.S.C. § 151 (1976), providing homestead opportunity for persons to settle federal lands; Kentucky Equal Opportunities Act, Kentucky Revised Statutes § 207.130 (1971), providing opportunities to persons "within the state"; 42 U.S.C. § 30001 (1976), providing opportunities to "older people."

[9] Campbell, "Equality of Opportunity," pp. 51–52.

[10] Macleod, "Equality of Opportunity," p. 1077 (original emphasis). See also O'Neill, "How Do We Know When Opportunities Are Equal?" p. 178 ("All opportunities are opportunities to do or enjoy some benefit or activity").

[11] See, e.g., 42 U.S.C. § 2003 (1976), prescribing opportunities for employment; 20 U.S.C. § 1221e(a) (1) (1983 Supp.), prescribing opportunities for education; 10 U.S.C. § 1076 (1976), prescribing opportunities for medical care; 47 U.S.C. § 315(a) (1976), prescribing opportunities for candidates for public office; 43 U.S.C. § 151

fer from one opportunity to another, but every opportunity is a relationship of a specific agent or class of agents (explicit or implicit) to a specific goal or set of goals (explicit or implicit).

It is sometimes said that goals to which opportunities are directed must be "desirable" in themselves.[12] Yet that is not necessarily the case. A prison warden, for example, could sensibly say of a prisoner, "In the course of his confinement here, he will have many opportunities to escape"—without in any way implying that *either* the warden *or* the prisoner considers escape to be desirable. Just as people can possess opportunities without taking advantage of them, they can possess opportunities without regarding the goals toward which the opportunities are directed as desirable. It is also said that 'opportunity' implies an exercise of both "choice" and "effort" on the part of an agent.[13] Yet that is not necessarily so either. Assume, for example, that a philanthropist promises a prize to a citizen whose name is drawn at random. The philanthropist could sensibly say that every citizen has an "opportunity" to win the drawing, even though winning involves neither a choice nor an effort on the part of the winner.

Obstacles

The third and most elusive of the elements is the relationship that connects the agent of an opportunity, say, X, to the goal of the opportunity, say, Y. An opportunity of X to attain Y is not necessarily a guarantee that X will succeed in attaining Y if he so chooses.[14] Every child born in America, for example, has an "op-

---

(1976), prescribing opportunities for homesteading public lands; 42 U.S.C. § 5318 (1977 Supp.), prescribing opportunities for housing; 31 U.S.C. § 744 (1983), prescribing opportunities for the purchase of public bonds; 14 U.S.C. § 276 (1976), prescribing opportunities for military promotion; Rawls, *A Theory of Justice*, p. 73, advocating opportunities for persons for lives of "culture"; Tawney, *Equality*, pp. 103–4, advocating opportunities for members of the community to use to the full their "natural endowments of physique, or character, and of intelligence."

[12] See, e.g., Campbell, "Equality of Opportunity," p. 51 ("An opportunity may be said to occur when an agent is in a situation in which he may choose whether or not to perform some effortful act which is considered desirable in itself"); Thomas, "Competitive Equality of Opportunity," p. 388 ("For something to be regarded as an opportunity, it must, in addition, be seen as to some extent good").

[13] See note 12 above. See also Campbell, "Equality of Opportunity," p. 54 ("It is not only inappropriate, it is nonsensical to say that an agent has an opportunity to do something that he is compelled to do, for an opportunity is something which the agent may or may not take advantage of depending on whether or not he chooses to do so").

[14] But see Green, "Competitive Equality of Opportunity," p. 10 and n. 15 ("an opportunity, formally defined, occurs when an agent is capable by his actions of

portunity" to become president of the United States; but none has a guarantee of becoming president if he so chooses, because none has an assurance that he will overcome the many obstacles that stand in the way. To be sure, an agent's opportunity to attain Y can take the form of a guarantee that he will attain it if he chooses it. Thus, a president-elect who has an opportunity of becoming president by choosing to take the oath of office also has a guarantee of becoming president if he chooses to take the oath. But, although opportunities can be guarantees, they are not always guarantees.[15]

Conversely, while an opportunity can be something less than a guarantee, it is something more than a mere possibility—more, that is, than merely the possible absence of all obstacles between a given agent and a given goal. We might say, for example, that every foreign-born citizen of the United States has the "possibility" of becoming president because it is possible to remove the constitutional requirement that candidates for president be native-born. Yet we would not say foreign-born citizens have an opportunity to become president, because an opportunity requires something more than the possible absence of all obstacles between a given agent and a given goal.

An opportunity thus falls somewhere between a guarantee and a possibility—that is, somewhere between the absence of all possible obstacles, on the one hand, and the possible absence of all obstacles, on the other. It might be argued that an opportunity is the absence of a *specified* obstacle between an agent, X, and a goal, Y. But that is not so, because one can remove a specified obstacle in the way of X's attaining Y without granting X an "opportunity" to attain Y. For example, assume that having required candidates

doing or having something if he chooses, and of not doing or having something if he chooses to abstain from that action which would have secured the good in question"); Thomas, "Competitive Equality of Opportunity," p. 388 ("One has an opportunity to do something or have something provided one can do it or have it if one chooses").

[15] Michel Rosenfeld argues that, not only is an opportunity not *always* a guarantee that a person can have something if he chooses it, it is *never* a guarantee of that sort. See Rosenfeld, "Substantive Equality and Equal Opportunity," pp. 1690–91. I have taken that same position myself; see Westen, "The Concept of Equal Opportunity," p. 839. I now believe, however, that my earlier views were mistaken. I believe it is true that a person does not have an "opportunity" for Y when he is guaranteed Y whether or not he chooses it. But it does not follow that he cannot have an "opportunity" for Y when he is guaranteed Y if he *does* choose it. (Nor does it follow that because a person does not have an "opportunity" when he is *guaranteed* Y regardless of whether he chooses it, he cannot have an "opportunity" when he has a *chance* of Y regardless of whether he chooses it.)

for governor to be native-born males, a state removes the gender requirement, thus leaving the governorship open to all native-born men and women. We might then say that, by removing one specific obstacle in the way of foreign-born women, the state has given foreign-born women an increased possibility of becoming governor. But we would not say that the state has given foreign-born women an "opportunity" to become governor because, by retaining the requirement that candidates be native-born, the state has explicitly left an insurmountable obstacle in their way—an obstacle which, unless removed, precludes foreign-born women from attaining the goal of becoming governor. It thus seems that an opportunity requires at a minimum that an agent have a "chance"[16] to attain his goal, that is, that no insurmountable obstacles explicitly stand in the way of his attaining his goal.[17]

This may suggest that an opportunity, being no less than a chance, is also no more than a chance, that is, no more than the absence of *insurmountable* obstacles in the way of X's attaining Y, "insurmountable" obstacles being ones which can be overcome only by being removed. But that is not so either, for opportunities are not confined to the absence of obstacles that can be overcome only by being removed. Suppose, for example, that having required airline stewardesses to be unmarried women, an airline removes the marital obstacle, thus opening stewardess jobs to all women. The marital obstacle differs from insurmountable obstacles like race, color, and sex that can be overcome only by being removed, because a person can overcome the marital obstacle without removing it by changing marital status. Yet we would surely say that, by removing the marital obstacle, the airline company has given married women an "opportunity" to become airline stewardesses.

What, then, is the relationship between the agent of an opportunity and its goal? The answer should now be clear. An opportunity is not solely the absence of a specified obstacle, or solely the

[16] See Levin, "Equality of Opportunity," p. 110 ("An opportunity for a job is a *chance* at it"); O'Neill, "Opportunities, Equalities, and Education," p. 276 ("If A has no chance of doing X whenever he chooses, then he has no opportunity to do X").

[17] By "explicit" obstacles, I mean obstacles that are actually under discussion. Thus, when we make the statement "Any child born in the United States has an opportunity to become president," we do not mean that there are no insurmountable obstacles of any kind in the way of any child's becoming president, for there are inevitably children who are so ill that they will never overcome the obstacle of poor health. We mean, rather, that there are no insurmountable obstacles of the kind that happen to be under discussion when we make the statement, such as obstacles of race, religion, or sex.

absence of insurmountable obstacles. It is a combination of both. 'Opportunity' is the word we use to refer to *the absence of a specified obstacle or set of obstacles, the absence of which leaves no insurmountable barriers explicitly in the way of X's attaining Y.*[18] We say someone has an opportunity when we have in mind a particular obstacle or set of obstacles, the absence of which gives X a chance he did not previously possess to attain Y. The particular obstacle or set of obstacles that an opportunity removes may be insurmountable (e.g., race, sex, or ancestry) or surmountable (e.g., religious belief, wealth, marital status, minimum age, high school diploma, or residence) or a combination of both. The obstacle may be one whose removal creates a "negative" freedom or a "positive" freedom.[19] Thus, the obstacle may consist of exclusion from a competitive race; or, if one is allowed to compete, of being forced to compete under disadvantageous conditions; or, if one is afforded competitive conditions, of being impeded by "socially relative initial disadvantages"[20] such as poor training, nutrition, or motivation; or, if one is not burdened by social disadvantage, of being impeded by lesser "natural" ability;[21] or, if one is not impeded by lesser natural ability, of having to overcome other features that distinguish one person from another.[22] The particular obstacle will differ from one opportunity to another, but every opportunity is a chance of a specified agent or class of agents, X, to attain a speci-

[18] Cf. Campbell, "Equality of Opportunity," p. 57 ("We might say that for any two persons equality of opportunity exists when they are free from the same limitations or obstacles which would have prevented them from . . . achieving the same objective").

[19] Michel Rosenfeld infers that I mean to argue that the obstacles that opportunities remove are those which, when removed, create what Isaiah Berlin calls "negative freedoms" as opposed to what he calls "positive freedoms." See Rosenfeld, "Substantive Equality and Equal Opportunity," pp. 1689–91. I do not mean to take that position. By 'obstacle', I mean any impediment, whatever its source or cause, which, when removed, gives an agent a chance he did not previously possess to attain a specified goal. See, generally, MacCallum, "Negative and Positive Freedom," p. 312.

[20] See Goldman, "The Principle of Equal Opportunity," p. 475 (advocating a standard of opportunity by which people are given handicaps to correct for "socially relative initial disadvantages").

[21] Compare Frankel, "Equality of Opportunity," p. 204 (advocating a standard of opportunity in which people are judged on the basis of their "abilities"), with Goldman, "The Principle of Equal Opportunity," p. 474 (discussing a "sense" of opportunity by which people are allowed to compete without the obstacles of their "natural" disadvantages).

[22] See Dorn, *Rules and Racial Equality*, p. 112 (advocating a standard of opportunity by which people have a chance to attain their goals without any hindrance other than those of pure lottery).

fied goal or set of goals, Y, without the hindrance of a specified obstacle or set of obstacles, Z.

An Illustrative Example

As an illustration, consider the Illinois Human Rights Act of 1979. The act provides opportunities for people in Illinois by making it unlawful for labor organizations to limit the employment of persons in Illinois by discriminating against them on the basis of "race, color, religion, sex, national origin, ancestry, age, marital status, [or] physical or mental handicap."[23] Like all opportunities, the Illinois statutory opportunity consists of a specified agent, X, a specified goal, Y, and a specified obstacle, Z, the absence of which gives X a chance he did not previously possess to attain Y. The agents are the class of persons in Illinois, the goal is employment, and the obstacle is discrimination by labor organizations on the basis of race, color, religion, sex, national origin, ancestry, marital status, or physical or mental handicap. Moreover, like all opportunities, the statutory opportunity consists of a certain relationship between agents, goals, and obstacles. The relationship is less than a guarantee and more than a possibility: less than a guarantee because the act provides for less than the removal of all possible obstacles to employment, more than a possibility because the act provides for more than the possible removal of obstacles. The relationship does more than simply remove a specified obstacle because it does so in such a way as to leave no insurmountable obstacles explicitly in the way of X's attaining Y; it also removes more than insurmountable obstacles because it removes some obstacles (e.g., marital status) that are not insurmountable. In a word (indeed, in the words of the act), the relationship constitutes an "opportunit[y]." It gives people in Illinois a chance they did not previously possess to attain employment by removing specified obstacles that would otherwise stand in their way.

Legislatures do not always specify as explicitly as Illinois does the precise terms of the opportunities they mean to prescribe. Indeed, the ambiguities of 'opportunity' result from stating opportunities without specifying their constituent terms. Consider, for example, the statement "Every child in America should have an opportunity to graduate from high school." Like all statements of

[23] Illinois Human Rights Act, Illinois Annotated Statutes chap. 68, § 1–101 (1979) (Smith-Hurd 1982 Supp.).

opportunity, it states a relationship between an agent, a goal, and an obstacle. The agents and the goal are explicit: the agents are the class of all children in America, and the goal is graduation from high school. The obstacle that the opportunity removes, however, is unstated, and hence the statement is ambiguous. The obstacle may be something educationally noncontroversial, such as obstacles of indigence or race, or it may be something educationally controversial, like the obstacle of passing a competency examination. By leaving the obstacle unstated, the statement masks a wide range of possible prescriptions, from the most acceptable prescription of opportunity to the most controversial.

'Opportunity', then, is a word much like 'equal'. It designates both a single concept and a multiplicity of conceptions. Each opportunity is like every other in that all opportunities reflect a certain formal relationship among agents, obstacles, and goals; but each opportunity also differs from other opportunities in that each is a relationship among particular agents, particular obstacles, and particular goals. Moreover, just as creating one equality may mean denying another, so, too, creating one opportunity may mean denying another. Thus, whenever a society creates an opportunity by removing an obstacle that affects people differentially, it denies people the opportunity to benefit from the differential. And, whenever a society creates an opportunity by removing human obstacles, it denies people the opportunity to exploit those obstacles. This does not mean that societies should refrain from creating opportunities. It means, rather, that just as the significant question for equality is not "Whether equality?" but "Which equalities?" the significant question for opportunity is not "Whether opportunity?" but "Which opportunities?"

The Meaning of 'Equal Opportunity'

Like all statements of "equality," statements of "equal opportunity" presuppose standards of comparison: to say that two opportunities are equal presupposes a "measure"[24] or "predicate"[25] by which opportunities can be compared and found to be identical. The standard by which particular opportunities are measured and compared is itself an opportunity, that is, it is a "specification"[26] of the three variable terms of which opportunities consist—a spec-

[24] Levin, "Equality of Opportunity," p. 110.
[25] O'Neill, "How Do We Know When Opportunities Are Equal?" pp. 177–78.
[26] Macleod, "Equality of Opportunity," p. 1083.

ification of relevant agents, relevant obstacles, and relevant goals. Two or more opportunities are equal if they are identical in those relevant respects. By the same token, two or more people have equal opportunities if they all fall within a class of agents who have a chance to attain the same relevant goal without the hindrance of the same relevant obstacles.

The standards by which opportunities are measured, in turn, may be "descriptive" or "prescriptive." Descriptive standards of opportunity measure people with respect to opportunities they actually have. Thus, descriptively, people have equal opportunity if they fall within a class of agents who are actually free, due to the absence of specified obstacles, to pursue specified goals. Prescriptive standards measure people with respect to the opportunities they *ought* to have. Prescriptively, people have equal opportunity if they fall within a class of agents who ought to be free from specified obstacles that would hinder the pursuit of specified goals. In both cases, we tend to say that people "have" equal opportunity, although we mean different things by it. In the former case we mean that they are "actually" free from certain obstacles that would prevent them from pursuing certain goals, whether or not we believe they ought to be; in the latter case we mean that they "ought" to be free in that way, regardless of whether they actually are. In both cases, however, to say opportunities are "equal" means that they are identical in relevant respects, that is, identical by reference to a controlling standard for measuring opportunities.

To say that people have an "equal" opportunity, therefore, does not mean that they have the "same" opportunity—if by 'same' one means the absence of identical obstacles. Two people can have equal opportunities even though each faces different obstacles, provided that they are both free from the obstacles specified as relevant by the controlling standard. Assume, for example, that two runners with different training and talent are both given a chance to win a race, by both being allowed to start at the same time and place and to run the same distance; assume, too, that the controlling measure of opportunity is the chance to win the race without the obstacles of starting at different times and running different distances.[27] In this event, the two runners can be said to have an equal opportunity to win the race because, even though they face differential obstacles of training and talent which give

[27] Felix Oppenheim, for example, takes this to be the relevant measure of competitive opportunity; see Oppenheim, *Political Concepts*, p. 116 ("Athletes have an equal opportunity to win the race since they all start from the same line").

them different probabilities of winning, they are identical in both being free from the same relevant obstacles. Conversely, two persons can lack an equal opportunity even though they are free from the same obstacles, if the obstacles from which they are free are *not* specified as relevant by the controlling standard. Thus, if the controlling standard for measuring the opportunity of runners is the absence of different "probabilities" of winning,[28] the two runners do *not* have an equal opportunity to win the race, even though they both start at the same time and place.

"Equal opportunity" thus depends upon the standards by which opportunities are measured. Whether a society regards a particular descriptive standard of opportunity as controlling depends upon its purposes in comparing opportunities. Whether a society regards a particular prescriptive standard as controlling depends upon its normative views. Thus, whether a society chooses to measure opportunities by "meritarian" as opposed to "utilitarian" standards of opportunity,[29] or by what John Rawls calls "fair" opportunity as opposed to what others call "formal" opportunity,[30] or by still other standards, depends upon which conception best furthers its particular values.

The Ambiguity of Equal Opportunity

We have already examined one of the ambiguities of equal opportunity. The statement that people "have" equal opportunity is ambiguous as to whether it is descriptive or prescriptive: it may mean

[28] Edwin Dorn and Onora O'Neill, for example, take "probability" to be the relevant measure of opportunity; see Dorn, *Rules and Racial Equality*, p. 112 ("Equal opportunity means, that, given some scarce divisible good, X, and N persons wanting X, the probability that any person will get X, is 1/N"); O'Neill, "How Do We Know When Opportunities Are Equal?" p. 184 ("The substantive interpretation of equal opportunity builds on a central feature of the idea of opportunity. To have an opportunity to do X is to have a chance to do X, and for A and B to have an equal opportunity to do X is for them to be equally likely [qua members of certain reference classes] to do X"). See also Rae, *Equalities*, p. 65 (defining "prospect-regarding" equality of opportunity as one in which "two persons, j and k, . . . each have the same probability of attaining X").

[29] See Campbell, "Equality of Opportunity," p. 68 (contrasting "meritarian" with "utilitarian" conceptions of equal opportunity).

[30] Compare Fullinwider, *The Reverse Discrimination Controversy*, p. 101 (A and B have "formal" equality of opportunity to attain Y when "neither faces a legal or quasi-legal barrier [to attaining Y] the other does not face"), with Rawls, *A Theory of Justice*, p. 73 ("fair" equality of opportunity exists when "those with similar abilities and skills . . . have similar life chances . . . irrespective of the income class into which they are born"). For more on the distinction between "formal" and "fair" equality of opportunity, see Daniels, "Merit and Meritocracy," p. 217.

that, descriptively, people are indeed free from relevant obstacles that would hinder the pursuit of relevant goals (regardless of whether they *should* be free from them); or it may mean that, prescriptively, people should be free in those relevant respects (regardless of whether they actually are). Statements of equal opportunity can also mask the specific obstacles and the specific agents to which they refer, thereby creating ambiguity as to their specific terms. These ambiguities arise in the same way under both descriptive and prescriptive statements of opportunity. For purposes of analysis, however, we shall confine our discussion to statements of prescriptive opportunity. With reference, then, to prescriptive opportunities, the ambiguities take two principal forms: (1) statements of the form "A shall have an equal opportunity with B to attain goal Y"; and (2) statements of the form "A and B shall have an equal opportunity to attain goal Y."

"A Shall Have Equal Opportunity with B"

Prescriptions of the form "A shall have equal opportunity with B" are indeterminate because, while they specify the agents of the prescribed opportunity (A and B) and the goal of the opportunity (Y), they do not specify the precise obstacle the prescribed opportunity removes. By using 'equal' to refer to the removal of the unstated obstacle, they imply that the obstacle consists of discrimination of some sort. Unfortunately, there are at least two different kinds of discrimination the removal of which would render A and B "equal" in their opportunities: discrimination against A vis-à-vis B, or discrimination against *either* A vis-à-vis B *or* B vis-à-vis A. By failing to specify which obstacle they mean to remove, the prescriptions mask their content.

To illustrate, assume that a statute takes the following form:

> American women shall have the same opportunity as American men to serve as astronauts in the space-shuttle program.

The statute specifies two terms of the prescribed opportunity. It specifies the agents who possess the prescribed opportunity (American men and women) and the goal of the opportunity (participation in the space-shuttle program). It also uses the term 'equal' in conjunction with 'men' and 'women' as a surrogate for the third term, thereby implying that the obstacle the statute removes is sex discrimination of some sort. Unfortunately, because at least two different kinds of sex discrimination prevent women

174

from having "equal opportunity" with men, the statute could be prescribing either of two different kinds of opportunity:

O_1: American women shall have whatever chances are otherwise extended to men to serve as astronauts in the space-shuttle program without the hindrance of any preference for men.

O_2: American women and men shall have a chance to serve as astronauts in the space shuttle program without the hindrance of any preference for persons of the opposite sex.

The foregoing prescriptions of opportunity differ significantly. O_1 protects women, but not men, from discrimination, while O_2 protects both men and women from discrimination. Yet both give women equal opportunities with men because each creates a class of agents consisting of men and women who possess a common opportunity. Each prescription also squares with the language of the underlying statute. To know which prescription corresponds with the *intent* of the underlying statute, one would have to pierce the "vague"[31] language of equal opportunity to disclose the unspecified obstacle to which it means to refer.

"A and B Shall Have Equal Opportunity to Attain Y"

The second ambiguity occurs with prescriptions of the form "A and B shall have an equal opportunity to attain Y." Such prescriptions of opportunity are ambiguous because they fail to specify either the agents who possess the prescribed opportunity or the obstacle the opportunity removes. The prescriptions mask at least two distinct prescriptive standards of opportunity by which A and B may be equal: (1) A and B shall be equal in their chances to attain Y without being disfavored vis-à-vis one another; and (2) A and B shall be equal to an unnamed but implied third-party agent, C, in their chances to attain Y without being disfavored vis-à-vis C.

The Export Expansion Act of 1971 is a good example of this sort of ambiguity.[32] The act requires the Export-Import Bank (Eximbank) to accord "equal opportunity" to "independent export firms [and] small commercial banks" to participate in Eximbank programs. The act specifies the goal of the prescribed opportunity (i.e., participation in Eximbank programs), and it uses "equal opportunity" in conjunction with "independent export firms" and

---

[31] Lucas, *The Principles of Politics*, p. 247.
[32] Export Expansion Finance Act, 12 U.S.C. § 635(b) (1) (B) (1983 Supp.) (1971).

"small commercial banks" in such a way as to raise implications about both the agents who possess the prescribed opportunity and the obstacles the opportunity removes, but its implications are sufficiently ambiguous to encompass at least two distinct prescriptions of opportunity:

O_1: Independent export agents and small commercial banks shall have a chance to participate in Eximbank programs without being disfavored vis-à-vis one another.

O_2: Independent export agents and small commercial banks shall have a chance to participate in Eximbank programs on whatever terms are otherwise available to *large commercial banks* without being disfavored vis-à-vis large commercial banks.

Both of the foregoing prescriptions create a class of agents who are identical—hence, equal—in their chances to attain specified goals without the hindrance of specified obstacles. Each class includes both independent export agents and small commercial banks. Yet the two opportunities differ significantly. The legislative history of the Export Expansion Act suggests that it was designed to codify O_2 rather than O_1.[33] Without independent information of that sort, however, one would have no way of knowing from the language of equal opportunity it employs which of the two opportunities the act intended to prescribe.

Conclusion

The "universal popularity"[34] of equal opportunity is problematic on several levels. For one thing, equal opportunity is often inconsistent with other equalities, particularly that of equal outcomes. An "opportunity" to attain a goal is a chance to attain a goal, not necessarily a guarantee of attaining it. Insofar as people have opportunities that are less than guarantees of what they wish, some of them will inevitably attain goals that others fail to attain. To create equal opportunity, therefore, is virtually always to allow

[33] See House Report No. 92–303, accompanying H.R. 8181, 92d Congress, 1st Sess., in *1971 U.S. Congressional and Administrative News* (St. Paul, Minn.: West, 1971), vol. 2, pp. 1414, 1427; Hearings on H.R. 8181, House Subcommittee on International Trade, 92d Congress, 1st Sess., pp. 513, 514, 517, 522–23, 524.

[34] Frankel, "Equality of Opportunity," p. 192.

people "to become unequal by competing against [their] fellows."[35] As J. Lucas puts the point:

> Every competition must result in some being successful and
> others not: and therefore, if the competition proceeds on a ra-
> tional basis, it not only creates a new inequality, but reveals
> an antecedent one. A competition in which there is equality
> of opportunity is one in which the best man wins, and there-
> fore one in which the winner is deemed to have been the best
> man, and in that crucial respect unequal.[36]

Furthermore, equal opportunity not only competes with other
equalities, it also competes with itself. When a society creates opportunities for some by removing human obstacles, it necessarily
denies others the opportunity to exploit those obstacles for their
own benefit. When a society creates opportunities by removing
obstacles that affect people differentially, it necessarily denies an
opportunity to people who benefit from the differential.[37]

Finally, the popularity of equal opportunity is difficult to square
with the nature of equal opportunity. "Equality of opportunity" is
the identity which obtains among persons by virtue of their being
both free from the same specified obstacle and free to attain the
same specified goal. The desirability of their equality of opportunity depends in each case on the desirability of their being free
from the respective obstacle in order to pursue the respective goal.
Thus, the equal descriptive opportunity of Americans to commit
homicide without the hindrance of a handgun shortage seems undesirable; their equal descriptive opportunity to live without the
fear of contracting smallpox seems desirable. The equal prescriptive opportunity once possessed by American property holders
under the *Dred Scott* decision to take chattel property into free ter-

---

[35] Schaar, "Equality of Opportunity, and Beyond," p. 241 ("The idea of equality
of opportunity is a poor tool for understanding even those sectors of life to which
the notion of equality is applicable. It is a poor tool in that, whereas it seems to
defend equality, it really only defends the equal right to become unequal by competing against one's fellows"). See also Nelson, "Equal Opportunity," p. 164
("equal opportunity, whether conceived as fair competition or as equal chances will
not necessarily result in more equal outcomes at all").

[36] Lucas, *The Principles of Politics*, p. 249.

[37] Cf. Rae, *Equalities*, p. 69 ("Given strictly unequal talents, every policy of
means-regarding equal opportunity must violate equality of prospects, and every
prospect-regarding equal opportunity must violate equality of means"); Nelson,
"Equal Opportunity," p. 158 ("Whichever side one takes on this issue [of the
proper measure of opportunity], there is some conception of equal opportunity one
rejects").

ritories today seems undesirable; the equal prescriptive opportunity they still possess to receive compensation for state appropriations of their property seems desirable. Equality of opportunity is only as desirable as the underlying descriptions and prescriptions from which it derives.

Despite all of this, however, the term 'equal opportunity' continues to have laudatory connotations. One reason is that both its constituent terms have favorable connotations. 'Opportunity', designating a kind of freedom, has the same laudatory connotations as 'freedom'.[38] 'Equal' has favorable connotations of its own, as we shall see in Chapter 11. In addition, 'equal opportunity' has two features which combine to give it special rhetorical force. The first is that the language of 'equal opportunity' has an inherent normative bias, which is a function of the two forms that statements of equal opportunity take. Statements of equal opportunity are either descriptive or prescriptive. As descriptive statements, they express an "is"; as prescriptive statements, they express an "ought to be." In neither event, however, do they express an "ought *not* to be." As a result, to the extent that statements of "equal opportunity" have normative content, the content is always *in favor of* equal opportunity, not against it.

This is not to say that language prevents speakers from condemning particular kinds of equal opportunity. Critics of equal opportunity are perfectly capable of expressing disapproval. The point is, rather, that in order to express disapproval of equal opportunity, a speaker must say so explicitly. Otherwise, he will be understood to be doing one of two things that the language of 'equal opportunity' does—either describing an equal opportunity, or prescribing an equal opportunity, but not criticizing one.

The bias of 'equal opportunity' would be less pronounced were it not combined with a second feature, i.e., the tendency to use the same words to refer to both descriptive and prescriptive opportunities. If speakers were careful to distinguish between statements of "is" and statements of "ought to be," the favorable con-

---

[38] Freedom, too, is a triadic relationship in which an agent, X, is unconstrained by Z to do or receive Y. See MacCallum, "Negative and Positive Freedom," p. 312. Opportunity differs from the broader concept of freedom, however, in at least two respects: (1) only animate agents may have opportunities, while both animate and inanimate objects can be free; (2) an opportunity is a relationship of freedom in which an agent has a "chance" to attain Y, while an agent may be free from Z to do or receive Y without yet having a chance to do or receive Y. For an inquiry into the reasons why 'freedom' has laudatory connotations, see Westen, " 'Freedom' and 'Coercion'," p. 541.

notations of the latter would not carry over to the former. Instead, speakers tend to use them interchangeably. Thus, instead of distinguishing between equal descriptive opportunities and equal prescriptive opportunities, we speak simply of equal opportunities. And, instead of saying that people "have" descriptive opportunities and "ought to have" prescriptive opportunities, we use the same words to refer to both: we say that "A and B *have* an equal opportunity." As a consequence, instead of being seen as a formal relationship of agents, obstacles, and goals, which is sometimes descriptive and sometimes prescriptive, equal opportunity comes to be regarded as a "substantive principle" of justice—as an "ideal."[39]

[39] Charvet, "The Idea of Equality as a Substantive Principle of Society," p. 2 (referring to equal opportunity as a "substantive principle"); Frankel, "Equality of Opportunity," p. 192 (referring to equal opportunity as something people regard as a "significant ideal").

PRECEPTS OF EQUALITY

'Equality', as we have seen, has two meanings—one general, the other specific. Generally, 'equality' refers to the relationship which obtains among persons or things which have been measured and found to be identical by reference to such standards of comparison as are deemed relevant to the inquiry at hand. Specifically, 'equality' refers to the relationship of identity which obtains among persons or things by reference to a particular standard of comparison, which the speaker asserts to be relevant under the circumstances. The former is the concept of equality, the latter a conception of equality.

In addition, 'equality' is sometimes used as a form of shorthand to refer, not to relationships *of* equality, but to certain precepts *about* equality—certain normative axioms whose truth is said to inhere in or follow from the concept of equality. These axioms are the so-called formal principle of equality and the presumption of equality:

> *Formal principle of equality*: Equals should be treated equally, and unequals should be treated unequally.

> *Presumption of equality*: People should be treated equally in the absence of good reasons for treating them unequally.

At first glance, these precepts would appear to fall beyond the purview of this study, for they are explicitly normative statements about how people "should" be treated. In that respect, they look very much like other normative propositions that are sometimes advanced about equality. The most celebrated recent example is what John Rawls has called the "difference principle," namely, the moral proposition that

> social and economic inequalities, for example inequalities of wealth and authority, are just only if they result in compen-

sating benefits for everyone, and in particular for the least advantaged members of society.[1]

Like all moral propositions, Rawls's difference principle is morally contestable[2] and, hence, raises what Alan White calls "evaluative" questions rather than the kind of "analytic" questions we are exploring here.[3]

On the other hand, the formal principle of equality and the presumption of equality also differ from Rawls's difference principle and other moral propositions about equality[4] in ways that render them appropriate subjects for analysis. The distinction is in the sources of their asserted truths. The difference principle is a moral proposition whose truth is candidly conceded to rest on a contestable combination of practical reason and intuition. In contrast, the formal principle and presumption of equality are normative propositions that are asserted to be rationally *incontestable*. Thus, the formal principle of equality is said to be a "principle of reason," a "premise of rational thought," and a "law of thought,"[5] while the presumption of equality is said to be a "logical rule of moral and prudential thinking," a principle "implicit in the notion of rational decision," and a "meta-moral axiom," i.e., "a rule for adopting rules" as opposed to a substantive ethical principle.[6] Indeed, it is

---

[1] Rawls, *A Theory of Justice*, pp. 14–15, 75–83. See also p. 302 ("Social and economic inequalities are to be arranged so that they are . . . to the greatest benefit of the least advantaged, consistent with the just savings principle"). For a more recent statement by Rawls of his views of equality, see "A Kantian Conception of Equality," p. 94.

[2] For criticism of the difference principle, see McDonald, "Rawlsian Contractarianism," p. 71.

[3] White, *Grounds of Liability*, pp. 1–6. See the Preface, note 17.

[4] Kai Nielsen has proposed a rival principle, which he regards as "more egalitarian" than Rawls's difference principle:

> After provisions are made for common social (community) values, for capital overhead to preserve the society's productive capacity, allowances made for differing unmanipulated needs and preferences, and due weight is given to the just entitlements of individuals, the income and wealth (the common stock of means) is to be so divided that each person will have a right to an equal share. The necessary burdens requisite to enhance human well-being are also to be equally shared, subject, of course, to limitations by differing abilities and differing situations.

Nielsen, *Equality and Liberty*, p. 48. But see Kamooneh, "Justice as Fairness or as Equality?" p. 65 (criticizing Nielsen).

[5] Feinberg, "Noncomparative Justice," p. 319 ("a principle of reason"); Freund, "The Philosophy of Equality," p. 14; Kelsen, "Aristotle's Theory of Justice," p. 134 ("a law of thought").

[6] See Graham, "Liberty and Equality," pp. 63–64 ("a logical rule of moral and prudential thinking"); Benn, "Equality, Moral and Social," p. 40 ("implicit in the

said not only that the two precepts are logical truths, but that the second can be logically derived from the first.[7]

In the following two chapters, we shall investigate the supposed analytic truth of these precepts of equality as well as the supposed logical relationship between them.

---

notion of rational decision"); Beardsley, "Equality and Obedience to Law," pp. 35–36 ("a meta-moral axiom," i.e., "a rule for adopting rules," as opposed to a "positive rule of ethics").

[7] For commentators who derive the "presumption of equality" from the proposition that "equals should be treated equally," see Benn and Peters, *The Principles of Political Thought*, pp. 124–28; Evans, "Equality, Ambiguity, and Public Choice," p. 1386; Flathman, "Equality and Generalization," p. 55; Frankena, "The Concept of Social Justice," pp. 10–13; Rawls, "Justice as Fairness," pp. 166–67; Spaemann, "Remarks on the Problem of Equality," p. 364; Wasserstrom, "Rights, Human Rights, and Racial Discrimination," pp. 634–37.

N I N E

THE FORMAL PRINCIPLE OF EQUALITY

Aristotle, building on prior work by Plato, said three things about equality that have influenced Western thought ever since:

(1) It is just to treat people who are equal equally.

(2) It is also just to treat people who are *unequal unequally.*

(3) The foregoing propositions are self-evident, being "universally accepted even without the support of argument."[1]

Ironically, what Aristotle regarded as self-evident, others consider to be not merely false but *patently* false. To treat equals equally, they say, can be grossly unjust. Consider those who are equal before the law. "If a ruler were to boil his subjects in oil, jumping in afterwards himself," William Frankena says, "it would be an injustice, but it would be no inequality of treatment."[2] Or consider a case that Phillip Montague asks us to imagine: A, B, and C comprise a class of persons who all justly deserve a certain benefit. One member of the class, A, is unjustly denied the benefit he deserves. The question thus becomes, how should B and C now

---

[1] Aristotle, *Nicomachean Ethics* V.3.1131a10–b15 (trans. Thomson). In the *Nicomachean Ethics* Aristotle expresses the three propositions in the following form: he says, first, that it is "universally accepted even without the support of argument" that what is "just" is "equal" and vice versa (1131a10–15); he then explains what 'equal' means, namely, giving "equal shares" to people who are "equal" and "unequal shares" to those who are "not equal" (1131a15–25). In the *Politics* Aristotle repeats the lessons of the *Nicomachean Ethics*:

> Thus it is thought that justice is equality; and so it is, but not for all persons, only for those that are equal. Inequality also is thought to be just; and so it is, but not for all, only for the unequal. . . . Now all men believe that justice means equality in some sense, and they are in limited agreement with the philosophy of justice which I explained in my *Ethics*: they hold that justice is some entity which is relative to persons, and that equality must be equal for equals.

Aristotle, *Politics* III.9.1280a8–15, III.12.1282b18–23 (trans. Sinclair).
For Plato's similar views, see Plato, *Laws* VI.757; Plato, *Republic* VIII.558c.
[2] Frankena, "The Concept of Social Justice," pp. 1, 17.

be treated? If it were just to treat equals equally, Montague says, then it would be just to inflict on B and C the injustice already inflicted on A. Yet, surely, that would be "plainly unacceptable."[3]

Aristotle's second proposition is even more controverted because, as some commentators argue, even if the precept "equals should be treated equally" is true, the proposition "unequals should be treated unequally" is clearly false.[4] A. M. Honoré, for example, who accepts the first precept, asks us to imagine a society that accepts the norm "all adult males shall be allowed to vote." It follows from the norm, he says, that adult males, being equally entitled to vote, should all be allowed to vote. It also follows that, by granting males something it does not grant to women, the rule regards men and women as unequal. Yet it does not follow, he says, that because the norm grants men the right to vote it must therefore deny women the right to vote, or that because men and women are not equal under the norm they must be treated unequally.[5]

These differences of opinion between Aristotle and others appear to be substantive in nature. They appear to be normative disputes about whether citizens should be boiled in oil, whether two wrongs make a right, or whether, having granted men the right to vote, a society should deny it to women. In reality, the disputes are not substantive but conceptual in nature. They are disputes, not about right and wrong, but about the meaning of 'equal' and 'unequal'. By analyzing the meaning of Aristotle's statements as he understood them, we shall see that they possess both more truth and less content than is sometimes supposed: more truth because they not only happen to be true but are necessarily true; less content because, being necessarily true, they add nothing to what we already know.

The Meaning of "Equals Should Be Treated Equally"

Aristotle believed that "treating equals equally" always produces just conduct. His critics have argued that, while "treating equals equally" is necessary to just conduct, it is not sufficient in itself.[6]

---

[3] Montague, "Comparative and Noncomparative Justice," p. 133.

[4] See, e.g., Flew, The Politics of Procrustes, p. 36; Wolgast, Equality and the Rights of Women, p. 77.

[5] Honoré, "Social Justice," pp. 83–84.

[6] See Carr, "The Concept of Formal Justice," pp. 211, 212 (Aristotle's maxim is "a necessary but not a sufficient condition for doing justice").

This is so, they say, because, although treating equals *unequally* is always unjust, treating equals *equally* is sometimes unjust as well, e.g., when people who are equal before the law are treated equally by all being boiled in oil.

This dispute between Aristotle and his critics, which appears to be substantive, is in fact a dispute about language, about what the words 'equal' and 'equally' mean in the precept "people who are equal should be treated equally." Let us begin with the word 'equal'. To what does 'equal' refer? There are two possibilities. 'Equal' may refer to people who are *prescriptively* equal, that is, to people who are identical with respect to the treatments that they ought to receive; or it may refer to people who are solely *descriptively* equal, that is, to people who are identical by standards *other than*, and *to the exclusion of*, those prescribing treatments they ought to receive. We can call these two possibilities "equal$_{pres}$" and "equal$_{des}$":

Equal$_{pres}$: Identical with respect to the treatments they ought to receive.

Equal$_{des}$: Identical in respects other than, and to the exclusion of, in respect of the treatments they ought to receive.

If the precept "people who are equal should be treated equally" is valid, the term 'equal' cannot mean "equal$_{des}$," for that would yield the contradictory precept "people who are *identical in respects other than, and to the exclusion of, in respect of the treatments they ought to receive* ought to be treated equally." Moreover, if 'equal' means "equal$_{pres}$," it must refer to people who are identical by reference to a relevant norm, or rule, of conduct prescribing certain treatment for people of a certain description; for, as we have seen, that is what it means to say people are identical with respect to the treatments they ought to receive. It follows, therefore, that *if* Aristotle's precept is valid (which is something yet to be established), it is valid by virtue of referring to people who are identical by reference to a relevant rule of conduct.

Now let us turn to the meaning of 'equally'. To say that people who are equal should be treated equally is to specify the kind of treatment they should receive. The adverb 'equally' necessarily incorporates one of two possible standards for comparing treatments: the same rule of treatment by which such people are classified as being equal; or some descriptive standard of treatment *other* than that defining the treatments prescribed for them by the rule by which they are classified as being equal. Under such standards, people would be treated as follows:

Equally$_{pres}$: Identically with respect to the treatments prescribed for them by the rule by which they are equal.

Equally$_{des}$: Identically in some respect other than in respect of the treatments prescribed for them by the rule by which they are classified as being equal.

Again, it is obvious that if Aristotle's precept is valid, 'equally' cannot mean "equally$_{des}$," because that would yield the contradictory statement "People who are equal should be treated *identically in some respect other than in respect of the treatments prescribed for them by the rule by which they are classified as being equal.*" Rather, if the precept is valid, 'equally' must mean "equally$_{pres}$." That is to say, to the extent that the precept is valid, 'equal' and 'equally' must both refer to a common prescriptive standard—a common rule (or set of rules) of conduct prescribing treatment of a certain description for people of a certain description. In short, "People who are equal should be treated equally" must at least mean:

People who are "identical with respect to the treatments they ought to receive" should be treated "identically with respect to the treatments prescribed for them by the rule by which they are equal."

or

People who are "identical by reference to relevant rules of conduct" should be treated "identically by reference to such rules."

Significantly, the dispute between Aristotle and his critics is not about the accuracy of the foregoing restatements of Aristotle's precept, for, if our reasoning has been sound, the alternative restatements are contradictory. The dispute, rather, is one of language, taking one of two alternative forms. On the one hand, the dispute is sometimes about the *kinds of rules* to which the word 'equal' refers in the precept "people who are *equal* should be treated equally." Aristotle, believing the precept to be coextensive with the precept "to each his due," intended the word 'equal' to be defined by reference to the totality of all rules a society regards as just, including comparative and noncomparative rules alike. Some of his critics, however, take the position that the word 'equal' in the precept—like prescriptive equality generally—ought to be understood as defined, not by reference to all relevant rules of conduct, but only by reference to a certain subclass of comparative rules, namely, *antidiscrimination* rules.[7] That is to say, they believe that the precept "equals should be treated equally" should be understood to mean that people who are prescriptively identical by reference to antidiscrimination rules ought to be treated identically by reference to such rules. An antidiscrimination rule is one that extends to members of a protected class whatever treatment is accorded to members of the reference class, whether that means granting or denying both classes the treatments to which they may otherwise be entitled. It follows that, although Aristotle and these latter critics agree that "treating equals equally" means complying with relevant rules of conduct, they disagree about the scope of the precept: Aristotle believed that the precept encompassed all relevant rules, whereas his critics assume that the precept is confined to a subclass of rules, a class of antidiscrimination rules the enforcement of which is consistent with the nondiscriminatory denial of the treatment to which persons are otherwise entitled.

Alternatively, the dispute is sometimes about what it means to treat people "equally" by reference to a relevant rule of conduct. The disagreement arises because, as we have seen in Chapters 3 and 4, there are two distinct ways in which rules of conduct can be used to measure and compare treatments:

—directly, as prescriptive standards of comparison, that is, as standards for measuring whether treatments are identical or nonidentical in the precise ways they ought to be identical or nonidentical;

—indirectly, as baselines within descriptive standards for measuring whether treatments are identical or nonidentical in the extent, if any, to which they depart from what they ought to be.

To say that treatments are identical by reference to a rule of conduct that is used directly as a standard of comparison means that they are identical in being what they ought to be, that is, identical in *complying* with the prescribed rule. To say that treatments are identical by reference to a rule of conduct that is used as a baseline within a descriptive standard of comparison means that they are

---

[7] See, e.g., Simons, "Equality as a Comparative Right," pp. 387, 394–403, 413–15.

identical in *either complying with or violating* the baseline rule.[8] The difference between Aristotle and some of his critics is that Aristotle used "treated equally" solely in the former sense and they use it in the latter sense.

As a result, Aristotle's critics understand his precept to mean:

> People who are identical by reference to relevant rules of conduct should be treated identically by reference to such rules— *meaning* all should be either given or denied the treatments prescribed for them.

Thus, Frankena asserts that one can take people who are "equal" in their right to a certain minimum level of welfare and treat them "equally" *either* by assuring them all such welfare *or* by "boiling them all in oil."[9] This explains why he and others believe that "treating equals equally" is a necessary condition of just action, but an insufficient one: necessary because without it all people who deserve certain treatment would not receive that treatment; insufficient because it may result in all people being denied the treatment they deserve. This also explains why critics challenge the truth of Aristotle's assertion that it is always just to "treat equals equally": it is not always just, they say, because "treating equals equally" may sometimes mean denying all deserving people the treatment they deserve.

In contrast, Aristotle understood "treated equally" to mean treated identically *in compliance with* the rules by which people are prescriptively equal. Thus, he understood "people who are equal should be treated equally" to mean:

> People who are identical by reference to relevant rules of conduct should be treated identically by reference to such rules— *meaning* they should all be given the treatments prescribed for them.

[8] See Chapter 3, pp. 87–89, and Chapter 4, pp. 98–99.

[9] Although the rule that a just society must provide a certain minimum level of welfare for everyone may be construed as an offshoot of the rule of equality, violations of these negative principles are unjust but do not necessarily entail any inequality of treatment, direct or indirect. If a ruler were to boil his subjects in oil, jumping in afterward himself, it would be an injustice, but there would be no inequality of treatment.

Frankena, "The Concept of Social Justice," p. 17. See also del Vecchio, *Justice*, pp. 86–87; Vlastos, "Justice and Equality," p. 62; Lucas, *On Justice*, pp. 171–84.

This explains why Aristotle regarded "treating equals equally" not merely as just, but as self-evidently just—as something "universally accepted even without the support of argument." It is necessarily just because it is *defined* as being just. The precept "people who are equal ought to be treated equally" is a "truism," a "tautology,"[10] the equivalent of saying "all people who ought to receive certain treatment ought to receive such treatment" or "relevant rules ought to be applied to the people to whom they apply."

This raises several interesting questions. Why do perceptive commentators interpret Aristotle's normative precept in a way that can produce unjust results? Why, given the alternative construction, do they interpret it as stating something that is normatively necessary, but not sufficient, when they could just as easily interpret it as stating something necessary and sufficient? Why, in other words, do they assume that treating equals "equally" is measured by a descriptive standard based on a prescriptive baseline, rather than by a purely prescriptive standard? The answer to these questions, I believe, has two parts.

The first is an accident of language—a semantic incongruity in the way the terms 'equals' and 'equally' work in normative discourse. As we have seen, treating people as "equals" differs from treating them "equally" because the former can unambiguously be understood to refer to a purely prescriptive standard, while the latter is ambiguous as to whether it refers to a prescriptive standard, on the one hand, or a descriptive standard based on a prescriptive baseline, on the other. Thus, we can unambiguously say of people who are boiled in oil in lieu of receiving the minimum level of welfare they deserve, "perhaps they are being treated equally, but they are not being treated as equals," meaning "perhaps they are being treated identically by reference to the baseline of what they deserve (in that they are all being denied it), but they are not being treated as people who are identically entitled to a

---

[10] See von Leyden, *Aristotle on Equality and Justice*, p. 5 (Aristotle's maxim is a "truism"); Cauthen, *The Passion for Equality*, p. 5 (a "tautology"). See also Kelsen, "Aristotle's Theory of Justice," pp. 110, 134 (referring to the precept "equals should be treated equally" as "a law of thought"); Kelsen, *General Theory of Law and State*, p. 439 ("The idea of equality . . . , the principle that equal things must be treated equally or, in other words, that equals deserve equality, *suum cuique*, does not actually proclaim anything more than the logical principle of identity or the principle of contradiction"); Recasens-Siches, "Dignity, Liberty and Equality," pp. 3, 17 ("[H]uman beings should be treated unequally as to the diversities that in justice should be taken into account. This . . . principle . . . theoretically is obvious").

certain minimum level of welfare." We cannot unambiguously say of such persons "they are not being treated equally" because in a sense they *are* being treated equally: measured by the baseline of what they deserve, they are descriptively identical in all being denied what they deserve. To avoid ambiguity, we would have to say "they are not being given the equal treatment they deserve" or "they are not being treated as the equals they are."[11]

Part of the answer, then, is that "treating people equally" is ambiguous. That, however, explains only why commentators are *able* to differ with Aristotle on the interpretation of his precept. It does not explain why they *prefer* their interpretation to his. One reason for their preference may be that the standard by which they measure equal treatment (that is, whether treatments are descriptively identical in the extent, if any, to which they depart from a prescribed baseline) is more versatile than Aristotle's prescriptive standard. We have seen that, for *any* two things to be equal or unequal, they must be amenable to a common standard of measurement. Aristotle's prescriptive standard is capable only of measuring treatments that *comply* with applicable rules, because it measures treatments only to determine whether they are identical as opposed to nonidentical (equal as opposed to unequal) in the ways in which they ought to be identical. In contrast, a descriptive standard that contains a prescriptive baseline can measure all treatments, whether they comply with or violate controlling rules, by measuring them by reference to whether they are identical or nonidentical in the extent, if any, to which they depart from controlling rules. This makes the critics' standard more versatile than Aristotle's, for under it all treatments are either equal or unequal: treatments that are not equal *must* be unequal, and vice versa. In contrast, treatments that depart from what they ought to be are *neither equal nor unequal* by Aristotle's standard because they are incapable of being measured by it: treatments that are not equal in Aristotle's terms by virtue of departing from what they ought to be are not unequal either.

It seems, then, that critics really disagree with Aristotle about whether it is just to "treat equals equally" not because they have different moral views but because they understand different things by it. They claim that Aristotle's faulty analysis led him to

[11] Aristotle appears to have avoided the ambiguity by speaking not of the right of equals to be "treated equally" or to "equal treatment," but rather of their right to "equality" and to "equal shares."

say things that are false, but in reality it is the language of 'equality' that creates, and perpetuates, an illusion of controversy.

The Truth of "Equals Should Be Treated Equally"

The truth of the precept "equals should be treated equally" is analytic. Whether interpreted as Aristotle understood it or as his critics understand it, its truth inheres in its meaning. Aristotle and his critics agree that the precept is true; they differ only regarding its sufficiency. On Aristotle's interpretation, it is a true statement that fully suffices as a formula for justice. On his critics' interpretation, it is a true statement that is necessary to justice but not sufficient for it.

In contrast, some commentators deny that the precept is true. That is, they deny that "treating equals equally" is a necessary condition of distributive justice. Norman Bowie, for example, denies that equals should be treated equally when people have an equal claim to commodities that are either indivisible or, if divided, leave everyone with an inadequate amount.[12] Bowie asks us to imagine that two men are trapped on an ice floe under circumstances in which sufficient food can be supplied to keep only one of them alive. Under those circumstances, he says, it would be "unjust" to treat them equally by giving them equal shares of food because equal distributions would cause both to die under circumstances in which one can be saved. To that extent, he says, equals should *not* be treated equally.

Bowie's apparent disagreement with Aristotle and his critics is entirely semantic. He disagrees about the justice of "treating equals equally" because he interprets the precept to mean something different. Aristotle and his critics understand it to mean:

People who are identical with respect to the treatments they ought to receive should be treated identically with respect to the treatments they ought to receive.

Bowie understands it to mean:

People who are identical with respect to the treatments they ought to receive should be treated identically *by being given per-capita shares*—regardless of whether they all ought to receive per-capita shares.

[12] Bowie, "Equality and Distributive Justice," p. 140.

As a result, the two interpretations inevitably produce different results in every case in which people are prescriptively identical in some respect *other* than in deserving per-capita shares.

The problem with Bowie's interpretation is that it attributes a meaning to "treating equals equally" that the phrase cannot plausibly possess. Consider his example of the two men on an ice floe. What does Bowie mean in saying that the two men have equal claims on the available food without having a right to equal shares? Presumably he means that they either have equal claims to having the food distributed by lot or have equal claims to having the food withheld altogether. If "treating equals equally" is to make normative sense, therefore, it must mean treating the men equally in the respects in which Bowie implicitly assumes them to be normatively equal—that is, with respect either to distributing the food by lot or to withholding it altogether. It cannot plausibly mean treating the men equally in a respect in which they are *not* normatively equal.

The Supposed Content of "Equals Should Be Treated Equally"

We have seen that Aristotle's precept lends itself to two distinct interpretations, and that the truth of each can be found in the precept's constituent terms. As Aristotle interprets it, the precept is both self-evidently just and uninformative: self-evidently just because "equals" are defined as persons who under just normative rules ought to receive certain treatment; uninformative because, rather than making a statement about the world, or revealing something previously unknown, it merely restates the import of the term 'equals', namely, that such persons ought to receive the treatment that just rules prescribe for them. As Aristotle's critics interpret it, the precept also says something analytic; yet what it says is not always just—namely, that people who deserve certain identical treatment should always receive either *that* or some *other* identical treatment (as opposed to *not* receiving identical treatment). In neither case, however, does the precept add to our knowledge of justice. Aristotle's interpretation contains no new moral information because it merely states that complying with just rules is itself just. The critics' interpretation adds nothing new because it merely states that one cannot be just *without* complying with just rules.

Interestingly, some commentators believe that Aristotle's precept *does* provide independent moral guidance—that it tells us

194

something new about how we ought to behave. Kent Greenawalt has expressed such a view with particular care and sophistication. He believes that the precept "equals should be treated equally" has independent "moral content" over and above whatever comparative and noncomparative rules a particular society may accept as just. He argues that the precept can direct our normative judgments in two distinct ways: first, it can come into play *before* settled rules are formulated by providing "genuine direction" about what moral or legal rules to adopt; and, second, it can come into play *after* rules are formulated by providing additional reasons for complying with just rules.

Before Rules Have Been Formulated

Let us begin with Greenawalt's suggestion that Aristotle's precept can operate before rules are formulated to influence their eventual content. Greenawalt asks us to imagine a case in which "identical twins" commit a burglary for which they share joint responsibility. The sentencing judge, who is uncertain about what sentences to impose, knows only two things for certain: first, the appropriate sentences for defendants under such circumstances lie somewhere between a term of imprisonment and a term of probation; and, second, there are "no distinguishing features" that warrant different sentences for the twins. Under those circumstances, Greenawalt says, Aristotle's precept comes into play to "affect the substantive judgment" the judge eventually makes because it tells the judge that, whatever sentences he eventually imposes, he should give the same sentence to both twins. Indeed, the "moral force" of the precept is so strong that it requires the judge to give the same sentence to both even though the judge believes that giving one twin probation and the other a term of imprisonment would make "a useful experiment" of the penological values of the two sentences: "Recognizing that each twin would strongly prefer to be placed on probation, the judge [should] hold back [from imposing differential sentences], sensing that treating two 'equals' so unequally would be unfair, even if an independent reason for doing so supports differential treatment."[13]

Greenawalt's judge, believing that the twins possess "no distinguishing features," concludes that it would be "unfair" to sentence one twin to prison and the other to probation. Greenawalt is

---

[13] Greenawalt, "How Empty Is the Idea of Equality?" p. 1171.

correct that, if the twins possess no distinguishing features, it would be unfair to sentence them differently. He is not so clearly correct, however, about the source of the judge's knowledge that it would be unfair to give the twins different sentences. Greenawalt believes that the origin of the judge's moral knowledge is the precept "equals should be treated equally." Yet, as we have seen, to say that two people are equal *means* that they fall within a class of persons for whom a relevant rule prescribes the same treatment. Thus, if the twins are "equals," it must be by virtue of an extant rule prescribing identical treatment for persons of their description. In this case, the pertinent rule is the unstated rule of criminal law that informs the judge's determination that "no distinguishing feature warrants different sentences for the two [twins]"—a rule of sentencing which, as applied to the twins, regards them as indistinguishable. Although the judge does not make the rule explicit, he appears to have something like the following in mind:

R_1: No criminal sentence shall either exceed or fall short of the sentence that most closely corresponds in gravity to the defendant's degree of blameworthiness.

or

R_2: No criminal sentence shall either exceed or fall short of the sentence that would most effectively deter the defendant or others from committing such crimes.

or

R_3: No criminal sentence shall either exceed or fall short of the sentence that would most effectively deter the defendant or others from committing such crimes, provided that the sentence does not exceed in gravity the defendant's degree of blameworthiness.

It is R_1, R_2, or R_3—not Aristotle—that supplies the judge with the knowledge that it would be "unfair" to give the twins different sentences, because it is R_1, R_2, or R_3 (or something like them) that informs the judge's determination that the twins, being indistinguishable regarding blameworthiness or deterrence value, are normatively "indistinguishable" and, hence, "equal" with respect to the sentences they ought to receive. These rules do not themselves instruct the judge whether to sentence the twins to prison or to probation because they do not specify which sentence corresponds to their degree of blameworthiness or to the desired deterrence. But they do tell the judge that whatever the appropriate sentence for the twins may be (whether imprisonment or probation), it must be the same for both.

To illustrate the significance of such antecedent rules, imagine that the twins had committed their crime in a jurisdiction which holds that, although it is never appropriate to impose sentences that *exceed* what defendants deserve in regard to blameworthiness or deterrence, it may be appropriate to impose sentences that are *less* than what defendants deserve. The jurisdiction holds that judges and prosecutors may be justified in reducing a sentence below what a defendant deserves for a variety of penological purposes, e.g., in order to induce a minor offender to cooperate in testifying against a major offender, or to induce a defendant to enter a guilty plea rather than put the state through a protracted trial, or to achieve the goals of amnesty, or to gather experimental data on the relative effectiveness of various sentencing options. Thus, rather than adhering to rules R_1–R_3, the jurisdiction embraces the following rule:

R_4: No criminal sentence shall exceed the sentence that corresponds in gravity to the defendant's degree of blameworthiness [or that would optimally deter the defendant or others]— but a sentence may be reduced below that level for penological purposes, including persuading witnesses to testify, inducing defendants to enter guilty pleas, achieving amnesty, and gathering experimental data regarding optimum sentencing practices.

In a jurisdiction that regards rule R_4 as just, as some jurisdictions do,[14] it would not be "unfair," all things considered, for a judge to

[14] Most jurisdictions in the United States allow prosecutors and judges to exercise leniency in order to persuade witnesses to testify and to induce defendants to plead guilty. See generally Newman, *Conviction*. Some jurisdictions allow courts to exercise selective leniency in the interests of gathering data on optimal sentencing practices. See Lipton, Martinson, and Wilks, *The Effectiveness of Correctional Treatment*, pp. 90–91 (discussing the "California" and "Bernstein" experiments on the relative utility of long and short sentences); pp. 75–77, 100–102, 424–26 (discussing the "Warren" experiments on the relative utility of incarceration and probation); Empey and Erickson, *The Provo Experiment*, pp. 23–38 (discussing the "Provo" experiment on the relative utility of incarceration and supervised living, and the relative utility of supervised living and probation); Karpardis and Farrington, "An Experimental Study of Sentencing by Magistrates," p. 109 (referring to a "real-life experiment" by Berg and McGuire in which juvenile truants were randomly selected to be adjourned, on the one hand, or supervised, on the other). Cf. *Aguayo v. Richardson*, 473 F.2d 1090, 1108–12 (2d Cir., 1973) (Friendly, J.) (a state may constitutionally

randomly select one twin for imprisonment and the other for probation, any more than it would be "unfair" to reduce a defendant's sentence in return for his cooperation. Nor would the judge be treating "equals" unequally, because, in invoking R_4, the judge would be concluding that the two *do* possess "distinguishing features"—namely, that one twin has been selected at random for an important experiment that will fail if both twins are used.[15] If the judge in Greenawalt's hypothetical case feels differently, it is because, even though the judge has not formulated *all* the rules that suffice for sentencing the twins, he has implicitly formulated at least *one* rule to which the precept "equals should be treated equally" may refer, namely, a rule such as rule R_1 from which it follows that the twins possess "no distinguishing feature."

To be sure, Greenawalt might disagree about the fairness of rule R_4. He might argue in response that there is always an element of unfairness in giving a defendant a lesser sentence than he deserves; that a judge should do so only under extraordinary circumstances where considerations of great public need override considerations of fairness; and that, although inducing one of the twins

---

experiment on welfare recipients by randomly placing some of them in experimental work project programs for the purpose of gathering information about optimum income maintenance policy), cert. denied sub nom *Aguayo v. Weinberger*, 414 U.S. 1146 (1974). For an analysis of the justice of giving defendants lesser sentences than they deserve, see Garcia, "Two Concepts of Desert."

[15] Jeffrie Murphy discusses an analogous case in his treatment of the question: Does a good Samaritan, who wishes to bestow charity on a mendicant, Jones, because of Jones's possession of characteristic C but who cannot afford to bestow charity on all mendicants possessing characteristic C, violate the axiom that "equals should be treated equally" by bestowing charity on Jones while withholding it from mendicant Smith who also possesses characteristic C? Murphy concludes that the good Samaritan does *not* violate the axiom because, under the circumstances, mendicants Jones and Smith are not "equals." They may be equal in possessing characteristic C, but they are not equal, all things considered, because one of them has been selected at random, and the other has not, by a benefactor who is morally justified in setting limits to his philanthropy:

> [I]f I show mercy to C-bearing Jones, how can I consistently (morally?) fail to show mercy to equally C-bearing Smith? If moral conventions are viewed as agreements based on rational self-interest, then the impact *on me* of my continued showings of mercy would become relevant. Thus, what relevantly distinguishes the Jones case from the Smith case will not be some feature that distinguishes Jones from Smith but, rather, some feature that distinguishes the impact on me of mercy to Jones from the impact on me of mercy to Smith. The mere fact that Jones got there first (or I noticed him first) might then make a great deal of difference. Smith, who is also pitiful to degree P, also owes me five dollars. I do not show him mercy, however, because, though I can afford the loss of five dollars, I cannot afford the loss of ten.

Murphy, "Mercy and Legal Justice," p. 59.

to cooperate with the prosecution or enter a guilty plea might be a matter of great public need justifying different sentences, gathering experimental data on sentencing practices is not. This argument has considerable force and, in the end, may reflect common intuitions more fully than the intuitions embodied in rule R_4. Nevertheless, even if one accepts the argument, it does not mean that, in balking at giving the twins different sentences for experimental reasons, Greenawalt's judge is deriving content from "equals should be treated equally" that *antedates* or *precedes* rules by which "equals" are defined. It means, rather, that in determining that the twins are "equals," the judge is adjudging the twins by some modification of rule R_4, a modified rule that would distinguish among twins in the interests of plea bargaining but not in the interests of gathering experimental information, such as:

> R_5: No criminal sentence shall exceed the sentence that corresponds in gravity to the defendant's degree of blameworthiness [or that would optimally deter the defendant or others]— but a sentence may be reduced below that level for penological purposes, including persuading witnesses to testify, inducing defendants to enter guilty pleas, and achieving amnesty, *but not including the gathering of experimental data regarding optimum sentencing practices.*

At the very instant at which the judge adjudges the twins to be "equals"—that is, adjudges them to possess "no distinguishing features" for sentencing purposes—the judge must also have embraced a rule something like rule R_5, because otherwise, the judge would have no way of knowing that, although the twins might be unequals for purposes of plea bargaining, they are equals for the purposes at hand.

After Rules Have Been Formulated

Now let us consider Greenawalt's second assertion, namely, that "equals should be treated equally" can come into play after rules of conduct have been formulated to provide an "additional moral reason" for complying with a rule. To illustrate, he posits the following situation:

Final Exams

A group of students take an examination in a class in which a score of 71 is established as a passing grade. Two of the students, B and C, both receive scores of 71. When their grades are recorded, however, they discover that, while C has received a passing grade in compliance with established school rules, B has received a failing grade in violation of established school rules.

Greenawalt argues that the teacher has wronged B in two ways: first, the teacher has given B a grade he does not deserve in violation of established school rules; second, the teacher has treated B differently from C, thereby violating the principle that "equals should be treated equally." The latter violation is a "separate aspect of the wrong" suffered by B, he says, because it "magnifie[s]" the wrong:

> If established criteria require that B, with a grade of seventy-one, be passed, then B has suffered a wrong if he is failed; but the *wrong may be magnified* if C, also with a grade of seventy-one is passed. Here, the formal principle [of equality] does not bear on how B should be treated (only redundantly indicating what treatment is called for by established criteria); but it does focus attention on a separate aspect of the wrong that is done to B if the criteria are not followed.[16]

Indeed, he says, the "separate aspect" of the wrong a person suffers by being treated unequally in violation of an established rule may even suffice to justify rejecting the established rule altogether. Thus, he continues, if "soft-hearted teachers" violate the school rule by passing six students with failing scores of 69, a hard-hearted teacher may thus become obliged to pass a seventh student with a score of 69 rather than allow "equals" to be treated unequally.

Greenawalt's reasoning here follows a pattern we analyzed earlier. He is correct about the *existence* of additional elements of fairness but not about their *source*. He believes that the additional elements of fairness derive from the precept "equals should be treated equally," while in reality the content of the precept derives entirely from the school's rules. Thus, Greenawalt is correct when he concludes that, having given B a failing grade, B's teacher "magnified" the wrong to B by giving a passing grade to C. He is wrong, however, about the source of the wrong. He believes that the wrong derives partly from the teacher's violation of established school rules and partly from a violation of the precept "equals

---

[16] Greenawalt, "How Empty Is the Idea of Equality?" p. 1173.

should be treated equally"; in reality, it derives entirely from the violation of school rules.

To see why, let us consider the school's rules regarding grading. Although Greenawalt does not state the rule explicitly, he appears to have something like the following in mind:

> Grading: An exam score of 71 is necessary and sufficient for a passing grade. No student shall be given a grade that is higher or lower than is justified by his score.

The "grading" rule can be assumed to embody two distinct policies—one noncomparative, the other comparative. The noncomparative policy is to enable a student to qualify for further instruction and for graduation by demonstrating that he or she has learned enough in a particular course to receive a score of 71. The latter policy is noncomparative because neither its fulfillment nor its violation depends upon how other students are treated. Thus, by denying B a passing grade despite his score of 71, the teacher violated the latter policy and wronged B. The violation and the wrong were complete at the moment the teacher denied B a passing grade, and do not depend upon how the teacher treated other students with scores of 71. If the teacher had denied all students with scores of 71 a passing grade, he would have wronged all of them to the same extent he wronged B.

The "grading" rule can also be assumed to embody a comparative policy based on the fact that in modern societies academic credits give competitive advantages to those who possess them vis-à-vis those who lack them. The policy is to prevent one student from acquiring an unfair competitive advantage over another. It is comparative because its fulfillment and its violation *do* depend directly on how other students are treated. Thus, let us imagine (as Greenawalt does) that after soft-hearted teachers give passing grades to six students with scores of 69, a hard-hearted teacher gives a failing grade to a seventh student, X, with a score of 69. The hard-hearted teacher does not violate the school's noncomparative policy by giving X a failing grade, nor does he wrong X in that respect, for X has not acquired sufficient knowledge to earn a passing grade. Yet, by giving X a failing grade, the hard-hearted teacher frustrates the school's comparative policy because he places X in a unfair position vis-à-vis the other six students. (We shall postpone for a moment discussion of whether the hard-hearted teacher was nevertheless right to give X a failing grade, as well as the relationship of that question to Aristotle's precept.)

201

This distinction between the school's two implicit policies is significant because it explains the relationship between the "original" wrong to B (denying B a passing grade on a score of 71) and the "magnified" wrong to B (giving C a passing grade on the same score). By giving B a failing grade, the teacher violated the school's noncomparative policy and, to that extent, wronged B. Thereafter, by giving C a passing grade on the same score, the teacher "magnified" the wrong to B (and created a "separate aspect of the wrong") by violating the school's comparative policy against giving one student an unfair advantage vis-à-vis another. Greenawalt believes that this "separate aspect of the wrong" originates, not in a violation of school rules, but in a violation of the principle that "equals should be treated equally." Yet that is not the case, because in the absence of the school's comparative policy, there would have been no "separate aspect of the wrong."

To illustrate the relationship between the school's comparative policy and the "separate aspect of the wrong," consider the following situation:

A Free Physical Examination

A public school in California establishes a rule to the effect that every student is entitled to a free physical examination. The purpose of the rule is to inform each student of the state of his health, not to prevent one student from gaining a comparative advantage over another. Along with other public institutions, the school is bound by the Fourteenth Amendment rule that it not stigmatize persons on grounds of race.

In the course of the year, the school complies with its rule with respect to every student, except that

—the school deliberately denies a black student, Y, a free physical examination because it has less regard for his interests than for those of its white students; and

—the school mistakenly denies a white student, Z, a free physical exam by confusing him with another white student of the same name.

The black student, Y, is in much the same situation as Greenawalt's student, B. By denying him a free physical examination, the school violates the noncomparative policy underlying its rule, a violation that would obtain even if the school also denied all its white students a free physical exam. Moreover, by denying him an examination on grounds of *race*, the school "compounds" the wrong by violating the comparative policy underlying the Fourteenth Amendment rule against depreciating persons on grounds of race. In the end, the school treats Y unequally, in violation of the precept "equals should be treated equally," in *two* distinct respects: first, by denying him the free physical exam given to others; and, second, by depreciating his interests vis-à-vis those of others on grounds of race.[17] Indeed, the only difference for our purposes between "A Free Physical Examination" and Greenawalt's case "Final Exams" is that in the former case a noncomparative wrong is "compounded" by the violation of a comparative policy found in an independent rule (the Fourteenth Amendment), and in Greenawalt's case a noncomparative wrong is "magnified" by the violation of a comparative policy found in the same rule as the noncomparative policy (the school's "grading" rule).

The white student, Z, is in a very different situation. In denying Z a free physical examination, the school wrongs Z by violating its noncomparative policy regarding free physical exams, a violation that would obtain even if the school denied the exam to all its students. Notice, however, what happens to the wrong to Z—or, more accurately, what does *not* happen—when the school grants other students the free physical exam it inadvertently denied Z. What happens is—nothing. The wrong to Z is neither "magnified" nor "compounded" by the school's decision to give free physical exams to the other students, because the school's treatment of other students violates no comparative policy for the protection of Z. By giving other students what it denies Z, the school wrongly treats Z unequally in violation of the precept "equals should be treated equally." The latter wrong, however, is not distinct from the first wrong; it is the *same* wrong—the wrong of denying Z the free physical exam to which he is entitled. In Z's case, "violating the rule" and "treating equals unequally" are alternative ways of talking about the same wrong to Z.

[17] The same analysis would obtain in the case of a jurisdiction that intentionally denies a white student a free physical exam simply because it does not care as much about his interests as about those of his fellow white students, provided, of course, that the jurisdiction adheres to a rule of law or morals to the effect that each person's well-being ought to count as much as everyone else's: by intentionally denying the white student a free physical exam that it extends to other white students, the jurisdiction violates both the noncomparative policy in favor of giving every student a physical *and* the comparative policy in favor of counting each person's well-being as much as everyone else's.

In contrast, if in Greenawalt's "Final Exams" the noncomparative wrong to B is "magnified"—if "treating equals unequally" is not merely an alternative way of talking about the initial wrong—it is because "treating equals unequally" is an alternative way of talking about a *further* wrong to B, the wrong of violating the school's separate comparative policy against unfairly disadvantaging one student vis-à-vis another. It follows, therefore, that the total wrong to B does not originate partly in the "grading" rule and partly in the precept "equals should be treated equally" but entirely in the two policies underlying the "grading" rule.

This brings us to the final questions Greenawalt raises. After soft-hearted teachers have passed six students with scores of 69, how should a hard-hearted teacher treat a seventh student, X, with an identical score of 69? In making his decision, what guidance can the teacher derive from the precept "equals should be treated equally"? Ironically, these questions are identical to the first question Greenawalt raised—namely, what is the content of Aristotle's precept *before* rules have been formulated? The questions are identical because the hard-hearted teacher must decide what *new* rule—what *remedial* rule—to adopt in the event that the two policies underlying the "grading" rule can no longer both be fulfilled. To decide what remedial rule to adopt, the teacher must decide which of the school's two policies ought to predominate in the event they conflict: if the teacher decides that the school's noncomparative policy is the more important of the two, he ought to respond by giving X a failing grade; if, on the other hand, he decides that the school's comparative policy is the more important, he ought to respond by giving X a passing grade. Whatever he decides, the teacher cannot derive any guidance from the precept "equals should be treated equally" because the precept cannot come into play before a remedial rule has been formulated to respond to the new situation. For, as we have seen, a teacher cannot know whether one student is prescriptively "equal" or "unequal" to others before he decides what rule of conduct to follow.

The Meaning of "Unequals Should Be Treated Unequally"

Aristotle's second precept involves many of the problems of the first. Yet it also raises questions of its own. Some commentators suggest, for example, that while equals should indeed be treated equally, unequals should *not* always be treated unequally.

The Relationship between "Equals Should Be Treated Equally"
and "Unequals Should Be Treated Unequally"

Much of what is true of the precept "equals should be treated
equally" is also true of "unequals should be treated unequally."
Thus, if Aristotle's second precept is true, then the noun 'unequals' must at least refer to people who are prescriptively unequal, that is, to people who are nonidentical with respect to the
treatments they ought to receive. By the same token, if the second
precept is true, the adverb 'unequally' must at least incorporate
the same prescriptive standard of treatment by which such people
have been ascertained to be unequal. Accordingly, if it is to make
any sense at all, the precept "people who are unequal should be
treated unequally" must at least mean:

People who are "nonidentical with respect to the treatments
they ought to receive" should be treated "nonidentically with
respect to the treatments they ought to receive."

or

People who are "nonidentical by reference to a relevant rule
of conduct" should be treated "nonidentically by reference to
that rule of conduct."

Just as the phrase "treated equally" renders Aristotle's first precept ambiguous, the phrase "treated unequally" renders the second precept ambiguous. To say people are "treated unequally
with respect to the treatments they ought to receive" may mean
either that they are treated unequally *in accord with* the unequal
treatment to which they are entitled or that they are treated unequally *in violation* of the unequal treatment to which they are entitled. Accordingly, "people who are unequal should be treated
unequally" can plausibly be understood in two ways:

People who are nonidentical by reference to relevant rules of
conduct should be treated nonidentically by reference to such
rules—meaning that such persons should all be *granted* the
nonidentical treatment that relevant rules prescribe for them.

or

People who are nonidentical by reference to relevant rules of
conduct should be treated nonidentically by reference to such

rules—whether it means *granting* them all or *denying* them all the nonidentical treatment that relevant rules prescribe for them.

The former interpretation (which is Aristotle's) yields a precept that is always just. The latter yields a precept that is a necessary basis for just action but is not sufficient for it. Both interpretations, though different, are true in their own respective ways.

It is no coincidence that these two interpretations correspond with those of Aristotle's first precept, for "equals should be treated equally" *necessarily entails* that "unequals should be treated unequally." The former precept entails the latter because every rule of conduct by which "equals" and "unequals" are measured can be stated at two levels of generality. One can say that the rule creates subclasses of persons who, being in subclasses, are "unequal," and, hence, should be treated "unequally." One can also say that the rule creates a single class of persons who, being all entitled to the benefit of the rule as a whole, are "equal" and should be treated "equally." Both statements are true because they are alternative ways of referring to the same normative relationships.

To illustrate, suppose that the state of New York enacts a statute guaranteeing indigent families with dependent children a monthly payment of $100 per child. Suppose further that two indigent mothers, Mary and Sue, have three and one dependent children, respectively, and are thus entitled to respective monthly payments of $300 and $100. The New York rule can be stated in two alternative ways, so the relationships between Mary and Sue can be stated in two alternative ways as well. One can state the New York law as the rule

> Indigent families with three dependent children shall receive $300 per month, while indigent families with one dependent child shall receive $100 per month.

In that event, one would say that Mary and Sue are prescriptively "unequal" and should be treated "unequally"—meaning that Mary and Sue are entitled to unequal monthly payments and should be treated unequally in that respect. Alternatively, one can state the New York rule as

> Indigent families with dependent children shall receive $100 per month per child.

In that event, one would say that Mary and Sue are prescriptively "equal" and should be treated "equally"—meaning Mary and Sue are both entitled to $100 per child and should be treated equally in that respect. Each statement is true because they are alternative ways of expressing the same prescriptive relationship.

It is not surprising that Aristotle's first precept regarding "equals" subsumes the second regarding "unequals," because, as we have seen, the formula of proportional equality is broad enough to encompass all just relationships, whether they are proportions of 1:1 or proportions of 3:1 (as with Mary and Sue). That is why Aristotle sometimes says that justice means *both* "treating equals equally" *and* "treating unequals unequally" and at other times says that justice means "equality."[18] A person who believes that "equals should be treated equally" must be committed to believing that "unequals should be treated unequally," for the former implies the latter.

Dissenting Views

Some commentators agree that "equals" should be treated equally, but disagree with the converse, arguing that *unequals* should sometimes be treated *equally*.

Greenawalt, for example, argues that the term 'unequals' is "ordinarily" understood to relate to the treatments persons would receive if the purposes behind particular programs could be "perfectly" carried out, and that when such purposes cannot be perfectly carried out we may be justified in treating "unequals" equally.[19] He gives the example of a decision made by Lord Halifax during World War II. Lord Halifax traced a leak of national security secrets from the Foreign Office to a particular typing pool but could trace it no further. Unable to identify the culprit, and unwilling to risk further leaks, he felt he had no choice but to sack everyone in the typing pool. Greenawalt regards Lord Halifax's decision as an instance in which "unequals" (in this case the guilty and innocent members of the typing pool) may justifiably be treated equally because of the realistic difficulties involved in treating them unequally.

Greenawalt believes he has found a flaw in Aristotle's second

[18] Compare Aristotle, *Politics* III.5.1280a1–10 (justice is treating equals equally and unequals unequally), with Aristotle, *Nicomachean Ethics* V.3.1131a10–30 (justice is equality).
[19] See Greenawalt, "How Empty Is the Idea of Equality"? pp. 1174–75.

precept, but instead he has given it a meaning it cannot plausibly have. We have seen that, if the precept is valid, it must mean that "people who are unequal by reference to a relevant rule of conduct should be treated unequally by reference to the rule." In contrast, Greenawalt implicitly takes it to mean that "people who are unequal by reference to an *irrelevant* rule of conduct should be treated unequally by reference to the rule." For, if the members of the typing pool are prescriptively unequal, it is by virtue of a rule that Greenawalt does not believe to be relevant under the circumstances.

Greenawalt begins by asserting that the guilty and innocent members of the typing pool are prescriptively unequal. If he is right, it must be by virtue of a rule that treats the guilty and the innocent differently, for example:

R_1: No employer shall discharge a person for breaches of national security unless the person can be shown to have committed the breach.

Yet, at the same time, Greenawalt implicitly asserts that R_1 is an irrelevant rule because he believes that Lord Halifax was justified in firing the guilty and the innocent alike. If Lord Halifax was so justified, it must be by virtue of a rule that does not distinguish between the guilty and the innocent, for example:

R_2: No employer shall discharge an innocent person for breaches of national security unless, based on all the information reasonably available, the person falls within the smallest class of persons whose discharge is absolutely necessary to eliminate the person responsible for the breach.

Measured by the prescriptive standards of R_2, the guilty and innocent members of the pool are equals, not unequals. Consequently, to say (as Greenawalt does) that Lord Halifax's conduct demonstrates that "unequals" should not always be treated "unequally" is to attribute a meaning to Aristotle's second precept that it cannot plausibly have—namely, that people who are "unequal" by a rule that is *irrelevant* under the circumstances (i.e., R_1) should be treated unequally by reference to the irrelevant rule.

A. M. Honoré challenges the validity of Aristotle's second precept on other grounds. Honoré agrees that to treat equals equally is to treat them in accord with the relevant rules by which they are classified as members of a single class, and that the "principle of treating like cases alike" is therefore a principle of "social justice."

Yet he denies that the principle "treat unlike cases unlike" is "part of the notion of justice, or of social justice in particular."[20] His reasoning is straightforward: He asks the reader to imagine a society which possesses a rule that explicitly gives men the right to vote without explicitly giving the right to vote to women—a rule that is consistent with the existence of collateral rules giving women the right to vote. To say that men and women are "unequal" under the rule means that the rule distinguishes between them by entitling men to vote without also entitling women to vote. To treat men and women "unequally," however, means allowing men to vote while *prohibiting* women from voting. The precept "unequals should be treated unequally" is unjust, therefore, because it goes beyond what a just society might wish to prescribe by precluding the possibility of collateral rules (in this case, rules giving women the right to vote).

The fallacy in Honoré's argument is nearly the converse of Greenawalt's. Honoré appears to assume that Aristotle's second precept means "people who are unequal by reference to a relevant rule of conduct ought to be treated unequally by reference to an *irrelevant* rule." Thus, he takes people who are "unequal" by reference to a relevant rule of conduct,

R_1: Men are herewith entitled to vote, while women are *not* herewith entitled to vote.

and assumes that they must therefore be treated unequally by reference to some other rule of conduct,

R_2: Men are herewith entitled to vote, while women are herewith *prohibited* from voting.

In doing this, Honoré, like Greenawalt, attributes to Aristotle's precept a meaning it cannot plausibly possess. If the precept is valid, it means that "people who are unequal by reference to a relevant rule of conduct ought to be treated unequally by reference to *that* rule." Thus, if R_1 is the relevant rule, then men and women are unequal and ought to be treated unequally by reference to R_1— meaning that, while men have a right to vote under R_1, women have no right to vote under R_1 (although they may have a right to vote under some other, collateral rule). If, on the other hand, R_2 is the relevant rule, then, again, men and women are unequal and ought to be treated unequally by reference to that rule—meaning

---

[20] Honoré, "Social Justice," pp. 83–84.

that, while men have a right to vote under R_2, women are prohibited by R_2 from voting (and thereby have no right to vote under other, collateral rules). Yet no one seriously suggests that men and women who are "unequal" by a relevant rule ought to be treated unequally by an irrelevant rule—or that a rule that treats women as "unequal" to men by *not entitling* women to vote should be understood to *prohibit* women from voting.

The Requirement of "Consistency"

Some commentators assert that the principle "equals should be treated equally" does something that underlying rules of conduct cannot do, namely, it ensures that rules of conduct are applied "consistently." Thus, Erwin Chemerinsky observes that every rule "inevitab[ly]" accords some "discretion" to decisionmakers charged with administering it. Yet, he adds, in exercising discretion, decisionmakers are also obliged to administer rules in a "consistent" and "even-hande[d]" manner. It would seem to follow, he says, that since the obligation to apply rules consistently does not derive from the rules themselves, it must derive from the independent requirement that "equals be treated equally."[21]

Other commentators go further, arguing that, with respect to decisions over time, the norm of consistency mandates a regime of precedent, that is, a regime in which earlier decisions constrain later decisions. This is so because later decisions can be made to conform to earlier decisions, but earlier decisions cannot be changed to conform to later decisions. It follows, they say, that if "equals" are to be treated "equally," the mere existence of an earlier decision requires a decisionmaker to decide later cases accordingly. According to Ronald Dworkin:

> The gravitational force of precedent may be explained by appeal not to the wisdom of enforcing enactments, but to the fairness of treating like cases alike. A precedent is the report of an earlier political decision; the very fact of that decision, as a piece of political history, provides some reason for deciding other cases in a similar way in the future.[22]

Commentators differ regarding the form of precedential decisions. Some argue that a precedent consists of an earlier decisionmaker's explicit reasoning in support of his decision; others argue that it

[21] Chemerinsky, "In Defense of Equality," pp. 580–81.
[22] Dworkin, *Taking Rights Seriously*, p. 113.

consists solely of the judicial order the earlier judge entered upon the facts as they are now understood.[23] In either event, however, the force of precedent is said to rest, not only on pragmatic considerations of efficiency, predictability, and protection against covert bias, but on the principled consideration—the "almost universal sense of justice"[24]—that "equals should be treated equally."[25]

I believe that the foregoing views of consistency and precedent are erroneous. The norm of consistency does not originate in the precept "equals should be treated equally." It originates entirely in underlying rules whose administration is at issue. Precedent does not have force apart from the pragmatic considerations that justify it; rather, its force derives solely from such considerations. When precedent has force, the precedent consists not in the decisionmaker's reasoning or disposition alone, but typically in both his reasoning and his disposition of the issue. To support these assertions, I shall proceed by analyzing consistency, first in the context of coeval decisions, and then in the context of decisions over time.

Coeval Consistency

The issue of consistency is not confined to decisionmaking over time; it also arises when a decisionmaker renders coeval, or contemporaneous, decisions. The issue of coeval consistency can arise in the context of two kinds of rules: mandatory rules, which leave a decisionmaker no room for discretion, and discretionary rules, which leave the decisionmaker some room to formulate policy. Although it is sometimes suggested that the issue of consistency arises only in the context of discretionary rules,[26] we shall see that the nature of consistency is the same in both contexts.

Let us begin with an example of a mandatory rule. Assume that a judge jointly convicts two defendants for illegally possessing firearms under a criminal statute that carries a mandatory sentence of one year in jail. The judge, announcing his intention to impose

[23] Compare Goodhart, "Determining the *Ratio Decidendi* of a Case," pp. 25–26 (arguing that precedent consists of the order the earlier judge entered upon the facts that the earlier judge regarded as normatively relevant), with Dworkin, *Law's Empire*, pp. 228–38, and *A Matter of Principle*, pp. 158–62 (arguing that precedent consists, not in what facts the earlier judge regarded as normatively relevant, but in the judgment the earlier judge entered upon the facts as the subsequent judge understands them).
[24] Llewellyn, "Case Law," p. 249.
[25] See Dworkin, *Taking Rights Seriously*, p. 135.
[26] See Chemerinsky, "In Defense of Equality," pp. 579–81.

sentences that are "consistent," sentences each defendant to one year in jail. What does it mean to say that these sentences are consistent? Sentences are consistent to the extent that they *both hold to the same principle or practice.*[27] Further, sentences are *normatively* consistent to the extent that they both adhere to the principle or practice *to which they ought to adhere.*[28] In this case, the principle to which sentences ought to adhere is obvious, namely, the principle that persons convicted of illegally possessing firearms shall be committed to jail for one year. In this case, therefore, to act consistently in normative respects is to hold to the rule to which one ought to hold.

It is sometimes thought that the problems of consistency change as one moves from mandatory rules to discretionary rules.[29] They do not. A decisionmaker's obligation to act consistently remains the same in both contexts, viz., to hold to the rule or rules to which he or she ought to hold. Recall Greenawalt's hypothetical case of the identical twins who are found equally blameworthy of burglary under a statute that permits a judge to use his best judgment in adopting sentences ranging anywhere from probation to one year in jail. The judge simultaneously sentences one twin to probation and the other to one year in jail, believing that, while both deserve up to one year in jail, it would constitute a useful experiment to sentence one of them to probation. The twin who receives the jail sentence complains that the sentences are not "consistent." What can the judge say in response? Are the sentences normatively consistent or inconsistent? The answer depends on which principle of sentencing the judge ought to be applying—or, in this case, which principle reflects his "best judgment" regarding sentencing. Thus, if the judge, using his best judgment, adopts the principle R_1:

R_1: No criminal sentence shall either exceed or fall short of the sentence that most closely corresponds in gravity to the defendant's degree of blameworthiness.

then the sentences are normatively inconsistent. This is so because, if the judge held to R_1 with respect to both twins, he would

[27] 'Consistent' is defined as "holding to the same principles or practice." *Webster's New World Dictionary*, p. 134.

[28] J. M. Brennan defines normative consistency as, not "fidelity to rules of conduct," but "fidelity to . . . the *rationale* behind the rule[s]." Brennan, *The Open-Texture of Moral Concepts*, p. 157.

[29] See note 26 above.

212

have to give them both the same sentence. On the other hand, if the judge, using his best judgment, adopts the principle R_2:

R_2: No criminal sentence shall be made to exceed the sentence that most closely corresponds in gravity to the defendant's degree of blameworthiness—but a sentence may be reduced below that level for penological purposes, including the gathering of experimental data regarding optimum sentencing practices.

then the sentences are normatively consistent, for both hold to the principle of sentencing to which they ought to hold under the circumstances.

Decisions that are normatively consistent by reference to R_2 will be descriptively inconsistent as measured by the standards of R_1. Indeed, it will always be true that decisions that are consistent as measured by one rule will be descriptively inconsistent as measured by others. The normative question, however, is not whether decisions are consistent by just any standard, but whether they are consistent by reference to the standard contained in the rule to which the decisionmaker ought to be adhering.

Consistency over Time

To illustrate the nature of consistency over time, consider a variation on Greenawalt's hypothetical case:

The Mercurial Judge

Identical triplets are jointly convicted of conspiracy to commit a burglary for which they are equally blameworthy. The burglary statute authorizes sentences ranging from probation to five years in prison.

The judge sets separate sentencing hearings for each of the triplets, scheduling them one week apart. In the course of each of the hearings the judge does two things: he announces his "opinion" in the case, that is, his reasons for imposing the particular sentence at issue; and he announces an "order" in the case, that is, a particular sentence he enters against the defendant. The disposition of the three cases is as follows:

Case 1—*Opinion*: "I believe that defendants who conspire to commit burglary under these circumstances deserve a maximum one-year sentence. I also believe that defendants should always be given the maximum sentence they deserve." *Order*: One year in prison.

Case 2—*Opinion*: "I have changed my mind. I now believe that, while defendants should never receive sentences that exceed what they deserve, they may be given sentences that are less than they deserve, provided that such lesser sentences serve a penological purpose. I also believe that it serves a penological purpose in this case to experiment with the use of probation." *Order*: Probation.

Case 3—*Opinion*: "I have changed my mind again. I now believe that defendants should be given sentences that exceed what they deserve, provided that such higher sentences are needed to deter others from committing similar crimes. I also believe that a sentence of at least two years in prison is needed to deter others from committing burglary." *Order*: Two years in prison.

Consistency over time is like coeval consistency—a matter of holding to a common principle or practice. Whether cases 1–3 are normatively consistent, therefore, depends upon the principle or practice to which the judge ought to hold in sentencing the triplets. There are at least three principles to which the judge might plausibly be obliged to adhere: (1) within the range of the minimum and maximum sentences permitted by statute, a judge at the time of sentencing ought to impose whatever sentence he in his best judgment and in good faith regards as the most appropriate under the circumstances; (2) having expressed an opinion about the meaning of a criminal statute in the past, a judge ought to impose sentences that are in accord with his previous opinion; and (3) having entered orders of sentence under a criminal statute in the past, a judge ought to impose sentences that he can reconcile with his previous orders.

Now it should be obvious that measured by principle (1), the sentences in cases 1–3 are perfectly consistent, because each represents the judge's best judgment, at the time, of the sentence he ought to impose under the circumstances. Measured by principle (2), the three sentences are wholly inconsistent, because the sentence in case 2 does not accord with the opinion in case 1, and the sentence in case 3 does not accord with the opinion in either case 1 or case 2. And, measured by principle (3), the sentences in cases 1 and 2 are consistent with one another but inconsistent with the sentence in case 3, because the judge in his opinion in case 2 reconciles the sentence there with the order he entered in case 1, but he does not reconcile the sentence in case 3 with the orders he entered in cases 1 and 2. It should also be obvious that while principle (1) is *not* based on precedent, principles (2) and (3) *are* based on precedent. It follows that the real question is not whether the sentences are normatively consistent, for they are consistent by reference to one principle and inconsistent by reference to the others. The question is whether, as a measure of consistency, the judge is obliged to hold to a principle of precedent.

Precedent

It is sometimes said that to be "consistent" over time, or to "treat equals equally" over time, is to act on the basis of precedent.[30] As we have just seen, that is not so. A decisionmaker can act consistently over time (and thus treat equals equally over time) without regard to precedent, provided that the principle to which he holds (the principle by which "equals" are measured) is itself nonprecedential in nature. Moreover, as John Coons has shown in his penetrating essay "Consistency,"[31] principles of decisionmaking often are nonprecedential. A good example of nonprecedential decisionmaking in law is the use of juries to ascertain normative standards of "reasonable care" in negligence cases. When a jury decides whether it is reasonable for a driver to operate a car without two or more functioning rearview mirrors, the jury is formulating an *ex post* rule of conduct applicable to the defendant before it. Yet the jury is required to formulate the rule without regard to precedent because the jury is prohibited from knowing how previous juries have decided in similar cases. Consequently, when various juries formulate divergent *ex post* rules of conduct for different defendants in accord with the procedures by which they are expected to deliberate, their behavior can be characterized in two ways: one can say that their actions are "inconsistent," meaning that the actions *would* contradict one another *if* juries were obliged to base their judgments on precedent;[32] or one can say that their

---

[30] See Dworkin, *Taking Rights Seriously*, p. 113; MacCormick, *Legal Reasoning and Legal Theory*, pp. 73ff.; Golding, *Legal Reasoning*, p. 98.

[31] See Coons, "Consistency."

[32] This is what Coons means by "inconsistent" rules. Inconsistent rules, he says, are rules that would be in "moral conflict" if all rulemakers were obliged to hold to the same moral values. Coons, "Consistency," p. 70. Notice, however, that rules that are inconsistent in Coons's sense may be normatively consistent in the sense

actions are normatively "consistent," meaning that the juries have all held to the principle of deliberation to which juries are obliged to adhere, namely, that they use their best judgment to formulate *ex post* rules of conduct in negligence cases without regard to precedent.

In other cases decisionmakers are obliged to respect precedent. They are obliged to do so when the pragmatic or instrumental advantages of respecting precedent (e.g., reliability, stability, efficiency, allocation of power, respect for the past, avoidance of undiscoverable bias or caprice, enlisting multiple decisionmakers with accumulating experience to develop rules incrementally against the backdrop of a multiplicity of concrete cases, and the hortatory effect on judges of knowing that their present decisions shall carry future weight) are regarded as outweighing the advantages of ignoring precedent (e.g., experimentalism, individual responsibility, citizen participation, and pluralism).[33] Commentators differ, however, on the *measure* of precedent. Some argue that precedent is measured by what the prior decisionmaker *said* he was doing, that is, by his stated opinion in support of his decision.[34] Others argue that precedent is measured by what the prior decisionmaker *did* under the circumstances as they appear in the record, that is, by the judicial order the prior decisionmaker entered on the facts as they are now understood from the record to have been.[35] In reality, the measure of precedent in most common-law jurisdictions is neither the one nor the other but a combination of *both*. A judge in a common-law jurisdiction has two obligations: first, a prima facie obligation to enter an order that is consistent with explicit *opinions* in previous cases; and, second, when the judge chooses to repudiate previous opinions, an independent obligation to enter an order which he or she can explain to be nor-

---

that they may be formulated by rulemakers who are *not* obliged to hold to the same values.

[33] I rely here on Coons's and Frederick Schauer's analyses of the considerations favoring and disfavoring precedent. See Coons, "Consistency," pp. 61, 107–13; Schauer, "Precedent," pp. 594–602. I am indebted to my colleague Leo Katz for the observation that some of the same advantages that allegedly favor precedent (i.e., predictability, efficiency, and elimination of bias) are also said to be served by non-precedential systems of decisionmaking such as arbitration.

[34] See, e.g., Cross, "The House of Lords and the Rules of Precedent," p. 183; Montrose, "*Ratio Decidendi* and the House of Lords," pp. 124–25; Montrose, "The *Ratio Decidendi* of a Case," pp. 588–89, 594–95; MacCormick, *Legal Reasoning and Legal Theory*, p. 83; Raz, *The Authority of Law*.

[35] See Levi, "The Nature of Judicial Reasoning," pp. 272–73; Stone, "The *Ratio* of the *Ratio Decidendi*," p. 597.

matively consistent with *orders* entered in previous cases.[36] The mechanism of precedent thus consists of a combination of what we previously stated as principles (2) and (3), a combination in which overcoming the prima facie obligation of principle (2) triggers the more rigorous obligation of principle (3). The *force* of precedent, in turn, consists of the degree to which a judge feels obliged to follow an earlier opinion with which he or she disagrees plus the degree to which he or she feels obliged to enter an order which can be explained to be consistent with prior orders with which he or she disagrees—both of which degrees of obligation are a product of the extent to which the pragmatic advantages of precedential decisionmaking override its disadvantages.

To illustrate, recall the judge who convicts three identical triplets for a burglary for which they are equally blameworthy. At the end of the first week, he sentences the first triplet as follows:

Case 1—*Opinion*: "I believe that defendants who conspire to commit burglary under these circumstances deserve a maximum one-year sentence. I also believe that defendants should always be given the maximum sentence they deserve." *Order*: One year in prison.

One week later, the judge faces the second of the triplets. By that time, the judge has changed his mind regarding sentencing practice. He now believes that, while defendants should never receive sentences that exceed what they deserve, they may be given lesser sentences if such sentences serve a penological purpose. He also believes that it would serve such a purpose to sentence the second triplet to probation as an experiment. Assuming that the judge is bound by precedent, what is his obligation regarding case 1? Is case 2 "like" case 1 or not?

The answer is that precedent imposes two obligations on the sentencing judge, hence creating two standards of "likeness." To

[36] See Eisenberg, *The Nature of the Common Law*, pp. 62–68. See also Lyons, "Formal Justice and Judicial Precedent," p. 503 (suggesting that the "practice of precedent" can perhaps be best understood as being based on "both" principle [2] and principle [3]—or what Lyons calls, respectively, "historical" and "normative" conceptions of precedent); Schauer, "Precedent," p. 580 (distinguishing the "argumentative burden" of adhering to prior opinions from the further burden that arises when a judge repudiates prior opinions—namely, the burden of entering an order that the judge can show to be consistent with prior orders); Simpson, "The *Ratio Decidendi* of a Case and the Doctrine of Binding Precedent," p. 148 (suggesting that, while the *ratio* of a case is what the precedent court took the rule of law to be, the *ratio* is "binding" on the decisionmaker only to the extent that, if he does not follow it, he must distinguish it).

begin with, the judge has a prima facie obligation to enter an order that is consistent with his stated opinions in previous cases; to that extent, the opinion in case 1 constitutes the measure of likeness. According to the opinion in case 1, all defendants who conspire to commit burglary "under these circumstances" are alike with respect to the sentences they should receive:

> *Opinion*: ". . . defendants who conspire to commit burglary under these circumstances deserve a maximum one-year sentence. . . . defendants should always be given the maximum sentence they deserve."

By that standard of likeness, the two cases are alike and hence should be decided alike. According to the dual norms of precedent, however, a judge who disagrees with an opinion in an earlier case may reject it if, on the basis of the facts in the record of the earlier case, he can reconcile the order the first judge entered with the order he presently wishes to enter. The judge in case 2 does so by writing an opinion in which he justifies both the earlier one-year sentence and a present sentence of probation:

> Case 2—*Opinion*: "I have changed my mind. I now believe that, while defendants should never receive sentences that exceed what they deserve, they may be given sentences that are less than they deserve, provided that such lesser sentences serve a penological purpose. I also believe that it serves a penological purpose in this case to experiment with the use of probation."

In that respect, the opinion in case 2 constitutes the measure of likeness needed to justify the judge's subsequent order. As measured by this standard, the two cases are prescriptively different and so may be decided differently.

Circumstances can arise in common-law jurisdictions which may justify a judge in overruling a prior decision altogether, that is, in entering a judicial order that is explicitly inconsistent with prior orders. That is what the mercurial judge did when he sentenced the third triplet:

> Case 3—*Opinion*: "I have changed my mind again. I now believe that defendants should be given sentences that exceed what they deserve, provided that such higher sentences are needed to deter others from committing similar crimes. I also believe that a sentence of at least two years in prison is needed

to deter others from committing burglary." *Order*: Two years in prison.

The judge's opinion in case 3 overrules altogether his decision in the earlier cases because it is predicated on an opinion which, if it had prevailed at the time cases 1 and 2 were decided, would have resulted in different sentencing orders. It is, again, the judge's opinion in the case at hand that constitutes the measure of "likeness"—and that is why an overruling case is *never* "like" the overruled cases. The difference between the overruling in case 3 and the judge's action in case 2 is that, when a judge overrules a prior decision altogether, he implicitly declares himself to be unable to write an acceptable opinion reconciling his present order with the judicial order entered in the overruled case.

Reasoning by Analogy

Some legal commentators, of whom Edward Levi is the leading spokesman, claim that judgments of "likeness" play a significant and distinctive role in the formulation of legal rules—a role that not only distinguishes legal reasoning from other varieties of practical reasoning but essentially characterizes it.[37] The claim consists of four essential steps:

(1) The adjudication of disputes in English and American law is largely based on precedent.

(2) In reasoning from precedent, a judge must either adopt the opinions of judges in prior cases and apply them deductively to the case at hand, or (if the judge finds prior opinions un-

---

[37] See Levi, *An Introduction to Legal Reasoning*, pp. 1–6. See also Fried, "The Artificial Reason of the Law," p. 57:

> So what is it that lawyers and judges know that philosophers and economists do not? The answer is simple: the law. They are masters of "the artificial Reason of the law." There really is a distinct and special subject matter for our profession. And there is a distinct method down there in that last twenty feet. It is the method of analogy and precedent. Analogy and precedent are the stuff of the law because they are the only form of reasoning left to the law when general philosophical structures and deductive reasoning give out, overwhelmed by the mass of particular details. Analogy is the application of a trained, disciplined intuition where the manifold of particulars is too extensive to allow our minds to work on it deductively.

See also Murray, "The Role of Analogy in Legal Reasoning," p. 847 ("Reasoning by analogy is the most prevalent form of legal reasoning").

persuasive) enter a judgment that can be reconciled with orders entered in prior cases.

(3) Before he or she can enter an order that can be reconciled with prior orders, however, a judge must first engage in "analogical reasoning," that is, the judge must first identify the prior cases that are relevantly "similar" to the case at hand.

(4) Having identified prior cases that are relevantly similar to the case at hand, a judge possesses a body of data on the basis of which he or she can formulate a new rule of decision reconciling the present cases with prior cases.

Levi is surely correct in stating that judicial reasoning in English and American law is largely based on precedent, that the formulation of judicial rules of decision consistent with precedent involves analogical reasoning, and that analogical reasoning involves identifying cases that are relevantly similar. Levi is not correct, however, about the *nature* of analogical reasoning—or, more precisely, about the *temporal relationship* between the determination of relevantly similar cases (step 3), on the one hand, and the formulation of a rule of decision (step 4), on the other. Levi believes that the two steps are sequential, that one *first* identifies through analogical reasoning cases that are relevantly similar and *then* formulates a rule of decision that is consistent with both the orders the judge wishes to enter.[38] In reality, the two steps necessarily occur simultaneously. The determination that cases are relevantly similar presupposes a relevant rule of decision for comparing them, just as the formulation of a rule of decision for a series of cases presupposes a determination of relevant similarity. Each step presupposes the other because statements of relevant similarity and statements of how relevant rules apply in particular cases

[38] The basic pattern of legal reasoning is by example. It is reasoning from case to case. It is a three-step process. . . . The steps are these: [a key and controlling] similarity is seen between cases; next the rule of law inherent in the first case is announced; then the rule of law is made applicable to the second case.

Levi, *An Introduction to Legal Reasoning*, pp. 1–2. For the requirement that the "similarity" be "key" and "controlling," see pp. 3, 7. For commentators who appear to share Levi's view that the identification of relevant similarities *precedes* the formulation of rules, see Berman and Greiner, *The Nature and Functions of Law*, pp. 417, 419; Burton, *An Introduction to Law and Legal Reasoning*, pp. 59–82; Christie, "Objectivity in Law," p. 1337; Cross, *Precedent in English Law*, pp. 182–83; Guest, "Logic in the Law," pp. 190–91; Kovesi, *Moral Notions*, pp. 114–15; Murray, "The Role of Analogy in Legal Reasoning," pp. 870–71; Stone, "The *Ratio* of the *Ratio Decidendi*," p. 597; Stone, *Legal System and Lawyers' Reasonings*, p. 316.

are alternate ways of talking about the same underlying normative judgment.[39]

To illustrate, consider the case of *Carey v. Population Services International*.[40] The issue in *Carey* was whether an unmarried sixteen-year-old girl had a constitutional right to purchase nondangerous contraceptives without a prescription. The plaintiff relied on a prior case in which an unmarried adult was held to be constitutionally free to obtain nondangerous contraceptives without a prescription (*Eisenstadt v. Baird*). The defendant argued that *Eisenstadt* was irrelevant and that the relevant precedent was instead one in which persons sixteen years old or younger were held to have no constitutional right to purchase adult pornography (*Ginsberg v. New York*). Levi and his followers would presumably say that, before the court in *Carey* could formulate a rule of decision consistent with prior judgments, the court had to determine which of the two prior cases was relevantly similar to the case at hand. In reality the court in *Carey* could not identify the relevantly similar prior case without implicitly making reference to a relevant rule of decision by which to compare them. Thus, when the court eventually held in *Carey* that unmarried sixteen-year-old girls were *similar* to the unmarried adults in *Eisenstadt* who had a right to obtain contraceptives without a prescription, and *dissimilar* to the sixteen-year-olds in *Ginsberg* who had no right to buy adult pornography, it could do so only because it had also decided that the relevant rule of decision ought to be something like "Because of the unique importance of procreative freedom, all mature persons, adults or not, should be able to purchase nondangerous contraceptives without the necessity of a prescription."

[39] See Brennan, *The Open-Texture of Moral Concepts*, pp. 38–39:

> We cannot say that like cases are alike in a morally neutral way if we mean by this that someone could tell which cases are alike without any reference to the moral standards by which they are being judged, since the standards determine which respects are relevant. . . .
> Since it is only if one knows the appropriate moral standard that one can tell what counts as an action of a certain type, the similarity between these actions cannot be detected without a prior grasp of the moral standard.

See also Becker, "Analogy in Legal Reasoning"; Goodman, "Seven Strictures on Similarity," p. 441; Eisenberg, *The Nature of the Common Law*, p. 87 ("Essentially, reasoning by analogy in the common law is a special type of reasoning from standards, like reasoning from precedent and from principle"); MacCormick, *Legal Reasoning and Legal Theory*, pp. 163, 186; Moore, "Precedent, Induction, and Ethical Generalization," p. 192; Singer, *Generalization in Ethics*, p. 40 ("to invoke an analogy is to appeal to a general rule, to the generalization implicit in the argument").
[40] 431 U.S. 678 (1977).

To be sure, a court that has not yet formulated a rule of decision may be able to make preliminary or subsidiary determinations of prescriptive similarity. This can occur, however, only because the court has already formulated preliminary or subsidiary rules of decision for the issues at hand. R. M. Hare puts the point particularly well:

> [T]he decision to treat certain features of a situation as morally relevant is not independent of the decision to apply certain moral principles to it. . . . It is a great mistake to think that there can be a morally or evaluatively neutral process of picking out the relevant features of a situation, which can then be followed by the job of appraising or evaluating the situation morally. We can indeed *describe* a situation without committing ourselves to any moral judgments about it . . . ; nevertheless, when we decide what features of the description are morally relevant, we are already in the moral business. . . . [T]o call a feature morally relevant is already to imply that it is a reason for or against making some moral judgment; and to say this is already to invoke a moral principle. . . .
> The question, therefore, of what features can be relevant to moral appraisal is the same question as that of what features can figure in moral principles.[41]

Assume, for example, that before deciding the *Carey* case, the court made the following preliminary and subsidiary determinations:

> —"The fact that the teenager in this case is black, while the teenager in *Ginsberg* was white, is not a relevant dissimilarity."
> —"The fact that the plaintiff here and the plaintiff in *Eisenstadt* both wished to acquire contraceptives makes them presumptively similar."
> —"The fact that the teenager here wished to purchase contraceptives, while the teenager in *Ginsberg* wished to read pornography, is a significant dissimilarity."

The court could make such determinations only because it had already formulated preliminary or subsidiary rules from which the foregoing similarities and dissimilarities follow, for example:

[41] Hare, "Relevance," p. 75.

—"No black person shall be disadvantaged on the basis of race."

—"Every person has a presumptive right to control his or her procreation through contraception."

—"A person has a greater protected interest in controlling procreation through contraception than in reading pornographic books."

This is so because one cannot make determinations of prescriptive similarity and dissimilarity without reference to the prescriptions by which they are measured.

Gerald Dworkin has suggested that a judge may be able to "see the facts in a case as more similar in more important respects to the facts in one earlier case rather than another" without, however, being able to formulate "a general rule" for resolving them. Dworkin is quite right if by a "general rule" he means (as he appears to mean) a "grand principle" that simultaneously "is intuitively plausible, covers all foreseeable cases, gives the desired result in this case, and is not open to obvious counterexamples."[42] Judges can and rightly do adjudge cases to be similar without being able to articulate foundational principles for resolving all foreseeable future cases. It does not follow, however, that in "seeing" the facts in one case to be "similar" to another, judges are not also formulating rules of decision—whether preliminary or subsidiary—for resolving the cases. Judges are not always conscious of the rules of decision that their judgments of similarity presuppose; and, if they are, they are not always ready to make the underlying rules explicit, or to commit themselves to one as opposed to another of several rules from which they could choose. But a judge cannot see two cases as similar without implicitly or explicitly formulating rules for resolving them, because judgments of prescriptive similarity entail prescriptive standards—or "rules"—by which similarity is ascertained.

The Requirement of Impartiality

Commentators sometimes equate the precept "equals should be treated equally" with the obligation to treat people "impartially."[43] Whether they are right to do so depends upon their understanding of the word 'impartiality'. What does it mean to treat people

[42] Dworkin, "Philosophy, Law, and Politics," p. 1357.
[43] Cauthen, *The Passion for Equality*, pp. 4–6.

impartially? Is impartial treatment always the same as equal treatment? Is it ever the same?

To act "impartially" is to act *without favoring* one person vis-à-vis others. The decision as to whether particular people ought to be favored depends, in turn, upon how people are classified under relevant moral and legal rules. It is the purpose of such rules to classify some people as deserving more favorable treatment than others. Thus, we believe that people who are innocent of crime ought to be favored over those who are guilty because we believe that the innocent are properly classified as deserving more favorable treatment. Needless to say, if there is a normative obligation to act impartially, it cannot consist of denying people the favors they ought to receive under relevant rules. Rather, such an obligation must consist of denying people the favors they ought *not* to receive under relevant rules. Like the obligation to "treat equals equally," the obligation to act impartially is tautologous: it instructs us to refrain from favoring such people as ought not to be favored.[44]

Like "equals should be treated equally," however, the obligation of "impartiality" can be understood in two distinct ways. It can be understood as Aristotle interpreted his precept, viz., as requiring that all people be granted the treatments they ought to receive. Or it can be understood as Aristotle's critics interpret his precept, viz., as requiring that people all be granted or all be denied the treatments they deserve. John Stuart Mill understood the obligation of "impartiality" as Aristotle understood "treat equals equally," that is, for Mill, to treat people impartially is to give them the treatments they ought to receive: "Impartiality, in short, as an obligation of justice, may be said to mean, being exclusively influenced by the considerations which it is supposed ought to influence the particular case at hand; and resisting the solicitation of any motives which prompt to conduct different from what those considerations would dictate."[45] It is not clear, however, that Mill accounts for ordinary usage. Assume, for example, as one of Aristotle's critics does, that a government prohibits everyone who is entitled to read *Doctor Zhivago* from reading it.[46] I should think most people would say that, although the government treated its citizens unjustly, it nevertheless treated them impartially. If so, then in ordinary usage, treating people "impartially" means what Aristotle's critics believe treating people "equally" means, viz.,

[44] See Carr, "The Concept of Formal Justice," pp. 222–23.
[45] Mill, *Utilitarianism*, p. 243.
[46] Vlastos, "Justice and Equality," p. 62.

treating them identically in the extent, if any, to which they are granted the treatment they ought to receive.

Kenneth Simons has argued that the obligation of impartiality is an obligation which is confined to comparative rules.[47] That is to say, he argues that a person fails to act impartially when, and only when, he violates a rule that itself makes reference to how others are treated. Again, I think ordinary usage differs. Assume, for example, that a piano teacher contracts separately with two students to give each sixty minutes of instruction a week. Instead of giving each student a full sixty minutes, however, the teacher regularly gives one student a few minutes less. The contractual right of the disadvantaged student to sixty minutes of instruction is a noncomparative right because it can be ascertained without reference to how others are treated. Yet we would commonly say, I believe, that by denying one student (and not the other) the sixty-minute lesson to which he is noncomparatively entitled, the teacher is not treating the two students "impartially."[48]

Conclusion

H.L.A. Hart makes two statements about the precept "equals should be treated equally" which are generally (though not universally)[49] accepted as true. He states first that in saying "equals should be treated equally," "*we need to add*" that "unequals should be treated unequally."[50] He then states that although the precept "equals should be treated equally" is "an empty form" until supplemented with "criteria of relevant resemblances and differences," once the formal precept is thus supplemented, it becomes a "determinate guide to conduct":

> [T]hough "Treat like cases alike and different cases differently" is a central element in the idea of justice, it is by itself

[47] Simons, "Equality as a Comparative Right," p. 412.

[48] For authority that the concepts of consistency and impartiality encompass noncomparative as well as comparative rules, see Carr, "The Concept of Formal Justice," pp. 222–23.

[49] Hart's first statement (that "equals should be treated equally" needs to be supplemented by "unequals should be treated unequally") is disputed, for example, by A. M. Honoré (see pp. 208–10 above). His second statement, that formal equality when supplemented by a material principle has content beyond the material principle, is powerfully disputed by Carr in "The Concept of Formal Justice," p. 211.

[50] Hart, The Concept of Law, p. 155 (emphasis added). Hart refers to the precept as "treat like cases alike," which I take to be equivalent to "treat equals equally."

incomplete and, until supplemented, cannot afford any determinate guide to conduct. This is so because any set of human beings will resemble each other in some respects and differ from each other in others and, until it is established what resemblances and differences are relevant, "Treat like cases alike" must remain an empty form. To fill it we must know when, for the purposes in hand, cases are to be regarded as alike and what differences are relevant.[51]

The validity of Hart's assertions depends upon whether they are understood in a strong or weak sense. It is true that, just as "equals should be treated equally," so also "unequals should be treated unequally," because the former logically entails the latter. But, because the former precept entails the latter, the latter is essentially redundant and in that sense is *not* something we "need to add." Indeed, because "treat unequals unequally" is redundant, many commentators either make no reference to it whatsoever or, having paid it lip service, proceed solely by reference to the obligation to "treat equals equally."[52]

"Treating equals equally" necessarily entails "treating unequals unequally" because every rule of conduct by which equals and unequals are measured can be stated at two levels of generality. The rule can be stated as creating subclasses of persons who, being in subclasses, are unequal and should be treated unequally. The rule can also be stated as creating a single class of persons who, being entitled to the benefit of the rule, are equal and should be treated equally. For example, the rule "to each according to his needs" can be stated as creating a single class of persons who are equal in being entitled to treatment on the basis of need. Or it can be stated as creating subclasses of persons who are unequal in their needs and ought to be treated unequally in that respect. The statements are alternative ways of referring to the same rule.

Hart's second statement, that the formal obligation to "treat equals equally" and substantive criteria of relevance together are a

---

[51] Hart, *The Concept of Law*, p. 155. Chaim Perelman takes the same two positions, namely, (1) that the principle "equals should be treated equally" is a purely "formal" concept until it is supplemented by "concrete formulas of justice," and (2) that once it is supplemented, it leads to "predictability and security." Perelman, *Justice, Law, and Argument*, pp. 1–23. For another comparison of "formal" and "material" concepts of justice, see Ross, *On Law and Justice*, p. 12.

[52] For an example of a student of justice who proceeds solely by reference to the first precept, see Gillespie, "On Treating Like Cases Differently." Hart himself, having made reference to the precept "unequals should be treated unequally," proceeds solely by reference to the precept "equals should be treated equally." See Hart, *The Concept of Law*, pp. 155–63.

"determinate guide to conduct," is also misleading because it suggests that the formal obligation to "treat equals equally" adds an element of justice to prescribed conduct over and above the substantive criteria of relevance.[53] In reality, substantive criteria of relevance are not only necessary to guide conduct but also entirely sufficient for it. They are sufficient because the phrase "criteria of relevant resemblances and differences" is simply an alternative way of referring to normative rules of conduct—referring to them by reference to the traits the rules require a person to possess in order to qualify for the treatments they prescribe. These rules of conduct may be noncomparative or comparative in nature, but, whichever they are, they tell us everything we need to know about how we ought to behave under given circumstances.

Consider, for example, Chaim Perelman's distinction between the formal and the material elements of justice.[54] Like Hart, Perelman argues that the formal element is the precept "equals should be treated equally," while the material element is a society's particular "conception of concrete justice," such as the rule "to each according to his needs." Perelman also suggests that, by virtue of "its requirement of uniformity," the formal element adds something significant to the particular material elements it incorporates.[55] Yet, once the material element is faithfully applied, there is no further role for the formal element to play, not even a role of uniformity, because the material element itself, when applied according to its terms, provides whatever uniformity its adherents desire. Thus, if the material element is "to each according to his needs," it tells us everything we need to know about the uniformity that ought to obtain, namely, that the rule ought to be applied to all persons in accord with their needs. Alternatively, if the material element is "to each debtor such forgiveness of debt as his

[53] Morris Ginsberg implies the same thing. He says that once one specifies the substantive content of rules, "it is necessary . . . to examine them in light of the formal principle of equality, the aim being to exclude every form of discrimination not justified by relevant differences"—thus implying that the formal principle of equality itself contains criteria of relevance over and above what substantive rules prescribe. See Ginsberg, *On Justice in Society*, p. 7. See also Frankena, "Some Beliefs about Justice," p. 94 (referring to the precept "equals should be treated equally" as a "necessary" element of justice).

[54] See Perelman, *The Idea of Justice and the Problem of Argument*, p. 15 (contrasting "formal" with "concrete" elements of justice); Perelman, *Justice, Law, and Argument*, pp. 1–23. For analysis of the meaning of "formal" concepts of justice, including the formal principle "equals should be treated equally," see Carr, "The Concept of Formal Justice."

[55] Perelman, *Justice, Law, and Argument*, p. 38 (the principle "likes should be treated alike," "with its requirement of uniformity, leads to predictability and security. It permits the coherent and stable functioning of a juridical order").

creditor is personally disposed to extend," it, too, tells us everything we need to know about uniformity, namely, that debts
ought to be forgiven to the extent creditors are so disposed. In
short, the formal element is not an independent component of justice over and above what the material elements of justice prescribe. It is simply an abstraction, or "generalization,"[56] of what it
means to treat people by reference to such material elements of
justice, or rules of conduct, as a society chooses to adopt.[57]

Hart argues that the precept "treat likes alike" cannot be equivalent to the notion of applying a rule according to its terms. If it
were, he says, we could never criticize the content of a rule for
failing to treat likes alike. Yet we do criticize "the laws themselves"
for failing to treat likes alike, as when we criticize racially discriminatory laws for excluding blacks from public parks.[58] Hart's anal-

[56] See Singer, *Generalization in Ethics*, p. 19.
[57] Craig Carr makes this point powerfully:

[E]quality of treatment . . . cannot be understood as a sufficient condition for
doing justice. And, once material principles of justice are introduced, they control the normative structure of our determinations of justice. Acting upon material principles of justice, of course, does involve fidelity to principle. But
these principles themselves imply the requirements of justice; it is quite unnecessary to think that we need a formal principle of justice to tell us that we
ought to obey these material principles. To think that the fidelity to principle
involved in doing justice reveals a formal dimension of what it means to do
justice, then, is to confuse a general point about the nature of rule-governed
activity with a specific point about the particular concerns of doing justice.

Carr, "The Concept of Formal Justice," p. 222. That is what commentators mean
when they say that the precept "equals should be treated equally" is "empty."
Carr, "The Concept of Formal Justice," p. 212 (Aristotle's maxim is "substantively
empty"); von Leyden, *Aristotle on Equality and Justice*, p. 5 (Aristotle's precept
"equals should be treated equally" is "tantalizingly empty"). The precept is
"empty" in the sense that it adds nothing to what is dictated by the substantive
notions of justice which it incorporates by reference. See Miller, *Social Justice*, p. 21
("It is therefore better to regard 'treat equals equally' simply as a corollary of the
more fundamental principle 'render to each his due' ").

[58] This close connection between justice in the administration of the law and
the very notion of a rule has tempted some famous thinkers to identify justice
with conformity to law. Yet plainly this is an error unless 'law' is given some
specially wide meaning; for such an account of justice leaves unexplained the
fact that criticism in the name of justice [i.e., in the name of "treating likes
alike"] is not confined to the administration of the law in particular cases, but
the laws themselves are often criticized as just or unjust. Indeed, there is no
absurdity in conceding that an unjust law forbidding the access of coloured
persons to the parks has been justly administered, in that only persons genuinely guilty of breaking the law were punished for it and then only after a fair
trial.

Hart, *The Concept of Law*, p. 157.

ysis of the relationship between "treat likes alike" and applying rules is, I believe, mistaken. His mistake is to use the meaning of "treat likes alike" in *morals* to assess its validity in *law*. To "treat likes alike" is to apply a rule according to its terms. The precept can have either a moral meaning or a legal meaning, depending upon whether one takes moral or legal rules as one's frame of reference. Thus, a person can justly "treat likes alike" *in law* by applying legal rules according to their terms. And he can justly "treat likes alike" *in morals* by applying moral rules according to their terms. What he cannot do is what Hart appears to do, namely, attempt to "treat likes alike" in morals by applying what he regards as immoral legal rules according to their terms. If Hart is right in his belief that racially discriminatory laws fail to treat likes alike, it is not because "treat likes alike" has normative content beyond the application of underlying rules; rather, it is because he is electing to measure "likes," not by the faithful application of laws of racial discrimination, but by the faithful application of independent moral rules of nondiscrimination.

TEN

THE PRESUMPTION OF EQUALITY

The so-called presumption of equality[1] can be expressed in various ways. Some speak of an *"onus probandi,"* or burden of proof, on those who wish to treat people unequally; others, of a "presumption against" treating people differently until grounds for distinction have been shown; still others, of a "prima facie" rule in favor of equality.[2] Essentially the various formulations come to the same thing, namely, that people ought to be treated equally until reasons are shown for treating them unequally. As Isaiah Berlin expresses it:

> The assumption is that equality needs no reasons, only in-
> equality does so; that uniformity, regularity, similarity, sym-
> metry . . . need not be specially accounted for, whereas dif-
> ferences, unsystematic behaviour, change in conduct, need
> explanation and, as a rule, justification. If I have a cake and
> there are ten persons among whom I wish to divide it, then if
> I give exactly one tenth to each, this will not . . . call for jus-

[1] It appears that Hugo Bedau was the first to employ the expression "presumption of equality," though not the first to entertain the thought. See Bedau, "Egalitarianism and the Idea of Equality," p. 19. But see Stephen, *Liberty, Equality, Fraternity,* p. 186 (referring to the "presumption in favour of equality"). ·

[2] Benn and Peters speak of "a presumption against" treating people unequally "until grounds for distinction have been shewn"; see Benn and Peters, *The Principles of Political Thought,* pp. 127–28. Bedau speaks of the rule that "social equalities need no special justification, whereas social inequalities always do"; see Bedau, "Egalitarianism and the Idea of Equality," p. 19. Browne speaks of the "presumption" that "in the absence of reasons for treating people unequally, they should be treated equally"; see Browne, "The Presumption of Equality," p. 46. Frankena speaks of a "prima facie" rule of equal treatment; see Frankena, "The Concept of Social Justice," p. 12. Graham speaks of the "burden of proof" being on the opponents of equality; see Graham, "Liberty and Equality," p. 59. Katzner speaks of "the principle . . . that with regard to distribution, all human beings must be treated the same until grounds for treating them differently can be shown"; see Katzner, "Presumptivist and Nonpresumptivist Principles of Formal Justice," p. 253. Sidgwick speaks of an *"onus probandi"* being on those who wish to treat people unequally; see Sidgwick, *The Methods of Ethics,* p. 380.

tification; whereas if I depart from this principle of equal division I am expected to produce a special reason.[3]

The presumption of equality is sometimes regarded as more than an ordinary rule of conduct. It is variously said to be "implicit in the notion of rational decision," a "logical rule of moral and prudential thinking," a "principle of all moralities which are not actually anti-rational," and a "meta-moral axiom," i.e., "a rule for adopting rules" as opposed to a substantive moral principle.[4] Moreover, it is frequently claimed to derive directly from the Aristotelian precept "equals should be treated equally." Thus, Bernard Williams writes:

> [T]he practical maxim of equality . . . claim[s] only that men should be treated alike in similar circumstances; and since 'circumstances' here must clearly include references to what a man is, as well as to his purely external situation, this comes very much to saying that for every difference in the way men are treated, some general reason or principle of differentiation must be given.[5]

Indeed, some commentators maintain that the presumption of equality is not only implied by Aristotle's "equals should be treated equally" but is something that Aristotle made explicit.[6]

We shall investigate the truth of these assertions. In the course of doing so, we shall examine the nature of presumptions, the relationship between the presumption of equality and the precept "equals should be treated equally," and the validity of the presumption itself.

[3] Berlin, "Equality as an Ideal," p. 137.

[4] Benn, "Equality, Moral and Social," p. 40 ("implicit in the notion of rational decision"); Graham, "Liberty and Equality," pp. 63–64 ("a logical rule of moral and prudential thinking"); Watkins, "Liberalism and Equality," p. 927 ("the formal principle of all moralities which are not actually anti-rational"); Beardsley, "Equality and Obedience to Law," p. 36 ("a meta-moral axiom," i.e., a "rule for adopting rules").

[5] Williams, "The Idea of Equality," p. 111.

[6] My point, then (and I believe Aristotle's too), is that the principle of equality in the context discussed admits of a weak and of a strong form. In its weak aspect, it enjoins that men should never be treated differently in any respect without justification, that is, until relevant grounds for the discrimination have been advanced.

Von Leyden, *Aristotle on Equality and Justice*, p. 9. See also Rees, *Equality*, pp. 92–93. Von Leyden and Rees do not support their assertions with any reference apart from Aristotle's statement that "equals should be treated equally, and unequals should be treated unequally."

The Nature of Presumptions

A "presumption" is a relationship between two propositions, A and B, such that "if A, then B."[7] The relationship between A and B may be irrebuttable, such that "if A, then *necessarily* B," or, more commonly, the relationship between A and B may be rebuttable, such that "if A, then B, *unless and until* X is shown to obtain." Thus, the presumption in the law of statutory rape, i.e., "If a girl is under the age of sixteen she is incapable of consenting to sexual intercourse," is irrebuttable because, once a girl is established to be under the age of sixteen, she is conclusively adjudged to be incapable of consenting to sexual intercourse, regardless of anything further that may be shown about her. In contrast, the so-called presumption of innocence—i.e., "If a person is charged with a crime, he shall be treated as innocent until he is shown beyond a reasonable doubt to be guilty"—is a rebuttable presumption because it requires that a person be treated as innocent *until* he is proven beyond a reasonable doubt to be guilty.

Presumptions consist of two propositions: a premise, A, and a conclusion, B. Each proposition may be descriptive or prescriptive. Thus, in the presumption "If a blood test is negative for the presence of HTLV-3 virus, the donor is probably not infected with AIDS," propositions A and B are both descriptive. In the presumption "If a person is found in the possession of recently stolen property, he will be deemed beyond a reasonable doubt to have known it was stolen until he proves the contrary," the premise is descriptive and the conclusion is prescriptive. In the presumption "If you owe a debt, you ought to repay it promptly," A and B are both prescriptive. And in the presumption "If you owe a debt, you will probably feel obliged to repay it," the premise is prescriptive and the conclusion is descriptive.

Within this taxonomy, the presumption of equality is rebuttable rather than irrebuttable: it is a statement of the form "If one deals with people, one ought to treat them equally *until* reasons are shown for treating them unequally." Moreover, it is a statement in which the premise is descriptive and the conclusion is prescriptive, taking the form "If it is descriptively the case that you are dealing with people, then it is prescriptively the case that you ought to treat them equally until you show reasons for treating

[7] See Cleary, ed., *McCormick on Evidence*, pp. 965–84.

them unequally." In short, the presumption of equality is a provisional rule of conduct, a rule about how one ought to behave until one has further, more precise information about how one ought to behave. It is a rule about how one ought to behave under circumstances of incomplete normative information—circumstances under which one knows one is dealing with people but does not yet know whether there are reasons for treating them unequally.

The Relationship between the Presumption of Equality and "Equals Should Be Treated Equally"

Some commentators argue that the presumption of equality can be logically derived from the precept "equals should be treated equally." They argue that, if equals should indeed be treated equally, it follows that people should be treated equally until reasons are shown for treating them differently.[8]

Louis Katzner and D. E. Browne have demonstrated that the presumption is not a corollary of "equals should be treated equally." It is not a precept that follows logically from "equals should be treated equally" without the necessity of further assumptions of fact or value.[9] There are two related reasons for this. For one thing, the two precepts presuppose very different backgrounds. The Aristotelian precept "equals should be treated equally" comes into play in the event that people are prescriptively equal: it states that if people are prescriptively equal they should be treated equally in that respect. In contrast, the presumption of equality can come into play *before* it is known whether people are equal, for it states that in the absence of evidence that people are prescriptively equal, they nevertheless should be treated equally.[10] Consequently, since the presumption of equality can op-

[8] See Benn and Peters, *The Principles of Political Thought*, pp. 124–28; Blackstone, "On the Meaning and Justification of the Equality Principle," p. 240; Evans, "Equality, Ambiguity, and Public Choice," p. 1386; Flathman, "Equality and Generalization," p. 55; Frankena, "The Concept of Social Justice," pp. 8–13; Gewirth, *Reason and Morality*, p. 186; Rawls, "Justice as Fairness," pp. 166–67; Singer, *Generalization in Ethics*, p. 31; Spaemann, "Remarks on the Problem of Equality," p. 364; Wasserstrom, "Rights, Human Rights, and Racial Discrimination," pp. 634–37; Watkins, "Liberalism and Equality," p. 927; Williams, "The Idea of Equality," p. 111.

[9] Browne, "The Presumption of Equality," p. 46; Katzner, "Presumptivist and Nonpresumptivist Principles of Formal Justice," p. 253. See also Nielsen, "On Not Needing to Justify Equality," pp. 58–61; White, "The Equality Principle," p. 53.

[10] This is not to say that the two precepts *always* operate on the basis of different factual presuppositions. There may be cases in which people are *known* to be unequal (thus satisfying Aristotle's maxim) without reasons having yet been *shown* for

erate in the absence of the very state of affairs that Aristotle's precept presupposes, the presumption of equality cannot logically be derived from Aristotle's precept unless one makes further assumptions of fact or value.[11]

Furthermore, Aristotle's precept and the presumption of equality are categorically different sorts of statements. "Equals should be treated equally" is a formal principle. It is an "empty form" (in H.L.A. Hart's words), which must be "supplemented" with material principles of justice before it can serve as a "determinate guide to conduct."[12] Rather than *being* a determinate rule of conduct, it is a *way of talking about* determinate rules of conduct, viz.,

---

treating them unequally (thus satisfying the presumption of equality). In that event, the two precepts will produce the same results on the same facts. The point is, rather, that there will also be cases in which reasons have not yet been shown for treating people unequally because such reasons are not yet known. In that event, the two precepts will produce different results.

[11] Nonpresumptivist principles of justice . . . rather than involving the notion of a 'burden of proof,' simply require that those who are the same be treated the same and that those who are different be treated differently. . . . Thus the application of the nonpresumptivist principle, unlike that of its presumptivist counterpart, does not rest solely upon what can and cannot be shown. What justifies difference of treatment in the case of the nonpresumptivist principle is that there is an actual (relevant) difference between the individuals involved (whether or not this distinction can be shown), whereas what justifies difference of treatment in the case of the presumptivist principle is being able to show grounds for distinction (whether or not this distinction actually exists).

Katzner, "Presumptivist and Nonpresumptivist Principles of Formal Justice," p. 253.

The presumption principle is to be carefully distinguished from what I shall call (following precedent) the Aristotelian formula of justice, viz: Equals are to be treated equally, unequals are to be treated unequally. It is important to appreciate that the Aristotelian formula does not state a *presumption* at all. We are not to presume either equality or inequality, but are directed to treat equally those who are equal, and to treat unequally those who are unequal.

Browne, "The Presumption of Equality," p. 47. See also Feinberg, *Social Philosophy*, pp. 100–101.

To say that the presumption of equality cannot be *derived* from Aristotle's precept is not to say that it is *incompatible* with it. On the contrary, we have seen that Aristotle's precept is a formula compatible with all normative propositions (including the presumption of equality) because Aristotle's precept is merely a way of talking about normative propositions. The presumption of equality is a normative proposition to the effect that all persons ought to be treated equally until good reasons are shown for treating them unequally. In terms of Aristotle's precept, the presumption states that "equals" (i.e., all persons) should be treated "equally" (i.e., should be treated as being entitled to be treated equally until reasons are shown for treating them unequally).

[12] Hart, *The Concept of Law*, p. 155 (referring to the principle "likes should be treated alike").

talking about them by reference to the prescriptive identities they create among people. R. M. Hare has done much to clarify the relationship between the use of normative terms, on the one hand, and implied rules, on the other. Hare has shown that to use certain moral terms is to commit oneself to a generalized rule of conduct. "The meaning of the word 'ought' and other moral words," he writes, "is such that a person who uses them commits himself thereby to a universal rule."[13] Thus, when a person says "Jack ought to give treatment X to Jill," he is implicitly committing himself to a rule, to the generalization "Everyone who is relevantly similarly situated to Jack ought to give treatment X to anyone who is relevantly similarly situated to Jill." Otherwise, Hare says, "he is abusing the word 'ought': he is implicitly contradicting himself."[14] To say that a person should "treat likes alike," then, is simply an alternative way of saying that he should adhere to whatever normative rule he necessarily implies in a particular use of 'ought'. In that sense, "equals should be treated equally" is indeed "an axiom of all rational ethics."[15]

The presumption of equality, in contrast, is not a formal principle of justice, for it need not be supplemented with material elements of justice before it can serve as a determinate guide to conduct. On the contrary, it purports to be sufficient in itself to guide an actor's conduct. As Katzner writes:

The [presumption of equality] is always a decisive guide to action. At any moment, one merely examines the information at his disposal. If it is enough to override the presumption of similar treatment, then one treats the individuals involved differently. If it is not enough to override the presumption of

[13] Hare, *Freedom and Reason*, p. 30. For perceptive discussions of what Hare calls "universalizability" and Marcus Singer calls "generalizability," see Flathman, "Equality and Generalization," p. 55; Locke, "The Trivializability of Universalizability," p. 25; Munro, "Consistency and Impartiality," p. 164.

[14] Hare, *Freedom and Reason*, p. 32.

[15] Ginsberg, *On Justice in Society*, p. 80 (it "is an axiom of all rational ethics and is implicit in the notion of a norm or law of action as such"). See also Feinberg, "Noncomparative Justice," p. 319 ("the principle that relevantly similar cases should be treated in similar ways . . . is a principle of reason"); Kelsen, "Aristotle's Theory of Justice," p. 134 (it is "a law of thought"); Freund, "The Philosophy of Equality," p. 14 (it is "a premise of rational thought"); Lucas, *The Principles of Politics*, p. 236 (it is "none other than the weak principle of universalizability, the principle of rationality"). As Browne puts it: "All rational theories have an element of formal equality because formal equality is inherent in the notion of rationality. If characteristic x is a sufficient reason to treat individual A in a particular manner, then it is a sufficient reason to treat B in the same manner." Browne, "The Presumption of Equality," p. 51.

similar treatment, then one treats them the same. Thus, in cases in which one has no idea as to what constitutes the grounds for similar or different treatment . . . or, knowing the grounds for similar or different treatment, does not know whether the individuals involved are similar or different in these respects . . . , the [presumption of equality] serves *by itself* as a decisive guide to action—it requires that the individuals involved be treated the same since grounds for distinction have not been shown.[16]

That it is not a formal principle does not mean that the presumption of equality is invalid. Rather, it means that, if the presumption is valid, it is valid in the way that other contestable moral principles are valid. The precept "Thou shalt not kill" is not a formal principle whose truth can be known by any person, whatever his morals and experiences in life. It is a normative principle based on a particular (hence, an essentially contestable) normative view of the nature of human life, a view derived from the experience of ourselves and other persons. The same is true of the presumption of equality. The presumption of equality is not an a priori principle whose logic can (or must) be accepted without regard to notions of right and wrong. It is "a normative principle"[17] based on a judgment about the nature of human beings, the features they share, and the ways in which they ought to be treated. According to James Fitzjames Stephen:

> The notion that apart from experience there is a presumption in favour of equality appears to me unfounded. A presumption is simply an avowedly imperfect generalization, and this must, of course, be founded on experience. . . . In precisely the same way the presumption (if any) to be made in favour of equality must be based on experience.[18]

The Meaning of the Presumption of Equality

The presumption of equality is a general proposition about equality, which coexists with a plethora of specific presumptions about equality. In American constitutional law, for example, the Fourteenth Amendment imposes rebuttable presumptions on state

[16] Katzner, "Presumptivist and Nonpresumptivist Principles of Formal Justice," pp. 256–57 (original emphasis).
[17] Browne, "The Presumption of Equality," p. 46.
[18] Stephen, *Liberty, Equality, Fraternity*, p. 186.

governments to treat whites and blacks, men and women, Protestants and Catholics equally. Yet the presumption of equality is not simply a generic name for what specific presumptions already prescribe; nor is it a mere extension to all "people" of what specific presumptions provide for specific people. Rather, the presumption of equality differs from specific presumptions in two respects. For one thing, while specific presumptions often require particularly weighty reasons to justify treating people unequally, the presumption of equality does not. Thus, while the Fourteenth Amendment requires a state to demonstrate "compelling" reasons for treating whites and blacks unequally, the presumption of equality simply requires *reasons*. Furthermore, while the "equality" that specific presumptions require seems evident, the "equality" that the general presumption requires is not. Thus, while treating blacks and whites "equally" evidently means eschewing making racial distinctions between them, treating all people "equally" has no such evident meaning.

The Meaning of Treating People "Equally"

The presumption of equality is a preference for treating people equally. An actor who treats people equally has no further obligations under the presumption; he can always satisfy the presumption simply by treating people equally. The question is: what does it mean to treat people "equally" for purposes of the presumption?

As we already know, to treat people equally is to treat them identically by reference to a given relevant standard of comparison. The question thus becomes: what is the relevant standard of comparison for purposes of the presumption of equality? One possibility is the standard *that the actor himself means to adopt*. Unfortunately, if that is what 'equally' means, the presumption of equality ceases to be a *criterion* for evaluating rules and becomes, instead, a vindication of whatever rule of conduct an actor chooses to adopt. Consider the rule that governed the status of the children of slaves in antebellum America. It was the American rule that the status of a newborn child followed the status of its mother. Accordingly, the child of a free mother (black or white) and a slave father was born free, while the child of a slave mother and a free father (black or white) was born a slave. If treating people equally for purposes of the presumption of equality means treating them identically in accord with rules that an actor chooses to adopt, a

237

slaveholder who followed the American rule of slave status could rightly claim to be treating all children equally.

It might be thought that the relevant standard of comparison is whatever rule of treatment is *morally just*. Yet that also is unsatisfactory. For one thing, people widely disagree about whether particular rules are just or unjust. If an actor is required to identify morally or legally just rules of conduct in order to know what it means to treat people equally, he faces a greater burden in treating people equally than in justifying departures from equal treatment. Furthermore, once an actor knows that a particular rule is just, the presumption of equality becomes superfluous, because once he knows a particular rule to be just, his proper course of conduct is *always* to treat people identically in accord with the rule—not (as the presumption of equality suggests) to treat them provisionally in a certain way until he learns more about how he ought to treat them.

Alternatively, treating people equally may mean treating them in accord with rules that draw no distinctions among them. At first glance, this, too, seems untenable because, as we have seen, nearly all rules distinguish among people in one way or another. Thus, the rule "to each according to his needs" distinguishes among people on the basis of their needs, while the rule "to each per capita" distinguishes among people by giving each person a distinctive share. The latter interpretation is more plausible, however, than it might at first seem. It is true, of course, that most rules (including, presumably, most just rules) distinguish among people in one way or another. It is also true that any principle that precludes an actor from distinguishing among people cannot be just. By its terms, however, the presumption of equality does not preclude an actor from treating people unequally; it merely requires that, when he does, he give reasons for doing so. The presumption of equality, therefore, can plausibly be understood to mean "People should always be treated without distinction until reasons are shown for distinguishing among them."

The Meaning of 'Reason'

The presumption of equality requires that reasons be shown for treating people unequally, but it does not explicitly state what constitutes a "reason." Some commentators suggest that, by not explicitly stating what counts as a reason, the presumption "leaves" it "open" to persons to define 'reason' in ways that "cover almost any type of situation."[19] Thus, Kenneth Simons says, if a parent takes two children to a movie but forgets to take a third, his "reason" for treating the third unequally can always be said to be his "lapse in memory."[20] A comparable argument is sometimes made regarding the legal counterpart in American constitutional law to the presumption of equality, viz., the constitutional presumption that all people should be treated equally until a state presents "rational" reasons for treating them unequally.[21] Some authorities argue that the "rationality" requirement is empty because the state's purpose can always be defined in such a way that its action is rationally related to its purpose.[22] Thus, Justice Rehnquist argued that the Illinois legislature's decision in *Trimble v. Gordon* to treat illegitimate children differently from legitimate children for purposes of intestate succession was rationally related to its purpose because "the purpose (in the ordinary sense of that word) of the Illinois Legislature in enacting the Illinois Probate Act was to make the language contained in that section a part of the Illinois law."[23]

Other commentators take a contrary position. To have a reason for treating people unequally, they say, is to have a "general" justification—as opposed to a personal preference—for doing so.[24] To say "I want"[25] to treat a person differently is not a reason for doing so. A reason does not count unless it is "relevant," and personal "preferences" do not count as relevant reasons for treating people unequally:

Does a parent's preference for one of his children justify his favouring that child over his other children? Does a teacher's preference for girls (or boys) justify his favouring them in his grading? Does a judge's preference for people who are short-

[19] Rees, *Equality*, p. 95 (quoting Isaiah Berlin). I am indebted to Rees for much of the discussion in this subsection.

[20] Simons, "Equality as a Comparative Right," p. 392.

[21] See, e.g., *Vince v. Bradley*, 440 U.S. 93, 97 (1979). For discussion of the so-called rational basis requirement, see Barrett, "The Rational Basis Standard for Equal Protection Review of Ordinary Legislative Classifications," p. 845; Bennett, " 'Mere' Rationality in Constitutional Law," p. 1049.

[22] Robert Nagel, as a law student, made this point powerfully in Note, "Legislative Purpose, Rationality, and Equal Protection," p. 132: "In every case in which the Court has construed a statutory goal in such a way that the statutory classification could be found to be not rationally related to the legislative purpose, it would have been equally possible to define the purpose so that the statute could have been found to be rational."

[23] *Trimble v. Gordon*, 430 U.S. 762, 782 (1977) (Rehnquist, J., dissenting).

[24] Wasserstrom, "Rights, Human Rights, and Racial Discrimination," pp. 634–35.

[25] Flathman, *The Public Interest*, pp. 75–76.

haired and neatly attired justify his favouring them in sentencing or fining? In none of these cases would a parent's, teacher's or judge's *preferences* make the individuals in question relevantly different from other persons in the same position *vis-à-vis* the judge, teacher or parent.[26]

Neither of the foregoing positions is entirely satisfactory. If, on the one hand, "reasons" include anything that happens to motivate an actor, the presumption will lose its force. It will become incapable of restraining an actor from doing anything he wishes to do. If, on the other hand, "reasons" exclude statements of "I want," the presumption will preclude an actor from discriminating among people on the basis of personal preferences in many areas in which it is presently regarded as appropriate to do so (in choosing friends and spouses, distributing alms, favoring authors and artists, and so on).[27]

Fortunately, the word 'reason' can be understood in a way that avoids these pitfalls. To do so, however, it is necessary to distinguish between "explanations" and "justifications." An explanation is a *causal* account of an event; a justification is a *moral* account of an event. Thus, if a repentant husband says that he assaulted his wife because he was drunk, he is explaining his conduct, not justifying it. He is giving a reason, which he believes causally accounts for the assault, without morally defending it. In contrast, if an unrepentant husband says that he assaulted his wife because she committed adultery, he is not only explaining his conduct but also justifying it, for he believes his reason ought to persuade people of the rightness of his conduct. Some people may reject his justification, finding it morally unacceptable. Even as they reject his proffered justification, however, they must recognize it for what it is—an effort to account for the morality of his conduct by giving reasons that he believes others ought to find morally persuasive.

The term 'reason' in the presumption of equality may intelligently be understood to mean "justification" in the foregoing

[26] Gillespie, "On Treating Like Cases Differently," p. 157. It should be noted that while Gillespie feels that the personal preferences of the actor do not render otherwise like cases "unalike," he nevertheless believes that such preferences alone may justify different treatment—or what he calls "treating like cases differently"—in some cases. Aristotle would surely say that if the personal preferences of the actor justify treating cases differently, then the cases are not "like" cases.

[27] See Rees, *Equality*, pp. 109–15, 129.

sense. If so, it avoids the pitfalls of the two interpretations we previously considered. It avoids the pitfall of encompassing any explanation an actor may happen to give, because it excludes reasons that are mere explanations, as opposed to justifications. It also avoids the pitfall of excluding reasons of personal preference, because it includes personal preferences in circumstances in which reasonable people might deem such preferences to be morally acceptable grounds for action. Thus, if 'reason' is understood in this way, the presumption of equality would preclude a teacher from favoring one student over another on the ground that he likes her better, but it would not preclude a teacher from marrying one acquaintance rather than another on the ground that he likes her better.

To be sure, giving reasons for one's conduct is not the same as fully justifying it. Most people who engage in morally controversial conduct can give some moral account of their actions. John Rees observes that "[i]t is the nature of the reasons themselves rather than a failure to have or to give them which is usually at issue: the Nazis had and gave reasons for persecuting the Jews, just as do the Soviet authorities for their treatment of Solzhenitsyn and other dissident intellectuals."[28] Nevertheless, the giving of reasons does something significant: it demonstrates awareness of a social obligation to account to others for the rightness of one's conduct.

It is sometimes assumed that 'reason' in the presumption of equality has a stronger meaning—that having reasons means not only having moral as opposed to amoral grounds for treating people unequally, but having moral reasons that fully suffice to justify treating people unequally. Thus, Kenneth Cauthen argues that nothing counts as a reason for purposes of the presumption of equality unless it is "sufficient" to justify unequal treatment.[29] Yet that interpretation renders the presumption of equality harder to

---

[28] Rees, *Equality*, p. 110.

[29] Cauthen, *The Passion for Equality*, p. 13. It is often said that the "reason" advanced to justify unequal treatment must be a "morally relevant" one. See Carritt, *Ethical and Political Thinking*, p. 99; Raphael, "Equality and Equity," p. 122; Wasserstrom, "Rights, Human Rights, and Racial Discrimination," pp. 634–35. Unfortunately, as D. H. Monro has shown, the term 'moral' is ambiguous. To say an actor must show a moral reason may mean that he must show a moral *as opposed to an amoral* reason, or it may mean that he must show a moral *as opposed to an immoral* reason, that is, a reason that is also morally "right." Monro, "Impartiality and Consistency," p. 161. By "morally relevant" reasons, I understand the commentators in question to mean "moral" reasons in the former sense.

rebut than it is commonly supposed to be. The presumption is commonly regarded as being "minimally substantive"[30] in nature—as requiring "rational" moral conduct, not necessarily "right" moral conduct.[31] If actors are required to show "sufficient" reasons for treating people unequally, they will rarely, if ever, be able to satisfy the presumption, because "the attempt to lay down conditions for what we shall regard as a *proper* justification will inevitably generate controversy."[32]

Ultimately, this difference of view as to what counts as a "reason" for rebutting the presumption of equality cannot be resolved without identifying what it is that gives the presumption its supposed force. The relationship within rebuttable presumptions between what is presumed and what rebuts is reciprocal: what counts as a rebuttal is a function of the force of the empirical or normative supposition that underlies the presumption. To understand what kinds of "reasons" suffice to rebut the presumption of equality, one must understand why being a person is a normative ground for being treated equally with other persons.

The Validity of the Presumption of Equality

The presumption of equality, as we have seen, is not a corollary of Aristotle's precept "equals should be treated equally," nor is it simply a matter of logic. *Not* having a normative reason for treating people unequally is not the same as *having* a normative reason for treating them equally, for it is possible that one may have no normative reasons for treating them either one way or the other.[33]

---

[30] Dixon, *Freedom and Equality*, p. 51.

[31] See Benn, "Equality, Moral and Social," p. 40 (characterizing the presumption of equality as being "implicit in the notion of rational decision"); Graham, "Liberty and Equality," pp. 63–64 (describing it as "a logical rule of moral and prudential thinking").

[32] Rees, *Equality*, p. 131. See also p. 121.

[33] Now it may be true, in some general sense, that inequalities are arbitrary if no reason can be given for them. However, it does not follow that equality is then any less arbitrary. All that follows, is that in the absence of reason, *any* pattern of distribution, equal or unequal, is arbitrary. . . . I do not see how, in the absence of any such reasons, there can be any positive "presumption of equality."

Norman, *Free and Equal*, pp. 57–58. See also Browne, "The Presumption of Equality," p. 53 ("What is *not* true is that the proposition that there is no reason for treating [people] differently entails the proposition that there is a reason for not treating them differently").

In contrast, A. C. Graham has argued that not having a reason to treat people

If the presumption is valid, then, it must be because reason and experience show that not distinguishing among people is the proper response to not having reasons to distinguish among them. To appreciate the possible grounds for such a judgment, we shall, first, identify within the larger range of cases in which an actor has no reasons for distinguishing among people the smaller subset of cases in which the presumption of equality arguably plays a role, i.e., cases in which an actor is uncertain whether to distinguish among persons. Second, regarding such cases of uncertainty, we will distinguish normative uncertainty from factual uncertainty. Third, we will analyze various reasons for responding to normative uncertainty in particular ways. Finally, applying what we have learned to the presumption of equality, we shall try to identify and determine the validity of the normative supposition that underlies the judgment that being a person is a normative ground for being treated equally with other persons.

---

unequally *is* itself a reason to treat them equally. See Graham, "Liberty and Equality," p. 59. His argument, in syllogistic form, seems to go as follows:

Premise A: The necessary alternative to distinguishing among people is to not distinguish among them.

Premise B: The necessity to do something is itself a reason for doing it.

Conclusion: An actor who has no reason for distinguishing among people necessarily has a reason for not distinguishing among them.

The problem with the syllogism is that it uses the word 'reason' in two different ways. In stating that "the necessity to do something is itself a reason for doing it," premise B uses 'reason' as a synonym for *causal explanation*. In stating that an actor has no "reason for distinguishing among people," the conclusion uses 'reason' as a synonym for *moral justification*. One cannot assume that, because an actor has no moral reason for doing something, he must have a causal reason for engaging in the alternative course of action. Nor can one assume that, because he has no moral reason for doing something, he must have a moral reason for engaging in the alternative course of action. He may lack moral reasons for engaging in either.

There is, perhaps, one interpretation of the presumption of equality that renders it equivalent to rational conduct, but it does so at the expense of neutralizing the presumption. Thus, it might be argued that to treat people equally means to treat them identically by reference to *all possible* prescriptive standards of comparison. Since no one can even theoretically treat people equally in that sense, it would follow that actors must always give reasons for what they do. The presumption of equality, in that event, would indeed mean "Give reasons for however you treat people." See Cooper, *The Illusions of Equality*, p. 15. Unfortunately, this would also neutralize the presumption *as a presumption*. For the nature of rebuttable presumptions is to favor one course of conduct over another. If treating people equally were interpreted to mean something that could never occur, the presumption of equality would lose its provisional capacity to favor equal treatment over unequal treatment. See Lucas, *On Justice*, p. 173 (the presumption loses its "bulldozing power" if it loses the capacity to separate treatments that require justification from those that do not).

243

The Range of Cases in Which an Actor Has No Reason to Distinguish among Persons

The range of cases in which an actor has no reason to treat people unequally can be divided into two subsets: (1) cases in which an actor is certain he should treat people equally because he has good reasons for treating them equally and no reasons for treating them unequally; and (2) cases in which an actor is uncertain whether he should treat people equally or unequally because he has no reasons for treating them one way as opposed to the other. The presumption of equality has no role to play in the first subset because the actor already possesses all the information he needs in order to know what he ought to do.

To illustrate cases in the first subset, assume that an employer follows the custom of giving each of his salesmen a one-month vacation each year. The practice is generally accepted within the industry as right and good. One day the employer reads about a Korean practice of awarding vacation time to salesmen in proportion to their annual sales. The employer is appalled by the latter practice, as are his employees. No one can think of any reason to adopt the Korean practice in lieu of the existing custom. What should the employer do? Should he continue to treat his employees equally or adopt the Korean practice of treating employees unequally? If he continues to treat his employees equally, why should he do so—because everyone considers it right and good or because of the presumption of equality? The answer seems clear. The employer should continue to give his employees a one-month vacation, and he should do so, not because the presumption of equality adds anything to what he already knows, but because he knows the existing practice to be right and good.

The employer in this case had an easy choice because he had predominant reasons for treating his employees equally with respect to vacations and no reasons he regarded as persuasive for treating them unequally. Significantly, a person will have the same easy choice in cases of factual uncertainty whenever established rules dictate that he resolve factual uncertainty in favor of equal treatment. Consider a case Kent Greenawalt imagines. A judge is called upon to sentence two criminal defendants for a crime in which they jointly participated. The judge knows that one of the defendants must be the more culpable (say, the one who pulled the trigger), but he has no way of identifying him. Greenawalt believes that, because the judge has no reason to suspect one defendant more than the other, the presumption of equality prohibits him from giving either defendant an aggravated sentence.[34] Greenawalt is surely right about what the judge ought to do but less so about why he ought to do it. The judge ought not to give one defendant (as opposed to the other) an aggravated sentence because shared and accepted notions of blaming dictate that, unless a judge considers it more likely than not, factually, that a particular defendant deserves to be condemned at an aggravated level, the judge ought not to impose such a sentence. This rule tells the judge everything he needs to know about what to do when he has no factual basis for giving one defendant an aggravated sentence.

It might be thought that the reason established rules mandate that factual uncertainty regarding aggravated sentences be resolved in favor of equality is that the presumption of equality itself requires that factual uncertainty always be resolved in favor of equal treatment. Yet this is not so. Factual uncertainty often is (and ought to be) resolved in favor of unequal treatment when equal treatment is believed to carry the greater risk of error. Assume, for example, that a jurisdiction requires judges to exercise mercy by giving defendants lower sentences than they deserve for their wrongdoing whenever judges can do so without any loss of deterrence. Now imagine that a judge is called upon to sentence two defendants for a crime for which they are equally culpable. The judge believes that deterrence requires that he give at least one of the defendants the full sentence deserved, but he is uncertain as to whether any further deterrence would be gained by giving full sentences to both. How should the judge proceed in the face of factual uncertainty regarding the requirements of deterrence? Should he resolve the doubt by giving both the higher sentence? Should he resolve it by showing mercy to a defendant whom he selects at random? There is no single answer to these questions. Jurisdictions may reasonably differ in their beliefs about the relative risks of error. Surely, however, a jurisdiction could sensibly decide that the risk of erroneously giving a higher than necessary sentence is greater than the risk of giving a lower than appropriate sentence, and, hence, it could decide to resolve factual doubts by exercising mercy in favor of a defendant selected at random.[35]

---

[34] Greenawalt, "How Empty Is the Idea of Equality?" p. 1176.

[35] In prescribing penalties for malefactors possessing the same levels of *mens rea*, states commonly distinguish among them by providing lower penalties for those

In short, the presumption of equality has no role to play in cases in which an actor believes he has good reasons for treating people equally and no reasons for treating them unequally, because he already possesses all the information he needs to conclude that he ought to treat people equally. If the presumption of equality has a meaningful role to play when an actor has no reason to treat people unequally, therefore, it must be in the remaining subset of cases, viz., cases in which an actor is uncertain whether to treat people equally or unequally by virtue of having no reasons for treating them one way as opposed to the other.

Cases in Which an Actor Is Uncertain Whether or Not to Distinguish among Persons

Cases in which an actor is uncertain about whether to treat people equally or unequally can be divided into two classes: (i) cases in which he is normatively uncertain whether to adopt a rule that treats people equally as opposed to unequally; and (ii) cases in which he is factually uncertain whether a person possesses a particular feature that justifies treating him unequally under established rules. The first class of cases is easily described. Consider

The Ambivalent Employer

The owner of a retail store wishes to return to his faithful employees some of the profits they have helped him earn during the year. But he is ambivalent about the formula of distribution he ought to institute.
—One possibility is to divide the profits by the number of employees and distribute the profits per capita.
—Another possibility is to distribute profits in proportion to employee seniority.

---

whose conduct does not result in actual harm. See Schulhofer, "Harm and Punishment," pp. 1498–99. The difference in treatment is commonly justified on grounds of "frugality," that is, on the ground that while no defendant shall ever receive a penalty in excess of what his conduct deserves, leniency may be randomly extended to some defendants (i.e., defendants whose conduct does not result in harm) because leniency serves the penological purpose of maximizing general deterrence at the lowest, or most "frugal," levels of punishment. See Schulhofer, "Harm and Punishment," pp. 1562–67, 1570–71, 1574–75. See also Model Penal Code § 5.05(1) comments, at 179 (Tentative Draft No. 10, 1960)(justifying punishment for crimes of attempt, solicitation, and conspiracy at lower levels than for the completed felonies to which they are directed, on the ground of "economizing" in the use of heavy sanctions for purposes of general deterrence).

—A third possibility is to distribute profits in proportion to existing salaries.

Each proposal treats employees equally in some sense and un-equally in others, although the proposal for per-capita distri-bution draws fewer distinctions among employees than the other proposals.

The employer studies the proposals carefully. He discovers that there is no industry custom on the matter. He also dis-covers that his employees are evenly divided in their prefer-ences. As for himself, he has no reasons for preferring one proposal over the others.

The employer's uncertainty is normative. Once he adopts a partic-ular proposal, he will have no difficulty applying it because he will have all the information he needs in order to execute it. His prob-lem is that he has no reasons for preferring one proposal over the others.

The second class of cases involves factual uncertainty about whether a particular person falls within a class of persons who ought to be treated differently under established rules. It is some-times suggested that these cases reflect factual uncertainty, *not* normative uncertainty.[36] In reality, while these cases differ signif-icantly from the former for purposes of the presumption of equal-ity, it is not because they lack normative uncertainty. Both classes of cases involve normative uncertainty about which of several pos-sible rules to adopt. The difference between them is that the am-bivalent employer faces only normative uncertainty, while the fac-tually uncertain actor faces uncertainty of two kinds—factual uncertainty about the applicability of established rules and nor-mative uncertainty about how to act in the event of factual uncer-tainty of that kind. To illustrate, assume that the ambivalent em-ployer finally decides to distribute a $3,000 bonus to each employee, with an extra $1,000 for those whose sales exceed their previous year's sales. But, because of the employer's faulty record-

---

[36] There are two important ways in which one might be unable to show simi-larities and/or differences between individuals. For one thing, one might be unable to decide which similarities and/or differences are relevant to a partic-ular case (*i.e.*, which material principle applies); and second, even if one knows which similarities and/or differences are relevant, he may be unable to deter-mine whether the individuals involved are similar or different in these re-spects.

Katzner, "Presumptivist and Nonpresumptivist Principles of Formal Justice," p. 255.

keeping, the records of salesman Sam's previous year's sales have been lost, and the employer cannot say whether it is more probable or not that Sam exceeded his previous year's sales. The employer now suffers from two kinds of uncertainty. First, there is factual uncertainty about how much merchandise Sam sold the previous year. Second, there is normative uncertainty as to which of two rules to adopt in the event of factual uncertainty about whether an extra bonus is deserved—a rule that resolves factual doubts in favor of paying Sam more than his fellow salesmen or a rule that resolves factual doubts in favor of paying him the same as his fellow salesmen.

It may be suggested that the ambivalent employer might already possess a rule of thumb for deciding contested issues of fact, a rule such as "In the event that the employer is unable to say that it is more likely than not that a salesman deserves an extra bonus, he shall not pay the salesman the extra bonus." That cannot be the case, however. For, if the employer already possessed such a rule, then, like Greenawalt's imaginary judge, the employer would no longer be in a position of uncertainty; rather, he would be in the position of possessing predominant reasons for giving Sam the same bonus as the other salesmen and no reasons for giving him more. It follows, then, that if an actor is genuinely uncertain about whether he should distinguish among people, he must, at least in part, be uncertain about what rule of conduct to adopt.

Nevertheless, it is important to differentiate between cases in which an actor is normatively uncertain about whether to distinguish among persons and cases in which he is factually uncertain as to a person's normative status under a rule that distinguishes among persons, for the presumption of equality has no role to play in the latter cases. The presumption has no role to play in resolving factual uncertainty regarding the normative status of a particular person under rules that distinguish among persons because, however such factual uncertainty is resolved, an actor must necessarily treat the person equally with regard to some people and unequally with regard to others. To illustrate, recall the ambivalent employer's uncertainty as to whether salesman Sam had exceeded his previous year's sales. The presumption of equality cannot resolve the employer's dilemma merely by directing him to treat people equally because, however the employer responds to his uncertainty, he must treat Sam equally with regard to some salesmen and unequally with regard to others. If, on the one hand, the employer pays Sam the extra $1,000, he treats Sam and those who exceeded their previous year's sales equally, and he treats Sam and those who did not exceed their previous year's sales unequally. If, on the other hand, the employer refuses to pay Sam the extra bonus, he treats Sam and those who did not earn the bonus equally, and Sam and those who did earn the bonus unequally. The same is true of every rule that distinguishes among people. Therefore, if the presumption of equality has a role to play in directing an actor's conduct, it must be confined to cases of normative uncertainty about which of two rules of distribution to adopt.

Reasons for Resolving Normative Uncertainty One Way as Opposed to Another

The object of the presumption of equality, then, is to help an actor decide which rule to adopt when he is normatively uncertain about whether to treat certain people equally or unequally. It does so by instructing him provisionally to adopt rules that treat people equally rather than unequally—that is, rules that refrain from distinguishing among persons of a particular class as opposed to rules that do distinguish among them. To understand the basis for that provisional instruction, it may be useful to examine various reasons for presumptively resolving normative uncertainty one way or another.

Rebuttable presumptions generally rest on the relative risks of error in choosing between two alternatives, P and Q.[37] Presumptions in favor of P are justified whenever the risk of erroneously choosing P is less than the risk of erroneously choosing Q. Two factors combine to constitute relative risks of error: the relative probabilities of error and the relative gravities of error. When there is a relatively lower probability of error in choosing P over Q, there is greater justification for presuming in favor of P; when there is relatively lesser harm in erroneously choosing P over Q, there is greater justification for presuming in favor of P.

---

[37] Risk of error is not the only possible basis for rebuttable presumptions. In an adversary system of justice, rebuttable presumptions can also reflect relative access to evidence. Thus, many states within the United States rebuttably presume that criminal defendants are sane until evidence of insanity is introduced. The presumption is justified, in part, on the grounds that, as between the prosecution and a defendant who possesses a privilege against self-incrimination, the defendant has better access to evidence of insanity than the prosecution and, hence, can be presumed to be sane for purposes of the prosecution's case until the defendant comes forward with evidence to the contrary.

These factors are easily illustrated. Consider the common presumption in criminal law that "unexplained possession of recently stolen property is evidence that its possessor knew it was stolen." The presumption is based on probability of error: a person who does not explain his possession of recently stolen property is likely to have known it was stolen, hence, an actor who presumes the person knew it was stolen is less likely to make an error than one who presumes the contrary. In contrast, the "presumption of innocence" is based upon the gravity of error: the harm of erroneously convicting an innocent person is regarded as so much graver than the harm of erroneously acquitting guilty persons that suspects are presumed to be innocent until sufficient incriminating evidence is presented to find them guilty "beyond a reasonable doubt."

It is important to distinguish between these rationales because they bear upon how presumptions are rebutted. A presumption that rests upon relative probability of error loses its force (or, in the language of lawyers, "bursts" or is "rebutted") to the extent that information exists which diminishes the underlying probability.[38] Thus, the presumption "Unexplained possession of recently stolen property is evidence that its possessor knew it was stolen" is rebutted to the extent that the fact-finder has information which suggests either that the possessor did not know the property was stolen or that he is unable to explain even innocent possession of it. In contrast, a presumption which rests on relative gravity of error is rebutted to the extent that information exists which renders the alternative harm equally grave under the circumstances. Thus, the presumption of innocence is rebutted to the extent that evidence of a defendant's guilt renders the harm of erroneously acquitting him as grave under the circumstances as the harm of erroneously convicting him.

Implications for the Presumption of Equality

Each of the foregoing factors—probability of error and gravity of error—may enter into, and explain, the judgment that "people ought to be treated equally unless reasons are shown for treating them differently." To the extent that they do, however, they pre-

---

[38] For an illuminating analysis of presumptions and related instruments in the law, see Allen, "Structuring Jury Decisionmaking in Criminal Cases."

suppose normative assumptions about which reasonable people may disagree.

Let us begin with an argument for the presumption of equality based on relative gravity of error. It has been said that "in modern western culture, people usually feel a more acute resentment when those they deem equal are treated better than they are . . . than when those they feel are relevantly less deserving are treated equally."[39] If that is true—if, indeed, people feel greater resentment at being erroneously treated unequally than at being erroneously treated equally—then treating people unequally creates a risk of greater harm than treating them equally. Yet in order to base a presumption of equality on that risk of greater harm, one must make a further normative assumption about which reasonable people may disagree, namely, that the resentment and envy which people feel over unequal treatment is a harm from which they ought to be protected.[40]

It can also be argued that all persons, by virtue of being persons, possess traits that create a probability of error if they are treated unequally. S. I. Benn makes such an argument. Once it is decided that "human beings" (as opposed, say, to "all mammals") are a class of creatures whose "interests are to count," he says, it is "implicit in the notion of rational decision" that they should be treated equally "until a case has been made for saying that some particular difference between them is relevant to the matter at hand."[41] Unfortunately, Benn's argument, as stated, is a non sequitur. That human beings constitute a class whose interests "count" is not a reason for presumptively treating them equally, for it does not follow from the fact that they possess interests that those interests are presumptively best served by treating them equally. As D. E. Browne explains:

> That questions of justice can only arise where the treatment of persons is concerned is true. But this truth has no normative implications. It is presupposed equally in those situations where justice requires *different* treatment of A and B, and in those situations where justice requires *the same* treatment of A and B. That A and B are both human beings is a necessary

[39] Greenawalt, "How Empty Is the Idea of Equality?" p. 1175.
[40] See Coons, "Consistency," p. 106, esp. n. 131 (questioning Kent Greenawalt's assumptions about the worthiness of resentment). On the varieties of envy and the extent to which they are morally worthy of protection, see Rawls, *A Theory of Justice*, pp. 530–41; Nozick, *Anarchy, State, and Utopia*, pp. 239–46.
[41] Benn, "Equality, Moral and Social," p. 40.

condition for *raising* the question of whether justice requires that they be treated equally or differently. But it does not *answer* that question.[42]

The argument Benn makes, however, can be stated in a stronger form. The stronger version starts from the normative assumption, not only that each person "counts," but also (as Jeremy Bentham puts it) that each person "count[s] for one."[43] In John Stuart Mill's words, "one person's happiness . . . [should be] counted for exactly as much as another's."[44] Some commentators have suggested that Bentham's normative premise by itself suffices to support the presumption of equality.[45] By itself, however, Bentham's starting premise is insufficient to support the presumption because, if people have different utility functions or if the utility of distributions does not diminish at the margin, per-capita distributions will not have the effect of maximizing utility for persons who all "count for one."[46] To support a general presumption in favor of per-capita distributions, therefore, one must make two further factual assumptions: first, that all persons have identical utility functions; and, second, that the utility of distributions of goods diminishes at the margin.[47] The presumption of equality thus finds some justification in Benthamite assumptions of utilitarianism. (By the same token, a Benthamite could rebut the presumption by showing that distinguishing among persons is likely to maximize aggregate or average well-being.)

Harry Frankfurt makes an argument against equal distributions of wealth that appears to militate against the foregoing justification for the presumption of equality. Frankfurt argues that in order to move from the premise that "everyone's happiness counts for one" to the conclusion that everyone has a right to an equal share of society's wealth, one must make two fundamental assumptions: (i) for each individual, the utility of money invariably diminishes at the margin, and (ii) with respect to money, or with respect to

[42] Browne, "The Presumption of Equality," p. 50 (original emphasis). See also Stone, "Justice Not Equality," p. 101.

[43] Mill, *Utilitarianism*, p. 257 (quoting Bentham). See also Bentham, "Plan of Parliamentary Reform," p. 459; Bentham, Introduction to "Constitutional Code," pp. 5–8.

[44] Mill, *Utilitarianism*, p. 257.

[45] See Vlastos, "Justice and Equality," pp. 38, 48–52, 72.

[46] See Richards, "Justice and Equality," p. 247 n. 14.

[47] To support a specific presumption of equality—that is, a presumption confined to a specific class of persons or to a specific class of goods—one would have to show that the specific class of persons has identical preference curves or that the utility of the specific class of goods diminishes at the margin.

the things money can buy, the utility functions of all individuals are the same.[48] Unless (i) and (ii) are true, he says, a rich person might obtain greater utility than a poor person from an extra increment of wealth. He proceeds to present good reasons for thinking that (i) and (ii) are both false, and concludes that giving each person as much wealth as everyone else does not necessarily maximize aggregate utility. Frankfurt's argument is relevant to the presumption of equality, but it is not conclusive, because it says nothing about the *frequency* with which propositions (i) and (ii) are false. The presumption of equality, after all, is not a hard and fast rule in favor of equal distributions; it is a rebuttable presumption based on relative probabilities. For purposes of the presumption of equality, therefore, the controlling question, as Robert Goodin observes, is not whether (i) and (ii) are always true, but whether they are true with sufficient frequency to support a rebuttable presumption in favor of equal treatment.[49]

Conclusion

R. M. Hare was quoted in an earlier chapter for his views about the justice of dividing a bar of chocolate among three people. Although it was not apparent then, his views were based on a broader belief about the presumption of equality. His broader statement is worth quoting in full:

> Suppose that three people are dividing a bar of chocolate between them, and suppose that they all have an equal liking for chocolate. And let us suppose that no other considerations such as age, sex, ownership of the chocolate, etc., are thought to be relevant. It seems to us obvious that the just way to divide the chocolate is equally. And the principle of universalizability gives us the logic of this conclusion. For if it be maintained that one of the three ought to have more than an equal share, there must be something about his case to make this difference—for otherwise we are making different moral judgments about similar cases. But there is *ex hypothesi* no relevant difference, and so the conclusion follows.[50]

Hare's statement touches upon several of the themes of this chapter. For one thing, he appears to accept the validity of the presumption of equality, for he states that, if an actor has no reasons

[48] Frankfurt, "Equality as a Moral Ideal," p. 25.
[49] Goodin, "Egalitarianism, Fetishistic and Otherwise," p. 48.
[50] Hare, *Freedom and Reason*, pp. 118–19.

for treating people differently, it "follows" that he should treat them "equally."[51] Furthermore, he argues that the principle of universalizability (by which he means "likes should be treated alike") provides the "logic" for the presumption of equality. As we have seen, however, that is not the case. The Aristotelian precept "likes should be treated alike" and the presumption of equality are very different kinds of propositions: the former is a formal proposition and the latter a normative proposition, hence the former cannot entail the latter. That an actor has no reason to treat people unequally does not mean he must have a reason to treat them equally, for he may have no reasons for treating them either one way or the other.

This is not to gainsay Hare's conclusion that the chocolate bar should presumptively be distributed among the three persons in equal shares. It means, rather, that his conclusion rests upon certain factual and normative assumptions he makes about people's preferences. The assumptions can be gleaned from the one signal fact Hare specifies about his three hypothetical persons, viz., that "they all have an equal liking for chocolate." If Hare is right in his assumption that having an "equal liking for chocolate" suffices to entitle a person to an equal share of chocolate in the absence of reasons to the contrary, it is because he is right in making two further assumptions about persons: first, that factually the utility of eating chocolate tends to diminish at the margin; and, second, that normatively the satisfaction of one person's preferences counts as much as the satisfaction of anyone else's. Or, as Hare puts it, quoting Bentham, "Everybody is to count for one, and nobody to count for more than one."[52] Bentham's normative assumption does give rise to a presumption in favor of per-capita distributions with respect to persons whose utility functions are known (or presumed) to be the same and for whom utility is known (or presumed) to diminish at the margin.

[51] Indeed, as part of the same discussion, Hare explicitly states "that everybody is entitled to equal consideration, and that if it is said that two people ought to be treated differently, some difference must be cited as the ground for these different moral judgments." Hare, *Freedom and Reason*, p. 118.

[52] Hare, *Freedom and Reason*, p. 118. Hare characterizes Bentham's maxim as a "purely formal principle of justice," which "follow[s] from the logical character of . . . moral words." But that cannot be so, for, if Bentham's maxim were a formal proposition, it would be incapable of serving as a guide to conduct without the insertion of independent norms. On the relationship between formal principles and the presumption of equality, see Browne, "The Presumption of Equality"; Katzner, "Presumptivist and Nonpresumptivist Principles of Formal Justice."

PART FOUR

THE RHETORIC OF EQUALITY

Douglas Rae opens his book *Equalities* by posing two fundamental questions. The first, to which he ultimately devotes his entire attention, concerns the meaning of 'equality'. As he puts it, "What, when it is brought [from theory to practice], does equality come to mean?" "Is equality the name of one coherent program or is it the name of a system of mutually antagonistic claims upon society and government?" He responds to that question by concluding that equality is a single name for "many distinct notions," some of which are "mutually exclusive," "antagonistic," and "incompatible."[1]

Rae's second question concerns equality's rhetorical force. How is it, he asks, if equality means different things to different people, that "[e]verywhere one hears praise for the idea of equality?" If equality has antagonistic and incompatible meanings; if favoring one equality also means opposing other equalities; if being a champion of equality also means being an enemy of equality—how, then, can it be that on balance "[a]lmost everyone seems somehow a partisan of equality"? Why, if everyone rejects equality in particular cases, does no one wish "to directly oppose equality in general"? What are the "rules of rhetoric" by which this one idea has become "the most powerful idea of our time"?[2]

Like Rae, we have focused thus far on the meaning of equality. In this final part we shall address the question Rae leaves unanswered. What does the meaning of equality tell us about the *rhetoric* of equality? Why do arguments for equality put opposing arguments "on the defensive"?[3] Why is it that "to our ears inequality has the ring of injustice, unfairness, and discrimina-

---

[1] Rae, *Equalities*, pp. 2, 4, 132, 138–40 (emphasis omitted).
[2] Rae, *Equalities*, pp. 2, 18, 19, 148 (emphasis omitted).
[3] Kristol, "Equality as an Ideal," p. 110.

tion"?[4] What is it that gives arguments of equality their "tremendous emotive force"?[5] Why are they so "influential,"[6] so "potent"?[7]

[4] Wolgast, *Equality and the Rights of Women*, p. 14.

[5] Chemerinsky, "In Defense of Equality," p. 590 ("tremendous emotive force"). Robert Nisbet refers to equality as a "spiritual dynamic." Nisbet, "The New Despotism," p. 33 ("Whatever else equality is, it is a spiritual dynamic").

[6] Bowie, "Equality and Distributive Justice," p. 140 ("The appeal to the value of equality" is "one of the most influential appeals in disputes concerning distributive justice").

[7] Temkin, "Inequality," p. 99 ("The notion of equality has long been among the most potent of human ideals").

ELEVEN

THE PERSUASIVENESS OF EQUALITY

> Equality every day confers a number of small enjoyments
> on every man. The charms of equality are every instant felt
> and are within the reach of all; the noblest hearts are not
> insensible to them, and the most vulgar souls exult in
> them. The passion that equality creates must therefore be
> at once strong and general. —*Tocqueville*[1]

Rhetoric is the art of persuasion.[2] The test of a rhetorical device, it
is said, is its ability "to produce change in the world."[3] By that
measure, "equality" has always enjoyed rhetorical power, because
it "has long been among the most potent of human ideals."[4] Aristotle, who first expounded the nature of rhetoric, noted that equality is the plea, not of the strong, who are satisfied with things as
they are, but of those who are seeking change.[5] Equality is a "politically aggressive idea."[6] It is a "protest ideal,"[7] a "rallying cry,"[8]
which possesses "built-in revolutionary force."[9] As "a weapon in
social, political and international struggles," it "has had a most
remarkable record of success in the story of modern Western soci-

[1] Tocqueville, *Democracy in America*, vol. 2, p. 101. See also Howells, "Equality as
the Basis of Good Society," p. 67 ("Equality is such a beautiful thing that I wonder
people can ever have any other ideal. It is the only social joy, the only comfort").

[2] Aristotle defines rhetoric as "the faculty of discovering in the particular case
what are the available means of persuasion." Aristotle, *Rhetoric* 7 (trans. Cooper).

[3] Bitzer, "The Rhetorical Situation," pp. 1, 3–4. See generally Campbell, *Critiques
of Contemporary Rhetoric*.

[4] Temkin, "Inequality," p. 99.

[5] Aristotle, *Politics* II.7.1266b14–1267b21, VI.3.1318b1–5. See also V.1.1301b26–27
("Inequality is everywhere at the bottom of faction, for in general faction arises
from men's striving for what is equal"; trans. Sinclair). As J. Pole puts it, "Equality
is normally the language of the underdog." Pole, *The Pursuit of Equality in American
History*, p. ix.

[6] Kristol, "Equality as an Ideal," pp. 108, 110 (equality is a "politically aggressive
idea").

[7] Sartori, *Democratic Theory*, pp. 326–27.

[8] Karst, "Why Equality Matters," p. 245.

[9] Nisbet, "The New Despotism," p. 34 ("Equality has built-in revolutionary
force").

eties,"[10] particularly in America.[11] It "facilitates important social and economic change; it . . . nurtures social mobilization; it can activate a quiescent citizenry."[12] It remains "the crucial issue underlying social change in political conflict in capitalist, socialist, and third-world societies."[13]

One measure of equality's rhetorical power is what advocates lose by forgoing it. An example is the current debate over "comparable worth" under Title VII of the Civil Rights Act of 1964. "Comparable worth" is a term of art for a legal claim, asserted principally by women, that they have a right to be paid what they are "worth" as measured by what their employers pay men with "comparable" skills.[14] The claim does not arise with respect to jobs

[10] Stone, "Justice Not Equality," p. 98:

[T]he notion of equality, used as a weapon in social, political and international struggles, has had a most remarkable record of success in the story of modern Western societies. It has had such success from the French and American Revolutions onward and still surges forward in 'liberation movements' of all kinds.

[11] The issue of equality is one that recurs throughout American history. The demand for equality has lain at the epicenter of the major upheavals that have erupted on the American political scene: the Revolution, the Jacksonian era, the Civil War and Reconstruction, the Populist-Progressive period, the New Deal, and the tumultuous 1960's and 1970's. Often these outbursts were fueled with fiery egalitarian rhetoric.

Verba and Orren, *Equality in America*, p. 21.

The idea of equality is one of the great themes in the culture of American public life. From the Declaration of Independence to the pledge of allegiance, the rhetoric of equality permeates our symbols of nationhood. Over and over in our history, from the earliest colonial beginnings, equality has been a rallying cry, a promise, an article of national faith.

Karst, *Belonging to America*, p. 1.

[12] [T]he equality principle . . . is the rock upon which our Constitution rests. Any defense of a constitutional democracy must begin with the equality principle, for the equality principle of our Constitution facilitates important social and economic change; it acts as the springboard for the realignment of unequal political forces toward economic and social equality. It nurtures social mobilization; it can activate a quiescent citizenry and it can recognize new and different forms of social organization.

Brennan, "The Equality Principle," p. 673.

[13] Beck, Foreword to *The Culture of Inequality*, p. iv ("[Equality] remains the crucial issue underlying social change in political conflict in capitalist, socialist, and third-world societies").

[14] Claims of "comparable worth," though originally raised and principally litigated by women, are theoretically available to members of any group protected by Title VII, including men and members of racial minorities. Some commentators have suggested, however, that comparable worth litigation is not a strategy that serves the economic interests of ethnic minorities. See Scales-Trent, "Comparable

in which men and women are evenly represented in an employer's work force. Nor does it arise with respect to female-dominated jobs for which an employer pays basically the same compensation as he or she pays employees with comparable skills in male-dominated or gender-integrated jobs. Rather, the claim arises with respect to female-dominated jobs for which an employer pays less than he or she pays employees with comparable skills in male-dominated or gender-integrated jobs.[15] The claim is that the employer and the marketplace combine to disvalue such jobs because they disvalue women and that, in doing so, they discriminate against employees on the basis of sex in violation of Title VII.

The argument for comparable worth is the kind of argument which, ordinarily, would be made in the language of 'equality'. As a claim for equality, the argument is straightforward: "An employer ought to pay people with equal skills equally without regard to sex." An accident of history, however, inhibits advocates from invoking the rhetoric of equality on behalf of comparable pay. The accident is that the earlier Equal Pay Act of 1963[16] appropriated the language of equality on behalf of a very different employment principle. The Equal Pay Act prohibits employers from paying women less than men for jobs *of the same description*. The authors of the Equal Pay Act, conscious of the impact of language,[17] deliberately framed their claim in terms of equality, demanding "equal pay" for "equal work." The term 'equal pay' has thus become a term of art in American labor law for the principle of equal pay for work of the same description—as opposed to equal pay for work requiring the same skills. As a consequence, the advocates of comparable worth, finding the term 'equal pay' foreclosed to them, have had to settle begrudgingly for the feebler plea for "comparable" pay.[18]

Worth." For the law of comparable worth, see Clauss, "Comparable Worth—the Theory, Its Legal Foundation, and the Feasibility of Implementation"; Weiler, "Wages of Sex."

[15] For an analysis of the two judicial tests currently available to measure an employee's "skills," see Rhode, "Occupational Equality," pp. 1228–30 (distinguishing between "relative worth" tests and "intrinsic worth" tests).

[16] Public Law 88-38, 77 Stat. 56 (1963), codified at 29 U.S.C. § 206(d)(1976).

[17] For the legislative history of the deliberate decision on the part of the authors of the Equal Pay Act to adopt the language of 'equality', see Williams and Bagby, "Comparable Worth."

[18] For discussion by its advocates of the unfortunate rhetoric of "comparable worth," see Brown, Baumann, and Melnick, "Equal Pay for Jobs of Comparable Worth"; Newman, Newell, and Kirkman, "The Lessons of AFSCME v. State of Washington," p. 484. Although they have had to settle for the rubric of "comparable worth," advocates of comparable worth still frame their claim in the language

Interestingly, although the fact of equality's rhetorical force is obvious, its source is not. One possibility, it might be thought, is that 'equality' is simply *defined* in favorable terms.[19] The terms 'justice', 'rights', 'fairness', and 'good' are "evaluative"[20] words of that kind. They are what J. Kovesi calls "complete" moral notions, that is, terms which are defined as referring to normatively desirable relationships.[21] Thus, a speaker who refers to something as being both "just" and "wicked" borders on contradicting himself. 'Equality', however, is not an evaluative word like 'justice' or 'rights'. 'Equality' can be used neutrally (e.g., "Jack and Jill are equal in height"), and it can be used pejoratively (e.g., "Hitler treated Jews and gypsies equally, by sending them all to concentration camps"). A speaker may contradict himself by arguing "against justice," but he does not contradict himself by arguing "against equality."[22]

Alternatively, it may be thought that 'equality' has favorable connotations because it happens to refer to something which in fact many (though not all) people find desirable. Conceptions of equality, however, are as diverse and incompatible as the standards by which they are measured.[23] Thus, rules of "equal oppor-

---

of 'equality'. See, e.g., Brown, Baumann, and Melnick, "Equal Pay for Jobs of Comparable Worth," p. 129 (emphasis added):

> Comparable pay theory addresses wage inequities that are associated with job segregation. The basic premise of comparable worth theory is that women should be able to substantiate a claim for equal wages by showing that their jobs and those of male workers are of *equal value* to their common employer.

[19] Some commentators appear to believe that 'equality' is an evaluative word of that kind. See de Cervera, "The Paradoxes of Equality," p. 238 (referring to equality as a "loaded word"). Cf. Benn, "Equality, Moral and Social," p. 41 ("the word 'inequality' has acquired . . . a pejorative force; 'inequalities' have come to mean *indefensible* differences in treatment")(original emphasis).

[20] See Wilson, *Equality*, p. 18.

[21] Kovesi, *Moral Notions*, p. 109.

[22] '[I]mpartial' is nearly always a value-word. 'Equal' may sometimes be used, even nowadays, as a word of praise; but in general it is purely descriptive. It would be natural to demand justice or impartiality as of right: these are things which by definition people ought to have. But whereas "Justice, O King!" is natural, "Equality, O King!" is not.

Wilson, *Equality*, p. 17.

For examples of argument "against" equality, see, e.g., Cooper, *The Illusions of Equality*, pp. 157–63; Flew, *The Politics of Procrustes*; Lucas, "Against Equality," p. 296; Lucas, "Against Equality Again"; Kristol, "About Equality," p. 42; Nietzsche, *Thus Spake Zarathustra*, Second Part, § 7, in *The Portable Nietzsche*, p. 211; Nisbet, "The New Despotism."

[23] See Rae, *Equalities*, pp. 138–40.

tunity" are incompatible with rules of "equal outcomes";[24] equality among groups is often incompatible with equality among individuals;[25] and equality according to need is incompatible with equality by lot. People who find one equality desirable will inevitably find others undesirable. The only relationship to which all equalities refer is a "formal" relationship—which, being formal, is neither desirable nor undesirable.

'Equality' designates what Kovesi calls an "incomplete" moral notion: it is a word which tends to have favorable connotations without being defined as having favorable connotations.[26] The question is, why? What is the source of its persuasiveness? Why does equality have "a laudatory connotation"?[27] Why does it "seem to be accepted almost everywhere as self-evidently and without qualification good"?[28]

Needless to say, the answers to these questions will not be found solely in a study of language. The sources of equality's rhetorical force are partly cultural, partly historical, and partly psychological. As James Boyd White has observed, claims of equality are premised on what claimants have in common with others and, hence, are assertions of brotherhood, sympathy, and community.[29] A person who makes a claim in the language of 'equality' thereby invokes something favorably associated with kinship and

---

[24] The idea of equal opportunity is a poor tool for understanding even those sectors of life to which the notion of equality is applicable . . . [because] whereas it seems to defend equality, it really only defends the equal right to become unequal by competing against one's fellows.

Schaar, "Equality of Opportunity, and Beyond," p. 233.

[W]hat I want to emphasize here is that even the highly egalitarian probabilistic conception of equality of opportunity just broached is incompatible with equality of outcome. They are not even extensionally equivalent. . . . The reason for the extensional inequivalence is simply that individuals with probabilistically equal opportunities can end up in quite different positions. They can have the same expectations, even the same curve, yet scale very different heights of success. This is a fact about probability.

Levin, "Equality of Opportunity," p. 114.

[25] On equality for groups in American constitutional law, see generally Fiss, "Groups and the Equal Protection Clause," p. 116.

[26] Kovesi, *Moral Notions*, p. 112.

[27] Oppenheim, "Egalitarianism as a Descriptive Concept," p. 143 ("The term 'equality' has a laudatory connotation").

[28] Flew, *The Politics of Procrustes*, p. 9. See also Zaitchik, "On Deserving to Deserve," p. 333 (referring to 'egalitarian' as an "honorific adjective").

[29] White, *When Words Lose Their Meaning*, pp. 77–79, 170, 224–28, 265–66, 272–74. See also Karst, "Why Equality Matters," pp. 280–87.

community. To a not insignificant extent, however, I believe the sources of equality's rhetorical power are also conceptual in nature. Without meaning to depreciate or subordinate other factors, I shall argue that the rhetorical force of 'equality' is in part the cumulative product of at least five conceptual factors: (1) the paradigm of equality in mathematics; (2) the grounding of prescriptive equalities in uncontroversial descriptive equalities; (3) the capacity of general statements of prescriptive equality to encompass a diversity of particular standards of comparison; (4) the unity of all equalities in a single concept of equality; and, perhaps most important, (5) the semantic bias which favors 'equality' over 'inequality'.

The Paradigm of Equality in Mathematics

Aristotle observed that political faction and instability stem from disagreements about equality. All people agree that a just society is an equal society, he says, but they differ in their conceptions of equality. The principal source of their disagreement is that, being equal (or unequal) in one respect, people believe they are equal (or unequal) in all respects. Thus, he says, democrats, being equal to other men in having been born free, believe that they are also equal in their rights to political office and authority. Oligarchs, having greater wealth than other men, believe that they should also have proportionately greater political privilege. As Aristotle expressed it in Book V of the *Politics*:

> Many constitutions have come about because, although everyone agrees on justice, i.e., proportional equality, they go wrong in achieving it, as mentioned before. Democracy arose from the idea that those who are equal in any respect are equal absolutely. All are alike free, therefore they claim that they are all equal absolutely. Oligarchy arose from the assumption that those who are *un*equal in some one respect are completely *unequal*: being unequal in wealth they assume themselves to be unequal absolutely. The next step is when the democrats, on the ground that they are equal, claim equal participation in everything; while the oligarchs, on the ground that they are unequal, seek to get a larger share, because 'larger' is unequal.[30]

[30] Aristotle, *Politics* V.1.1301a25–35 (trans. Sinclair). See also 1301b26–27, quoted in note 5 above.

The assumption that people who are equal in one or more relevant respects are equal in all respects is not peculiar to the ancient Greeks. It is potentially present every time A and B are asserted to be equal in X respect on the ground that they are equal in other respects. An example is the debate as to whether women have a right to compete against men in all-male athletic events. As an argument *against* integrating such events, it is sometimes asserted that if men and women are equal for purposes of competing in all-male events, men and women will also be equal for purposes of competing in all-female events, thereby denying a disproportionate number of women (who, as a class, are sometimes unable to compete effectively against men in athletic events) an opportunity to participate in athletics.[31]

This argument is based on the fallacy that people who are equal in one respect must be equal in other respects. To say that men and women are "equal" for purposes of competing in otherwise all-male athletic events presupposes a prescription, or a rule, by which men and women can be compared and found to be indistinguishable. A number of rules could have that effect, but the most plausible, socially, is an antidiscrimination rule of the following sort:

R_1: No woman shall be denied an opportunity to participate in athletic events on the basis of sex.

This rule establishes a certain equality between men and women, for it renders women equal to men, and, therefore, men equal to women, in their right to compete against members of the opposite sex in otherwise all-male athletic events in which they wish to compete. In areas in which men as a group have higher levels of skill than women (i.e., areas in which no rule can succeed in treating men and women equally regarding *both* the opportunity to compete against each other *and* the opportunity to compete in proportion to their share of the population), R_1 also has considerable social value, for it gives women an opportunity, if they so desire, to compete and excel at the highest levels of competition, without in any way impairing their opportunity to compete against a group of people with the same average skills.

Notice, however, that R_1 refrains from giving men a right to compete against women in otherwise all-female events in which

[31] See, e.g., *Clark v. Arizona Interscholastic Association*, 695 F.2d 1126 (9th Cir., 1982). See generally *Women, Philosophy, and Sport*, ed. Postow; Tokarz, "Separate but Unequal Educational Sports Programs," p. 201.

they wish to compete. It also refrains from creating equality among men and women in that respect. To create such prescriptive equality, one would need one of the following rules:

R_2: No *man* shall be denied an opportunity to participate in athletic events on the basis of sex.

or

R_3: No *man or woman* shall be denied an opportunity to participate in athletic events on the basis of sex.

or

R_4: No man [or, no man or woman] shall be denied an opportunity *to compete athletically against members of the opposite sex* on grounds of sex.[32]

Whatever their merits (and they are several), these rules would clearly frustrate the purposes of R_1. For if it is indeed true that men as a group have higher levels of athletic skill than women in certain sports, these rules would more drastically reduce the number of women who could participate in such sports than R_1 would reduce the number of men who could participate in them.[33] It follows, therefore, that one cannot infer R_2, R_3, or R_4 from R_1; nor can one infer the equalities created by the former rules from the equality created by R_1.

The significant issue for our purposes is not so much that people fallaciously infer one equality from another, but *why* they do so, and to *what effect*. The most likely reason is that they are making the "category mistake"[34] of confusing equality in mathematics

[32] R_4 differs from the other three rules because, while the other rules give members of a designated sex the right to complain if *they* are excluded from athletic events organized for members of the opposite sex, R_4 goes further and also gives the members of a designated sex the right to complain if members of the *opposite* sex are excluded from events in which they wish to participate.

[33] This is not to say that, because R_2–R_4 reduce the opportunities for women more than R_1 reduces them for men, R_1 is preferable. There are independent reasons to prefer R_3–R_4, namely, that they consistently treat people as individuals without regard to sex, rather than selectively privileging one group and disadvantaging another on the basis of sex.

[34] See Chapter 2, note 31. Elizabeth Wolgast may be making a mistake of this kind in arguing that claims of "equality" do not serve the interests of women because women possess some traits, e.g., the capacity to become pregnant, that significantly distinguish them from men and thus require that they be treated "unequally." See Wolgast, *Equality and the Rights of Women*. Wolgast's argument lends itself to two different interpretations. If she is arguing that because equality does not always further women's interests, equality is not something that women can

with equality elsewhere. As we have seen, mathematical entities that are equal in one respect are equal in all respects because the features they share are the features by which they are defined. To the extent that people accept mathematical equality as the paradigm for other equalities, therefore, they will be inclined to assume that people who are prescriptively equal in one respect are prescriptively equal in other respects. The effect is to give advocates of equality an undeserved rhetorical advantage whenever they urge equality on behalf of people who are already prescriptively equal in some respect. The category mistake enables such advocates to move from an existing equality to a desired equality without having to make an independent case for the latter.

The Grounding of Prescriptive Equalities in Descriptive Equalities

Statements of prescriptive equality consist of, and rhetorically benefit from, a distinctive relationship of "is" to "ought."

We have seen that equalities among persons are of two distinctive types—descriptive equalities and prescriptive equalities—of which descriptive equalities are relatively uncontroversial. We have also seen that statements of prescriptive equality contain two elements: one descriptive and the other prescriptive. The descriptive element is a description of a class of persons who are identical in possessing certain traits in common; the prescriptive element is the prescription of a certain common treatment for members of that class. The descriptive element, again, is relatively uncontroversial because, like all descriptive equalities, it is a statement of "is," rather than a statement of "ought."

This nexus between description and contestable prescription, between "is" and "ought," contributes to equality's persuasiveness in two ways. First, it appears to give statements of prescriptive equality a factual basis, a verifiable premise, which other normative statements lack. Or, as one commentator puts it, the descriptive equalities underlying prescriptive equalities appear to render them "open to empirical confirmation."[35] Second, and per-

exclusively rely upon, the point is uncontrovertible. If, however, she is arguing that because equality does not *always* further the rights of women, equality *never* serves their interests, she is making the mistake of assuming that because men and women are not *always* normatively equal, they are *never* normatively equal.

[35] Thomas, "Equality within the Limits of Reason Alone," p. 540. See also Stone, "Justice Not Equality," p. 98 ("The notion of equality [carries] a certain *soupçon* of logically or mathematically demonstrable certainty and objectivity").

haps more importantly, because prescriptive equalities are grounded in descriptive equalities, they are sometimes *inferred* from descriptive equalities, thus enabling advocates to "glide from the 'is' to the 'ought' "[36] without having to make an independent case for the "ought." As Bernard Williams puts it, prescriptive equalities "have force because they are regarded as affirming an equality which is believed in some sense already to exist."[37]

To understand why equality uniquely seems to possess the foregoing features, it may be useful to compare statements of prescriptive equality with other normative claims. In a sense, every claim of right presupposes empirically verifiable facts about the persons for whom the right is asserted. Thus, to say something is "deserved" presupposes "some possessed characteristic or prior activity"[38] of a person by virtue of which it is deserved, for otherwise one would have no way of identifying deserving persons. By the same token, to say that a certain class of persons has a "right" is to presuppose some "factual" characteristic that they uniquely possess in common.[39] The difference is that, in the case of equality, the factual premise and the normative conclusion are both stated *in the same terms*. The normative conclusion that people "ought to be treated equally" rests on the factual premise that they "are equal." Thus, while one cannot meaningfully say "we ought to be entitled to X because we are entitled to X," a speaker can meaningfully say "we *ought* to be treated equally because we *are* equal." In that fashion, the speaker explicitly grounds the "ought" of equality in the "is" of equality, emphasizing its firm empirical foundation.

The language of equality not only links "ought" to "is," but also tends to *reduce* "ought" to "is," thereby giving contestable statements of prescriptive equality the appearance of uncontroversial matters of fact. It does so by using the same terms to refer to both descriptive equals and prescriptive equals. Thus, the assertion "all

[36] Hawkins, *The Science and Ethics of Equality*, pp. 11–12 (referring to criticism of those who believe that equality is a formula for inferring an "ought" from an "is"). For an example of this fallacy, see Weale, *Equality and Social Policy*, p. 22. Cf. Williams, "The Idea of Equality," pp. 112–14 (suggesting that equality is a formula for moving from an "is" to an "ought" by virtue of rationality alone).

[37] Williams, "The Idea of Equality," pp. 111–12.

[38] Feinberg, "Justice and Personal Desert," p. 72.

[39] See Wasserstrom, "Rights, Human Rights, and Racial Discrimination," p. 633 ("It is evident, I think, that almost any argument for the acknowledgment of any rights as human rights starts with the factual assertion that there are certain respects in which all persons are alike or equal").

men are equal" is capable of stating both an "is" and an "ought": an "is" if it means "all men are descriptively equal in their possession of certain empirical traits"; an "ought" if it means "all men are prescriptively equal in certain ways in which they ought to be treated."[40] As a statement of fact it is uncontroversial because all men are factually equal in numerous ways, including their common possession of X chromosomes. As a statement of value, it is essentially contestable. However, since prescriptive statements take the same form as descriptive statements, and since the latter are generally uncontroversial, a speaker can make prescriptive assertions that *appear* to be incontrovertible. Felix Oppenheim makes this very point:

> There is a tendency to use factual statements for expressing normative views. We have seen that the allegation that "Men are equal" if taken in the factual sense, is either meaningless, or tautological, or false. However, this adage serves more often as a rhetorical device to disguise the normative principle that men should be treated equally—in some respect which is often left unspecified.[41]

The upshot is a form of argument in which people are inferred to be prescriptive equals *simply because they are descriptive equals*.[42]

The Ambiguity of Prescriptive Equalities

We have just examined the rhetorical advantages of one of equality's ambiguities: the ambiguity as to whether a speaker is making

[40] An example of the same ambiguity occurs in Aristotle's precept "people who are equal should be treated equally." We have seen that for Aristotle the precept was tautological, because he understood the phrase "people who are equal" *prescriptively*—that is, as equivalent to "people who are identical in the ways they ought to be treated." Yet commentators regularly criticize Aristotle for asserting the precept because they understand "people who are equal" *descriptively*—that is, as equivalent to "people who are factually identical in some empirical respect." See, e.g., Harvey, "Two Kinds of Equality," pp. 114–15; Hawkins, *The Science and Ethics of Equality*, pp. 11–12 (referring to Aristotle's critics).

[41] Oppenheim, "Egalitarianism as a Descriptive Concept," p. 152.

[42] The character of argument of those who assert human equality is roughly of this form: "all men are equal: and *therefore* they ought to be treated equally" (or "therefore the colour bar is bad," or "therefore you have to give very good reasons for different treatment"). This is supposed to be an *argument*: "therefore" is supposed to mean something.

Wilson, *Equality*, p. 19 (original emphasis).

267

a descriptive or a prescriptive assertion. Even when a speaker is clearly making a prescriptive assertion, however, the language of equality lends itself to a further ambiguity possessing advantages for those who use it—an ambiguity as to the precise prescriptive standard of comparison the speaker has in mind. As a consequence of this ambiguity, assertions of equality can create consensus that would collapse if prescriptive claims were made more explicit.

The ambiguities are of two kinds. A simple plea for "equality" is ambiguous as to whether the prescriptive rule on which it is based is an *antidiscrimination* rule or not.[43] The difference is significant because, generally, antidiscrimination rules permit greater flexibility than other rules. An antidiscrimination rule requires that, if B is granted a certain benefit, A must be granted it, too. Thus, a person can comply with an antidiscrimination rule *either* by granting the benefit to A and B *or* by denying it to A and B. In contrast, noncomparative rules are less flexible because they flatly require that A be granted certain benefits regardless of whether they are granted to B.[44] As a consequence, in advocating a noncomparative rule in the ambiguous language of equality, a speaker may gain the "rhetorical"[45] benefit of associating his (inherently inflexible) claim with the inherent flexibility of antidiscrimination claims.

Apart from the difference between comparative and noncomparative claims, statements of prescriptive equality can also be ambiguous as to the precise terms of the particular comparative or noncomparative rules on which they are based.[46] Of course, equality is not the only form of normative discourse that lends itself to ambiguity. Claims of rights and freedoms can also be stated ambiguously. Nevertheless, among such forms of discourse, statements of equality are particularly elliptical and, hence, particularly

[43] See Chapter 3, pp. 72–74. See also Raz, *The Morality of Freedom*, p. 233.

[44] Justice Robert Jackson of the U.S. Supreme Court has suggested that the Supreme Court ought to look more favorably on antidiscrimination claims than on noncomparative claims precisely because the former permit greater flexibility. See *Railway Express Agency, Inc. v. New York*, 336 U.S. 106, 112 (1949)(Jackson, J., concurring). For further discussion of the remedial aspects of violating antidiscrimination rules, see Ginsburg, "Some Thoughts on Judicial Authority to Repair Unconstitutional Legislation," pp. 322–24; Simons, "Equality as a Comparative Right," pp. 427–34.

[45] See Raz, *The Morality of Freedom*, p. 228 (referring to the "rhetorical" benefits of expressing noncomparative claims in the egalitarian language associated with antidiscrimination claims).

[46] See Chapter 3, pp. 74–79.

elusive. Thus, one cannot meaningfully assert a "right" without specifying more or less precisely *who* is entitled to *what* from *whom*. Nor can one meaningfully assert a prescriptive "freedom" without specifying more or less precisely who ought to be unconstrained by what to do what. Yet speakers regularly assert B and A to be "equal" without specifying anything about *the respect* in which they are equal—that is, without specifying any elements of the prescriptive standard by which they are equal, apart from the fact that B and A constitute the beneficiary class. As a result, insofar as B and A are equal by some prescriptive standard that is acceptable to an audience, a speaker has a chance to elicit agreement from listeners who, in reality, know very little about the specifics of the claim he is implicitly asserting.

An example is the recent dispute in American constitutional law about the validity, under the equal protection clause of the Fourteenth Amendment, of programs of racial affirmative action. During the 1950s and 1960s the U.S. Supreme Court resolved a series of cases in which state governments had stigmatized blacks by explicitly disparaging them on the basis of race. The Court consistently ruled for the black litigants, holding that blacks and whites are "equal" under the Fourteenth Amendment and, thus, ought to be treated equally. The Court's pronouncements of "equality" were generally applauded by people who, because they agreed with the results, did not have to specify the precise prescriptive standards by which they deemed blacks and whites to be equal. In the early 1970s a series of affirmative action cases revealed for the first time that the Court's generalized assertions of racial equality masked sharp disagreement among "egalitarians" over the prescriptive standard by which blacks and whites are equal. One faction argued that the equal protection clause prohibits states from disadvantaging any person, white or black, on grounds of race, thus prohibiting states from adopting affirmative action programs that disadvantage whites. Another faction argued that the equal protection clause prohibits states from disadvantaging blacks (and other commonly disparaged groups) on grounds of race, thus permitting states to adopt affirmative action programs that favor blacks.[47] Although the Court eventually resolved the dispute,[48] it

[47] For an excellent analysis of the dispute from a philosophical standpoint, see Fullinwider, *The Reverse Discrimination Controversy*. See also Brest, "Affirmative Action and the Constitution," p. 281.

[48] The Court resolved the dispute by means of its well-known compromise in *University of California v. Bakke*, 438 U.S. 265 (1978), holding in a plurality opinion

succeeded for years in uniting both factions by speaking elliptically of racial "equality," rather than specifying the precise prescriptive standard by which such equality was being measured.

This is not to deny the virtues of ambiguity. Ambiguity can serve a variety of purposes. On the one hand, as Charles Frankel observes, "a verbal formula which everybody employs, and which therefore creates the impression of general agreement on fundamentals, is often very useful politically."[49] It is probably the case, for example, that equality's very lack of specificity enabled the Supreme Court to create a working consensus in the United States in the fifties and sixties, during a time of considerable national stress. On the other hand, as Frankel also notes, ambiguous concepts "may also prevent the clear analysis of issues and the formulation of the choices that have to be made." Whether for good or for bad, equality in the end is a rhetorical device that tends to persuade

---

by Justice Powell that the Fourteenth Amendment embraces *both* standards, though perhaps with different degrees of rigor. The Court has more recently held that *all* racial discrimination by a state shall be subjected to the same Fourteenth Amendment test, namely, the test of whether it serves a "compelling" state interest, though there is still some question whether or not the results the Court reaches in *applying* that test will reflect the majority or minority status of the race being discriminated against. See *Richmond v. J. A. Croson Co.*, 109 *Supreme Court Reporter* 706 (1986).

[49] Frankel, "Equality of Opportunity," p. 192. Kenneth Karst has made the same point:

It is no accident that our most cherished constitutional values—including equality—are also diffuse rather than specific. Their very lack of specificity helps them to serve as symbols of community. The part of the brain that houses intuition and holistic ways of knowing is also the home of dreams, and tears, and laughter. For a value to endure, to do its work in binding a community, that value must not merely appeal to our interests but touch our emotions. Diffuse loyalty is the essence of community.

Karst, "Equality and Community," p. 206. Frederick Schauer, in contrast, argues that broad and vague concepts like equality enable a community to delegate authority to its leaders to make specific determinations of value as future events arise:

[M]uch of political life, here and elsewhere, places enormous importance on the use of a number of broad and vague expressions that are more symbolic than substantive. Examples that come immediately to mind include 'liberty', 'freedom', 'justice', and 'equality'. . . . To the extent that this language is tolerated or even encouraged as the dominant mode of discourse in political life, once again we can be said to have fostered an intentional rather than inevitable indeterminacy as a way of increasing the authority of our leaders to decide themselves how they will deal with the future when it arises.

Schauer, "Authority and Indeterminacy," p. 36. Cf. Connolly, "Modern Authority and Ambiguity," pp. 21–26.

precisely by virtue of "cloak[ing] strongly divergent ideas over which people do in fact disagree."[50]

The Unity of Equalities in a Common Concept of Equality

Advocates of equality, today, are the direct beneficiaries of the moral and legal triumphs which have been won in its name in the past. The triumphs are many and, to most people, glorious: the abolition of chattel slavery, the elimination of feudal privilege, the eradication of caste, the disestablishment of religion, the spread of universal suffrage, the opening of careers to talent, the outlawing of racial discrimination, the emancipation of women, and the provision of medical and social security. As a result of that tradition, a person who advocates something controversial today in the name of equality can plausibly argue that he is furthering a crusade that history has shown to be both right and "invincible."[51]

That contemporary advocates benefit from equality's prior triumphs, however, raises further questions. What, for instance, do seventeenth-century issues have to do with twentieth-century controversies? How, precisely, does the language of equality enable a person who favors, say, the emancipation of children from their parents to associate his cause with something as normatively distinct as the abolition of chattel slavery? The answer has several parts. To begin with, all conceptions of equality, however diverse, do have one thing in common: they are all grounded in the same concept, the concept of *equality*. Thus, the controversial equality of children and their parents has something significant in common with the equality of slaves and their masters: they are both identities which obtain among persons by reference to relevant standards of comparison. As a consequence, an advocate of the former can truly say that the two issues are essentially the same, because conceptually they are the same. Moreover, since nearly all ques-

---

[50] Frankel, "Equality of Opportunity," p. 192. See Raz, *The Morality of Freedom*, p. 228:

> The price we pay [for stating noncomparative rules in the language of equality] is intellectual confusion since their egalitarian formulation is less perspicacious, i.e., less revealing of their true grounds, than some non-egalitarian formulations of the same principles.

[51] Tocqueville, *Democracy in America*, vol. 2, p. 102 (describing the "passion" of democratic communities for equality as "ardent, insatiable, incessant, invincible").

tions of justice can be stated in the form of equalities (as Aristotle demonstrated through his formula of proportional equality), it follows that equality has the capacity to give a "spurious unity"[52] to the broadest spectrum of normative judgments.

This unifying feature of equality can be illustrated by the terms in which commentators assess Earl Warren's tenure as chief justice of the U.S. Supreme Court. During the period in which Warren served as chief justice, from 1954 to 1969, the Court transformed American constitutional law in a variety of areas. Among other things, the Court integrated public schools, reapportioned state legislatures, disestablished religion, provided the right to counsel to indigent defendants, limited the authority of the police to interrogate criminal suspects, reformed the law of libel, protected unpopular speech, and protected the free exercise of religion. The Court's decisions in one area often had little, if any, normative connection with decisions in other areas, apart from their common source in the Constitution. Thus, the decision to apportion the upper houses of state legislatures on the basis of population had nothing normative in common with the decision to require that criminal suspects be advised of their right to remain silent, and the decision to ban prayers in the public schools had nothing normative in common with the decision to protect seditious speech. Yet, upon Earl Warren's retirement, when respected commentators reviewed the Court's jurisprudence during his tenure, they were plausibly able to say that the diverse work of the Warren Court could be unified in a single theme. The unifying theme, they said, was *equality*—equality among voters, among criminal suspects, among criminal defendants, among political dissidents, among people of different races, and among religions.[53] Without realiz-

---

[52] Cooper, *The Illusions of Equality*, p. 2 (referring to the "spurious unity in the ranks of those who proclaim equality").

[53] See, e.g., Bickel, *The Supreme Court and the Idea of Progress*, p. 13; Cox, *The Warren Court*, pp. 5–8; Karst, "The Supreme Court, 1976 October Term—Foreword," p. 26. The forerunner of these assessments was Philip Kurland's essay "The Supreme Court, 1963 Term—Foreword," p. 143. Justice William Brennan makes the point directly:

[T]he judicial pursuit of equality is, in my view, properly regarded as the noblest mission of judges; it has been the primary task of judges since the repudiation of economic substantive due process as our central constitutional concern. This pursuit of shared moral values and their accurate translation in individual cases is what produced the United States Supreme Court decision in *Brown v. Board of Education*, *Baker v. Carr*, and *Gideon v. Wainwright*.

Brennan, "The Equality Principle," p. 674.

ing, perhaps, that the unity they detected was conceptual rather than normative, they were plausibly able to maintain that all of the Warren Court's diverse judgments essentially involved one and the same thing.

One feature, then, that gives diverse conceptions of equality the appearance of unity is that all are based on the same concept. Yet that feature alone is not a sufficient explanation, because other forms of normative discourse, which lack equality's capacity to unify, also have common conceptual frameworks. Issues of "justice," for example, can be reduced to the common conception *suum cuique*—"To each person his due."[54] Nevertheless, an advocate who urges something controversial in the name of justice derives little, if any, benefit from prior crusades for justice because his audience understands that 'justice' is a conclusory term for whatever a speaker regards as proper under the circumstances. 'Justice', by definition, is an evaluative term because it refers to relationships that speakers regard as desirable. Yet "almost no one will associate its evaluative or emotive force uncritically with any determinate set of facts" because "almost everyone knows that [application of] the concept is the subject of disagreement."[55]

The difference between the concepts of justice and equality is that, while justice signals its conclusory nature, equality conceals it. 'Justice' refers by definition to what a speaker regards as right and good; hence, when a speaker asserts something to be just, his audience understands him to be referring to something *he* regards as desirable, not necessarily something they will regard as desirable. In contrast, 'equality' is not defined as an evaluative term. It encompasses descriptive as well as prescriptive relationships. Moreover, when 'equality' refers to prescriptive relationships, it does so, not directly, but elliptically: it refers to prescriptions, not by their constituent terms, but by consequential relationships of identity and nonidentity, which the prescriptions produce among persons. As a consequence, the discourse of equality leads speakers and listeners alike to believe that what prescriptive equalities

[54] Justice is *suum cuique*, to each his due. The just state of affairs is that in which each individual has exactly those benefits and burdens which are due to him by virtue of his personal characteristics and circumstances. We have yet to inquire what those characteristics and circumstances may consist in, but the general definition leaves this question open.

Miller, *Social Justice*, p. 20.

[55] Waldron, "What Is Private Property?" p. 339 (referring to essentially contestable concepts in general, as opposed to justice in particular).

share is not a formal concept which incorporates exogenous values by reference, but a certain endogenous set of values—not a receptacle for receiving values but itself "a value."

All conceptions of equality thus have a single thing in common: they are all reifications of the same formal concept, differing only by reference to the standards by which likes and unlikes are measured. At the same time, prescriptive equalities tend to conceal the fact that what unites them is a formula for incorporating external values by reference rather than a determinate set of values. A person who advocates something controversial in the name of equality benefits from the other equalities that his audience accepts. He "gain[s] from the good name that 'equality' has in our culture,"[56] by creating the impression that the particular set of values he is expounding is "indivisibly"[57] linked to values his listeners already accept.

The Semantic Bias in Favor of 'Equality'

The "laudatory connotation"[58] of 'equality' does not flow solely from its association with popular causes. During the 1920s and 1930s in the United States, for example, many Americans associated 'equality' with highly unpopular causes. In an era of "Red scares," equality was associated with the economic and social leveling of the Russian Revolution, and at a time of pervasive racial discrimination, equality was also associated with unpopular principles of the Fourteenth Amendment. For those reasons, in part, claims for equality became (in the words of Oliver Wendell Holmes) a constitutional argument "of last resort."[59] Even then, however, the word 'equality' had favorable connotations vis-à-vis

[56] Raz, *The Morality of Freedom*, p. 228.
[57] Consider Verba and Orren's views of the normative commonality of diverse conceptions of equality:

> Equality can be analyzed into its many components, but these components are closely interconnected. Historically, the many aspects of equality have been linked in political discourse. The issue of economic equality has consistently appeared in the debates on political equality. The moral principle demanding equal treatment of one oppressed group inevitably spread to others, in [accord with] what Pole refers to as the "indivisibility" of the equality concept.

Verba and Orren, *Equality in America*, p. 25.
[58] Oppenheim, "Egalitarianism as a Descriptive Concept," p. 143 ("Like 'democracy' or 'freedom', 'equality' has a laudatory connotation").
[59] *Buck v. Bell*, 274 U.S. 205, 208 (1927)(referring to the equal protection clause as "the usual last resort of constitutional arguments").

'inequality' because there is an inherent semantic bias in favor of equality.

Some commentators maintain that 'equality' used in reference to persons is *defined* as a laudatory term.[60] As we have seen, that is not so. Equality among persons is the relationship of identity which obtains among them by reference to relevant standards of comparison. The standards may be descriptive, prescriptive, or a combination of descriptive standards and prescriptive baselines. When the standards are either descriptive alone or combine descriptive standards and noncomparative prescriptive baselines, the resulting identities are relationships of "is" from which no "ought" can be inferred. Moreover, even when the standards are prescriptive, a speaker may not mean to commend the resulting equalities because, if he is speaking of legal equalities, he may not consider the relevant legal standard to be *morally* relevant. Assume, for example, that a legally valid statute provides that "no person who has been convicted of a felony shall be allowed to practice law." Measured by the prescription contained in the statute, all felons are equal because all are disqualified from practicing law. From a legal standpoint, moreover, the statute is the relevant standard for comparing people who wish to practice law. Morally, however, a speaker may not consider the statute to be the relevant standard for comparing people who wish to practice law because he may consider it morally wrong to disqualify all felons from practicing law.[61]

Nevertheless, while 'equality' does not always refer to laudable relationships, it does so more frequently than 'inequality'. There are two reasons for this semantic bias in favor of equality—one deriving from the semantics of prescriptive equalities and inequalities, the other deriving from the semantics of descriptive equalities based on prescriptive baselines.

Prescriptive Equalities

'Equality' refers to commendable relationships whenever it is based on prescriptive standards that a speaker regards as normatively relevant, and speakers often use 'equality' in that sense. Advocates of equality, for example, always use 'equality' that way

[60] See, e.g., von Leyden, "On Justifying Inequality," p. 67 ("the true opposite of 'equality' is arbitrary").

[61] For this same point, see the discussion of H.L.A. Hart's hypothetical case of the racially discriminatory statute, in Chapter 9, pp. 228–29.

because they always use it to refer to the identities which obtain among people by reference to prescriptive standards they regard as just. Aristotle, too, uses 'equality' in that sense in saying "equals should be treated equally." By "equals," Aristotle does not mean people who are only descriptively equal or people who are prescriptively equal by legal standards that may or may not be morally just. He means people who are equal by reference to prescriptions that are themselves morally just, which, of course, is why he maintains that equality is always just.[62] Exponents of equality thus enjoy the favorable connotations of a word that their listeners are accustomed to using to refer to commendable relationships.

Now it might be argued that the semantics of 'inequality' would tend to create equally laudatory connotations in favor of inequality, too, thereby neutralizing any bias in favor of equality. After all, so the argument goes, equality and inequality are correlative concepts. Thus, just as 'equality' incorporates prescriptive as well as descriptive standards, 'inequality' does, too. By the same token, just as prescriptive equalities can incorporate *normatively* relevant prescriptions, prescriptive inequalities can, too. Aristotle himself recognized this. For, just as Aristotle asserts that "equals should be treated equally," he also insists that "unequals should be treated unequally"—meaning that people who are unequal by normatively relevant standards of comparison should be given unequal treatment.[63] It would seem to follow, then, that whatever laudatory connotations accrue in favor of equality will be counterbalanced by equally laudatory connotations in favor of inequality.

This argument overlooks a significant discontinuity between the concepts of equality and inequality. 'Equality' is semantically more comprehensive than 'inequality' because, while equality is broad enough to refer to all persons who are subject to rules, inequality can only refer to people who are treated differently by rules.[64] Assume, for example, that three persons (A, B, and C) with proportional needs of 2:1:1, respectively, reside in a jurisdiction that fol-

[62] See Chapter 9, pp. 185–91.

[63] See Aristotle, *Politics* III.5.1280a7–20; Aristotle, *Nicomachean Ethics* V.3.1131a20–25 ("this is the origin of quarrels and complaints—when either equals have and are awarded unequal shares, or unequals equal shares"; trans. Ross).

[64] This semantic feature—that 'inequality' has a narrower compass than 'equality'—does not affect the observation made in Chapter 9 that "equals should be treated equally" entails that "unequals should be treated unequally," for that observation was made with reference to rules that *classify* people and, hence, prescribe *both* equal *and* unequal treatment for those subject to them. See above, pp. 79–83, 205–10.

lows the rule "to each according to his needs." A speaker can use 'equality' to refer to all the prescriptive relationships among A, B, and C created by the rule. Thus, a speaker can use 'equality' to refer to the relationship between B and C alone, by saying "B and C are equal in their needs." He can also use 'equality' to refer to the relationship among all three, by saying "A, B, and C are equal in their right to receive distributions based on need." 'Equality' is a "protean"[65] word, which can be used to refer to any relationship that a rule creates among two or more persons. The word 'inequality' is much less versatile. A speaker may use 'inequality' to refer to the relationship that the rule creates between A, on the one hand, and B and C, on the other, but he cannot use 'inequality' to refer to the relationship between B and C because B and C do not differ by reference to the rule.

This discontinuity between the concepts of equality and inequality has a bearing on the usefulness of each. The concept of equality is the more useful because, while 'equality' can refer to every distribution to which 'inequality' refers, 'inequality' cannot refer to every distribution to which 'equality' refers. Therefore, speakers tend to use 'equality' more frequently to refer to the relationships which obtain under rules they regard as normatively relevant. Indeed, one sees the tendency in Aristotle and Plato, too. They both emphasized that, just as "equals should be treated equally," so should "unequals be treated unequally."[66] Yet, when they came to refer to the single principle underlying the two precepts, they resorted solely to the language of equality, declaring that justice is "equality."[67] That speakers use the word 'equality' more often than 'inequality' to refer to prescriptions that they consider normatively relevant creates a semantic bias in favor of 'equality': their doing so means that 'equality' is more likely than 'inequality' to refer to relationships that a speaker regards as just.

Descriptive Equalities Based on Prescriptive Baselines

As we have seen, the normative implications of 'equality' and 'inequality' are not confined to prescriptive standards of comparison.

---

[65] Schaar, "Equality of Opportunity, and Beyond," p. 228.

[66] See Plato, *Republic* VIII.558c; Aristotle, *Politics* III.9.1280a7–20.

[67] See Plato, *Laws* VI.757 ("justice [is] a true and real equality, meted out to unequals"; trans.); Aristotle, *Nicomachean Ethics* V.3.1131a10–15 ("We have shown that both the unjust man and the unjust act are . . . unequal. . . . If, then, the unjust is unequal, the just is equal, as all men suppose it to be"; trans. Ross); Aristotle, *Politics* III.12.1282b7–22 ("Now all men believe that justice means equality"; trans. Sinclair).

They also extend to the equalities and inequalities which result from descriptive standards based on prescriptive baselines—that is, on descriptive standards for measuring whether or not people are identical in receiving the treatments they ought to receive. Normative implications of the latter kind are also semantically skewed in favor of 'equality' and against 'inequality'. They are skewed because, while "equal" treatment by such standards is *often semantically positive*, "unequal" treatment is *always semantically negative*. Consider the antidiscrimination rule we discussed in Chapter 4, i.e., "no person shall be disadvantaged vis-à-vis others on the basis of race." Measured by the standard of whether people are identical in receiving the treatments they ought to receive, "equality" means that no one has been denied such treatment, while "inequality" means that some have been granted and some denied such treatment. The normative implications of violating noncomparative rules are slightly different: to say that people have been treated equally with respect to the enforcement of noncomparative rules may be semantically positive or negative, depending upon whether one means that they have all been granted or all been denied the noncomparative treatments they ought to receive. To say that they have been treated unequally, however, is always negative because it always means that some have been granted and some denied the treatments they ought to receive.

The semantic implications of this are significant. It means that, when equality and inequality are measured by the standard of whether people are identical in the extent to which they receive the treatments they ought to receive, 'unequal' is always pejorative because *by those standards* it is *defined* as being pejorative.[68] Consider Aristotle's observation that, just as equality is always just, inequality is always unjust.[69] Given what Aristotle means by "equality" and "inequality," the assertion is a tautology. By "equality," he means the relationship that obtains among people who are *prescriptively identical*—that is, identical as measured by the treatments they ought to receive. By "inequality," he means the relationship that obtains among people who are *descriptively nonidentical* as measured by the extent to which they receive the treatments they ought to receive. It is easy to understand why Ar-

[68] Perhaps that explains why some commentators assert that 'inequality' always has pejorative connotations. See Benn, "Equality, Moral and Social," pp. 38, 41 ("the word 'inequality' has acquired . . . a pejorative force; 'inequalities' have come to mean *indefensible* differences in treatment") (original emphasis).

[69] Aristotle, *Nicomachean Ethics* V.3.1131a10–15, quoted in note 67 above.

istotle regarded such inequalities as unjust: they are defined as being unjust.

These pejorative connotations of 'inequality' would have no overall rhetorical effect—that is, they would have no tendency to skew decisionmaking against purely descriptive inequalities—if the underlying standards of comparison were always made explicit, for then it would be obvious whether 'unequal' is being used descriptively or pejoratively. In practice, however, speakers often leave the standard unstated, which enables them to move from the "is" of descriptive inequality to the "ought not" of pejorative inequality without the need for normative argument. An example is John Ely's advice to constitutional advocates in his celebrated book *Democracy and Dissent*. Ely recognizes that the equal protection clause of the Fourteenth Amendment is a normative provision, expressing in the language of equality such implicit antidiscrimination rights as the right of protected minorities not to be disparaged or disadvantaged on grounds of race.[70] By the same token, he recognizes that to demand "equality" under the Fourteenth Amendment is to demand that states comply with those prescriptive rights. Yet, in commenting on litigation strategy, Ely observes that any competent lawyer can express *any* grievance his client may have in the language of "equal protection," merely by describing the difference between his client's situation and that of third persons who are more favorably situated:

> Any case, indeed any challenge, can be put in an equal protection framework by competent counsel. If you wish to challenge the fact that you're not getting good X (or are getting deprivation Y), it is extremely probable that you will be able to identify someone who *is* getting good X (or is not getting deprivation Y).[71]

Notice the implicit message. Ely implicitly suggests that advocates invoke any existing descriptive inequality as a basis for asserting what is essentially a prescriptive grievance, viz., that they are not getting the prescriptive equality to which they are entitled.[72] If the

[70] Ely, *Democracy and Dissent*, pp. 32, 251–52 n. 69.

[71] Ely, *Democracy and Dissent*, p. 32.

[72] Now it might be thought that Ely's suggestion is in fact based on a *prescriptive* view, i.e., the view that every descriptive inequality is prima facie evidence of prescriptive inequality under the Fourteenth Amendment. (For a discussion of the latter view—the so-called rational basis standard of equal protection—see Chapter 10, note 21.) If it were true that Ely accepted the latter view, his statement would not constitute a "glide" from an "is" to an "ought." However, Ely does not appear to

strategy succeeds, it is because the ambiguous language of 'inequality' permits advocates to use the same word to make uncontroversial statements of fact as they use to make prescriptive claims—i.e., by asserting that a state's treatment "is unequal"—thereby enabling advocates to move from an "is" to an "ought not" without having to engage in normative argument.

Conclusion

The event that transformed Abraham Lincoln from a regional lawyer into a political figure of national renown was his publicized series of debates with Stephen A. Douglas during the Illinois senatorial campaign of 1858. The two men focused in large part on the question of whether chattel slavery should be allowed to extend into the new territories of the United States. Their "forensic duel," perhaps the most momentous in American history,[73] is rhetorically interesting for our purposes because in it Lincoln maneuvered Douglas into debating the issue in the language of equality. The debates turned on the meaning of the statement in the Declaration of Independence that "all men are created equal."

Conceptually, Lincoln had little to gain by framing the question of slavery in the language of equality. The statement "all men are created equal" is incomplete without a specification of the descriptive or prescriptive respect in which they are allegedly equal. Descriptively, all men in 1858, including whites and blacks, were equal in some respects and unequal in others: equal in having skin color, unequal in the skin colors they had. Prescriptively, all men in 1858, including blacks and whites, were also equal and unequal: equal in having a right not to be murdered, but unequal in having a right to vote.[74] The real question for Lincoln and Douglas was

take the latter view of the equal protection clause. Rather, he takes the position that the so-called rational basis test of equal protection has no intelligible content, and that the equal protection clause presumptively prohibits only such statutory classifications as impinge upon specific rights the Court wishes to protect. See Ely, *Democracy and Dissent*, pp. 21, 251–52 n. 69.

[73] See Jaffa, *Crisis of the House Divided*, p. 19 ("It is doubtful that any forensic duel . . . ever held the power of decision over the future of a great people as these debates did").

[74] See, e.g., Georgia Code § 4953 (1861)("Any person who shall maliciously kill or maim a slave, shall suffer such punishment as would be inflicted if the like offense had been committed on a free white person"); Stampp, *The Peculiar Institution*, p. 227 ("The southern codes did not prescribe lighter penalties for slaves who murdered other slaves than for slaves who murdered whites").

Although some antebellum states did allow free blacks to vote, hold office, and enjoy the other privileges of citizenship, the overwhelming majority of states, both

not whether the Declaration of Independence declared all men to be prescriptively equal but in *what respect* it declared them equal, and, in particular, whether it rendered them equal in their right to be free from chattel slavery.

Rhetorically, however, Lincoln used 'equality' to his advantage by exploiting two of its persuasive features. He was able to demand equality without having to specify the precise rules by which such equality would be measured. Lincoln's racial views, in fact, were rather complicated. On the one hand, he did not believe that blacks should be granted citizenship or that they should be allowed to vote, sit on juries, hold public office, or intermarry with whites. On the other hand, he did believe that they should be free from the bondage of chattel slavery, at least in the new territories in which slavery had not yet taken hold.[75] By expressing his racial views in the elliptical language of equality, however, he could appeal to people possessing a range of racial views without alerting them to their potential differences. Indeed, Douglas complained that Lincoln's racial views lacked integrity—that Lincoln advocated one kind of equality to Abolitionist audiences in northern Illinois and another kind of equality to more conservative audiences in southern Illinois.[76]

More importantly, Lincoln exploited the favorable connotations of 'equality' and the pejorative connotations of 'inequality' by

---

North and South, denied blacks such privileges. See Berlin, *Slaves without Masters*, pp. 90–91, 129, 131; Litwak, *North of Slavery*, pp. 58, 60, 75, 93–94.

[75] See Speech of Abraham Lincoln at Charleston, 18 September 1858, in *The Political Debates between Hon. Abraham Lincoln and Hon. Stephen A. Douglas*, p. 136 (hereafter cited as *Debates*) ("I will say then that I am not, nor ever have been, in favor of bringing about in any way social and political equality of the white and black races—that I am not nor ever have been in favor of making voters . . . of Negroes"). For differing views of Lincoln's racial attitudes, compare Cox, *Lincoln and Black Freedom* (arguing that, while Lincoln believed that whites and blacks should be political equals, he also believed that, politically, the country in 1860 was not ready to accept such equality or to follow leaders who advocated it), with Frederickson, "A Man but Not a Brother," p. 39 (arguing that Lincoln did not really believe that blacks should be politically equal to whites but merely that blacks were human and, hence, unfit for slavery). See also Fehrenbacher, "Only His Stepchildren"; Quarles, *Lincoln and the Negro*.

It should be noted that while Lincoln expressed a personal repugnance toward slavery and held that the Declaration of Independence envisaged slavery's ultimate extinction, he emphasized that he did not wish to do anything to interfere with the institution of slavery in the states where it already existed but, rather, only wished to prevent its spread into the new territories. See Speech of Abraham Lincoln at Ottawa, 21 August 1859, in *Debates*, pp. 74–75.

[76] See Speech of Stephen A. Douglas at Charleston, 18 September 1858, in *Debates*, pp. 154–55. For discussion of Douglas's complaint, see Jaffa, *Crisis of the House Divided*, pp. 165–68.

making himself the champion of equality and Douglas the defender of inequality. Lincoln made himself the champion of equality by invoking the Declaration of Independence:

> I adhere to the Declaration of Independence. If Judge Douglas and his friends are not willing to stand by it, let them come up and amend it. Let them make it read that all men are created equal except negroes. Let us have it decided, whether the Declaration of Independence, in this blessed year of 1858, shall thus be amended.[77]

He also succeeded in causing Douglas to present himself as an advocate of inequality:

> I am aware that all the Abolition lecturers that you find traveling about through the country, are in the habit of reading the Declaration of Independence to prove that all men were created equal. . . . Mr. Lincoln is very much in the habit of . . . reading that part of the Declaration of Independence to prove that the negro was endowed by the Almighty with the inalienable right of equality with white men. Now, I say to you, my fellow citizens, that in my opinion, the signers of the Declaration had no reference to the negro whatever, when they declared all men to be created equal. They desired to express by that phrase white men, men of European birth and European descent, and had no reference either to the negro, the savage Indians, the Fejee, the Malay, or any other inferior and degraded race, when they spoke of the equality of men.[78]

Douglas may have made a mistake in thinking that because Lincoln advocated equality he himself had no choice but to defend inequality. He could have responded, not by defending inequality, but by advocating a *competing* equality such as the equal rights of the citizens of each state to decide for themselves whether to abolish slavery, or the equal right of all persons (free and slave, white and black) to receive the treatments to which they were entitled under state and federal laws. Instead, Douglas allowed Lincoln to maneuver him into the rhetorically unfavorable and ultimately unsuccessful position of opposing "equality"—and defending "inequality."

[77] Speech of Abraham Lincoln at Springfield, 17 July 1858, in *Debates*, p. 63.
[78] Speech of Stephen A. Douglas at Jonesboro, 15 September 1858, in *Debates*, p. 116. See also Speech of Stephen A. Douglas at Chicago, 9 July 1858, in *Debates*, p. 12 ("I am opposed to negro equality").

On the merits, of course, Lincoln had the better of the arguments, at least by today's standards. Lincoln's plea for the abolition of slavery was morally superior to Douglas's plea for states' rights, and, hence, Lincoln's conception of equality was morally superior to Douglas's. Since prescriptive equality is the equality that obtains among people by reference to the rules that ought to govern their treatment, it follows that, by today's standards at least, Lincoln was not only morally right in his assertion of equality, he was also conceptually correct in invoking prescriptive equality on his own behalf. Unfortunately, what seems morally obvious today seemed less so at the time. The people of Illinois disagreed as to which of the two speakers was expounding the morally preferable position, and, hence, they would also have disagreed about which was rightly invoking the language of equality.

CONCLUSION

This volume, by a conservative estimate, is one of 30 to 40 books about equality that can be expected to be published in English this year. It follows the publication of 46 books on equality in 1988, 65 in 1987, 50 in 1986, and 370 during the decade 1978–87. It will, if added to the card catalog of the Sterling Memorial Library at Yale University, join what are said to be 326 entries under the subject heading "equality."[1]

To make matters worse, there is a sense in which this book says nothing of interest about equality, for it says nothing about the issues of equality that tend to concern people the most. It is not a normative essay about the merits of competing equalities, a legal inquiry into the proper interpretation of constitutional or statutory equalities, an economic examination of the costs of achieving various equalities, a psychological survey about people's attitudes toward various equalities, a sociological study of distributions of wealth, or a historical account of particular conceptions of equality.

There is a sense, however, in which the book, if it accomplishes what it undertakes, says much of what one needs to know about equality. It is principally an effort to understand what equality *means*—that is, to identify what it is about the 326 entries in the card catalog that renders them books "about equality" (rather than, for example, about justice, rights, or liberties). It is also an effort to understand some of the sources of equality's rhetorical power, that is, to understand some of the reasons why it is, and always has been, easier to favor equality than to oppose it.

What we have discovered is a truth as old as Aristotle. "Equality," he writes, is a word the very "definition" of which is "equiv-

---

[1] The Research Libraries Information Network (RLIN) is a database containing the recent acquisitions of the major research libraries in the United States, including the Library of Congress. A search of RLIN for titles of books cataloged under the subject heading "equality" reveals approximately 46 titles for 1988, 65 titles for 1987, 50 titles for 1986, and 370 titles for the decade 1978–87, for an average of slightly more than 40 per year. In an essay published in 1987, Harry Frankfurt states that the card catalog of the Sterling Memorial Library at Yale contains 326 entries under the subject heading "equality." See Frankfurt, "Equality as a Moral Ideal," p. 23.

ocal.''[2] It is conceptually equivocal because it has both a single meaning and many diverse meanings—because its definition consists of fixed terms whose meanings remain constant, and a variable term, the meaning of which changes from one context to another. It is also normatively equivocal because it both *is* and *is not* value-laden: the concept of equality, the fixed formula that always remains constant, is itself normatively neutral; yet the variable terms, which are used to transform the concept of equality into particular conceptions of equality, can be inherently evaluative in nature.

These equivocations of 'equality' are further aggravated by the semantics of 'inequality'. Like equality, inequality is both a single concept and a multitude of conceptions. Like 'equal', the word 'unequal' can be purely descriptive or purely prescriptive (as Aristotle, for example, means it to be in asserting that "unequals should be treated unequally"). Yet there remains a significant semantic difference between 'equal' and 'unequal', a difference that occurs when they are used *both* descriptively *and* prescriptively. When 'equal' and 'unequal' are used purely descriptively, both are normatively neutral, as in the sentence "Jack and Jill are equal (or unequal) in height." When they are used purely prescriptively, both are normatively laudatory, as in "equals should be treated equally, and unequals unequally." Yet 'equal' and 'unequal' can also be used in a third way, a way that combines description with prescription: they can be used to indicate whether people are identical or nonidentical in having *actually* received the treatments they *ought* to receive. Thus, people are equal in this third sense if they are either all granted or all denied the treatments they ought to receive; they are unequal in this sense if some are granted and some denied the treatments they ought to receive.

When 'equal' and 'unequal' are used in this latter sense, their normative implications diverge: 'equality' can be either normatively positive or normatively negative, depending upon whether all are being granted or all are being denied the treatments they ought to receive. 'Inequality', however, is always negative because

---

[2] And here again may we not take up the same position and say that the term 'much' is equivocal? In fact there are some terms of which even the definitions are equivocal; e.g., if 'much' were defined as 'so much and more', 'so much' would mean something different in different cases: 'equal' is similarly equivocal.

Aristotle, *Physics* VII.4.248b11–22 (trans. Hardie and Gaye).

it always means that some people are not being given the treatments they ought to receive. Thus, when Plato charges that equal treatment of people who are morally unequal is ultimately "unequal," he is stating the obvious, because by "unequal" he means a relationship in which some people are granted more of what they ought to receive than others.[3] When they are used in that way, 'equality' and 'inequality' are semantically skewed: 'equality' is at times what Maurice Cranston calls a "hurrah-word," but 'inequality' is always a "boo-word."[4] In that respect, 'equality' owes its rhetorical advantage over 'inequality' not to distinct ideals they express but to language.

I have reserved a final set of questions for the end, partly because they presuppose an understanding of the propositions I have previously advanced, and partly because they are more personal than the matters I have previously discussed. They are questions about my motivations in undertaking this study. "Why," people may say, "have you undertaken this study? What has led you to dissect 'equality' in this critical way?"

These questions would be easier to answer if I were politically opposed or indifferent to the substance of claims that advocates today tend to make in the language of equality. But that is not the case. I feel deeply committed to many of the social causes that are commonly advanced in the name of equality, including rights for women, nondiscrimination on the basis of race, and redistribution of wealth. The questions would also be easier if I truly believed that from a strategic standpoint advocates could more effectively advance these social causes by substituting clearer expressions for the language of equality. Unfortunately, I am not confident that is so.

This leaves me in the uncomfortable position of having propounded a thesis that, if valid and if accepted, will deny a rhetorical advantage to people who are endeavoring to advance social causes with which I agree. I have made arguments that will tend to inhibit my ideological friends (as I feel myself being inhibited) from resorting to 'equality' to expound values we happen to share. I have advanced arguments that I know can be used—and, worse

[3] See Plato, *Laws* VI.757.
[4] See Cranston, *Freedom*, p. 16. See also Hare, "Liberty and Equality," p. 2 (referring to 'equality' as a "hurrah-word").

BIBLIOGRAPHY

Abernethy, George L., ed. *The Idea of Equality: An Anthology*. Richmond: John Knox, 1959.

Adler, Mortimer J. "Ideas of Relevance to Law." *West Virginia Law Review*, vol. 84, no. 1 (October 1981), 1–29.

———— and Robert M. Hutchins. "The Idea of Equality." In *The Great Ideas Today 1968*, 303–50. Ed. Mortimer J. Adler and Robert M. Hutchins. Chicago: Encyclopedia Brittanica, 1968.

Alexander, Larry A. "Modern Equal Protection Theories: A Metatheoretical Taxonomy and Critique." *Ohio State Law Journal*, vol. 42, no. 1 (1981), 3–68.

Allen, Ronald J. "Structuring Jury Decisionmaking in Criminal Cases: A Unified Constitutional Approach to Evidentiary Devices." *Harvard Law Review*, vol. 94, no. 2 (December 1980), 321–68.

Annas, Julia. "Plato's *Republic* and Feminism." *Philosophy*, vol. 51, no. 197 (July 1976), 307–21.

Argyle, A. W. *The Gospel according to Matthew*. Cambridge: Cambridge University Press, 1963.

Aristotle. *Ethica Eudemia*. In *The Works of Aristotle*, vol. 9. Trans. J. Solomon. Ed. W. D. Ross. Oxford: Clarendon Press, 1925.

————. *Ethica Nicomachea*. In *The Works of Aristotle*, vol. 9. Trans. and ed. W. D. Ross. Oxford: Clarendon Press, 1925.

————. *The Ethics of Aristotle: The Nicomachean Ethics*. Trans. J.A.K. Thomson. Rev. Hugh Tredennick. Middlesex, England: Penguin, 1986.

————. *Metaphysica*. In *The Works of Aristotle*, vol. 8. 2d ed. Trans. and ed. W. D. Ross. Oxford: Clarendon Press, 1928.

————. *Physica*. In *The Works of Aristotle*, vol. 2. Trans. R. P. Hardie and R. K. Gaye. Ed. W. D. Ross. Oxford: Clarendon Press, 1930.

————. *The Politics*. Trans. H. Rackham. London: William Heinemann, 1932.

————. *The Politics*. Trans. T. A. Sinclair. Rev. Trevor J. Saunders. New York: Penguin, 1981.

————. *The Politics of Aristotle*. Trans. Ernest Barker. Oxford: Clarendon Press, 1948.

Aristotle. *The Rhetoric of Aristotle*. Trans. Lane Cooper. New York: Appleton, 1932.

Bambrough, Renford. "Aristotle on Justice: A Paradigm of Philosophy." In *New Essays on Plato and Aristotle*, 159–74. Ed. Renford Bambrough. London: Routledge and Kegan Paul, 1965.

————. "Universals and Family Resemblances." *Proceedings of the Aristotelian Society*, New Series, vol. 61 (1961), 207–22.

Barrett, Edward L. "The Rational Basis Standard for Equal Protection Review of Ordinary Legislative Classifications." *Kentucky Law Journal*, vol. 68, no. 4 (1979–80), 845–78.

Barry, Brian. "A Grammar of Equality" (review of D. Rae et al., *Equalities*). *New Republic*, 12 May 1982, 36–39.

Bator, Paul M. "Equality as a Constitutional Value." *Harvard Journal of Law and Public Policy*, vol. 9, no. 1 (Winter 1986), 21–24.

Beardsley, Monroe C. "Equality and Obedience to Law." In *Law and Philosophy*, 35–42. Ed. Sidney Hook. New York: New York University Press, 1964.

Beck, Bernard. Foreword to Michael Lewis, *The Culture of Inequality*. Amherst: University of Massachusetts Press, 1978.

Becker, Lawrence. "Analogy in Legal Reasoning." *Ethics*, vol. 83, no. 3 (April 1973), 248–55.

Bedau, Hugo Adam. "Egalitarianism and the Idea of Equality." In *Equality*, Nomos IX, 3–27. Ed. J. Roland Pennock and John W. Chapman. New York: Atherton, 1967.

Belsey, Andrew and Catherine Belsey. "Sex, Equality and Mr. Lucas." *Philosophy*, vol. 55, no. 213 (July 1980), 386–91.

Belton, Robert. "Discrimination and Affirmative Action: An Analysis of Competing Theories of Equality and *Weber*." *North Carolina Law Review*, vol. 59, no. 3 (March 1981), 531–98.

Benn, Stanley I. "Egalitarianism and the Equal Consideration of Interest." In *Equality*, Nomos IX, 61–78. Ed. J. Roland Pennock and John W. Chapman. New York: Atherton, 1967.

————. "Equality, Moral and Social." *Encyclopedia of Philosophy*, vol. 3, 38–42. Ed. Paul Edwards. New York: Macmillan, 1967.

———— and R. S. Peters. *The Principles of Political Thought*. New York: Free Press, 1959.

Bennett, Robert W. " 'Mere' Rationality in Constitutional Law: Judicial Review and Democratic Theory." *California Law Review*, vol. 67, no. 5 (September 1979), 1049–1103.

Bentham, Jeremy. Introduction to "Constitutional Code." In *Works of Jeremy Bentham*, vol. 9, 3–8. Ed. John Bowring. Edinburgh: William Tait, 1843.

———. "Plan of Parliamentary Reform." In *Works of Jeremy Bentham*, vol. 3, 433, 459. Ed. John Bowring. Edinburgh: William Tait, 1843.

———. "Principles of the Civil Code." In *The Theory of Legislation*, 88–236. Ed. C. K. Ogden. New York: Harcourt, Brace, 1931.

Berger, Raoul. *Government by Judiciary: The Transformation of the Fourteenth Amendment*. Cambridge: Harvard University Press, 1977.

Berlin, Ira. *Slaves without Masters: The Free Negro in the Antebellum South*. New York: Pantheon, 1974.

Berlin, Isaiah. "Equality as an Ideal." In *Justice and Social Policy*, 128–50. Ed. Frederick A. Olafson. Englewood Cliffs, N.J.: Prentice-Hall, 1961.

Berman, Harold J. and William R. Greiner, eds. *The Nature and Functions of Law*. 3d ed. Mineola, N.Y.: Foundation, 1972.

Bernhardt, Stephen. "Frege on Identity." *Journal of Critical Analysis*, vol. 8, no. 3 (Summer/Fall 1980), 57–65.

Berry, Mary Francis. *Why ERA Failed: Politics, Women's Rights, and the Amending Process of the Constitution*. Bloomington: University of Indiana Press, 1986.

Bhattacharya, Rajlukshmee Debee. "Because He Is a Man." *Philosophy*, vol. 49, no. 187 (January 1974), 96.

Bible. *The Interpreter's Bible: The Holy Scriptures*. Ed. George Butrick. Vol. VII. New York: Abingdon-Cokesbury, 1951.

Bickel, Alexander M. *The Supreme Court and the Idea of Progress*. 1st ed. New York: Harper and Row, 1970.

Bitzer, Lloyd F. "The Rhetorical Situation." *Philosophy and Rhetoric*, vol. 1, no. 1 (Winter 1968), 1–14.

Blackstone, William. *Commentaries on the Laws of England*. Ed. John L. Wendell. Vol. 4. New York: Harper and Brothers, 1854.

Blackstone, William T. Introduction to *The Concept of Equality*, v–xiii. Ed. William T. Blackstone. Minneapolis: Burgess, 1969.

———. "On the Meaning and Justification of the Equality Principle." *Ethics*, vol. 77, no. 4 (July 1967), 239–53.

Bork, Robert H. "The Impossibility of Finding Welfare Rights in the Constitution." *Washington University Law Quarterly*, vol. 1979, no. 3 (Summer 1979), 695–701.

Bowie, Norman E. "Equality and Distributive Justice." *Philosophy*, vol. 45, no. 172 (April 1970), 140–48.

Brennan, J. M. *The Open-Texture of Moral Concepts*. London: Macmillan, 1977.

Brennan, William J., Jr. "The Equality Principle: A Foundation of

American Life." *U.C. Davis Law Review*, vol. 20, no. 4 (Summer 1987), 673–78.

Brest, Paul. "Affirmative Action and the Constitution: Three Theories." *Iowa Law Review*, vol. 71, no. 2 (January 1987), 281–85.

Bronough, Richard. Introduction to *Philosophical Law*, 47–51. Westport, Conn.: Greenwood, 1978.

Brown, Judith Olans, Phyllis Tropper Baumann, and Elaine Millar Melnick. "Equal Pay for Jobs of Comparable Worth: An Analysis of the Rhetoric." *Harvard Civil Rights–Civil Liberties Law Review*, vol. 21, no. 1 (Winter 1986), 127–70.

Brown, Raymond, ed. *The Jerome Biblical Commentary*. Vol. 2. Englewood Cliffs, N.J.: Prentice-Hall, 1969.

Browne, D. E. "Nonegalitarian Justice." *Australasian Journal of Philosophy*, vol. 56, no. 1 (May 1978), 48–60.

———. "The Presumption of Equality." *Australasian Journal of Philosophy*, vol. 53, no. 1 (May 1975), 46–53.

Burton, Steven J. *An Introduction to Law and Legal Reasoning*. Boston: Little, Brown, 1985.

Campbell, Karlyn Kohrs. *Critiques of Contemporary Rhetoric*. Belmont, Calif.: Wadsworth, 1972.

Campbell, T. D. "Equality of Opportunity." *Proceedings of the Aristotelian Society*, New Series, vol. 75 (1975), 51–68.

Carr, Craig L. "The Concept of Formal Justice." *Philosophical Studies*, vol. 39, no. 3 (April 1981), 211–26.

Carritt, E. F. *Ethical and Political Thinking*. Oxford: Clarendon Press, 1947.

Caton, C. E. "The Idea of Sameness Challenges Reflection." In *Studies on Frege II: Logic and Philosophy of Language*, 167–80. Ed. Matthias Schirn. Stuttgart-Bad Cannstatt: Friedrich Frommann, 1976.

Cauthen, Kenneth. *The Passion for Equality*. Totowa, N.J.: Rowman and Littlefield, 1987.

Chamallas, Martha. "Evolving Conceptions of Equality under Title VII: Disparate Impact Theory and the Demise of the Bottom Line Principle." *U.C.L.A. Law Review*, vol. 31, no. 2 (December 1983), 305–83.

Charvet, John. *A Critique of Freedom and Equality*. Cambridge: Cambridge University Press, 1981.

———. "The Idea of Equality as a Substantive Principle of Society." *Political Studies*, vol. 17, no. 1 (March 1969), 1–13.

Chemerinsky, Erwin. "In Defense of Equality: A Reply to Professor Westen." *Michigan Law Review*, vol. 81, no. 3 (January 1983), 575–99.

Christie, George C. "Objectivity in Law." *Yale Law Journal*, vol. 78, no. 8 (July 1969), 1311–50.

Civil Rights Act of 1964, Pub. L. No. 88–352, § 703(a)(2), 78 Stat. 241, 255 (codified as amended at 42 U.S.C. § 2000e–2(a)(2)(1982)).

Clarke, Barry. "Eccentrically Contested Concepts." *British Journal of Political Science*, vol. 9, pt. 1 (January 1979), 122–26.

Clauss, Carin Ann. "Comparable Worth—the Theory, Its Legal Foundation, and the Feasibility of Implementation." *University of Michigan Journal of Law Reform*, vol. 20, no. 1 (Fall 1986), 7–97.

Cleary, Edward W., ed. *McCormick on Evidence*, 3d ed. St. Paul, Minn.: West, 1984.

Cohen, G. A. "On the Currency of Egalitarian Justice." *Ethics*, vol. 99, no. 4 (July 1989), 906–44.

Connolly, William E. "Modern Authority and Ambiguity." In *Nomos XXIX: Authority Revisited*, 9–27. Ed. J. Roland Pennock and John W. Chapman. New York: New York University Press, 1987.

———. *The Terms of Political Discourse*. 2d ed. Princeton: Princeton University Press, 1983.

Coons, John E. "Consistency." *California Law Review*, vol. 75, no. 1 (January 1987), 59–113.

Cooper, David E. *The Illusions of Equality*. London and Boston: Routledge and Kegan Paul, 1980.

Cox, Archibald. *The Warren Court: Constitutional Decision as an Instrument of Reform*. Cambridge: Harvard University Press, 1968.

Cox, LaWanda C. Fenlason. *Lincoln and Black Freedom: A Study in Presidential Leadership*. 1st ed. Columbia: University of South Carolina Press, 1981.

Cranston, Maurice. *Freedom: A New Analysis*. London and New York: Longmans, Green, 1954.

Cross, Rupert. "The House of Lords and the Rules of Precedent." In *Law, Morality and Society: Essays in Honour of H.L.A. Hart*, 145–60. Ed. P.M.S. Hacker and J. Raz. Oxford: Clarendon Press, 1977.

———. *Precedent in English Law*. 3d ed. Oxford: Clarendon Press, 1977.

Dallmayr, Fred R. "Functionalism, Justice and Equality." *Ethics*, vol. 78, no. 1 (October 1967), 1–16.

Daniels, Norman. "Merit and Meritocracy." *Philosophy and Public Affairs*, vol. 7, no. 3 (Spring 1978), 206–23.

Davis, Michael. "Sentencing: Must Justice Be Even-Handed?" *Law and Philosophy*, vol. 1, no. 1 (April 1982), 77–117.

de Cervera, Alejo. "The Paradoxes of Equality." In *Equality and Freedom*, vol. 1, 237–43. Ed. Gray Dorsey. Dobbs Ferry, N.Y.: Oceana, 1977.

Del Vecchio, Giorgio. "Equality and Inequality in Relation to Justice." *Natural Law Forum*, vol. 11 (1966), 36–47.

———. *Justice: An Historical and Philosophical Essay*. Ed. A. H. Campbell. Edinburgh: Edinburgh University Press, 1952.

Dilman, Ilham. "Universals: Bambrough on Wittgenstein." *Proceedings of the Aristotelian Society*, New Series, vol. 79 (1978), 35–58.

Dilworth, Craig. "Identity, Equality, and Equivalence." *Dialectica*, vol. 42, no. 2 (1988), 83–92.

Dixon, Keith. *Freedom and Equality: The Moral Basis of Democratic Socialism*. London and Boston: Routledge and Kegan Paul, 1986.

Dorn, Edwin. *Rules and Racial Equality*. New Haven: Yale University Press, 1979.

Driscoll, Dawn-Marie and Barbara J. Rouse. "Through a Glass Darkly: A Look at State Equal Rights Amendments." *Suffolk University Law Review*, vol. 12, no. 5 (Fall 1978), 1282–1311.

Dworkin, Gerald. "Philosophy, Law, and Politics." *Iowa Law Review*, vol. 72, no. 5 (July 1987), 1355–58.

Dworkin, Ronald. *Law's Empire*. Cambridge: Harvard University Press, 1986.

———. "Liberalism." In *Public and Private Morality*, 113–43. Ed. Stuart Hampshire. Cambridge: Cambridge University Press, 1978.

———. *A Matter of Principle*. Cambridge: Harvard University Press, 1985.

———. *Taking Rights Seriously*. Cambridge: Harvard University Press, 1978.

———. "What Is Equality?": "Part 1, Equality of Welfare." *Philosophy and Public Affairs*, vol. 10, no. 3 (Summer 1981), 185–246. "Part 2, Equality of Resources." *Philosophy and Public Affairs*, vol. 10, no. 4 (Fall 1981), 283–345. "Part 3: The Place of Liberty." *Iowa Law Review*, vol. 73, no. 1 (October 1987), 1–54. "Part 4: Political Equality." *University of San Francisco Law Review*, vol. 22, no. 1 (Fall 1987), 1–30.

Eisenberg, Melvin Aron. *The Nature of the Common Law*. Cambridge: Harvard University Press, 1988.

Ely, John Hart. *Democracy and Distrust: A Theory of Judicial Review.* Cambridge: Harvard University Press, 1980.

Emerson, Thomas I. and Barbara G. Lifton. "Should E.R.A. Be Ratified?" *Connecticut Bar Journal*, vol. 55, no. 3 (June 1981), 227–37.

Empey, LaMar and Maynard Erickson. *The Provo Experiment: Evaluating Community Control of Delinquency.* Lexington, Mass.: Heath, 1972.

Euclid. *The Thirteen Books of Euclid's Elements.* 2d ed. Trans. Thomas L. Heath. New York: Dover, 1956.

Evans, Bette Novit. "Equality, Ambiguity, and Public Choice." *Creighton Law Review*, vol. 14, no. 4 (Supp. 1981), 1385–1408.

———. "Thinking Clearly about Equality: Conceptual Premises and Why They Make a Difference." In *Elusive Equality: Liberalism, Affirmative Action, and Social Change in America*, 101–14. Ed. James C. Foster and Mary C. Segers. Port Washington, N.Y.: Associated Faculty Press, 1983.

Fehrenbacher, Don E. "Only His Stepchildren: Lincoln and the Negro." *Civil War History*, vol. 20, no. 4 (December 1974), 293–310.

Feinberg, Joel. "Justice and Personal Desert." In *Justice*, Nomos VI, 69–97. Ed. Carl J. Friedrich and John W. Chapman. New York: Atherton, 1963.

———. "The Nature and Value of Rights." In *Rights, Justice, and the Bounds of Liberty: Essays in Social Philosophy*, 143–58. Princeton: Princeton University Press, 1980.

———. "Noncomparative Justice." *Philosophical Review*, vol. 83, no. 3 (July 1974), 297–338.

———. *Social Philosophy.* Englewood Cliffs, N.J.: Prentice-Hall, 1973.

Finnis, John. *Natural Law and Natural Rights.* Oxford: Clarendon Press, 1980.

Fishkin, James S. *Justice, Equal Opportunity, and the Family.* New Haven: Yale University Press, 1983.

Fiss, Owen M. "Groups and the Equal Protection Clause." In *Equality and Preferential Treatment*, 84–154. Ed. Marshall Cohen, Thomas Nagel, and Thomas Scanlon. Princeton: Princeton University Press, 1977.

———. "A Theory of Fair Employment Law." *University of Chicago Law Review*, vol. 38, no. 2 (Winter 1971), 235–314.

Flathman, Richard E. "Equality and Generalization: A Formal

Analysis." In *Equality*, Nomos IX, 38–60. Ed. J. Roland Pennock and John W. Chapman. New York: Atherton, 1967.

———. *The Public Interest: An Essay concerning the Normative Discourse of Politics*. New York: Wiley, 1966.

Flew, Anthony. *The Politics of Procrustes: Contradictions of Enforced Equality*. Buffalo: Prometheus, 1981.

Frankel, Charles. "Equality of Opportunity." *Ethics*, vol. 81, no. 3 (April 1971), 191–211.

Frankena, William K. "The Concept of Social Justice." In *Social Justice*, 1–29. Ed. Richard B. Brandt. Englewood Cliffs, N.J.: Prentice-Hall, 1962.

———. "Some Beliefs about Justice." In *Perspectives on Morality: Essays by William K. Frankena*, 93–106. Ed. K. E. Goodpastor. Notre Dame: University of Notre Dame Press, 1976.

Frankfurt, Harry. "Equality as a Moral Ideal." *Ethics*, vol. 98, no. 1 (October 1987), 21–43.

Frederickson, George M. "A Man but Not a Brother: Abraham Lincoln and Racial Equality." *Journal of Southern History*, vol. 41, no. 1 (February 1975), 39–58.

Frege, Gottlob. "Function and Concept." In *Translations from the Philosophical Writings of Gottlob Frege*, 21–41. Ed. Peter Geach and Max Black. Oxford: Blackwell, 1980.

Freund, Paul A. "The Philosophy of Equality." *Washington University Law Quarterly*, vol. 1979, no. 1 (Winter 1979), 11–23.

Fried, Charles. "The Artificial Reason of the Law, or: What Lawyers Know." *Texas Law Review*, vol. 60, no. 1 (December 1981), 35–58.

Friedman, Joel W. "Redefining Equality, Discrimination, and Affirmative Action under Title VII: The Access Principle." *Texas Law Review*, vol. 65, no. 1 (December 1986), 41–99.

Friedman, Lawrence M. "Legal Rules and the Process of Legal Change." *Stanford Law Review*, vol. 19, no. 4 (April 1967), 786–840.

Fullinwider, Robert K. *The Reverse Discrimination Controversy: A Moral and Legal Analysis*. Totowa, N.J.: Rowman and Littlefield, 1980.

Gallie, W. B. "Essentially Contested Concepts." *Proceedings of the Aristotelian Society*, New Series, vol. 56 (1956), 167–98.

Gallop, David. *Plato: Phaedo*. Oxford: Clarendon Press, 1975.

Galston, William. "Equality of Opportunity and Liberal Theory." In *Justice and Equality Here and Now*, 89–107. Ed. Frank S. Lucash. Ithaca, N.Y.: Cornell University Press, 1986.

Garcia, J.L.A. "Two Concepts of Desert." *Law and Philosophy*, vol. 5, no. 2 (August 1986), 219–35.

Gewirth, Alan. "The Basis and Content of Human Rights." In *Human Rights*, Nomos XXIII, 119–47. Ed. J. Roland Pennock and John W. Chapman. New York: New York University Press, 1981.

———. "Political Justice." In *Social Justice*, 119–69. Ed. Richard B. Brandt. Englewood Cliffs, N.J.: Prentice-Hall, 1962.

———. *Reason and Morality*. Chicago: University of Chicago Press, 1978.

Gillespie, Norman C. "On Treating Like Cases Differently." *Philosophical Quarterly*, vol. 25, no. 99 (April 1975), 151–58.

Ginsberg, Morris. *On Justice in Society*. Ithaca, N.Y.: Cornell University Press, 1965.

Ginsburg, Ruth Bader. "Some Thoughts on Judicial Authority to Repair Unconstitutional Legislation." *Cleveland State Law Review*, vol. 28, no. 3 (1979), 301–24.

Gold, Michael Evan. "*Griggs'* Folly: An Essay on the Theory, Problems, and Origin of the Adverse Impact Definition of Employment Discrimination and a Recommendation for Reform." *Industrial Relations Law Journal*, vol. 7, no. 4 (1985), 429–598.

Golding, Martin P. *Legal Reasoning*. New York: Knopf, 1984.

Goldman, Alan H. "The Justification of Equal Opportunity." *Social Philosophy and Policy*, vol. 5, no. 1 (Autumn 1987), 88–103.

———. "The Principles of Equal Opportunity." *Southern Journal of Philosophy*, vol. 15, no. 4 (Winter 1977), 473–85.

Goodhart, Arthur. "Determining the *Ratio Decidendi* of a Case." In *Essays in Jurisprudence and the Common Law*, 1–26. Cambridge: Cambridge University Press, 1931.

Goodin, Robert E. "Egalitarianism, Fetishistic and Otherwise." *Ethics*, vol. 98, no. 1 (October 1987), 44–49.

———. "Epiphenomenal Egalitarianism." *Social Research*, vol. 52, no. 1 (Spring 1985), 99–117.

Goodman, Nelson. "Seven Strictures on Similarity." In *Problems and Projects*, 437–46. Indianapolis: Bobbs-Merrill, 1972.

Gottlieb, Gidon. *The Logic of Choice: An Investigation of the Concepts of Rule and Rationality*. London: Allen and Unwin, 1968.

Govier, Trudy R. "Woman's Place." *Philosophy*, vol. 49, no. 189 (July 1974), 303–9.

Graham, A. C. "Liberty and Equality." *Mind*, vol. 74, no. 293 (January 1976), 59–65.

Gray, John. "On Liberty, Liberalism, and Essential Contestability." *British Journal of Political Science*, vol. 8, pt. 4 (October 1978), 385–402.

Gray, John Chipman. *The Nature and Sources of the Law*. 2d ed. New York: Macmillan, 1938.

Greely, Hank. "The Equality of Allocation by Lot." *Harvard Civil Rights and Civil Liberties Review*, vol. 12, no. 1 (Winter 1977), 113–41.

Green, Philip. *The Pursuit of Inequality*. 1st ed. New York: Pantheon, 1981.

Green, S.J.D. "Competitive Equality of Opportunity: A Defense." *Ethics*, vol. 100, no. 1 (October 1989), 5–32.

Greenawalt, Kent. "How Empty Is the Idea of Equality?" *Columbia Law Review*, vol. 83, no. 5 (June 1983), 1167–85.

Guest, A. G. "Logic in the Law." In *Oxford Essays in Jurisprudence: A Collaborative Work*, 176–97. Ed. A. G. Guest. Oxford: Clarendon Press, 1961.

Gutmann, Amy. *Liberal Equality*. Cambridge: Cambridge University Press, 1980.

Haack, Susan. "On the Moral Relevance of Sex." *Philosophy*, vol. 49, no. 187 (January 1974), 90–95.

Hare, R. M. *Freedom and Reason*. Oxford: Clarendon Press, 1963.

———. "Liberty and Equality: How Politics Masquerades as Philosophy." *Social Philosophy and Policy*, vol. 2, no. 1 (Autumn 1984), 1–11.

———. "Relevance." In *Values and Morals: Essays in Honor of William Frankena, Charles Stevenson, and Richard Brandt*, 73–90. Ed. Alvin I. Goldman and Jaegwon Kim. Dordrecht: Reidel, 1978.

Harrison, Jonathan. *Hume's Theory of Justice*. Oxford: Clarendon Press, 1981.

Hart, H.L.A. "Between Utility and Rights." *Columbia Law Review*, vol. 79, no. 5 (June 1979), 828–46.

———. *The Concept of Law*. Oxford: Clarendon Press, 1961.

———. "Definition and Theory in Jurisprudence." In *Essays in Jurisprudence and Philosophy*, 21–47. Oxford: Clarendon Press, 1983.

Harvey, F. D. "Two Kinds of Equality." *Classica et Mediaevalia*, vol. 26 (1965), 101–46.

Hawkins, David. *The Science and Ethics of Equality*. New York: Basic Books, 1977.

Haynes, Richard P. "The Form Equality, as a Set of Equals: *Phaedo* 74b–c." *Phronesis*, vol. 9, no. 1 (1964), 17–26.

Heyd, David. *Supererogation: Its Status in Ethical Theory*. Cambridge: Cambridge University Press, 1982.

Hobbes, Thomas. *Leviathan*. Reprint of 1651 ed. Ed. Michael Oakeshott. Oxford: Blackwell, 1946.

Hohfeld, Wesley Newcomb. *Fundamental Legal Conceptions as Applied in Judicial Reasoning*. Ed. Walter Wheeler Cook. New Haven: Yale University Press, 1964.

Honoré, A. M. "Social Justice." *McGill Law Journal*, vol. 8, no. 2 (1962), 77–105.

Howells, William Dean. "Equality as the Basis of Good Society." *Century Magazine*, vol. 51 (November 1895), 63–67.

Isocrates. *Areopagiticus*. In *Isocrates*, vol. 2, 100–157. Trans. George Norlin. Cambridge: Harvard University Press, 1956.

Jacobs, Louis A. "A Constitutional Route to Discriminatory Impact Statutory Liability for State and Local Government Employers: All Roads Lead to Rome." *Ohio State Law Journal*, vol. 41, no. 2 (1980), 301–48.

Jaffa, Harry V. *Crisis of the House Divided: An Interpretation of the Lincoln-Douglas Debates*. Garden City, N.Y.: Doubleday, 1959.

Jefferson, Thomas. *Papers of Thomas Jefferson*. Vol. 2. Ed. Julian P. Boyd. Princeton: Princeton University Press, 1950.

Kamooneh, Kaveh. "Justice as Fairness or as Equality?" *Journal of Value Inquiry*, vol. 21 (1987), 65–71.

Kant, Immanuel. "The Fundamental Principles of the Metaphysics of Morals." Excerpted in *The Idea of Equality*, 153–55. Ed. George L. Abernethy. Richmond: John Knox, 1959.

Karasik, Sidney. "Equal Protection of the Law under the Federal and Illinois Constitutions: A Contrast in Unequal Protection." *DePaul Law Review*, vol. 30, no. 2 (Winter 1981), 263–94.

Karpardis, Andreas and David Farrington. "An Experimental Study of Sentencing by Magistrates." *Law and Human Behavior*, vol. 5, nos. 2–3 (1981), 107–39.

Karst, Kenneth L. *Belonging to America: Equal Citizenship and the Constitution*. New Haven: Yale University Press, 1989.

———. "Equality and Community: Lessons from the Civil Rights Era." *Notre Dame Lawyer*, vol. 56, no. 2 (December 1980), 183–214.

———. "Equality as a Central Principle in the First Amendment." *University of Chicago Law Review*, vol. 43, no. 1 (Fall 1975), 20–68.

———. "The Supreme Court, 1976 October Term—Foreword: Equal Citizenship under the Fourteenth Amendment." *Harvard Law Review*, vol. 91, no. 1 (November 1977), 1–68.

———. "Why Equality Matters." *Georgia Law Review*, vol. 17, no. 2 (Winter 1983), 245–89.

Katzner, Louis I. "Presumptivist and Nonpresumptivist Principles of Formal Justice." *Ethics*, vol. 81, no. 3 (April 1971), 253–58.

Kay, Herma Hill. "Equality and Difference: The Case of Pregnancy." *Berkeley Women's Law Journal*, vol. 1, no. 1 (Fall 1985), 1–38.

———. "Models of Equality." *University of Illinois Law Review*, vol. 1985, no. 1 (1985), 39–88.

Kelsen, Hans. "Aristotle's Theory of Justice." In *What Is Justice?* Berkeley and Los Angeles: University of California Press, 1957.

———. *General Theory of Law and State*. Cambridge: Harvard University Press, 1945.

Kovesi, Julius. *Moral Notions*. London: Routledge and Kegan Paul, 1967.

Kristol, Irving. "About Equality." *Commentary*, vol. 56, no. 5 (5 November 1972), 41–47.

———. "Equality as an Ideal." In *International Encyclopedia of the Social Sciences*, vol. 5, 108–11. Ed. David Sills. New York: Macmillan, 1968.

Kurland, Philip B. "Ruminations on the Quality of Equality." *Brigham Young University Law Review*, vol. 1979, no. 1 (1979), 1–23.

———. "The Supreme Court, 1963 Term—Foreword: Equal in Origin and Equal in Title to the Legislative and Executive Branches of Government." *Harvard Law Review*, vol. 78, no. 1 (November 1964), 143–76.

Lakoff, Sanford A. "Christianity and Equality." In *Equality*, Nomos IX, 115–33. Ed. J. Roland Pennock and John W. Chapman. New York: Atherton Press, 1967.

———. *Equality in Political Philosophy*. Cambridge: Harvard University Press, 1964.

Laski, Harold. "Liberty and Equality." In *Social Problems and Public Policy: Inequality and Justice*, 26–31. Ed. Lee Rainwater. Chicago: Aldine, 1974.

Laymon, Charles, ed. *The Interpreter's One-Volume Commentary on the Bible*. Nashville: Abingdon, 1971.

Lee, Rex E. *A Lawyer Looks at the Equal Rights Amendment*. Provo, Utah: Brigham Young University Press, 1980.

Levi, Edward H. *An Introduction to Legal Reasoning*. Chicago: University of Chicago Press, 1949.

———. "The Nature of Judicial Reasoning." In *Law and Philosophy*, 263–81. Ed. Sidney Hook. New York: New York University Press, 1964.

Levin, Michael E. "Equality of Opportunity." *Philosophical Quarterly*, vol. 31, no. 123 (April 1981), 110–25.

Lincoln, Abraham. *The Political Debates between Hon. Abraham Lincoln and Hon. Stephen A. Douglas*. Columbus: Follett, Foster, 1860.

Lipton, Douglas, Robert Martinson, and Judith Wilks. *The Effectiveness of Correctional Treatment: A Survey of Treatment Evaluation Studies*. New York: Praeger, 1975.

Litwak, Leon F. *North of Slavery: The Negro in the Free States*. Chicago: University of Chicago Press, 1961.

Llewellyn, Karl. "Case Law." In *Encyclopedia of Social Sciences*, vol. 3, 249–51. New York: Macmillan, 1930.

Lloyd, Dennis. *Introduction to Jurisprudence*. 3d ed. London: Stevens, 1972.

Locke, Don. "The Trivializability of Universalizability." *Philosophical Review*, vol. 77, no. 1 (January 1968), 25–44.

Lucas, J. R. "Against Equality." *Philosophy*, vol. 40, no. 154 (October 1965), 296–307.

―――. "Against Equality Again." *Philosophy*, vol. 52, no. 201 (July 1977), 255–80.

―――. *On Justice*. Oxford: Clarendon Press, 1966.

―――. *The Principles of Politics*. Oxford: Clarendon Press, 1966.

Lukes, Steven. *Individualism*. Oxford: Blackwell, 1973.

―――. *Power: A Radical View*. London and New York: Macmillan, 1974.

―――. "Relativism: Cognitive and Moral." *Proceedings of the Aristotelian Society*, New Series, vol. 48 (1974), 165–89.

―――. "Reply to MacDonald." *British Journal of Political Science*, vol. 7, pt. 3 (July 1977), 418–19.

Lupu, Ira C. "Untangling the Strands of the Fourteenth Amendment." *Michigan Law Review*, vol. 77, no. 4 (April 1979), 981–1077.

Lyons, David. "Formal Justice and Judicial Precedent." *Vanderbilt Law Review*, vol. 38, no. 3 (April 1985), 495–512.

MacCallum, Gerald C., Jr. "Negative and Positive Freedom." *Philosophical Review*, vol. 76, no. 3 (July 1967), 312–34.

MacCormick, Neil. *Legal Reasoning and Legal Theory*. Oxford: Clarendon Press, 1978.

MacDonald, K. I. "Is 'Power' Essentially Contested?" *British Journal of Political Science*, vol. 6, pt. 3 (July 1976), 380–82.

MacKinnon, Catharine. "Difference and Dominance: On Sex Discrimination." In *Feminism Unmodified*, 32–45. Cambridge: Harvard University Press, 1987.

Macleod, A. M. "Equality of Opportunity: Some Ambiguities in the Ideal." In *Equality and Freedom*, vol. 3, 1077–98. Ed. Gray Dorsey. Dobbs Ferry, New York: Oceana, 1977.

Mansbridge, Jane J. *Why We Lost the ERA*. Chicago: University of Chicago Press, 1986.

Marc-Wogau, K. "Aristotle's Theory of Corrective Justice and Reciprocity." In *Philosophical Essays: History of Philosophy, Perception, and Historical Explanation*, 21–40. Ed. Philosophical Society of Uppsala. Copenhagen: Ejnar Munksgaard, 1967.

Maritain, Jacques. "Human Equality." In *Ransoming the Time*, 1–32. Trans. Harry Lorin Bihsse. New York: Scribner, 1941.

Marshall, Geoffrey. "Notes on the Rule of Equal Law." In *Equality*, Nomos IX, 261–76. Ed. J. Roland Pennock and John W. Chapman. New York: Atherton, 1967.

Marx, Karl. "The Critique of the Gotha Programme." Excerpted in *Capital, The Communist Manifesto, and Other Writings*, 2–7. Ed. Max Eastman. New York: Modern Library, 1932.

McCloskey, H. J. "Egalitarianism, Equality, and Justice." *Australasian Journal of Philosophy*, vol. 44, no. 1 (May 1966), 50–69.

————. "Rights—Some Conceptual Issues." *Australasian Journal of Philosophy*, vol. 54, no. 2 (August 1976), 99–115.

————. "Utilitarian and Retributive Punishment." *Journal of Philosophy*, vol. 64, no. 3 (February 1967), 91–110.

McDonald, Virginia. "Rawlsian Contractarianism: Liberal Equality or Inequality?" *Canadian Journal of Philosophy*, supp. vol. 3 (1977), 71–94.

Menne, Albert. "Identity, Equality, Similarity: A Logico-Philosophical Analysis." *Ratio*, vol. 4, no. 1 (June 1961), 50–61.

Michelman, Frank. "The Supreme Court 1968 Term—Foreword on Protecting the Poor through the Fourteenth Amendment." *Harvard Law Review*, vol. 83, no. 1 (November 1969), 7–59.

Mill, John Stuart. *Utilitarianism*. In *Collected Works of John Stuart Mill*, vol. 10, 203–59. Ed. F.E.L. Priestley. Toronto: University of Toronto Press, 1969.

Miller, David. "Arguments for Equality." In *Midwest Studies in Philosophy*, vol. 7, 73–87. Ed. Peter A. French, Theodore E. Uehling, Jr., and Howard K. Wettstein. Minneapolis: University of Minnesota Press, 1982.

————. *Social Justice*. Oxford: Clarendon Press, 1976.

Milne, Heather. "Desert, Effort, and Equality." *Journal of Applied Philosophy*, vol. 3, no. 2 (1986), 235–43.

Monro, D. H. "Impartiality and Consistency." *Philosophy*, vol. 36, no. 137 (April–July 1961), 161–76.

Montague, Phillip. "Comparative and Noncomparative Justice." *Philosophical Quarterly*, vol. 30, no. 119 (April 1980), 131–40.

Montrose, J. L. "*Ratio Decidendi* and the House of Lords." *Modern Law Review*, vol. 20, no. 2 (March 1957), 124–30.

————. "The *Ratio Decidendi* of a Case." *Modern Law Review*, vol. 20, no. 6 (November 1957), 587–95.

Moore, Michael S. "Precedent, Induction, and Ethical Generalization." In *Precedent in Law*, 183–216. Ed. Laurence Goldstein. Oxford: Clarendon Press, 1987.

Mortimore, G. W. "An Ideal of Equality." *Mind*, vol. 77, no. 306 (April 1968), 222–42.

Munzer, Stephen R. "A Theory of Retroactive Legislation." *Texas Law Review*, vol. 61, no. 3 (November 1962), 425–80.

Murphy, Jeffrie. "Mercy and Legal Justice." *Social Philosophy and Policy*, vol. 4, no. 1 (Autumn 1986), 1–46.

Murray, James R. "The Role of Analogy in Legal Reasoning." *U.C.L.A. Law Review*, vol. 29, no. 4 (April 1982), 833–71.

Nagel, Thomas. "The Meaning of Equality." *Washington University Law Quarterly*, vol. 1979, no. 1 (Winter 1979), 25–31.

Nelson, William. "Equal Opportunity." *Social Theory and Practice*, vol. 10, no. 1 (Summer 1984), 157–84.

Newman, Donald J. *Conviction: The Determination of Guilt or Innocence without Trial*. Boston: Little, Brown, 1966.

Newman, Winn, Lisa Newell, and Alice Kirkman. "The Lessons of AFSCME v. State of Washington." *New York University Review of Law and Social Change*, vol. 13, no. 2 (1984–85), 475–97.

Nielsen, Kai. *Equality and Liberty: A Defense of Radical Egalitarianism*. Totowa, N.J.: Rowman and Allanheld, 1985.

————. "On Marx Not Being an Egalitarian." *Studies in Soviet Thought*, vol. 35, no. 4 (May 1988), 287–326.

————. "On Not Needing to Justify Equality." *International Studies in Philosophy*, vol. 20, no. 3 (Fall 1988), 55–71.

Nietzsche, Friedrich Wilhelm. *The Portable Nietzsche*. Trans. Walter Kaufmann. New York: Viking, 1954.

Nisbet, Robert A. "The New Despotism." *Commentary*, vol. 59, no. 6 (June 1975), 31–43.

Norman, Richard. *Free and Equal: A Philosophical Examination of Political Values*. Oxford: Clarendon Press, 1987.

Note, "Developments in the Law—Equal Protection." *Harvard Law Review*, vol. 82, no. 1 (March 1969), 1065–1192.

Note, "Equal Pay, Comparable Work, and Job Evaluation." *Yale Law Journal*, vol. 90, no. 3 (January 1981), 657–80.

Note, "Justice Stevens' Equal Protection Jurisprudence." *Harvard Law Review*, vol. 100, no. 5 (March 1987), 1146–65.

Note, "Legislative Purpose, Rationality, and Equal Protection." *Yale Law Journal*, vol. 82, no. 1 (November 1972), 123–54.

Nowak, John E., Ronald D. Rotunda, and J. Nelson Young. *Constitutional Law*. 2d ed. St. Paul, Minn.: West, 1983.

Nozick, Robert. *Anarchy, State, and Utopia*. New York: Basic Books, 1974.

O'Neill, Onora. "How Do We Know When Opportunities Are Equal?" In *Feminism and Philosophy*, 177–89. Ed. Mary Vetterling-Braggin, Frederick A. Elliston, and Jane English. Totowa, N.J.: Rowman and Littlefield, 1977.

———. "Opportunities, Equalities, and Education." *Theory and Decision*, vol. 7, no. 4 (October 1976), 275–95.

Oppenheim, Felix. "The Concept of Equality." In *International Encyclopedia of the Social Sciences*, vol. 5, 102–8. Ed. David Sills. New York: Macmillan, 1968.

———. "Egalitarianism as a Descriptive Concept." *American Philosophical Quarterly*, vol. 7, no. 2 (April 1970), 143–52.

———. *Political Concepts: A Reconstruction*. Chicago: University of Chicago Press, 1981.

Orwell, George. *Animal Farm*. 1st ed. New York: Harcourt, Brace, 1946.

Pennock, J. Roland. Introduction to *Equality*, Nomos IX. Ed. J. Roland Pennock and John W. Chapman. New York: Atherton, 1967.

Perelman, Chaim. *The Idea of Justice and the Problem of Argument*. Trans. John Petrie. London: Routledge and Kegan Paul, 1963.

———. *Justice, Law, and Argument: Essays on Moral and Legal Reasoning*. Trans. John Petrie et al. Dordrecht: Reidel, 1980.

——— and L. Olbrechts-Tyteca. *The New Rhetoric: A Treatise on Argumentation*. 2d ed. Brussels: Editions de l'Institut de Sociologie de l'Université Libre de Bruxelles, 1970.

Perry, Michael J. "Modern Equal Protection: A Conceptualization and Appraisal." *Columbia Law Review*, vol. 79, no. 6 (October 1979), 1023–84.

Piaget, Jean. *Judgment and Reasoning in the Child*. London: Routledge and Kegan Paul, 1965.

———. *The Moral Judgment of the Child*. Trans. Marjorie Gabain. Glencoe, Ill.: Free Press, 1948.

Plato. *Gorgias*. Trans. W. D. Woodhead. In *The Collected Dialogues of Plato*. Trans. Lane Cooper et al. Ed. Edith Hamilton and Huntington Cairns. Princeton: Princeton University Press, 1961.

———. *Laws*. Trans. A. E. Taylor. In *The Collected Dialogues of Plato*. Trans. Lane Cooper et al. Ed. Edith Hamilton and Huntington Cairns. Princeton: Princeton University Press, 1961.

———. *Parmenides*. Trans. F. M. Cornford. In *The Collected Dialogues of Plato*. Trans. Lane Cooper et al. Ed. Edith Hamilton and Huntington Cairns. Princeton: Princeton University Press, 1961.

———. *Phaedo*. Trans. Hugh Tredennick. In *The Collected Dialogues of Plato*. Trans. Lane Cooper et al. Ed. Edith Hamilton and Huntington Cairns. Princeton: Princeton University Press, 1961.

Pole, J. R. *The Pursuit of Equality in American History*. Berkeley and Los Angeles: University of California Press, 1978.

Popper, Karl. *The Open Society and Its Enemies*. Princeton: Princeton University Press, 1971.

Postema, Gerald J. "Liberty in Equality's Empire." *Iowa Law Review*, vol. 73, no. 12 (October 1987), 55–95.

Postow, Betsy. "An Afterword on Equal Opportunity." In *Women, Philosophy and Sport: A Collection of New Essays*, 61–68. Ed. Betsy Postow. Metuchen, N.J.: Scarecrow, 1983.

Quarles, Benjamin. *Lincoln and the Negro*. New York: Oxford University Press, 1962.

Rabinowicz, Wlodzimierz. *Universalizability: A Study in Morals and Metaphysics*. Dordrecht and Boston: Reidel, 1979.

Rae, Douglas et al. *Equalities*. Cambridge: Harvard University Press, 1981.

Raphael, D. Daiches. "Equality and Equity." *Philosophy*, vol. 21, no. 79 (July 1946), 118–32.

Rawls, John. "Justice as Fairness." *Philosophical Review*, vol. 67, no. 2 (April 1958), 164–94.

———. "A Kantian Conception of Equality." *Cambridge Review*, vol. 96, no. 2225 (February 1975), 94–99.

———. *A Theory of Justice*. Cambridge: Harvard University Press, 1971.

Raz, Joseph. *The Authority of Law: Essays on Law and Morality*. Oxford: Clarendon Press, 1979.

———. *The Morality of Freedom*. Oxford: Clarendon Press, 1986.

———. "Principles of Equality." *Mind*, vol. 87, no. 347 (July 1978), 321–42.

———. Joseph. "Professor Dworkin's Theory of Rights." *Political Studies*, vol. 26, no. 1 (March 1978), 123–37.

Recasens-Siches, Luis. "Dignity, Liberty and Equality." In *Equality and Freedom*, vol. 1, 3–25. Ed. Gray Dorsey. Dobbs Ferry, N.Y.: Oceana, 1977.

Rees, John. *Equality*. New York: Praeger, 1971.

Rhode, Deborah. "Occupational Equality." *Duke Law Journal*, vol. 1988, No. 6 (December 1988), 1207–41.

Richards, David A. J. "Justice and Equality." In *And Justice for All: New Introductory Essays in Ethics and Public Policy*, 241–63. Ed. Tom Regan and Donald VanDeVeer. Totowa, N.J.: Rowman and Littlefield, 1982.

Rosenfeld, Michel. "Substantive Equality and Equal Opportunity: A Jurisprudential Appraisal." *California Law Review*, Vol. 74, no. 5 (October 1986), 1687–1712.

Ross, Alf. *On Law and Justice*. Berkeley and Los Angeles: University of California Press, 1959.

Russell, Bertrand. *The Principles of Mathematics*. Vol. 1. Cambridge: Cambridge University Press, 1903.

Rutherglen, George. "Disparate Impact under Title VII: An Objective Theory of Discrimination." *Virginia Law Review*, vol. 73, no. 7 (October 1987), 1297–1345.

Ryan, William. *Equality*. 1st ed. New York: Pantheon, 1981.

Ryle, Gilbert. *The Concept of Mind*. Harmondsworth: Penguin, 1966.

———. *Philosophical Arguments*. Oxford: Clarendon Press, 1945.

Sartori, Giovanni. *Democratic Theory*. Detroit: Wayne State University Press, 1962.

Scales-Trent, Judy. "Comparable Worth: Is This a Theory for Black Workers?" *Women's Rights Law Reporter*, vol. 8, nos. 1–2 (Winter 1984), 51–58.

Schaar, John. "Equality of Opportunity, and Beyond." In *Equality*, Nomos IX, 228–49. Ed. J. Roland Pennock and John W. Chapman. New York: Atherton, 1967.

Schauer, Frederick. "Authority and Indeterminacy." In *Authority Revisited*, Nomos XXIX, 28–38. Ed. J. Roland Pennock and John W. Chapman. New York: New York University Press, 1987.

———. "Precedent." *Stanford Law Review*, vol. 39, no. 3 (February 1987), 571–605.

Schlag, Pierre. "Rules and Standards." *U.C.L.A. Law Review*, vol. 33, no. 2 (December 1985), 379–430.

Schneider, Elizabeth M. "The Dialectic of Rights and Politics: Perspectives from the Women's Movement." *New York University Law Review*, vol. 61, no. 4 (October 1986), 589–652.

Schulhofer, Stephen J. "Harm and Punishment: A Critique of Emphasis on the Results of Conduct in the Criminal Law." *University of Pennsylvania Law Review*, vol. 122, no. 6 (June 1974), 1497–1607.

Sealander, Judith. "Feminist against Feminist: The First Phase of the Equal Rights Amendment Debate, 1923–1963." *South Atlantic Quarterly*, vol. 84, no. 2 (Spring 1982), 147–61.

Sen, Amartya. "Equality of What?" In *Liberty, Equality, and Law: Selected Tanner Lectures on Moral Philosophy*, 237–62. Ed. Sterling M. McMurrin. Salt Lake City: University of Utah Press, 1987.

Sidgwick, Henry. *The Methods of Ethics*. 7th ed. London: Macmillan, 1907.

————. *The Principles of Political Economy*. London: Macmillan, 1883.

Sigmund, Paul E. "Hierarchy, Equality, and Consent in Medieval Christian Thought." In *Equality*, Nomos IX, 134–53. Ed. J. Roland Pennock and John W. Chapman. New York: Atherton, 1967.

Simons, Kenneth W. "Equality as a Comparative Right." *Boston University Law Review*, vol. 65, no. 3 (May 1985), 387–482.

Simpson, A.W.B. "The *Ratio Decidendi* of a Case and the Doctrine of Binding Precedent." In *Oxford Essays in Jurisprudence: A Collaborative Work*, 148–75. Ed. A. G. Guest. Oxford: Clarendon Press, 1961.

Singer, Marcus George. *Generalization in Ethics: An Essay in the Logic of Ethics with the Rudiments of a System of Moral Philosophy*. New York: Knopf, 1961.

Smith, J. C. *Legal Obligation*. London: Athlone, 1976.

Smith, Rogers M. *Liberalism and American Constitutional Law*. Cambridge: Harvard University Press, 1985.

Sowell, Thomas. "We're Not Really 'Equal.' " *Newsweek*, 7 September 1981, 13.

Spaemann, Robert. "Remarks on the Problem of Equality." *Ethics*, vol. 87, no. 4 (July 1977), 363–69.

Spielberg, Herbert. "A Defense of Human Equality." *Philosophical Review*, vol. 53, no. 2 (March 1944), 101–24.

Stampp, Kenneth. *The Peculiar Institution: Slavery in the Antebellum South*. New York: Knopf, 1956.

Steiner, Gilbert Yale. *Constitutional Inequality: The Political Fortunes of the Equal Rights Amendment*. Washington, D.C.: Brookings, 1985.

Stephen, James Fitzjames. *Liberty, Equality, Fraternity.* Ed. R. J. White. Cambridge: Cambridge University Press, 1967.

Stevenson, Charles Leslie. "Persuasive Definitions." *Mind*, vol. 47, no. 187 (July 1938), 331–50.

Still, Jonathan W. "Political Equality and Election Systems." *Ethics*, vol. 91, no. 3 (April 1981), 375–94.

Stone, Julius. "Equal Protection and the Search for Justice." *Arizona Law Review*, vol. 22, no. 1 (1980), 1–17.

————. "Justice Not Equality." In *Justice*, 97–115. Ed. Eugene Kamenka and Alice Erh-Soon Tay. London: Edward Arnold, 1979.

————. *Legal System and Lawyers' Reasonings.* Stanford: Stanford University Press, 1964.

————. "The *Ratio* of the *Ratio Decidendi*." *Modern Law Review*, vol. 22, no. 6 (November 1959), 597–620.

Swanton, Christine. "Is the Difference Principle a Principle of Justice?" *Mind*, vol. 90, no. 359 (July 1981), 415–21.

————. "On the 'Essential Contestedness' of Political Concepts." *Ethics*, vol. 95, no. 4 (July 1985), 811–27.

Tawney, R. H. *Equality.* Rev. ed. London: George Allen and Unwin, 1964.

Taylor, Charles. "The Nature and Scope of Distributive Justice." In *Justice and Equality Here and Now*, 34–67. Ed. Frank S. Lucash. Ithaca, N.Y.: Cornell University Press, 1986.

Temkin, Larry S. "Inequality." *Philosophy and Public Affairs*, vol. 15, no. 2 (Spring 1986), 99–121.

Thomas, D. A. Lloyd. "Competitive Equality of Opportunity." *Mind*, vol. 86, no. 343 (July 1977), 388–404.

————. "Equality within the Limits of Reason Alone." *Mind*, vol. 88, no. 352 (October 1979), 538–53.

Thomson, David. *Equality.* Cambridge: Cambridge University Press, 1949.

Tocqueville, Alexis de. *Democracy in America.* Trans. Henry Reeve. Ed. Phillips Bradley. New York: Knopf, 1945.

Tokarz, Karen L. "Separate but Unequal Educational Sports Programs." *Berkeley Women's Law Journal*, vol. 1, no. 1 (Fall 1985), 201–45.

Twining, William and David Miers. *How to Do Things with Rules: A Primer of Interpretation.* 2d ed. London: Weidenfeld and Nicolson, 1982.

Verba, Sidney and Gary R. Orren. *Equality in America: The View from the Top.* Cambridge: Harvard University Press, 1985.

Vlastos, Gregory. "Justice and Equality." *Social Justice*, 31–72. Ed. Richard B. Brandt. Englewood Cliffs, N.J.: Prentice-Hall, 1962.

von Leyden, Wolfgang. *Aristotle on Equality and Justice: His Political Argument*. Houndsmills, Basingstoke: Macmillan, 1985.

———. "On Justifying Inequality." *Political Studies*, vol. 11, no. 1 (February 1963), 56–70.

Waismann, Frederick. *Introduction to Mathematical Thinking: The Formation of Concepts in Modern Mathematics*. Trans. Theodore J. Benac. New York: Unger, 1951.

Waldron, Jeremy. "What Is Private Property?" *Oxford Journal of Legal Studies*, vol. 5, no. 3 (Winter 1985), 313–49.

Wasserstrom, Richard. "Rights, Human Rights, and Racial Discrimination." *Journal of Philosophy*, vol. 61, no. 20 (October 1964), 628–41.

Watkins, J.W.N. "Liberalism and Equality." *Spectator*, vol. 197 (28 December 1956), 927–28.

Weale, Albert. *Equality and Social Policy*. London: Routledge and Kegan Paul, 1978.

Webster's New World Dictionary. 2d college ed. Ed. David B. Guralnik. Cleveland: Collins, 1980.

Webster's Third New International Dictionary of the English Language. Unabridged. Ed. Philip Babcock Gove. Springfield, Mass.: Merriman, 1966.

Weiler, Paul. "Wages of Sex: The Uses and Limits of Comparable Worth." *Harvard Law Review*, vol. 99, no. 8 (June 1986), 1728–1807.

Wellman, Carl. *A Theory of Rights: Persons under Laws, Institutions, and Morals*. Totowa, N.J.: Rowman and Allanheld, 1985.

Westen, Peter. "The Concept of Equal Opportunity." *Ethics*, vol. 95, no. 4 (July 1985), 837–50.

———. " 'Freedom' and 'Coercion': Virtue Words and Vice Words." *Duke Law Journal*, vol. 1985, nos. 3–4 (June–September 1985), 541–93.

———. "The Meaning of 'Equality' in Law, Science, Math and Morals: A Reply." *Michigan Law Review*, vol. 81, no. 3 (January 1983), 604–63.

White, Alan R. *Grounds of Liability: An Introduction to the Philosophy of Law*. New York: Oxford University Press, 1985.

White, James Boyd. "Thinking about Language." *Yale Law Journal*, vol. 96, no. 8 (July 1987), 1960–83.

———. *When Words Lose Their Meaning*. Chicago: University of Chicago Press, 1984.

White, Stephen W. "The Equality Principle: Is It Linguistically Justifiable?" *Personalist*, vol. 55, no. 1 (Winter 1974), 53–60.

Williams, Bernard. "The Idea of Equality." In *Philosophy, Politics and Society*, Second Series, 110–31. Ed. Peter Laslett and W. G. Runciman. Oxford: Blackwell, 1962.

Williams, Robert E. and Thomas R. Bagby. "Comparable Worth: The Legal Framework." In *Comparable Worth: Issues and Alternatives*, 197–266. Ed. E. Robert Livernash. 2d ed. Washington, D.C.: Equal Employment Advisory Council, 1984.

Williams, Robert F. "Equality Guarantees in State Constitutional Law." *Texas Law Review*, vol. 63, nos. 6–7 (March/April 1985), 1195–1224.

Williams, Wendy. "The Equality Crisis: Some Reflections on Culture, Courts, and Feminism." *Women's Rights Law Reporter*, vol. 7, no. 3 (Spring 1982), 175–200.

———. "Equality's Riddle: Pregnancy and the Equal Treatment/Special Treatment Debate." *New York University Review of Law and Social Change*, vol. 13, no. 2 (1984–85), 325–80.

Wilson, John. *Equality*. New York: Harcourt, Brace and World, 1966.

Wittgenstein, Ludwig. *The Blue Book*. In *The Blue and Brown Books*, 1–74. 2d ed. Oxford: Blackwell, 1960.

———. *Philosophical Investigations*. 3d ed. Trans. G.E.M. Anscombe. New York: Macmillan, 1968.

Wolgast, Elizabeth. *Equality and the Rights of Women*. Ithaca, N.Y.: Cornell University Press, 1980.

Wright, J. Skelley. "Judicial Review and the Equal Protection Clause." *Harvard Civil Rights–Civil Liberties Law Review*, vol. 15, no. 1 (April 1980), 1–28.

Yudkin, M. S. "Difference Be Damned." *Philosophy*, vol. 55, no. 213 (July 1980), 392–95.

Zaitchik, Alan. "On Deserving to Deserve." *Philosophy and Public Affairs*, vol. 6, no. 4 (Summer 1977), 370–88.

INDEX

Absolute equality: in given dimension, 22–24; identical in all respects concept, 24–25; Plato's conception of, 20–21, 21.n12

Adler, Mortimer, 16, 42

Affirmative action: equality and, 6–7; validity of, 269–70

Agents of equal opportunity, 165

Ambiguity: of antidiscrimination rights, 144–45; of equal opportunity, 173–76; of equal treatment of equals principle, 99–102, 117, 192; of prescriptive equality, 71–79, 267–71

Ambivalent employer analogy, presumption of quality and, 246–49

Analogical reasoning, formal principles of equality and, 219–23

Analog scales: descriptive equality and, 11–12, 33–36; pound cake analogy, 11–12

Animal Farm, 129–30

Anticonceptualism, mathematical equality and, 47–52

Antidiscrimination rights, 131–45; ambiguity of, 268; defined, 132n.2; due process and, 132–34, 133n.4; equality, comparisons and comparative rights, 134–39; equal treatment of equals principle, 139–42, 188–90; Twenty-sixth amendment, 137–39

Arabic numerals, mathematical equality, 44–45

Aristocracy, proportional equality and, 57

Aristotle: on distributive equality, 150–53; equal treatment of equals, 186–91, 193–94; "first among equals" concept, 129–30; formal principle of equality and, 185–86; on impartiality, 224; on "is/ought" distinction, 70–71; on "more or less" measurement, 15–17; on prescriptive equality, 91, 267n.40; presumption of equality, 231–36; on proportional equality, 52–57, 155–56; proportional standard of comparison, 105–6; on rhetoric of equality, 257–58, 262–65; on same-

ness and equality, 14n.5; semantic bias of equality and, 276–80; social justice defined by, xiv; unequal treatment of unequals, 204–10

Athletic events, sexual equality in, 263–64

Balance scales: comparative measurements, 18–19; noncomparative measurements, 18–19, 40–41; per capita distribution and, 157–58

Barry, Brian, 159–62

Baseline standards: for descriptive equalities, 86–89, 277–80; equal treatment, 117; equal treatment of equals, 189–91; prescriptive, 86–89, 98–99, 117, 189–91, 277–80, 286–87

Bedau, Hugo: on descriptive equality, 13, 26; on identity, 13; presumption of equality, 230n.1

Benn, S. I., 251–52

Bentham, Jeremy, 252–53

Berlin, Isaiah, 169n.19

Bias, of equal opportunity, 178–79; semantics, 276–80

Binary measurement standards, 16–17; per capita distribution and, 157–58

Bowie, Norman, 193–94

Browne, D. E., 233

Burden of proof, presumption of equality and, 230–31

Campbell, T. D., 165

Carey v. Population Services International, 221–23

Carr, Craig, 228n.57

Category mistakes, 58; rhetoric of equality and, 264–65

Cauthen, Kenneth, 241–42

Chamallas, Martha, 109–10

Charity, equal treatment and, 116

Chemerinsky, Erwin, 210

Chesterton, G. K., 158

Chocolate bar analogy, presumption of equality and, 253–54

Civil Rights Act of 1964, 109–10; comparable worth provision, 258–59

The Princeton University Press series "Studies in Moral, Political, and Legal Philosophy" is under the general editorship of Marshall Cohen, Professor of Philosophy and Law and Dean of Humanities at the University of Southern California. The series includes the following titles, in chronological order of publication:

Critical Legal Studies: A Liberal Critique by A. Altman (1989)

Finding the Mean: Theory and Practice in Aristotelian Political Philosophy by S. G. Salkever (1990)

Marxism, Morality, and Social Justice by R. G. Peffer (1990)

Speaking of Equality: An Analysis of the Rhetorical Force of 'Equality' in Moral and Legal Discourse by P. Westen (1990)

Friedrich Nietzsche and the Politics of the Soul: A Study of Heroic Individualism by L. P. Thiele (1990)